THE SOCIOGONY

Studies in Critical Social Sciences Book Series

Haymarket Books is proud to be working with Brill Academic Publishers (www.brill.nl) to republish the *Studies in Critical Social Sciences* book series in paperback editions. This peer-reviewed book series offers insights into our current reality by exploring the content and consequences of power relationships under capitalism, and by considering the spaces of opposition and resistance to these changes that have been defining our new age. Our full catalog of *SCSS* volumes can be viewed at https://www.haymarketbooks .org/series_collections/4-studies-in-critical-social-sciences.

THE SOCIOGONY

Social Facts and the Ontology of Objects, Things, and Monsters

MARK P. WORRELL

Haymarket Books
Chicago, IL

First published in 2018 by Brill Academic Publishers, The Netherlands.
© 2018 Koninklijke Brill NV, Leiden, The Netherlands

Published in paperback in 2020 by
Haymarket Books
P.O. Box 180165
Chicago, IL 60618
773-583-7884
www.haymarketbooks.org

ISBN: 978-1-64259-070-8

Distributed to the trade in the US through Consortium Book Sales and
Distribution (www.cbsd.com) and internationally through Ingram Publisher
Services International (www.ingramcontent.com).

This book was published with the generous support of Lannan Foundation and
Wallace Action Fund.

Special discounts are available for bulk purchases by organizations and
institutions. Please call 773-583-7884 or email info@haymarketbooks.org for
more information.

Cover design by Jamie Kerry and Ragina Johnson.

Printed in United States.

10 9 8 7 6 5 4 3 2 1

Library of Congress Cataloging-in-Publication Data is available.

For my sister Kay, with amaranthine gratitude

⋰

Contents

Preface

The Sociogony is the first volume in a larger project entitled *Sacrifice and Self-Defeat* that sets out to accomplish three broad results: lay out the terms and conditions (Volume One) under which we may explicate the moral geometry of collective consciousness (Volume Two) in a social system dominated by the commodity form (Volume Three). Specifically, the present and first volume deals with "social facts" and the distinction between objects and things as moments within a genetic procession or *sociogony* characterized by differing degrees of liquidity and crystallization, transparency and reification, with an eye toward the moments of derealization and transvaluation in which society partially or totally decomposes into the night of monsters. The specific goal of the second volume is to map the currents and modalities of self-destruction within the modern social system. Here we will develop the concept of the *social octahedron* or what amounts to a geometry of collective consciousness that assists theorizing the late imperialist epoch of neoliberal social disintegration and extreme polarizations. The final, twofold aim of the third volume is the examination of the Calvinistic logic of ascetic labor in a calling as a "vanishing medium" (Karl Rosenkranz, in Hegel 2002: 264) escorting Spirit into the modern epoch of mass death and, secondly, extending the idea of the "social octahedron" from volume two in an effort to reconstruct and expand Marx's general formula for capital (for this I have constructed a "New General Formula") that enables an exposition of the "octagonal" structure of the commodity.

What you have in front of you was originally conceived as a slim volume of love letters for dead theorists but, whatever the original impetus, I have obviously loved them to death. My colleague and long-time collaborator Daniel Krier says that this book reminds him of the Pequod: "A cannibal of a craft, tricking herself forth in the chased bones of her enemies" (Melville [1851] 1988: 90). Cannibalism is a fitting motif to describe what I have done here and there is no way to conceal the crime. Bergson says that the author should make the reader forget they are using words (1920: 57) but my readers will unfortunately never forget. It's not a fun read and one that is sure to annoy partisans and outrage purists. Marx, Weber, and Durkheim figure prominently in this work but in synthesizing these currents into a composite they figure less as autonomous problem solvers and more like dismembered atrocities bolted together into a monstrosity named Max von Marxheim. But make no mistake, at the end of the day the real driving force behind the whole thing is the primacy of Marx's theory of the commodity. Marx is unsurpassed is in his critique of political economy, dialectical analysis of the commodity, and phenomenology of value

forms, however, his underdeveloped vision of communism, the social psychology of the proletariat and the dialectics of solidarity, as well as his attack on the
social division of labor and institutionalized social mediation all pose serious
problems that generations of critical social theorists have wrestled with but
heretofore not solved.

Marx has been fused with just about every intellectual current under the sun
but few have attempted to forge the particular alloy I have in mind. This theoretical blindspot is due to the fact that the overwhelming majority of liberal
and radical thinkers "cannot see a Durkheimian world as anything other than
a moral abomination" (Haidt 2012: 193). A rare exception is James O'Connor
who says:

> The failure of Durkheim's successors [Mayo and Parsons] to critically
> address the problem of social solidarity ... should not dissuade us from
> studying Durkheim's own views on that subject. The reason is that, unlike
> the works of modern bourgeois sociologists, Durkheim's thought cannot
> be understood as a lower species of ideology.... Durkheim was a devoted,
> skilled scholar with a firm belief in science on the one hand and a solid
> commitment to creating a society based on individual self-development
> on the other. His work is an example of the best that bourgeois thought
> has to offer, or what bourgeois thought is capable of when it is stretched
> to its limit in the hands of one of its leading practitioners. This is the
> general reason why it is worthwhile for Marxists to study Durkheim ...
>   1980: 60

The paradox of freedom and solidarity has plagued the entire history of neo
Marxism and bourgeois liberalism. Today, we know that we are doomed with
out the regulating function of the social absolute but we cannot stand to have
our autonomy limited. "A Durkheimian world ... places limits on people's
autonomy and it endorses traditions.... For liberals, such a vision must be com-
bated, not respected" (Haidt 2012: 193).

In the aftermath of the First World War, Marxists turned in a number of directions to comprehend the enigma of the proletariat, most notably to Freud,
but they never considered the master theorist of solidarity. Durkheim has
something to offer progressives, radicals, and social democrats and I think we
should take seriously the claim made by Wexler that Durkheim is "among the
most unclaimed important theoretical forebears of social psychology" (1996:
37). Wexler did not mean social psychology in general but specifically *critical*
social psychology. I have coined the "Marxheim" neologism but I am by no
means the inventor of this way of thinking – as far as I am concerned that

distinction lies primarily with David Norman Smith at the University of Kansas who taught me that the comprehension of the commodity and exchange-value is enhanced by recourse to Durkheim's theory of the totem and mana as well as Weber's theory of the calling and charisma. Historical precursors to this way of thinking include Gurvitch, Bataille, Goux, and perhaps even Althusser to an extent. Bataille once said, "Emile Durkheim seems to me to be unjustly disparaged nowadays. I take my distance from his doctrine [?] but not without retaining its essential lessons" (1989: 123). More recently, O'Connor (cited above) makes the case that Marxists should not only take Durkheim seriously but that an interpenetration of the two thinkers leads to an enrichment and mutual strengthening (1980). A positive antipodal soulmate is O'Keefe's *Stolen Lightning* (1982) that bears on the problem of magic; Karatani's recent work on exchange and the intersection of Maussian gift theory with Marx (2014) is relevant; Gangas suggestively draws out some important parallels between Durkheim and Hegel (2007; see also Therborn 1980) as well as Durkheim's untapped potential for critical social theory (2017: 551–53); and not least of all, Stephen Wilson provides a sterling example of the power of combining neo-Marxist social psychology (Adorno) with Durkheimian sociology in his monumental theorization of French antisemitic ideology during the Dreyfus Affair (1982: 602–51). Hopefully, the volumes that comprise *Sacrifice and Self-Defeat* will not only make a contribution to our understanding of the commodity world but probe the limits and potentials for rational solidarity and reasonable social control in a world that seems to be falling apart.

Acknowledgements

I have the good fortune of being supported by a loving family and a close circle of colleagues that have supported and encouraged my work over the years. Many thanks to Robert J. Antonio, Harry Dahms, David Fasenfest, Dan Krier, David Norman Smith, Tony Smith, and all the participants of The Symposium for New Directions in Critical Social Theory at Iowa State University. With sadness I mark the passing of Ben Agger who did much to propagate my work.

Abbreviations

A number of sources have been referenced so frequently that abbreviations are relied upon for the sake of tidiness. I have also abbreviated some reference works such as encyclopedias and dictionaries the details of which are listed below:

AJ   *Ancient Judaism*, Max Weber (1952).

C   *Capital*, Karl Marx. *Vol. 1* ([1867] 1976); C, 2: *Vol. 2* ([1884] 1978); C, 3: *Vol. 3* ([1894] 1981). A reference to page 150 in volume 3, for example, would appear as: (C, 3: 150).

C, 2   See above.

C, 3   See above.

CPE   *A Contribution to the Critique of Political Economy*, Karl Marx ([1859] 1970).

DOL   *The Division of Labor in Society*, Emile Durkheim ([1893] 1984).

EFRL   *The Elementary Forms of Religious Life*, Emile Durkheim, translated by K. Fields ([1912] 1995).

EP   *Encyclopedia of Philosophy*, (1967). A reference to page 150 in volume 3, for example, would appear as: (EP, 3: 150).

ES   *Economy and Society, Volume 1*, Max Weber, (1978); ES, 2: *Volume 2*. A reference to page 150 in volume 2, for example, would appear as: (ES, 2: 150).

ESS   *Encyclopedia of the Social Sciences*, edited by Edwin R.A. Seligman ([1930–1934] 1933–1937). A reference to page 150 in volume 3, for example, would appear as: (ESS, 3: 150).

FMW   *From Max Weber*, edited by Hans H. Gerth and C. Wright Mills (1946).

G   *Grundrisse*, Karl Marx ([1857] 1973).

MECW   *Collected Works of Marx and Engels*, Karl Marx and Frederick Engels ([1835–1895] 1975–2004). A reference to page 150 in volume 44, for example, would appear as: (MECW, 44: 150).

OED   *Oxford English Dictionary* (1989).

PESC   *The Protestant Ethic and the Spirit of Capitalism*, Max Weber (1930).

PM   *The Economic and Philosophical Manuscripts of 1844*, Karl Marx ([1844] 1964).

PR   *Elements of the Philosophy of Right*, G.W.F. Hegel ([1821] 1991).

PS   *Phenomenology of Spirit*, G.W.F. Hegel ([1807] 1977).

RSM   *The Rules of Sociological Method*, Emile Durkheim (1982).

S   *Suicide*, Emile Durkheim ([1897] 1951).

SGS   *The Sociology of Georg Simmel* (1950).

Introduction: Toward a "Marxheimian" Sociology

The Greek fascination with the material things of this world gave way in the post-Socratic and Christian epoch to an all-absorbing subjectivity and intellectual inwardness. The beginning of the bourgeois epoch in the early 16th Century witnessed a rejection of Humanistic textuality and a return to "thingness" and utilitarian realism (Durkheim 1977: 278–91). The ensuing subjective reaction, peaking in the 19th Century, took an interesting turn when post-Kantian German philosophy placed the mind and praxis on a self-consciously *social* foundation. Though not the creator of Absolute Idealism,[1] Hegel is considered the primary exponent of this form of idealistic thought, lifting it up over the course of his career into a novel, speculative form that decisively transformed the way people think about society and history – even if they are not aware of it. In Hegel's philosophy we find a self-conscious social philosophy complete with a social ontology and a method that did not merely thread the needle between materialism and idealism but sublated both tendencies into a new *sui generis* form, at once greater than and different than the sum of its parts. A central feature of Hegel's thought is the peregrination of the Concept (*Begriff*) – not an innate organ of the mind, nor the emanation of some disembodied transcendental ego, nor an empty container for naming and linking words, but a social and historical achievement invested with authority. The actualization of the concept or the Idea, i.e., not the concept per se or in-itself but "the objective or real Concept" (SL: 755), provides the socially integrated individual an objective form of consciousness that has the wherewithal to raise itself above sensual immediacy while also resisting the lure of self-destructive mysticism.

The most contested European intellectual debates during the 19th Century revolved around the proper ontological and epistemological presuppositions of the historian and the social scientist. The "rationalist" orientation that unifies the work of Marx, Durkheim, and Weber is rooted in Hegel – whether they

---

1   In simple terms, absolute idealism (commonly categorized as a form of objective idealism) does not reduce the world to subjectivity but "grants the *objectivity* of that world with reference to *finite* conscious individuals, such as human beings. For Objective Idealism, this 'world,' with all its relations, events, objects, and qualities, may be the manifestation of One Infinite Spirit, but it *is not* the mere sensations or ideas of *finite* spirits" (Spaulding 1918: 309).

know it or not.[2] Hegel's speculative idealism,[3] a philosophy that attempts to locate the universal equivalent of the universal equivalents (Goux 1990: 46–47) in the odyssey of Spirit found its culmination in the work of Marx and Durkheim, each representing two contrasting lines of "completion" of the Hegelian project. Marx's famous renovation of the Hegelian dialectic pins down the universal of the universal in the modes and relations of energy extraction, productive transformations, exchange dynamics, consumption, and the accumulation of symbolic surpluses whereas Durkheim, apparently ignorant of the ins and outs of Hegelian philosophy,[4] found the universal of the universal in the shimmering, effervescent web of devotion and sacrifice to the collective representation. A "Marxheimian" sociology locates the common denominator of surplus moral energy beneath the money-totem homology: money, the god of all other commodities (CPE: 125; Goux 1990: 18) and the totem qua proto-god of clan and tribal life. However, the greatest sociological achievements of the 19th and 20th centuries, Marx's *Capital* (1867) and Durkheim's *Elementary Forms of Religious Life* (1912), were undone between the world wars. The inevitable proletarian revolution prophesied by Marx and his orthodox followers was reduced to absurdity as the workers of the world slaughtered one another on the battlefields of Europe. And what remained of the Durkheimian school after WWI was almost completely destroyed after the invasion of France during WWII.

---

2 Weber's relationship to Hegel is obscure. The consensus among Weberians is that he was a neo-Kantian yet Ernst Troeltsch, who knew him *exceedingly* well, points especially to *Hegel and Marx* as the guiding spirits. Weber, says Troeltsch, put together "a great total view of history of development and sociology, contemplating anew and in a quite original manner, ever if essentially sociologically, Hegel's and Marx's ideas; and thereby giving to history new views of the greatest importance" (1922: 233).

3 "Speculative" has a vague tone but "speculative" is the English word sometimes used to translate the German *begreifendes* (e.g., PS: 36) which is commonly translated as "comprehensible." What is important is that we comprehend or grasp something conceptually. The concept (*Begriff*) is the self of the object in its own coming-to-be process whereby the subject finds that through its own activities that it is actually identical with what was imagined to be external alien substance. Coarser forms of thought such as picture-thinking are sublated and raised up beyond mere understanding (standing under) to the freedom of reason. For example, sociologically, we see both Marx and Durkheim performing the work of conceptual critique on the reified collective representations that animate and regulate common sense and alienated consciousness. These representations impede reason due to their moral gravity and mass (see PS: 37) and it is the task of sociology to illuminate their origins and logic in order to free thought from the prison that it has made for itself.

4 See Anderson (1993) for a brief discussion on Durkheim's (and Weber's) attitude toward Hegel and Hegelianism.

Modelling itself on the prestige and profitability of the natural sciences during the postwar era, sociology went long on quantification, grand systematic abstractions, and positive-empirical studies in an attempt to work itself up into a genuine social physics that, after a generation of effort, led to growing sense of futility and failure.[5] Writing the year of Prague Spring, the Tet Offensive, and the assassinations of Dr. King and Bobby Kennedy, Bosserman says:

> In recent years the social sciences have become aware of a general malaise among many of their fraternity. The reason is that there is growing concern the brotherhood is failing to answer the really significant questions facing humanity. The *why* and *whither* have taken on a will-o-the-wisp character. Tools for statistical research have been developing rapidly, but the solutions fail to come. The drilling has produced no moisture for an arid land. The research seems to be barren and fruitless. It is a vast desert of abstracted theory, or empiricism, or concern with trivia.
>
> 1968: 87

Perhaps the biggest problem with sociological scientism is the loss of a concept of authority and the unhinging of the concept of social freedom from its substantive ground. As Seligman indicates not only does the epistemology of the mainstream social sciences lack a concept of authority there is actual aversion and outright hostility toward the idea and, consequently, these sciences are simply incapable of explaining human experience and action (2000: 3). The social prime mover is either disavowed altogether or pushed into an inaccessible domain reserved for noumenal mysteries. This development is unsurprising. On the one hand, much of the thinking behind networks, social evolution, and the principle of self-organization as it is applied to complex social systems is contaminated with residual vitalism.[6] On the other hand, and more seriously,

---

5   With 20th Century warfare it was "the end of everything that isn't quantifiable" (Gary 2017: 53). The first to attempt a social physics was Quetelet, the father of the "Average Man" who pioneered the use of averages applied to human beings and groups. The paradox of quantification and averaging is that they deprive individuals of any being. "He declared that the individual person was synonymous with error, while the average person represented the true human being" (Rose 2016). Since individuals necessarily deviate from averages this leaves empirically-existing people reduced to the status of deviants and perverts (Bering 2013). The "average man" or "average Joe" is a construct. Interviewed by Emilio Granzotto, Lacan said "First off, let's get rid of this average Joe, who does not exist. He is a statistical fiction. There are individuals, and that is all" (1974: n.p.; cf. S: 300 ff.).

6   "[Frederic] Laloux wrote the following lines, capturing a widely held conventional wisdom: 'Life in all its evolutionary wisdom, manages ecosystems of unfathomable beauty, ever evolving towards wholeness, complexity and consciousness. Change in nature happens

no modern event did more to drive a nail into the idea of authority than World
War I.[7] However, authority as such has been on the ropes for several centuries. Truth be told, for nearly 500 years Western civilization has been in open
revolt to, first, the various forms that authority has assumed and, finally, the
very "principle itself" (Dewey 1946: 93; see also Frankel 1956). Reason was once
used to liquidate unjust domination and, now, the authority of reason is itself
melting away. "The whole modern world is at war with reason; and the tower
already reels" (Chesterton 1986: 235).

1   Authority and Authoritarianism

The word "authority" seems to resonate on the same frequency as superstition,
oppression, and tradition (Royce 1969: 301). The suspicion is that authority is
synonymous with authoritarianism (Smith 2016) and that authority is hostile
to progress, freedom,[8] and social democracy.[9] The rejection of the principle of
authority leads us, however, toward a moral vacuum that provides the perfect

---

everywhere, all the time, in a self-organizing urge that comes from every cell and every organism, with no need for central command and control to give orders or pull levers.' Here we
find the twenty-first-century version of the late-nineteenth-century notion of the élan vital,
a mystical property to be found in all things" (Mulgan 2018: 77).

7   "In our minds the idea of authority – which is what they [parents, teachers, etc.] represented –
implied deeper insights and a more humane wisdom. But the first dead man that we saw
shattered this conviction…. Our first experience of heavy artillery fire showed us our mistake
and the view of life that their teaching had given us fell to pieces under that bombardment"
(Remarque [1929] 2010: 13). "A sudden fright, an unexpected happiness, a blow of fate beyond
the ordinary can dispel at once all the delusions of the misdirected reason … e.g., in August
1914 the word 'fatherland' and all the theories of 'essence' dissolved into nothing" (Rosenzweig [1945] 1999: 56). Perhaps it is wrong to implicate "misdirected reason" when a better
case can be made that reason was not so much "misdirected" as perverted through a negative
process of hyper-rationality or over-rationalization. For example, antisemitic ideology that
would play such an outsized role in the following world war seems purely irrational, but, "If
anything, it is over-rational rather than 'irrational,' as Adorno himself realized, writing in The
Authoritarian Personality: 'Anti-Semitic writers and agitators … have always maintained that
the existence of the Jews is the key to everything … they speak as if they were in the know
and had solved a riddle otherwise unsolved by mankind'" (Wilson 1982: 604). Alienated from
morality and ethics, reason is liable to devolve into a one-sided technical form that can be
hitched to any end – from industrial efficiency to mass murder.

8   "He alone has his own way who, to compass it, does not need the arm of another to lengthen
his own. Consequently freedom, and not authority, is the greatest good. A man who desires
only what he can do for himself is really free to do whatever he pleases" (Rousseau 1889: 44).

9   See Nietzsche (1968: 123–24) on the connection between socialism and the hostility to authority (cf. Neumann 1944: 128).

breeding ground for the reentry of sadomasochistic politics. The moral virtu-
oso might not require physical restraint in order to live:[10] "To invoke authority
is always to invite opposition, especially in the minds of youth. But the human
past shines upon us like a great light, and there is no need to invoke authority....
There are other sources of reverence besides the declarations of Scripture or
the pronouncements of the church. Men like William Morris and Walt Whitman have loved and reverenced the life of man on earth, and have found inspiration and guidance in the contemplation of its relationships" (Breasted 1933:
411). However, we will not have reverence for our fellow human being and our
world if those representations themselves lack authority gifted by ourselves.
When authority has been undermined and the light of the past fades we have
to choose between life and death, the choice between some kind of authority
over chaos or simple resignation and the celebration of dissolution as freedom. "'One lives for today, one lives very fast – one lives very irresponsibly:
it is precisely this which one calls "freedom." That which makes institutions
institutions is despised, hated, rejected: whenever the word "authority" is so
much as heard one believes oneself in danger of a new slavery'" (Nietzsche, in
Antonio 1995: 9).[11] Hobbes clearly saw that when a people grows ignorant of
rights and necessities the resulting vacuum fills with power and money as individuals climbing over top of one another to ascend to the apex of the diseased
social and political order (1889: 4). In that abyssal vortex the individual gropes
for something objective and powerful to cling to and "gladly debases himself
to servitude and total subjection simply in order to escape the torment of va-
cuity and negativity" (Hegel [1821] 1991: 186). Does "authority" always mean

---

10   Some people can function for a while in the absence of the absolute or with one that
     "comes and goes" (C: 183). Some individuals are imbued with confidence and rocksteady
     faith in the permanence of something that can never be seen or embrace empirical
     reality as the objectivation not of humanity or nature but the work of a mysterious Other.
     "We sit as in a boundless Phantasmagoria and Dream-grotto; boundless, for the faint-
     est star, the remotest century, lies not even nearer the verge thereof: sounds and many-
     coloured visions flit round our sense; but Him, the Unslumbering, whose work both
     Dream and Dreamer are, we see not; except in rare half-waking moments, suspect not.
     Creation, says one, lies before us, like a glorious Rainbow; but the Sun that made it lies
     behind us, hidden from us" (Carlyle [1836] 1987: 42–43).
        Others think that they need no overarching normative regulator ("Down with the ab-
     solute!") as they improvise their self-destruction on a day to day basis. Durkheim saw
     clearly that pragmatism is a suicidal ideology dressed up in fantastic and alluring visions
     of fluid and free life.
11   Nietzsche, the father of modern cultural critique, was not anti-authority. Rather, modern
     capitalism leads to the "complete evaporation of legitimate authority [providing] nearly
     unlimited opportunities for the ascent of frauds..." (Antonio 1995: 11).

subjection? There is a very good reason for the identification of authority and authoritarianism.

Both authority and authoritarianism appear to share an identical structure. Authority, says Haidt, involves looking in two directions simultaneously: "up toward superiors and down toward subordinates" (2012: 168). Having spent my entire professional career studying authoritarianism and the authoritarian syndrome my gut reaction to this "authority" is revulsion. It immediately calls to mind the bending and kicking of the authoritarian personality. Reich called this complex the top sergeant mentality (*Feldwebelnatur*) that "cringes upward and dominates downward" (in Samelson 1993: 25) whereas Adorno likened it to the *Radfahrernatur* or a cyclist nature "back bent toward those above, kicking down at those below" (Frankfurt Institute of Social Research 1972: 176).[12] However, subordination per se does not automatically imply or impose authority (EFRL: 35) and it follows that one who is subordinated is not automatically reduced to impurity nor degraded to the status of a tool.[13] Temperamentally I abide by the good gray poet who recommends that we resist much and obey as little as possible (Whitman [1892] 1992: 7). We should always keep foregrounded the idea that disobedience to authority is necessary for a healthy and vibrant authoritative system and that those who are committed to a rational social organization are thereby also committed to disobedience. Let me rephrase that: those who love society and recognize the necessity of moral authority must also be committed to disobedience. The disobedient radical is one that constantly probes the lines of authority and discovers what is rational and what is bunkum. Wilde is undoubtedly correct that disobedience is a "virtue" and the resistance against authority is already its own kind of authority

---

12   Marx may have been the original inspiration for this bowing and kicking metaphor. In *The Eighteenth Brumaire* he notes that "Each party kicks from behind at that driving forward and in front leans over towards the party which presses backwards" ([1869] 1963: 42–43).

13   "Subordination" sounds terrible to us because it is intimately connected to "inferiority" and liberal progressivism is hostile to the principles of subordination, inferiority, and the implicit ranking of groups. Of course, liberals are opposed to these principles while also defending old ranks or busy constructing new forms of superordination in the name of anti-subordination. A more troubling pseudo-progressive impulse is the masochistic degradation of all humans to a subordinate position – we are implored to get over ourselves and just embrace the fact that we are just animals, reducible to genes or unmediated evolutionary processes. This form of subordination amounts to the stripping of human consciousness (Spirit) of its "ordained" status – if we cannot all be ordained than none of shall be. As an egoist it pains me to see others treated like dogs but I don't think the solution is for me to climb under the porch and gnaw on bones. This self-degradation ethos resonates with some hipsters warring for justice but it also assumes a distinct form in the hands of libertarians who advocate for the destruction of the state and the elimination of social welfare programs.

([1891] 2003). But when disobedience is couched in the authority of the ego and the autonomy of the individual the conditions are ripe for catastrophe. While in the US we tend to celebrate the rebel it is actually the good little boys and girls that wind up being the most resistant to demagoguery.[14]

Self-identifying progressives and radicals are generally opposed to hierarchy and subordination of any kind because their morality revolves around individual autonomy, equality, justice, and inalienable personal rights. Anarchists push this logic to the extreme: all authority must be obliterated because authority in every form is synonymous with domination (cf. Marx and Engels 1972: 662–65). The reason we equate authority with authoritarianism is that, under it all, authority rests on strength of one form or another (Sennett 1980: 18) and where there is strength there must be weakness and inequality. The whole authoritarianism complex swings primarily on this polarity of the strong and the weak. Even if one fails to go as far as the anarchists there is still a feeling of repulsion toward authority; our immediate reaction is to equate authority with domination but authority is actually anti-domination. Unlike domination, simple coercion, and chicanery, authority *flows from the bottom*

---

14   "I genuinely believe that a certain amount of evil is being perpetuated through the use of the concept of authority. I believe that, as the person responsible for *The [Authoritarian] Personality,* I have a certain right to point that out. First, authority itself is essentially a social-psychological concept and does not directly mean the social reality itself. In addition, there is a technical authority – i.e., the fact that one person understands something better than another – that cannot simply be disregarded. Instead, the concept of authority derives its value from the social context in which it occurs. However, since you have just brought up the subject of authority, I would like to mention something about the socialization process in early childhood. This theme concerns the relation of social, educational, and psychological categories. The way one attains psychological autonomy is not simply by protesting against every kind of authority. Empirical studies in America, as carried out by my late colleague Else Frenkel·Brunswik, have shown precisely the opposite, namely, that so-called well·behaved children tend to become autonomous and critical men and women more so than refractory children, who then as adults immediately gather 'round the beer table with their teachers to rally 'round the same slogans. But the process is such that children – called the normal development – generally identify with a figure, i.e., an authority, they internalize it, appropriate it, and then in a very painful process that leaves scars, they learn that the father or father figure does not correspond to the ego-ideal that they learned from him: and thus they break away from him. Only in this way do children become mature people. I believe the factor of authority is presupposed as a genetic factor in the process of maturation. But this fact must by no means be used to glorify and remain satisfied with this stage. Were this to occur... not only would psychological deformities result. but also manifestations of immaturity in the sense of the artificially induced stupefaction that today is omnipresent" (Adorno, in Adorno and Becker 1983: 106–07).

up,[15] is conferred upon leadership from their "followers." As Marx would say, when you get right down to it, the master really is the servant (PM: 168–69).[16] Submission in this sense is not demanded by powerful leaders, rather, it is the leaders that actually submit to the collective will. Take for example a minor personal anecdote from the undocumented history of the United States Marine Corps.

As every Marine recruit learns, the Corps has never lost a single battle (not one!) since its inception in 1775. There may have been some cases of "retrograde combat" (i.e., "fighting in reverse" and reverse fighting is definitely not "retreating" since Marines never retreat either) but, no, Marines never lose on the battlefield. Another thing that has never happened in the long history of the Marines is that, unlike the Navy, there has never been a mutiny. Not one mutiny. However, in the mid-80s, a 19-year-old lance corporeal had endured enough of an incompetent platoon sergeant and convinced his low-ranking comrades to fight back by putting in for a collective transfer. This lance corporal obtained request forms for every private, private first class, and lance corporal in the platoon and delivered the completed forms to the company clerk. All hell broke loose and the little radical was brought up in front of the company gunnery sergeant, executive officer, and the commanding officer. He was informed of his impending indictment for mutiny and that he faced life in prison or the death penalty if found guilty – and he was guilty. Unfazed, the insurgent informed the company "gunny" that he seriously doubted that any of that would come to pass since, as everyone knows, there had never been a mutiny in the history of the Marines and it was very much unlikely that the commanding officer wanted the notoriety for opening that new chapter in US military history. That put an end to the bluster and, in less than a day, the platoon sergeant was transferred. Not only was there no "mutiny" but the little reformer that created the mess was awarded a meritorious mast and promoted shortly thereafter. In retrospect, the company "gunny" came to see things in a different light: the mutinous "shithead" was transformed into a "gungy sonofabitch" (gung ho)

---

15   There is quite a discrepancy between the logic of authoritarianism whereby a person or group consents to being humiliated and beaten so long as they are presented with a compensatory object to beat and defile.

16   Of course, people never get what they deserve but, when it comes to political representation and delegation, they get what they themselves bring into existence. "Only he who *wills* to be *coerced* can be coerced into anything" (PR: 120). For example, we may not *deserve* a corpulent, vulgar, abusive and self-destructive baby as our national executive but who seriously doubts that this monstrosity is not the most fitting representation for neoliberal America? This is what the absolute vomits up in the moments preceding its final descent into the abyss.

It would be difficult to imagine an institution in American life more authoritarian and hierarchical than the Marines, yet, even in the Marines, any good "leader" knows to keep track of the moral pulse of the troops and not push them beyond where they are willing to go. Even in the Marines, authority flows from the bottom up and actual leaders follow their troops – they lead from behind.

About the same time the US Marines did not suffer its first and only mutiny, critical theorists had been worrying about the self-defeating logic of liberalism as democratic politics were shifting toward a neoliberal form.[17] The grave errors of their fulminations were the fetishisms of populism, exceptional moments, Eventism, and the native wisdom of that pernicious abstraction, Average Joe. Worse still was the fascination with Medieval corporatism and war charisma. Critical theory realized the self-defeating logic of the unrelenting war on moral authority but had nothing much to offer except backward glances and nostalgia. Still, without authority there can be no social organization better than a prison and reaction is served when, no longer able to rule ourselves, we are subjected to a despotism of unimaginable depth and breadth (Marx and Engels 1972: 662–65). Without authority we are left with nothing more than power politics, rebellion, rationalizations, propaganda, and mass death events – Durkheim describes the condition as one of oscillations between anarchy and authoritarianism.[18]

Critical social theory, though it often claims to be rooted in the Hegelian tradition, seldom concerns itself with the problems of social order, engaged as it is, in extending the war on authoritarianism, domination, and hegemony in every direction.[19] A voice on the Left says, well, of course Durkheim "was no doubt right" when it comes to the issue of the transmission of social values

---

17   I teach at an important "scene of the crime" in the history of critical social theory (Worrell and Dangler 2011).

18   Liberals, progressives, and radicals are almost exclusively inhabitants of Western Europe and North America and represent a "statistical outlier" in relation to the rest of the world and the sum total of human history. For us, the social atom, the individual, is the whole and there can be nothing greater than the whole. "And with this abandonment of man's native rapport with the whole, the nerve of worth in his own living and acting silently ceases to function. Here, I venture to think, is the root of our malady" (Hocking 1956: 23). Pushed to the extreme, the good fight against authoritarianism, knowing no limits, easily develops into a world not only devoid of the good but one plagued by a nightmare of what Durkheim called "will mania" (1915) that leads inevitably to its opposite, fatalism, combined with acute social disorder (e.g., the iron cage of commodity fetishism or Protestant anti-authoritarianism that devolves into predestination, fatalism, and brutal social control).

19   I realize a statement like this puts me in harrowing proximity to someone like Michael Novak where "Hegel is back upright, and Marx flipped over" (Kintz 1997: 222).

(Miliband 1969: 243) but the "values" the working class are fed by the lapdogs of their capitalist masters are not real social values at all but ideological bobbles. At the root of this conception is the erroneous but weirdly shared assumption that commodity exchange is the base and "privileged determiner of practical norms" (Winfield 1988: 82). From this point of view, all norms in capitalist society are reducible to self-serving, ideological reflections of the dominant class. After all, it does appear that capitalism eliminates all values from the world except for exchange-value. But Marx says that the ruling class is the producer of dominant ideas, not all ideas, and modern people are certainly not "cheerful robots" (Mills) nor do they fit the model of pure "automaton conformity" (Fromm) – at least not yet.

It stands to reason that as mainstream sociology committed intellectual suicide through a commitment to grant acquisitions, mindless empirical studies, quantification, variabilization, and bloated grand theories, revolutionary theory made its own contributions to the negation and decay of intellectual life. In its ideal negation of bourgeois civilization orthodoxy can be said to have made not the slightest dent in the predicate while contributing a great deal further to the disintegration of the subject. In the name of solidarity and freedom, Marxism, the negative sibling of capitalism, delivers the exploited individual to either the gulag, revolutionary terror,[20] the iron will of the party, or, paradoxically, to the domain of hyper-individualism (the animating philosophy of egoism and utilitarianism) and private interests over collective necessities; hence, the source of Durkheim's dismissal of "historical materialism" as infantile and regressive. One of the contradictions of most forms of social critique is that it does not actually diminish the concentration of power in the hands of the few as hoped but unintentionally assists in its concentration. The more we negate the principle of authority in the struggle against authoritarianism and the sanctity of I-rights and personal entitlements the more we are left with a flat ontological plane of social atoms jostling for position and seeking status attention because "authority" is swept away. In this context, the strong easily defeat the weak. As O'Connor points out, the discourse and forms of class struggle in the West, ideal-typically expressed in the US, are marinated in the same individualism embraced by capital, and that this shared individualism is "an important source modern economic and social crises" (1984: 5). The negation of authority pushed to the extreme undermines the foundations for communal life in general and ends up devouring itself because, as Marx,

---

20   Engels did not flinch from the authoritarianism and even terrorism of revolution and
      revolutionary organization and the discipline that revolution entails (in Marx and Engels
      1972: 665).

Durkheim, and Weber demonstrate in their own unique ways, capitalism only "works" if the buyers and sellers of labor power are operating within the same universe of solidarity and authority (see O'Connor 1984: 119). As we undermine the legitimacy of the system of the production for exchange we simultaneously and unintentionally undermine the bases of social solidarity that were founded on the same moral ground. As critical theory imagines that it is liquidating capitalist domination (which it is not) it is actually digging an intellectual grave for those that it would enlighten[21] and, in the process, devalues its own theoretical voice via internal irrationality. Indeed, from the more general view, where there is no authority there cannot even be a sociology since its ultimate problematic is, in the final analysis, the study of authority (EFRL: 210–11).

The social organization of authority is an essential problem. If we wish to avoid complete social chaos, if we wish to actually live in a society, authority has to be embodied and respected. Various institutions and classes have been nominated for this task, from the state, the aristocracy, the working class, and technocracy, and so on (Arnold [1869] 1990: 82–85). The Enlightenment answer to this problem was reason (Royce 1969: 300–01) or its deification, Reason. The main problem with this Reason and the idolatry of the mind in general was that it was based not on a synthetic, non-linear *social* reason, a reason that emerges out of human association or combination, but on the analytic, positive, and linear reasoning of the reflective individual mind in isolation (see Haidt 2012: 105). This is the major defect of idealism prior to Hegel who elevates reason from the flat plane of egoism, self-reflection, and logical propositions, to the drama of history and social conflict. For Hegel, "the structure of reason was social" (Pinkard 2002: 249). Anyone who has contemplated the mystery of the disjunctive syllogism in Hegel's *Logic* will sooner or later arrive at the realization that what is mapped out in that decisive passage is the transformation of the abstract universal into a synthetic absolute through the sublation of the individual into a collective representation. All at once, humanity becomes a god to itself (S: 334).[22]

2   Reason and Mediation

Spirit worked itself up to a new shape in the 19th Century and, if not everywhere, was finally capable of objective scientific thinking. Hegel's rationalism

---

21   The humane person "will eventually curse an art which seems to implant in the souls of men a predilection for belittling and doubt" (Nietzsche 2015: 4).

22   Of course, the shift from Christ to Christ Incorporated happened rather quickly, arguably at some point between *Adversus Haereses* and Constantine.

is far different than the rationalism of the Enlightenment and while his
Science represents the apogee and perhaps the apotheosis of reason, his science (*Wissenschaft*) is far different from the pinched, empirical scientism and
the fetishism for abstraction we find in the contemporary social sciences.[23]
The logic and rationality applicable to matter and animals is inapplicable to
the most essential aspects of humans as social beings. We have a profane,
material side but that is not where society is located (Bougle [1926] 1970: 74).
Where Hegel, Marx, and Durkheim converge is the rationalist insight that "beneath" the shell of profane matter, social relations and institutions exhibit syllogistic forms (PR; G: 89; CPE: 94; EFRL: 426).[24]

> There is an understandable resistance to the Hegelian notion that the
> structure and evolution of society conform to a rational pattern, a re-
> sistance remarked on by Hegel himself in the famous preface to the
> *Philosophy of Right*. Men and women are willing to grant there is logic
> in the movement of the heavens or the migration of the Canada goose.
> Human social arrangements, however, are supposed to be the product
> of chance and caprice leavened, perhaps, with a modicum of reason.
> Even less attractive is the conception that society and the state, with
> all their faults and perversions, could be related in any way to ones
> own thought and action. Yet everyone agrees that human language and
> its grammar constitute a rational system, even though language, like
> society itself, arises from practical and accidental circumstance. Nor is
> there much mystery involved in the active identity (and distinction)
> between the thinking individual and his or her language. But if words,
> phrases, and even grammatical forms have been created over a vast pe-
> riod of time by individual men and women, the underlying grammatical
> structure and interrelationships of language are mostly derived from an
> *unconscious rationality* which is discovered only after its emergence and
> development.
>
> MACGREGOR [1984] 2015: 22

---

23   Scientism is the "religion of science" and is "open to doubt as all the other religions. It is
      also less poetic than the others – and more stupid, since it bypasses the very problem it
      purports to solve" (Comte-Sponville 2007: 102).
24   "Marx could not have done his job without Hegel. By exhibiting the workings of his dia-
      lectic in such detail and so comprehensively, Marx's 'great teacher' had given us a faithful
      map of our jail" (Cyril Smith 1994: n.p.).

The syllogism[25] appears to most of us to be something applicable only to formal logic games[26] or "an empty piece of book learning" (Hegel [1830] 1991: 260) but the syllogism is reason *in the world*[27] and, as far as sociology goes, syllogism relates to how ideas and collective representations are brought into relation with one another, how these ideas form sui generis hierarchies whereby images and ideas subsume and contain other images and ideas, or come to be subsumed and contained by others, and, finally, how these processes are regulated by social norms regarding what passes for rational and valid thinking. Syllogism enables a breaking into a "unitary phenomenon" and disentangling the various moments and interconnections "stored up within" it (Mannheim 1982: 205).

When we seek a vocation for ourselves, affirm the best way to get ahead in life is to work hard, deliberate between two objects as the best qualified to

---

25 "Syllogism" comes from the Greek "*sullogizesthai*" which gives us "*logizesthai*" (to reason) which is itself rooted in the Greek *logos* (reason). The syllogism is the dance of Logos. Specifically, however, syllogism is *analogical* reasoning. Analogy comes from the Greek *analogia* meaning "proportion." Analogy is the act of transferring meaning from one particular subject to another particular subject and analogies are akin to "conceptual metaphors" that enable us to port the knowledge from one domain over to another. It is the making of analogies that "lies at the heart of intelligence" (Hofstadter 1995: 63). Our taxonomies, classifications systems, mental hierarchies, and metaphors all rely on the syllogism. Our metaphors are thoughts that allow us to draw further analogies. "The concepts that govern our thought are not just matters of the intellect. They also govern our everyday functioning, down to the most mundane details. Our concepts structure what we perceive, how we get around in the world, and how we relate to other people. Our conceptual system thus plays a central role in defining our everyday realities. If we are right in suggesting that our conceptual system is largely metaphorical, then the way we think, what we experience, and what we do every day is very much a matter of metaphor" (Lakoff and Johnson [1980] 2003: 4). A people that worships the singular and preaches the immediate is doomed to wander aimlessly because it is in the mediating term, the middle that connects individuals to the domain of universality, where commonality and logos are situated (see Everett 1882). Where mediators frequently "vanish" Spirit will remain concealed from itself and it will be continuously plagued by monsters.

26 This would be the merely boring and "subjective form" of the syllogism (SL: 669).

27 "Like the judgment, the syllogism is also in the world (and not merely in our heads and our thought). Yet where the judgment is merely a thing in the outside world, it seems more appropriate to grasp the syllogism as an event. 'The several forms of syllogism make themselves constantly felt in our cognition. If any one, when awakening on a winter morning, hears the creaking of the carriages on the street, and is thus led to conclude that it has frozen hard in the night, he has gone through a syllogistic operation – an operation which is every day repeated under the greatest variety of conditions....' In reality, however, it is the very world of this early morning in Berlin so many years ago which has performed a syllogism" (Jameson 2009: 97).

satisfy our desires, or feel that one is equally an "American" regardless of
whether or not one is a Christian, or a Jew, or a Muslim, etc., but not an atheist, etc., one is engaging in syllogistic thinking. Syllogisms are, for us, not just
formal deductions but how socially generated ideas form unfolding matrices
of meaning. Syllogistic thinking, reasoning, encompasses not only the whole
of the social proper but the supra-social as well as the infra-social, or, individual psychology. Depending upon one's "unit of analysis" we can generate an
integrated system of facts, from the most aggregate (the "superior" or "higher
orders") to the most infinitesimal.

   If the rational is syllogistic, we know that when someone claims, no doubt
for their own benefit, that there is no such thing as society – only individual
people and their families truly exist – we know that this claim falls short of
rationality and fails to raise itself above distorting ideology. Indeed, to not be
conscious of the need for society or to deny it (and the necessity for it) is to
fall below the level of human rationality into simple understandings, personal
interests, or even animality – to think like sheep (MECW, 5: 44). The same could
be said for those that say institutional regulations are irrelevant in a world driv-
en by a self-correcting system of impersonal market imperatives. Such a claim
is by definition irrational and is therefore mere propaganda used to benefit
some particular class of individuals. Likewise, the suffering egoist who says
they don't need anybody else in their life because they have all the things they
want or, by contrast, the religious or economic fanatic who destroys other people for the benefit of the big Other (god, the party, etc.) fails to act on the basis of rationality. It is not merely coincidental that many non-denominational
Protestant sectarians condemn reason as satanic. No one is more rational than
the devil. In Goethe's *Faust*, Mephistopheles is the spirit of negation and reason incarnate – the devil is literally the only character in that work that can
think straight.

   Any number of syllogisms can be constructed according to the problem
and the point of view from the religious, political, economic, technological, vocational, and cultural, etc., and with different "units of analysis" such
as world systems, international affairs, states, regional dynamics, urban life
and so on. Sociology proper has generally not concerned itself with the most
aggregate nor the most granular (the grand abstraction of "humanity" as an
undifferentiated whole nor the infinite vortex of the isolated psyche) but the
sweeping "middle range" from civilizations to dyadic interactions where we
find our problems and explanations (Durkheim and Mauss [1913] 2006: 35–39).
The result is not merely an arbitrary string of superficial syllogisms but a vast
unrepresentable constellation of spiraling and interconnected concepts (each
containing syllogisms of their own).

Social reality is rational or has a rationality about it and everything rational is syllogistic (SL: 664–65; see also Hegel [1830] 1991: 256). Hegel even goes so far as to say that "Everything is a syllogism..." (SL: 669). No good sociological explanation is possible without the "triangulation" and interpenetrations enabled by the concept, driven by syllogistic structural development (e.g., Marx's analysis of the value forms in the first chapter of *Capital*). If we wish to raise our grasp of society and history to an objective level then it is through the syllogism (Hegel [1830] 1991: 257). Tony Smith tells us that, deep down, Hegel's syllogisms are really about how our thoughts are regulated by principles and that we project our reasons into the principled (1993a: 7–21). In other words, there is a logic to social life: "these conceptions of the general medium and process of social life are pushed home into the actual formative operation of the social mind and will. Society, we are told, may be compared not ... to an organism, but rather to a mind; it is a co-operative mind, a syllogism, in which the principles held by one part are modified and applied by another" (Bosanquet [1923] 1965: 41; see also Bouglé [1926] 1970: 255–56; Durkheim 1973: 13; and Gangas 2007 who, rare among writers today, draws upon the neglected Bosanquet). According to Tarde, society inclines toward "great agglomerations, great centralizations, to the formation of majestic and perpetually growing systems where Social Logic marvels at itself, in pyramids of syllogisms higher and stronger than any tomb of the Pharaohs" (in Davis 1906: 23).[28] Each science that attempts to grasp nature or society is itself a syllogism (Durkheim 2004: 197).[29] This sounds rather abstract and superfluous to everyday concerns, however, if we wish to see consciousness raise itself out of mere existence or understanding where it is pushed around by uncomprehended external causes (a short-circuiting of reason where a bunch of "becauses" and compulsions dominate) and, instead, grasp the internal necessity of some facts (see Findlay 1958: 240) by virtue of reflection ("speculation")[30] and conceptual reasoning, syllogisms are not only relevant but essential to sociology. As Durkheim put it

---

28   The second volume of the present work, the book on suicide, will be an exploration of the inner dynamics of one of these "pyramids."

29   The individual sciences are "an immense prosyllogism, and, unless the utility of these sciences is denied and it's asserted that there's nothing more in the most complex formulas they arrive at than there is in the definitions that serve as their base, the utility of syllogistic reasoning must be recognized" (Durkheim 2004: 197). A prosyllogism is "an argument composed to two syllogisms such that the conclusion of the former becomes the major premise of the latter. We could also have a prosyllogism composed of multiple syllogisms such that the conclusion of each one of them becomes the major premise of the one following" (Durkheim 2004: 196).

30   "For in Hegel the concept of speculation, removed from its terminological shell, means in turn none other than life forced to turn inward..." (Adorno 1993: 91).

in his philosophy lectures, an abyss stretches out between the individual and
the universal, "an abyss that induction leaps across – but by means of what
principle?" (2004: 201). The principle is causality.[31] Where there is causality or
cause there is reason (rational grounds) and action.[32]

If I insist that the salt in front of me is black when clearly it is white no one
will ask for a *reason* for such a misjudgment, rather, they will seek only, and at
best, an explanation for my statement, wonder what is wrong with me, or wait
for the punchline. The assertion that salt is black is an error of perception and
judgement but I have not run into a moral dilemma or committed a mortal
sin because the color of salt is a problem of the understanding or comedy. But
once we move into the sphere of moral or immoral actions, e.g., separating
green-eyed people from the blue-eyed people for discriminatory purposes, we
demand to know the reason or rationale for such an action.[33] Understanding is
thinking as it applies to the world of profane and individual judgements.
Seeking an *understanding* leads nowhere beyond subjectivism and personal
attitudes. The irony of "understanding" is that once we can no longer reason
properly we have nothing substantial left to metaphorically stand under; the
sky's the limit and society falls into anomic drift. Hegel compares the understanding to a table of contents standing at the head of the real substance (PS:
32). Understanding by itself is schematic and lifeless. Reason, on the other
hand, and as Durkheim illustrates in *Elementary Forms*, is authoritative thinking or thought that pertains to things sacred, the rationale and structure of

31   To shift paradigms: "At the core of the historical-materialist conception of social determi-
      nation ... is the idea, no matter how qualified, that social phenomena are *causally* related
      to one another. One of the primary challenges for explanation is thus to go beyond the
      mere description of how social forms are constructed to identification of the complex
      hierarchy of causal forces and principles" (Mohanty 1997: 51–52). Causality, from cause
      (*chose*) is literally *thingality* in our sense of *thing* (relation) to be developed further. An-
      other point worth drawing out here is that explanation has to go beyond not only descrip-
      tions but beyond explanation itself. To explain something is to do no more than make
      things intelligible by spreading or flattening them out (the Latin *explānāre* = to spread
      out flat, flatten out, to make intelligible). Reason includes explanations but it goes beyond
      this in composing the right causal narrative; reason is the voice of the absolute made
      intelligible for itself.
32   Like reason, the absolute, and the syllogism, the concept of "cause" and the idea of deter-
      mination are somewhat outdated terms (see Carr 1961: 115).
33   The *understanding* of "behavior can only be achieved from the viewpoint of the subjec-
      tive experiences, ideas, and purposes of the individuals concerned – in sort, from the
      viewpoint of the religious behavior's 'meaning'" (ES, 1: 399). However, we are not inter-
      ested in "behavior" and wish to go beyond subjectivism. When we shift from attitudes to
      motivated action and social "factors" we are searching for expressions of the *reason* why
      people perform such and such actions (ES, 1: 400). And this search is capable of yielding
      objective knowledge (Ibid.).

which is sunk in long-extinct or partially extinct religious practices. Reason bursts onto the scene with the unfolding organization of society. And, more importantly, reason is the world not of subjective attitudes but one of motivated conduct on the part of groups and the individuals subsumed by those groups. Totem worshippers were essentially worshipping *concepts* and *categories* as proto-gods. The apex of this system of worship was the concept in the appearance of the emblem of the animal species. Totemism, and its elementary form of syllogistic thinking, is *the original cult of reason* weaving together a descending spiral of totemic becoming:[34]

U	P	S		
Confederacy	Tribe	Phratry		
	U	P	S	
	Tribe	Phratry	Clan	
		U	P	S
		Phratry	Clan	Personal
			U	P	S
			Clan	Personal	Optional

If, as Durkheim says, the "totem is wakan" for the clan member (EFRL: 198) then what holds for the totem holds also for mana/wakan/orenda and so on. Prior to the emergence of a universal totem reflecting a development of social organization beyond the clan matrix of relatively autonomous and externally related groups, reason does not have the ground from which to *erupt* and transform social principles of clan life (Ibid: 199) or develop beyond "mere understanding" and the lingo of understanding (the binary juxtaposition of "general" things and "individual" things) awaits the arrival of reasoning. There really is nothing truly universal (absolute) yet and actual social *particularity* as a moral function within the intersubjective matrix is lacking. "Under these conditions, it would occur to no one that these heterogeneous worlds were only different manifestations of one and the same fundamental force" (Ibid: 198–99). Do not misunderstand: we are not idealists saying that reason or the Idea creates society but that the dynamism, projective and objectivating practices, constant social reorganizations, and the systems of autonomous (reified) representations necessitate a development of social thinking beyond understanding. In this sense it is literally true that society is a conceptual being and reason is

---

34   On the forms of syllogism as they pertain to ascension and descent see Kant (1929: 321).

the absolute framework of society (Harms 1981). If society disintegrates at the hands of a class of liquidators we can expect reason and morality to falter and action devolve into a war of private interests or, at best, disaggregated ethical codes. And, indeed, the contemporary American political culture on both the left and right is devoid of a universal dimension – all that remains are punishing mobs and self-absorbed victims (Lilla 2017).

Reason, unlike other individual cognitive capacities such as perception and understanding, is a social product that only manifests itself or erupts from organized social life that has worked itself up to a certain level (e.g., a unified tribe). If the totem (collective representation) unfolds according to the syllogism once we arrive at the tribal form, mana (energy) also spreads out in a syllogism:

U	P	S
Universal Mana	Specialized Mana	Personal Mana
Tribe	Clan/Realm	Realm Things

The phrase "realm things" sounds odd but it is keeping with the spirit and letter of the text in that it refers simply to the things and individuals "assigned to each clan" and therefore belonging to a distinct "realm" (Ibid: 198). Each totemic group is but a single "chapel of the tribal Church." But each chapel enjoys its own relevant independence and autonomy, each clan and cult constitutes its own *realm*. Cults are juxtaposed and not interpenetrating. The sacred things of the clan realm are individualities (singularities) and irreducible to other group things but, overall, each clan is not actually sufficient unto itself in any absolute sense. A network of groups exists at this point being externally related, i.e., they are alienated to a certain extent. Each clan and its collection of sacred things is a distinct realm unto itself. Each group has its own authority and regulatory principles – reflected in the etymology of the concept of realm. However, once the tribal unit has developed it absorbs all the clans "more or less completely" and all the separate realms are gathered together under a universal sign. Yet, singularity does not vanish but is preserved (Ibid: 197, 198–99).[35]

35   Weber is incorrect that syllogism succeeds analogy and that analogic thinking grew out of rationalized magic. If this were true, syllogistic constructs would then be a later development of something that syllogism actually had a hand in producing, or, metaphorically, was on hand to witness its own birth. On the contrary, magic is a latter development and presupposes a fairly developed social organization and one that has worked itself up to the notion of universal mana and the tribal totem. We would not even say that magic and syllogism develop in parallel since the completion of the tribal syllogism is a

Sociology is interested in collective action or group life and a group is only interesting or sociologically relevant once it has divided itself in at least some rudimentary manner (EFRL: 169). Once a division or collective self-alienation has occurred we are no longer in the presence of a jumble of individuals (some kind of "primal horde" ruled by terror) but a social organism that produces moral forces and principles for self-organization. Sociology seeks an explanation for such things, this is true, but real sociological theory seeks *more than explanations,* it seeks the reasons for such things. Once consciousness can reason on the basis of the concept genuine causes can be separated from ideologies and rationalizations.

Hegel's syllogistic renovations were important: "Hegel hit on the idea of translating the elements of the Aristotelian logical mechanism back into genuine philosophical conceptualities. So successful was this operation indeed that Hegel is scarcely ever mentioned in the history of logic, as though he had somehow suppressed the method and the mechanics which made it 'logic' in the first place" (Jameson 2009: 76). Hegel's innovation was carried forward by Marx, and Durkheim, sometimes consciously (Marx's phenomenology of the value form) and sometimes unconsciously (Durkheim's tribal syllogism).

> Society acquires the status of a 'syllogism' characterized by cooperation and interdependence of parts.... Although Hegel ascribes to the state the status of a syllogism ... clarifying within it moments of 'particularity,' 'singularity' and 'universality,' Durkheim's modelling of organic solidarity can be reconstructed as a syllogism. In his classic work on religion, Durkheim comes very close to the conception of society as a syllogism, when he writes: 'If society is something *universal* in relation to the individual, it is none the less an *individuality* itself, which has its own personal physiognomy and idiosyncrasies; it is a *particular* subject and consequently *particularizes* whatever it thinks of'.... These 'moments' constitute the path through which the complex web of mediations leads to the idea of 'unity-in-difference.' Clearly, Durkheim lacks the systematic character of Hegel's exposition. Yet, organic solidarity may be reconstructed as the culmination of this logical configuration since it preserves unity (solidarity) and difference (the freedom of the individual in his or her right to a *particular* life and vocation).
>
> GANGAS 2007: 325

---

precondition for the emergence of magic, a negative universal power. Magic "is a tribal and even intertribal institution" (EFRL: 199). Magical forces "hover above the divisions and subdivisions of the social organization" (Ibid: 200). Where there is magic, then, the syllogism is always already there.

The particularities that mediate relations and undergird universality are not empty and lifeless categories or abstractions but the subject-substance that is collective consciousness and without the correct syllogistic structure we are left without organization or hope. In both Hegel and Durkheim, the syllogism is coterminous with society and is inescapable. For Marx, however, where there is syllogism there is always the sacrifice of a middle term – under capitalism, the "vanished mediated" (C: 187) includes living labor power.

The contradictions of the capitalist mode of production incline toward a breakdown of mediation altogether. It is no longer the case that the laboring mediator is extinguished in the fires of the labor process but that labor is no longer what we think of as labor. The worker in the automatic industrial setting no longer mediates the production process (G: 705ff.). With the growing irrelevance of the individual worker, all knowledge and skill can be absorbed by capital (general intellect) and, once the working class rises up to dispossess the capitalists of the means of production and subsistence, liberated humanity can enjoy directly and immediately, the fruits of the automatic system of needs-satisfaction under new ownership.

Modern, bourgeois liberal thought attempts to repress the structure of syllogistic reasoning by not only denying the substance of universals but also by collapsing the moment of particularity into individuality. One frequently encounters flip juxtapositions between universals and particulars as if a particular and a singularity were synonymous functions. We should reject the term "individual" because individual means, literally, undividable whereas a *singularity* is a thing divided – it has undergone a constitutive alienation (sacrifice) and doubling that will function, not as a vanishing mediator (C: 187) but as a durable conduit to connect people to the universal moral domain. Individuals have only *interests* whereas groups have ethics and society as a totality is the realm of *morality*. The connection and mediation between interests and morality are the *ethical* codes that regulate the moments of particularity.[36] The commodified mind is allergic to the concept of mediation beyond dollars: what every autonomous being demands is immediate universality – a direct connection to the big Other, the perverse affirmation of the anarchy of personal interests as morally good.

The long-term danger to humanity is that social logic is repressed to such an extent that it can no longer be recovered, relegated to the devalued arts and

---

36   Readers familiar with Hegel's *Philosophy of Right* will be excused for misunderstanding the relationship between morality and ethics. Ethical life is not a "higher" form of conduct but is the institutional ground upon which morality is based. Hegel's critique of morality in *Philosophy of Right* is aimed specifically at Kantian morality.

Humanities, and we are subjected to an alien, machine logic of pure, mathematical rationality applicable only to the domination of matter. The old problem of humans being reduced to servants of machines in the capitalist mode of production is on the cusp of a more horrifying alienation of involuntary machine control from within on the nanoscale level of integration. Either we will learn to live within the limits of our own self-imposed social authority or we will be reduced to soulless tools. The contradictions of social life under our own authority means that we cannot always do what we like or like what we do but this tension is preferable to the total negation of liking anything at all ever again. Every time I hear somebody utter the phrase "Liberal Fascist" I wince in pain because, even though they don't know it, there is a kernel of rationality to the idea that a morality whittled down to autonomy, justice, and rights is generated and sustained within the cultural matrix of the capitalist necroverse that eventually leads in only two directions: into the abyss of self-destruction or pure mechanical determination. Our horror at the cretins of America who would put the "Stable Genius" in the White House only masks our own ignorance of the moral geometry of a good society. Our war on authority has led us into the dead end of an inability to even understand the normal thoughts and feelings of the rest of humanity. When we hear Americans speak we only hear "the crazy" and flee in terror from the ordinary person.

> Consider what it is to listen and understand someone speaking to us. In a certain sense we have to become the other person; or rather, we let him become part of us for a brief second. We suspend our own identities, after which we come back to ourselves and accept or reject what he has said. But that brief second of dawdling identity is the nature of understanding language; and if that language is a command, the identification of understanding becomes the obedience. To hear is actually a kind of obedience. Indeed, both words come from the same root and therefore were probably the same word originally. This is true in Greek, Latin, Hebrew, French, German, Russian, as well as in English, where 'obey' comes from the Latin *obedire*, which is a composite of *ob* + *audire*, to hear facing someone.
>
> JAYNES 1990: 97

We can no longer stand to listen to or understand one another because we cannot tolerate any form of intrusion upon the self. And since we are constitutionally incapable of accepting authority of our own making we are assuredly and inevitably well on our way to a moral downfall. Just when we need a rounded multidimensional morality that is not alienated from the rest of humanity and a critical theory that is free from intellectual and political tribalism, which

always produces victims, we have instead demons, scapegoats, and punishers –
and we have no morality or theory at all (see Habermas 1970: 33).[37]

3   The Concept

We live in an age of minimalist intellectual aspirations and skepticism towards
anything synthetic and prefer the titillations of eclectic play and identity politics.
In the natural sciences, the status quo "often suppresses fundamental novelties
because they are necessarily subversive of its basic commitments" (Kuhn 1970: 5)
but in contemporary sociology, it is the work of subversive novelties that plays its
part in suppressing objective insights into the structures and processes of capitalist society. Concepts are not only useless for sociology today, they are actually
perceived to be threats to the status quo. In the pursuit of grants and titles, sociology eschews concepts because they cannot be plugged into the work of mainstream, quantitative sociology engaged as it is in multivariate regressions. In the
postwar era American social scientists were positively giddy over the super-
abundance of cash streams available from public and private sources, especially for survey research (e.g., Alpert 1958). The social sciences of today that
mimic the methods of the natural sciences require not concepts but variables
or *dehydrated concepts*. In the best of times, concepts were viewed in postwar
sociology as nothing more than "tools" for empirical research – operationalized
and disposable means to assist the sociologist in informing people how best to
conform and adapt to industrial civilization. Every day we encounter a pervert
who describes some concept or another as a nice addition to their "tool kit."

If, as Hegel says in the preface to the *Phenomenology*, science and truth require concepts[38] then contemporary sociology has degenerated to the point of
absurdity.

> It is the governing ideal of much specialized social science to abstract
> out single variables and, on the natural science model, try to figure out
> what their effects would be if everything else were held constant. Yet in
> the social world, single variables are seldom independent enough to be
> consistently predictive. It is only in the context of society as a whole
> with its possibilities, its limitations, and its aspirations, that particular

---

37   Of "Actor Network Theory" Latour says "ANT is not a theory of the social, any more than
     it is a theory of the subject, or a theory of God, or a theory of nature. It is a theory of the
     space or fluids circulating in a non-modern situation" (1998: 22).
38   The "concepts" of modern empirical and positivistic science are not at all concepts per
     se but arbitrary "conceptual fictions" or what Croce referred to as "pseudo-concepts"
     (Collingwood 1946: 198).

variables can be understood. Narrowly professional social science, particularly in its most reductionist form, may indeed deny that there is any
whole. It may push a radical nominalism to the point of seeing society
as a heap of disparate individuals and groups lacking either a common
culture or a coherent social organization.[39]

BELLAH ET AL. 1985: 300

Variables in this strange world have quantitative and analytic value (not to
mention those famous "wooing glances" of exchange-value) and conceptual
thought has been rendered valueless. This is especially troublesome because
reason and normative life cannot function without conceptual articulation
(Brandom 2013: 16; see also Weber 1949: 107). If variables are dried out, lifeless concepts, reasoning on the basis of quantitative analysis fails to rise above
mummified schematics. Human combination (as Marx puts it) gives rise to
weird effects, as does the fusion of concepts and representations, however, and
this is something that quantitative analysis has not begun to even imagine,
the assemblage of variables fails to generate any sublime product; sociology
should make you bleed, not drain the blood from the world. Not only does
thinking with variables and hypotheses fall below the threshold established by
Marx for changing the world but even below that established by Weber whereby sociology merely interprets and understands the world – there's nothing left
to even stand under.

Even in the critical domain, the apparent need for operationalization leaves
concepts on the side of the road. Whatever Marx's theory of value may or may
not be, we are told, it is irrelevant from the standpoint of economism (e.g.,
Reuten 1993) where we find value reduced to a metaphor that cannot operate at
the level of *Begriff* and must, instead, operate along the ontologically flat plane
of indices. Bortkiewicz, for example, famously stated: "value is merely the index of an exchange relationship" ([1907] 1952: 5–6). The result of this zeal for
indexicality and the mania for mathmaticovariableization is the loss of systematic and objective thought on the social logic of the commodity and the contradictions of capitalist society. The hard work of Hegel, Marx, and Durkheim
to solidify a socially realistic ontology was jettisoned for more glittering prospects. With the loss of conceptual thought, a dialectical method, and the abandonment of a socially realistic paradigm, we now find ourselves in a situation
akin to the separation of Marx's theory of the commodity from the reformist
labor movement of Bernstein: the loss of an "axis of intellectual crystallization around which isolated facts group themselves in the organic whole of a

---

39   In the *repression* of philosophy and *denial* of totality, two separate forms of negation, the
      contemporary social sciences have doubled their intellectual insanity.

coherent conception of the world" (Luxemburg [1900] 1970: 57). Without conceptual objectivity grounded in social and institutional processes ontology re-
gresses into determinism and naive empiricism, on the one hand, and mystical
realism that finds moral substances in the fabric of nature. Both currents, for
example, are presently tearing the world of linguistics apart but we can find the
same dual regression working itself out across the entire liberal arts spectrum.

4   The Absolute

Hegel says that, "Spirit often seems to have forgotten and lost itself, but inwardly opposed to itself, it is inwardly working ever forward..." ([1840] 1995:
546–47). We can replace "Spirit" with society and make the same argument. It
may not be the case that every move that Spirit makes is progress or is a station
along a teleology but there is a "reason" behind a social form nonetheless. The
irrationality of the present condition is incomprehensible without discovering its inner rationality but contemporary sociology and social philosophy, far
from offering rational critiques of the existing state of society, seem content
on reproducing in thought and models an abstract reflection of the observable
which, since it is not directly observable, lacks the dimension of the organic
absolute. This is saying nothing more than the bourgeois spirit pursues equilibrium while delivering chaos, "the striving after a mean between the countless
extremes and opposites that arise in human conduct" while simultaneously
rejecting the dimension of the absolute as abhorrent (Hesse 1963: 56–57). As a
consequence, luck and destiny come at us from all sides.

> Man is not the mechanism he is too often described as being, who auto-
> matically pursues his interest in all areas. It takes a higher urge, a com-
> monly recognized experience, reason which eludes all reason. It takes a
> motivation which we not only feel inscribed within us but which also
> imposes itself upon us like the love urge. A social group can exist only if
> all its members are included in a common 'reason,' are subject to an im-
> perative recognized as transcendent. They must be living in a community
> relationship, not one, of course, which is constant or openly recognized
> but one which is latent, and so basic that it can bloom outwardly only in
> rare moments. Yet everybody shares in this order.[40]
>
> ELLUL 1975: 53

---

40   "A social morality based upon convention or contact between personalities breaks down
     as soon as an individual or a group becomes sufficiently powerful to violate the compact
     with impunity. A social morality based on authority or revelation is compatible with the

One result of this regressive dualism is the actual loss of society as a concept. It is one thing to deny the existence of society, that is common enough in the case of Enlightenment materialists, bourgeois ideologues, the estranged, and the anomic, but it is another thing altogether to elevate the negation of society to a philosophical or methodological principle that, intentional or not, undermines the "spiritual" life of a collectivity.[41] We may negate all day and night as part of a critique of existing society plagued by problems and antinomies but, in the final analysis, we do not leave things as an indeterminate heap of facts and dismembered parts but, as Marx does in *Capital*, construct an objective and compelling judgement that informs subjects as to how they might act, think, and feel if they wish to live freely. Marx's error was substituting an implicit theory of instinctual restoration symbiotically integrated with a general intellect crystallized in the post-capitalist mechanical complex where there should have been a will to society. At the end of the day, critique and negation must retain a "will to society" (Bouglé [1926] 1970: 220) and to will society is to will an absolute.

One could argue that the further one goes back in history, the closer the unity between society and its universal image, to the point even of a practical unity. The totem, for example, is the absolute representation of the clan such that the totem, clan, and members are all submerged in a primal identity: the universal tribal totem encompasses both the particularity of the clan and the individuality of each member who, qualified to do so, bears the mark of their individual totem). In the modern world, the absolute and society can become radically disconnected or split off from one another or the gap between the two may widen to the point that one or both seem to vanish altogether. This disappearance can be due to the workings of purely impersonal forces and tendencies but it may also be due to personal antipathies and political revenge. After the second world war many émigré (e.g., Popper) and Anglo writers continued to prosecute German thought by excoriating the concept of the absolute and, especially, the bogeyman most associated with promulgating the "big, queer thing – the Absolute", Hegel (White [1955] 1957: 25).[42]

---

autonomy of moral action. Yet a social morality *must be grounded on some objective order*. It cannot be the order of nature" (Moses Hess in Hook 1934: n.p.).

41   Contractualism, Hobbesianism, Rossueaianism, Utilitarianism, etc., are all "in agreement in viewing society as fundamentally a post-individual phenomenon" (Alpert 1939: 138).

42   "During the World Wars, Hegel's popularity, like that of many German thinkers, was at low ebb in the English-speaking world. First in L.T. Hobhouse's antipathetic *The Metaphysical Theory of the State*, Hegel's 'wicked doctrine' was made responsible for the ills of the First World War. Later, Karl Popper picked up where Hobhouse left off and performed the same function of saddling Hegel with the atrocities of World War II. He galvanized the already negative sentiment against Hegel and spread it beyond all previous dimensions with his

When he was not dismissed as a wooden and perhaps nauseating oddity in the history of Western intellectual history (e.g., Brinton 1950: 424, 444) Hegel was condemned as the justifier of Prussian absolutism, a fetishizer of the state, a romantic reactionary, and a proto-architect of German authoritarianism, and, more troubling, those who seemed most keen on Hegel were Marxists. Even into the mid-6os, a decade after even Nietzsche had begun his "rehabilitation" at the hands of establishment academics, it was still common to find papier-mâché versions of the "ominous" Hegel (Muller 1966), that perverse antipoce to Goethe and the German Enlightenment, as the monster responsible, at least in part, for conjuring up totalitarianism.[43]

The separation of the absolute and society (the disintegration of society into understandings and misunderstandings, idols and errors) only makes sense when we see that, in such a case, the "absolute" under consideration is the absolute that has divided itself into three moments: two sides of the abstract absolute alienated from concrete and organic social reality which no longer knows itself as such. In a society that is thrown off balance, has suffered some tremendous blow such that mediating institutional authority loses its holc, facticity appears as fiction, fictions as facts, and massive devaluation sets in; a population becomes estranged, alienated from itself and the absolute decom-poses into a night of horrors. The terrors of our time are not due to an irrational insistence on an emotional-ideological absolute (Rank 1941: 23) but, rather, a divestment in energy and coherence in the mediating particularities (callings, institutions, etc.) that render the absolute rational by connecting individuals to a universal system of moral necessity. Ah, we cannot abide necessity. If we believe that to be fully human it is necessary to be free then we also have to recognize the "freedom of necessity.... This is freedom according to Spinoza, to Hegel and no doubt according to Marx and Freud: freedom as an understood necessity..." (Comte-Sponville 2004: 67). This necessity applies not only to the

---

well-known book *The Open Society and Its Enemies*. In the second tome of that work, Pop-per, in a rather untempered tone, argues that Hegel's political philosophy amounts to nothing less than a straightforward totalitarianism that has certain affinities with Naz Germany. Thus, Hegel, like Nietzsche, suffered the fate of being branded as a forerunne of German national socialism, and this unfortunate association had a profound impact a the particular historical moment. This justly criticized reading was, despite its scholarly shortcomings, taken up uncritically by a number of scholars on both sides of the Atlantic (Stewart 1996: 6; see also Carr 1961: 119–21).

43   "Since the state was the embodiment of what [Hegel] termed the 'divine idea,' the essence of morality, the individual could lead a truly ethical life only by identifying himself with the state. By submitting to the state and rendering it unconditional obedience, the indi-vidual could realize true freedom" (Breunig 1970: 161).

analytic realm but the synthetic as well. Sans moral necessity or moral facticity reason dies or fails to develop fully (PS: 53).[44]

Our aversion to "necessity" is paradoxical because our default position in bourgeois society is one of willing necessity. According to Durkheim "We hold to the profane world with every fiber of our flesh. Our sensuous nature attaches us to it; our [physical] life depends upon it" (EFRL: 317). This "death drive" – the fighting tooth and nail to return to the realm of the profane has great implications for the fate of the absolute – it means, in short, that the absolute is inherently prone to dissolution. However, when the absolute is in tip-top shape the "death drive" assumes another form.

> Who but an Englishman, the legendary Sir John Franklin, could have managed to die of starvation and scurvy along with all 129 of his men in a region of the Canadian Arctic whose game had supported an Eskimo colony for centuries? When the corpses of some of Franklin's officers and crew were later discovered, miles from their ships, the men were found to have left behind their guns but to have lugged such essentials as monogrammed silver cutlery, a backgammon board, a cigar case, a clothes brush, a tin of button polish, and a copy of The Vicar of Wakefield. These men may have been incompetent bunglers, but, by God, they were gentlemen.
>
> FADIMAN 1998: 24–25

We all die but some perish while sticking to, if not their guns, at least their principles. In a famous letter to Freud, Albert Einstein wrote that human

---

44   It is the norm to find individuals fetishizing things like nations or parties, etc., whereby they arrive at "wrong" (Hegel) syllogistic structures whereby particularities ("America" or "Christian") assume the position of universals within a syllogism such that things like an international order or a brotherhood of humanity cease to exist as anything more than balderdash cooked up by talkers. For the cosmopolitan "talker" types, universality may mean anything up to the genus *Homo* whereas for the provincial "doer" civilization is synonymous with nation. "The conviction that what we call civilization is a national product has entered people's minds to the extent that it has become a foundation for territorial claims. It is almost comic to see some ill-known, ill-studied folkloric elements being invoked during the [Versailles] Peace Conference as evidence that such and such nation should extend here or there, on the grounds that we can still find there such or such shape of house or some bizarre custom" (Mauss [1920/1950] 2006: 43). Territorial disputes between nations is literally a dispute over the syllogistic middle term. "The same thing happens in diplomatic negotiations ... for example, when various powers lay claim to one and the same piece of land. In this case, the right of inheritance, the geographic lie of the land, the descent and language of its inhabitants, or any other ground, can be brought up as a *medius terminus*" (Hegel [1830] 1991: 261).

associations are as a matter of course degenerate and diseased but that, all
the same, we have an "imperative duty" to rise to the occasion in spite of the
imperfections (1982: 105).

In our state of deranged separation and alienation, either the concrete or
the abstract appear to consciousness as non-existent even though this appearance is deceptive. It is deceptive because what appears as the systemic failure
of a whole social system is not merely the death or end of one constellation
but also the birth of a new form, imperceptible except in its obscure outline.
Concluding his last lecture in Jena, Hegel said:

> Ours is a significant epoch, a time of ferment, when the spirit has made a
> jerk, transcended its previous form, and is gaining a new one. The whole
> mass of previous notions, Concepts, the bonds of the world, have dis-
> solved and collapse like a dream image. A new emergence of the spirit is
> at hand.
>
>   in KAUFMANN 1965A: 96–97

What we lack is the optimism of Hegel that even when it appears that a social
order is on the cusp of going into the night, a new daybreak is imminent. We
lack the historical distance to know whether we are at the end of something
or the beginning of something new and hopefully better. Keep in mind that
social disorganization does not necessarily mean that a whole social system is
broken down and going into the abyss but that the normal modes of mobiliz-
ing people and energies no longer work as they did in the past (see Blumer
1969: 77).

5   Ersatz Absolutes

How one views the structure of the social order depends upon one's coordinates and one's goal.[45] If, for example, you would like to dismember society
and turn it into hoardable cash then there is no such thing as a "will to society"
but merely a desire to sacrifice individuals and their families. Here we have the
classic bourgeois liberal unmediated unity of the concrete universal that seeks
to get the state off the backs of those heroic entrepreneurs who want nothing

---

45   There is, in even some forms of critical social theory, an inability or unwillingness to
      maintain a dialectical ("stereoscopic") vision that does not block out some dimension of
      social life, whether it is that of the individual, intersubjectivity, or structures and totalities
      (see Dews 1987: 285).

more than to help humanity while helping themselves. Critical sociology sees through this mumbo jumbo as a world dominated by a bad absolute (capital). However, the Marxist counter to capital has been to *substitute* various other "good" absolutes such as History, The Revolution, The Worker, or The International, etc., that also have the effect of dismembering and rebuilding society. Naturally, when we survey the world around us we find only individuals and their individual minds, there is no group brain or transcendental ego hiding behind the moon that all these individuals are wired into for their thinking, but the result of this individualism (ontological and epistemological) is the collapse of the mind into a simple or rather undifferentiated thinking machine or tool that the person uses to make their way in the world in pursuit of singular interests.

The stronger version of this flattened world, let us call it flat intersubjectivity, is one where there is no reality beyond individuals and interacting individuals engaged in symbolic dances, slapdash agreements, negotiations, and contracts. Here, there is no Big Other of any kind other than a linguistic fiction retained by naive fools. This is the scale of analysis in which we find red hot constructionism, relationalism, intentionality, and pragmatic fluidity (see Worrell and Krier 2018). An extended variation of this intersubjective model admits of a universal dimension but the universal is so unsubstantial that it cannot rise even to the level of a collective representation but merely pops up from time to time like repetitive musical motifs in our transactions as interpretive schemas. Here, a Big Other is a linguistic skeleton or an empty signifier, at best a metaphor filling in the cognitive blanks to make reality bearable and where we are enabled to enjoy our neurotic symptoms in the futile pursuit of desires. We tune into this universal because we see the advantage of mutual understandings and being regarded as polite and civilized. At another ontic scale (triadic intersubjectivity) we find those that allow for a permanent universal dimension but, all the same, the universal is a schematic of the understanding and amounts to a kind of transcendental nominalism.[46]

---

46 With nominalism, hypothesis replaces the Scholastic syllogism "as the foundation of science" and hypotheses are the best we can hope for (Gillespie 2008: 23). If all we are left with are hypotheses then the foundation of reason cannot assume any positive truth content; everything except for the certainty and free will of the transcendental god is radically contingent. Another way of looking at the problem in Hegelian-Marxist terms is that the mediating function of particular equivalency, that entity that grounds truth and connects the absolute with the contingent singular, is liquidated leaving the tie between the universal and the singular (as well as the signified and the signifier) at best distorted or, at worst, completely broken such that we have a breakdown of regulation, social control, authority and a breakdown of ontic stability for language and categories.

Here, though, we find a little more backbone in the "transcendental" third in the form of a commitment to *consensus* reality.[47] Of course, the three forms (subjectivity, dyadic-intersubjectivity of definitional situations, and the lifeless triadic-intersubjectivity of durable understandings, grammar, and generalized others) may overlap to create hybrid aporia and many theorists may even delude themselves that they are social *realists* when, in fact, their so-called "realism" fails to rise above the level of intellectual contractualism and pragmatic behaviorism. Pragmatism is catnip for the unhinged.[48] However, unlike most of my critical colleagues, I am unwilling to simply jettison pragmatism, constructionism, and affiliated strains as simply deranged, defective, and incapable of rehabilitation. They are half-baked and symptomatic perspectives (many of the greatest personalities to embrace pragmatism, for example, were self-destructive and disillusioned rascals) but they do express a real aspect of society.[49] Constructionism and relationalism, etc., are only "bad" when they do not function as moments within an "absolute sociology."

At the psychological level we can clearly see the effects of the reduction of human life down to the level of egos: there is no Big Other and there is no Other of the Other (Žižek, Fink, etc.). Here we find not only no ontology (that is fine) but no *social* ontology either, and a lacunae of this magnitude is another matter altogether. Yet, no sooner do we have the claim that there really is no Other nor Other of the Other we find the exact opposite demand:

Hypothesis, variables, empiricism, materialism, etc., are the negations of syllogism (realism) and represent moments in the negation of society itself. What does hypothesis really mean? Hypothesis comes form *hypo* (under or below) *thesis* (to place). We are left with nothing more than contingent propositions and probabilities falling below and trapped below an inaccessible domain of absolute truth (the broad, open space – the *plateia* – qua the mind of god). Nominalism and hypotheses reduces social and moral thought to literally a dualism of justified ignorance.

47   Be wary of those who spout "consensus" – that will be the justification used to haul you off to a gulag. "For the sake of consensus, comrade, board the train."

48   Bertrand Russell hits on something profound with the pragmatism of William James: "There is an impatience of authority, an unwillingness to condemn widespread prejudices, a tendency to decide philosophical questions by putting them to a vote, which contrast curiously with the usual dictatorial tone of philosophic writings.... A thing which simply is true, whether you like it or not, is to him as hateful as a Russian autocracy" (in Santayana 1913: 124).

49   Pragmatism, like relativism, denies "the validity of objective truth [and] ... may pave the way for the adoration of the existing. But at the same time they are debunking theories.... Positivism and pragmatism bow only to ascertained facts and, thereby, demand freedom to ascertain and analyze them" (Neumann 1944: 463).

> If we are to preserve some notion of a just Law above and beyond the particular laws of the land – given the current legitimation crisis of the legal, juridical, and executive branches of government – a just Law that is equitably and uniformly enforced, we must have an experience of Law at home which at least approaches that ideal to some degree.
>
> FINK 1997: 254

Without the Other (universal equivalent, the stability and authority of signification, i.e., logonomy) and, further, the Other of the Other (the universal equivalent of the universal equivalent, Authority, i.e., authority that endures beyond fluid intersubjective contacts across all domains of obligatory public life, religious, political, and economic), we are doomed to nothing more than prohibitions and little knots that tie together signifiers and the signified. They claim those little ties are "unshakable" but it seems to me that one needs additional bonds, the Bond of all Bonds, if one wants to avoid having the social order come unhinged.[50] So even though the Other behind language does not exist in an empirical and "scientific" sense we nonetheless must have one if we wish to survive. The Other must must be practically true even if it is not actually true, yet, it must function as more than an obvious fiction. We should not lose our heads over this term "absolute." We are not referring to a reified or transcendental monstrosity pulsating somewhere out there but the *concept* of the absolute which is no more substantially absolute than the concept of a circle is actually round (Comte-Sponville 2007).[51] As such, this absolute is not a thing that can limit our rational development (Becker 1973: 166). I hate to be the bearer of bad news but we need the absolute and we need social facts.[52] "There are things that are facts, in a statistical sense, on paper, on a

---

50 "[T]he autonomy of functional systems secured by their own binary codings excluded metaregulation by a moral supercode, and *morality itself accepted, indeed remoralized this condition*.... 'The higher amorality of functional codes was recognized by morality itself; but this also meant renouncing the idea of the moral integration of society'" (Luhmann, in Gagnas 2017: 562).

51 "The quality of being right-angled, acute-angled or equilateral, according to which triangles are classified, is not implicit in the determinateness of the triangle itself, that is, not in what is usually called the Notion [*Begriff*, concept] of the triangle..." (SL: 59–60; see also Mannheim 1982: 210).

52 Knowledge of the absolute is not synonymous with the knowledge of everything but knowing what the world is like "behind" its veil of appearances. "To gain absolute knowledge we do not have to know all the facts it is possible to know" (Singer 1983: 91). One is reminded of Weber who said it is not more facts we need but better interpretations. One will notice that with the term "absolute" the image of a grand thing (society) and its power to inspire as well as control is intermingled. This is not due to sloppy thinking

tape recorder, in evidence. And there are things that are facts because they have to be facts, because nothing makes any sense otherwise" (Chandler 1995: 847–48). In other words, there are some things that not only are facts but must be facts (self-evidently true, i.e., necessary) in order to prevent collective mental suicide. Without some minimal absolute there can be no universal morality, no particular or professional ethics, and no individual callings.[53] Since ordinary sociology can do nothing more than map the destruction of "society" and even participate in its downfall, and consequently the substitution of the "psychological man" (Becker 1973: 191)[54] for the sociological character, it therefore falls upon the shoulders of *critical* sociology (dialectical, historical-comparative, normative, etc.) to defend the concept of the social absolute and *moral necessity* because the alternative is just nihilism. This brings us to the reason we should not lose our heads over the "absolute." A science (systematic knowledge) that cannot lift itself up beyond the understanding and a matrix of competing interpretations is doomed to idolatry (PS: 32) because it lacks a commitment to the structure of reason (*Vernunft*) beyond the dichotomous relation between universals and individuals; in short, understanding (*Verstehen*) fails to consider itself a form of negative *particularity* and as a positive mediating function in the lives of individuals in their intersubjective and universal relations. Our disagreeable need for social authority is not the pseudo-authority of the individual nor the authority of the imperious absolute that does not comprehend itself but, rather, the authority of the mediating particularity that connects individuals to the social Other. The "'I' that is 'We' and the 'We' that is 'I'" (PS: 110) depends upon an unbreakable relation between singularities and their "particular equivalents" within the vocational-ethical matrix (DOL) and ecstatic cult life (EFRL) as drivers for a common social morality.

The time for one-sided deconstruction is over and we must enter into an era of negative reconstruction. If the social absolute fails to realize itself above the level of subjectivity and intersubjectivity it remains, as Hegel says, "a soft element prone to every possible kind of fantasy" (in Lukács 1926: n.p.).

---

but recognition that the absolute, absolute knowing, and absolute ideals have the same goal: rational solidarity and rational social control that opens a permanent space for individuality.

53   "'Ethics,' writes Alain, 'consists of knowing that one is of the spirit and, therefore, is obligated absolutely; *noblesse oblige*. There is nothing more to ethics than one's sense of one's own dignity'" (Comte-Sponville 2004: 10).

54   The rise in the value of psychology in bourgeois society serves as an index in the relative devaluation of sociology and the social sciences in general, as well as philosophy as the "collective consciousness" of science (DOL: 301).

A sociology which allows itself to be diverted, and which sacrifices the central category, that of society itself, for the sake of the idol of controllable data – thus the concept through which all these so-called facts of the data are first mediated, if not altogether constituted – would regress from its own conception and would thus join ranks with that spiritual regression which must be counted among the most threatening symptoms of total sociation.

FRANKFURT INSTITUTE FOR SOCIAL RESEARCH 1972: 33

Neither society nor the absolute are actually dead, they are merely "dead" to the perverted gaze of what passes for rational critical thinking today in the same way that the world has not actually ended when a heroin junkie overdoses and dies or a depressed individual dangles from the end of a rope.

6   Critical and Ordinary Sociology Circle the Invisible

Mainstream social sciences have already committed intellectual suicide or are engaged in embryonic forms of self-destruction through the jettisoning of theory, fetishizing methods and quantification, and money chasing. The last refuge lies in critical social theory and critical sociology to press for and compel the social spirit to recoil from the abyss.[55] Contemporary specialized social sciences not only cannot grasp the totality of social life they actually *disavow* any knowledge of the whole "or any part of the whole that lies beyond its strictly defined domain" (Bellah et al. 1985: 300). It is not the absolute that is dead but, we, on the contrary, are dead to the absolute.[56] In order to

---

55   Antonio says "our time is riven with emergent, profound social and ecological crises that threaten our world literally and make problematizing neoliberalism and forging an alternative regime compulsory if we are to save democracy and the planet as we have known it" (2017: 655). What I want to stress is that critical theory has a new *ethical* requirement to accompany permanent and immanent critique: the abyss of intellectual freedom that opens up at the hands of criticism is now obliged to point consciousness to new realities, obligations, necessities, facts, and ethics. Critique "is insufficient for positive construction; we must have actual results, methodical work, and positive issues; and the prophet of the twentieth century finds it necessary again [!] to emphasise the importance of objectivity" (Carus [1900] 1996: 451). If social thought decomposes any further into a hurricane of ideas, play, difference, anarchy, skepticism, nihilism, etc., then it will be complicitous not in the destruction of capitalism, empire, or fascism but of life itself.

56   "Either Western man is going to choose a new society – or a new society will choose, and abolish him" (Harrington 1965: 275). Harrington's *Accidental Century* is as old as I am but the book is more relevant now than when it was originally published. We cannot allow

function within the synergistic corporate-academic setting, modern positive (commercial, relevant, mainstream, recognized) social sciences sacrifice *Wissenschaft* to method supremacy and scientific production. If sociology were still a theoretically-driven field it would be forced to confront the repressed remainder that lies hidden behind the presumed *a priori* conditions that allows it to engage in symbolic discourse (Certeau 1984: 61) while acting as if the background logos that holds together the facticity of the world does not exist.

Where "society" is banished one can be sure that empiricists and positivists are in the driver's seat.[57] This is to be expected. As Kant indicates, where we find an energetic to and fro, simultaneous attractions and repulsions toward and away from a representation, we can be certain that we are in the presence of the sublime (1951: 97) which, to the alienated social atom, appears as a horrifying abyss to be avoided if the preciousness of the ego is to be preserved from contamination and devaluation. Of course, for the "socialist" the same representation is a source of salvation. One cannot, today, serve both money and society. The bad absolute of capital does not make society vanish but turns it into a bad society (a negative heaven) that has its own unique structure and processes when compared to the "positive hell" of good society.[58]

---

ourselves to "go with the flow" or we will passively elect to commit suicide. Sociology must return to a concept of the social totality (society) as its absolute and its calling, or it will go into the night along with the postmodernists, academics, and the entrepreneurs. Society is our divinity and the universal moment in the sociological syllogism or there will be nothing left (EFRL: 351; S: 312; Royce 1948: 394). When western civilization lose its traditional absolute in the 16th Century the result was the transformation of nearly the entire planet into forced labor camp. The results of society remaining in the place of the "mediator that vanishes" (Marx) as capitalism continues its descent into hell will include the sloughing off of hundreds of millions of surplus individuals as useless waste in the new system of work and leisure, production and consumption. What separates the contemporary sociologist from the classical masters is the reduction of society to a means or a mere verbal entity, no more than a piece of devalued paper currency (cf. Gruppe's positive nominalism, in Vaihinger 1924: 204–05) – in other words, sociology has become a reflection of perversity rather than its negation. When the "Social Order" is reduced to an "instrument" or "our plaything, and make our private fortunes the one object, then this social order rapidly becomes vile to us; we call it sordid, degraded, corrupt, unspiritual and ask how we may escape from it forever" (Royce 1948: 394).

57   "Some [critical, dialectical] apply to societal totality and its laws of movement, others, in pointed opposition, apply to individual social phenomena which one relates to a concept of society at the cost of ostracization for being speculative" (Adorno 1976: 68).

58   When everything is running smoothly, life is a veritable "positive hell."
      Sartre is correct, hell is other people ([1946] 1976), but to exist as a person this hell is inevitable. The options are to escape and die or "Keep your mind in hell, and despair not" (St. Silouan, in Cladis 2012: 98).

Under the capitalist regime of accumulation, society and collective consciousness become the register upon which the deeds of capital are written.

The new materialists and their mystical-empirico brethren (two sides of the same coin) have misplaced the social absolute in the pursuit of commercial and literary appeal and, consequently, their observations and speculations lead them to the conclusion that the notion of society (as a nominal entity) points to nothing real.[59] What is the absolute? "In Hegel's Absolutes there is imbedded, though in abstract form, the full development of what Marx would have called the *social* individual, and what Hegel called individuality 'purified of all that interfered with its universalism,' i.e., freedom itself" (Dunayevskaya 1965).

It might be worth considering the intentions of the pioneers of modern social thought. Hegel claimed to know the mind of god before creation (SL: 50); Comte promoted sociologists to the rank of priests of modernity; Marx the critical criticizer of German idealism and political economy is as much revolutionary prophet as theorist of the commodity; Durkheim, under the surface of positive science was a moral crusader and cult leader; Weber, our Gloomy Gus, was the only one that struck a resigned pose but his poorly grasped ideas on value-free sociology and objective research distorts the reality of the normative Weber.

I think to deny the existence of society on the part of sociology is, really, just a reassertion of its existence in some new guise or shape. As Seligman says, sociology follows the facticity of society "providing post hoc legitimacy and explanations of events it cannot critically comprehend, sharing as it does the epistemological premises of the society it purports to study" (2000: 33). Do we suffer from a sense of a missing absolute? That suffering is none other than the absolute as it is being experienced from a specific set of coordinates and interests within the social universe.

> We all of us experience the Absolute because the Absolute is in everything. And as it is in everything we do or suffer, we may even say that we experience it more fully than we experience anything else, especially as one profound characteristic runs through the whole. And that is, that the world does not let us along; it drives us from pillar to post, and the

---

59   Empirical positivism and the transcendental *a priori* amount to the same thing: an inaccessible and therefore unspeakable dimension of moral reality. Society as something greater than and different than the hustle and bustle of interacting individuals, is either an unverifiable fiction, and therefore not worth the trouble to articulate, or, conversely, beyond our reach and therefore incapable of being rendered symbolically.

very chapter of accidents, as we call it, confronts us with an extraordinary
mixture of opportunity and suffering, which is itself opportunity.
        BOSANQUET 1912: 27

As Žižek might say, where one claims that society is nothing, in reality, it is
less than nothing, i.e., the claim that it is nothing is based on it already being
something: it "has to be something in order to be able to achieve pure nothingness..." (2012: 4). Even as some thinkers deny the existence of society as an
ontological fact they practically refute their claim in their practical activities.
In their normal interactions with others they exhibit a degree of vicious insuf-
ficiency that we would expect from a world devoid of an enduring absolute.

It is not the case that society has ceased to exist or lost its analytic import,
but, rather, it has simply "become invisible" (Jameson 1990: 39). The idea that a
society can go "invisible" demands at least a minimal understanding of what s
meant by "society." At the very least a society, at any scale of existence from the
family, to political and religious associations, to the state, etc., entails a specific
normative representational structure such that individuals and relations (the
atomic singularities and the web of particular equivalents) create, maintain,
and draw sustenance (solidarity, law, language, etc.) from an absolute, an absolute or universal (or, really, an ultra-universal logic) that enables individuals
and groups to interact and pass easily from one domain of social life to another
and interact in multiple domains simultaneously on the basis of homological,
analogical, and metaphorical transpositions. As Goux says,

> The march of history is the evolution of the social organism as a whole
> toward its arrangement, in all domains, under the general [universal]
> equivalent. There is a historical *peak* (I do not say an end point) in the
> accession to a recognized, ratified hegemony of major symbols, the firmly
> established reign of general equivalents. Now it clearly appears that this
> reign has taken place. The summit of a certain history has come to pass. It
> ends in the mode of production based on monetary exchange, and what
> we are experiencing today is the aftershock of this culmination. This
> aftershock does not propel us down the other slope; it shakes the very
> foundations of this history, the very problematics of summit and base,
> including the very concept of the general equivalent.
>   1990: 41

There are moments when the "main thing" goes "invisible" but still functions
(unconsciously) behind the backs of individuals no longer adequately attached to institutions. All of this is a complicated way of stating what is really

simple: the person may drift away from society (loss of relation) but that does not mean society itself has ceased to exist, indeed, it is actually the person that has ceased to exist – i.e., the devaluation of individuality and the fall into egoism. The egoist sits in the wilderness believing that only its ego is real and valuable all the while it has ceased to be of any value whatsoever. The real world has disappeared for the deranged mind in isolation. But even for those who are still engaged, most of what counts as "social" operates invisibly – and, even when it appears physically or manifests itself in physical effects, what is essential is still invisible. For a prosaic but deeply disturbing example, take the world of circulating commodities: the exchange process renders the whole production process invisible to the buyer (Žižek 2012: 7). Likewise, the value of a commodity is completely "invisible" yet socially real and powerful (MECW, 35: 105) as are the bonds "uniting the various branches of trade" (MECW, 35: 359) and the chains of labor domination (MECW, 35: 573).[60] Are capitalism, value, and domination not really existing and problematic things? For a dramatic historical example, take the Calvinist encounter with the doctrine of predestination.

> The Father in heaven of the New Testament, so human and understanding, who rejoices over the repentance of a sinner as a woman over the lost piece of silver she has found, is gone. His place has been taken by a transcendental being, beyond the reach of human understanding, who with His quite incomprehensible decrees has decided the fate of every individual and regulated the tiniest details of the cosmos from eternity.... In its extreme inhumanity this doctrine must above all have had one consequence for the life of a generation which surrendered to its magnificent consistency.
>
> PESC: 60

One consequence of this doctrine was the devaluation or demonization of institutions and what appears to be the elimination of god from the scene. "Finally, even no god" (PESC: 61). The universal equivalent of universal equivalents, the absolute, withdrew from the scene, or really was pushed out and rendered invisible, but, in its more terrifying invisibility, became more terrifyingly powerful. While it appeared that god had absconded and took love with him, and that the diabolical was omnipresent, this was no post-imperial moment of realization through derealization that there is nothing here but us. The extreme anti-social way of acting, thinking, and feeling that characterized

---

60   For more on "invisibility" in the capitalist regime of production and accumulation: (MECW, 28: 230; MECW, 29: 308; MECW, 30: 27; and MECW, 35: 465, 540).

Calvinism (PESC: 60–64)[61] was nonetheless and despite appearances propelled by a negative absolute functioning as "head and capital of a divided territory from which it is barred as empty, omnipresent center" (Goux 1990: 44) and that resulted in creating the modern world order that we know today where, like never before, the absolute of absolutes continues to legislate. After all, the brutally transcendent god of the Calvinists who vanished behind the moon was only the hypostatic representation of their collective existence, the treasury of their hopes, fears, and dreams, and they did not fail to continue living collectively, to hope, dream, and fear because while it appeared that their god had abandoned them, in reality, their god had only changed: the new god that was so indifferent and brutally hyper-nomic was only the transubstantiation of an old god into a new god that appears to have acquired many of the most striking features of capital.

7   The Negative Absolute

In a social order that seems to be irredeemably divided to the point of pathology, say, one where the urban is pitted against the rural, the blue stands opposed to the red, and wind and coal cannot see eye to eye, etc., it would appear that a reconciling third has failed to materialize. True, dialectics tells us that these contradictory and warring dyads require a third to fuse and reconcile their contradictions in an ongoing process of upward cancellations, but it is also sometimes the case that the third works itself to a "higher" stage of development, that "the state of affairs ... enforces the distinction" (Miller 1982: 186). Contradictions and polar antagonisms are not the result of a lack of unity but the work of unity itself (Caird 1893: 128, 136). Where we think there is a problem because of a lack in the register of the third, a lack in the "triadic" structure, the appearance is faulty and diremption is following an invisible logic of universal disembroilment that escapes the analytic eye. Is society dead to us, or, are we dead to society? "Let the idea of society be extinguished in individual minds, let the beliefs, traditions, and aspirations of the collectivity be felt and shared by individuals no longer, and the society will die" (EFRL: 351).

   If sociology is propelling itself down the slope (to recall Goux), regressing to the scale of subjectivity, intersubjectivity, singular relativity and equivalencies, the random flux of networks, etc., it is not because it is following the logic

---

61   The great paradox, of course, is the superior form of social organization that emerges from such an anti-social ideology (PESC).

of society as it exists and functions, but is following money, the anti-society. Even critical theory is not free of contamination. "Marxism is is not immunized against its object. After a century of contact the critique of the commodity succumbs to the commodity" (Jacoby 1981: 1). Consider the anti-object. "It is commonly supposed that an atheist is a man who does not believe in the existence of God. This is wrong, for he is not so negative. He is a man who believes in the existence of not-God" (Pessoa 2012: 3). Like the atheist, the contemporary sociologist, in disbelief, is dedicated to the anti-society. Where there should be a sociological absolute there appears to be a void (the central theme of volume two) but this void is not strictly the absence of something but more like an oppressive black hole, a dark symbol of the energetic vortex of the disembroiling absolute in its autonomous reconstruction. As Hegel says in the big logic, "the process of *determining what the absolute is* has a negative outcome, and the absolute itself appears only as the negation of all predicates and as the void" (SL: 530).

What remains of the old social absolute appears as nothing more than "a multiplicity without unity" (SL: 475). The immediacy of ordinary thinking and of the current shape of the sociological imagination actually presupposes the absolute operating, if not consciously, then behind the backs of those deluded by the notion of an immediacy of social existence and absolute difference and diversity flourishing in the absence of unity.[62] But not only does social and intellectual difference presuppose a unity, observable or unobservable, but is itself an *expression* of that unity (Caird 1886: 136). In the career of any society or system self-evident immediacy secretly emerges from an unseen ground and spreads out in ways that elude a sense of a form that is in the process of developing.

8   Networks and Sideways Glances at Jittery Totalities

With the negation of society, we also find the fetishism of individuals (in the abstract) and relationalism (intersubjectivity) and the degradation of the universal dimension. Human thought is impossible without universals and universals can only be the product of collective thought.

The existence of universals implies the existence of society. A concept carries with it a social stance: not merely of some one other person, but

---

62   Operating without concepts and without theoretical interposition sociology gropes in the darkness of immediacy for the keys to institutional survival in the neoliberal, corporatized university setting (cf. MacIntyre 1984: 79).

> an open and universalizing viewpoint of a plurality of other persons. Just
> how many people this implies is not given. It is more than two; in fact
> it must be explicitly *unspecified* how many it comprises, since concepts
> imply meaningfulness for any and every personal stance at all.
>   COLLINS 1998: 859

The ontic risk, here, lies in quantitative pluralism, anti-dialectical flattening,
and an equalization of powers across realities. Perhaps we find pyramidal networks ranked from top to bottom on the basis of competencies and shared
consensus (learn more, climb higher in the world of mathematics). Collinsland
looks like a nice place to live: plastic networks, consensus, discourse, reflex-
ivity, negotiations, mild epistemological disagreements that William James
could solve with a wave of the hand, and maybe a few arguments from time
to time, coalitions, ritually energized interactions, and pragmatic decision-
making.

There is a connection between the modern academic social scientist and
the bourgeois narcissist: the provisional or even fictional status of social reality
(Worrell and Dangler 2011; see also Horney 1939: 92–93). Where "society" has
ceased to exist, intellectually, webs and networks pop up as substitutes.[63] But
networks, like markets, are merely "the surface of society" and a fetish expression for actual society and where appearance either replaces essence or constitute an identity (Dunayevskaya 1943). Essentially, the problem with network
theory is that it is deranged by virtue of being logically incoherent. Imagine if
Marx's analysis of the value form had pulled up short at the expanded form, the
contradictory, elastic network of partial and oscillating relatives and equivalents. The network, it is true, is a battleground of synthesis, but one where the
synthesis lacks unity and authority or, in the case where unity is present, it
is of only a temporary and negotiated form – here universality only "comes
and goes" as Marx says. One of the odd consequences of the marketing or net-
working mentality is that they expand or contract but not due to forces and
substances external to the market or network but due to the virtues or defi-
ciencies of the web itself. If the thing does encounter something that looks like
resistance it is only a competing market or network that must be overpowered
or, alternatively, the apathy of individuals who do not respond appropriately
to the demands of the market, etc. This is merely a bourgeois mentality that
finds nothing resembling society but merely an aggregate of individuals (Leach
1993: 387).

---

63   According to Collins, "networks are the primary movers" (1998: 626).

But anti-conceptualists cannot simply wish society away any more than we can wish money away; it is not simply a matter of subjective attitudes. In other words, the class of anti-conceptualists may carry on as if the Idea (the actualized concept) and the social absolute simply no longer exist, nothing more real than tooth fairies, but the Idea persists and works behind their backs nonetheless. The mind of a deluded empiricist focused only on the material singularities of the phenomenal realm may believe that he or she is the rational antipode of the lunatic transcendentalist filled to the brim with superstitions, however, unbeknownst to both the empiricist and the metaphysician, they are collaborating on the excavation of a secret tunnel that joins the two domains of disenchanted matter and enchanted noumena. As they claim to reject society and an absolute they are doing the work of the invisible and negative bourgeois absolute. Let us modify a passage from Hegel's major logic to fit our current needs by replacing the word "state" with "society."

> But if an object, for example, the concept of society, did not correspond at all to its Idea, that is, if in fact it was no the Idea of society at all, if its reality, which is the self-conscious individuals, did not correspond at all to the Concept, its soul and its body would have parted; the former would escape into the solitary regions of thought, the latter would have broken up into the single individualities. But because the Concept of society so essentially constitutes the nature of these individualities, it is present in them as an urge so powerful that they are impelled to translate it into reality, be it only in the form of external purposiveness, or to put up with it as it is, or else they must needs perish. The worst society, one whose reality least corresponds to the Concept [e.g., the neoliberal necroverse], in so far as it still exists, is still Idea; the individuals still obey a dominant Concept.
>   SL: 758, translation altered

Just as the depressed egoist engages in suicide believing that either they have rebelled against society or that they have acted in accordance with their individual conscience alone, they nonetheless have obeyed an impersonal command issued by a "higher" authority, that of society. And the modern, anti-conceptualist wheeler and dealer in variables, along with their compadres measuring networks and relations, have not only not liberated themselves from society but are actually engaged in intellectual suicide on behalf of an impersonal imperative issued from "on high" and operating behind their backs: murder the concept and embrace the variable for I have shown you the way to wealth and status.

The concept is the principle of life.[64]

HEGEL [1830] 1991: 236

Society is a conceptual being.

DURKHEIM, EFRL

Let us revolt against this rule of concepts.

MARX, MECW, 5: 23

Concepts are useless

CONTEMPORARY SOCIOLOGIST

The irony is that we have generations of researchers kicking about parts without perceived wholes. This could be the case because there are no longer wholes or totalities and that description is merely a more or less accurate description of the existent or, conversely, totality exists but is rendered invisible due to a breakdown of our concepts and interpretive frameworks. If they are broken or missing we have no choice but to build all new interpretations out of whole cloth, which leaves one overexposed to irrationality, or one can draw upon the past.

> Our ideas and concepts are the crystallization, the comprehensive essence of the whole of our experience, present and past. What was already fixed in the past in abstract mental forms must be included with such adaptations of the present as are necessary. New ideas thus appear to arise from two sources: present reality and the system of ideas transmitted from the past.
>
> PANNEKOEK 1937: Part III, n.p.

Again, the whole or totality[65] cannot exist in the mind once the unity of reality and the concept has been dissolved (SL: 757). To deny, reject, or ignore totality is to abandon society itself and once the category of categories (totality) has been rendered irrelevant coherent scientific reason breaks down.

---

64   For Hegel, the surmounting of externality (as it will be defined in the first chapter) is through the possession of the concept and the mind's concept of itself (2007: 27). When we confront the alien and external our first and last problem is not having the concept that enables a traversal of the gulf that separates subjectivity from the things of this world in such a way that we hang together cooperatively.

65   "The concept of totality is but the concept of society in the abstract form. It is the whole that includes all things, the supreme class that contains all other classes" (EFRL: 443).

It used to be that totality was "self-evident" as a presupposition in theories of knowledge (EFRL: 442) and now self-evidence has ceded to the evidence of the self perspective. As such, the mind may convince itself that it is observing individuals or perhaps a network of related individuals apart from any notion of an encompassing totality called "society" but the error is not in the conception of the whole or totality but the proliferation of uncoordinated, one-sided atheoretical glances that misapprehend the ontic depth of the social sphere as a boundless epistemic matrix.[66] As positivists, they cannot see depth, only surface (Jacoby 1981: 22); as soon as one admits depth one supposedly allows in a god or metaphysics (Burke 2010: xii). To paraphrase Bergson, this is not the social order we are looking for (in Jankélévitch 2012: 35).

We are supposedly living in a "post-social society" (Streeck 2016) and everywhere totality is being searched for. People have grown weary of deconstructions and reconstruction, critique has gone too far in some directions and not far enough in others, and one begins to suspect that our best thoughts have contributed to the erosion of the representations and forces that once provided sources of life and ebullience. We negate and negate day and night and, in the end, deprive the powerless of a "recourse" to a more reasonable world (McCarthy 1991: 112). All this, however, is to be expected: "As ... international life broadens, so does the collective horizon; society no longer appears as the whole, par excellence, and becomes part of a whole that is more vast, with frontiers that are indefinite and capable of rolling back indefinitely" (EFRL: 446). Note carefully, though, the word "appears" in this assessment from Durkheim's magnum opus. If sociology has lost sight of the social absolute as a distinct collective representation, as it does from time to time, this is not because society or societies have ceased to exist, but because the hypereducated and decadent self-consciousness of society has begun to daydream, has gotten lost, and, finding itself stranded in the wilderness, begins the arduous task of reorienting itself not by climbing a peak in order to take in the widest possible view but, conversely, to describe the triviality in its immediate empirical surroundings. Sociology might like to get back to its calling but, having forsaken its critical concepts and theoretical legacy, it is powerless to resist seeing things the way the negative and invisible prime mover dictates (EFRL: 62).[67]

---

66   "In fact, the law that governs the divergent perspectives is the structure of the social process as a preordained whole" (Adorno 1973: 37).

67   "Now, to maintain itself, society often needs us to see things from a certain standpoint and feel them in a certain way. It therefore modifies the ideas we would be inclined to have about them, and the feelings to which we would be inclined to have about them ... even to the extent of replacing them with quite opposite feelings" (EFRL: 62). It would be quite a trick for the "great social being" to distort the sociological gaze so far such that it

Mainstream sociologists and careerists can complain bitterly that concepts are non-falsifiable and that everywhere one finds theory one has come into contact with the smoke and mirrors, sorcerers, abstractions, and fictions. There is a kernel of truth to this. As Danto says, with theory one transports matter to another dimension, a realm of thought – the world of art is one of objects bearing theories and that without theory there is no art world but merely individual "artists" engaged in contingent production (the end of art thesis). If the mainstreamers at the Death to Concepts summer retreat are correct, concepts and theories are not merely useless abstractions, they can never be anything more than *fictions*. But this reduction of concepts and theories to fictions is only sensible from the standpoint of a model of contemporary science, dominated by the methods and assumptions of the natural sciences that, carried out to the extreme, "censor critical thought" (Jacoby 1981: 6). It is true that the "social sciences" died in some sense after the second world war when the methods of the "hard" sciences were embraced by the more difficult (soft) sciences. Following Bachelard we can see that this type of science, that substitutes reality with mathematized relations between variables, has no place for living, organic life and replaces life with abstract fabrications (Forrester 1981: 61).[68]

9   Marxist Association

Marxists still have a conception of society but, invariable, it is of a pejorative variety such that society is always *bourgeois* society and either automatically digging its own grave or, alternately, subject to revolutionary overthrow once the empirical proletariat catches up with the imagined proletariat of radical ideology. Interestingly, revolution leads not back to a good society but to no society at all. "Leave everything behind' appears as a permanent inscription above the door to Marxism" (Bloch 1988: 157).

---

cannot even locate the thing it is supposed to comprehend. Historically, it is usually the nominalist or the capitalist class that insists that society does not exist. In our era, it is cash-sniffing neoliberals who follow Margaret Thatcher when she said "There is no such thing as society. There is living tapestry of men and women and people and the beauty of that tapestry and the quality of our lives will depend upon how much each of us is prepared to take responsibility for ourselves and each of us prepared to turn round and help by our own efforts those who are unfortunate" (in Hinshaw and Stearns 2014: 577).

68   Today, sociology is like a science fiction fantasy where most people go with the flow and kill with numbers for money while a dwindling handful of bearded and robed mystics theorize on the fringes of the imperial system. Of course we can't forget the goofy fuzzballs that fill out the background scenery and provide us with "thick descriptions" and comic relief.

Marx spoke surprisingly little about "society" except in this negative way and the post-capitalist world was not a "society" per se but an ill-defined communist association lacking any sense of "transcendental meditation" (Worrell and Krier 2018). Here, we arrive at a surprising conjunction between neoliberal ideology and critical sociology: the flattened ontological plane of granular assemblages and actor networks with the reduction of social life to something that appears to be little more than erotic and contingent opportunism amongst amateurs liberated from the drudgery of everyday labor via ultra industrialization and the exploitability of unlimited natural resources (communism foregrounded as fishing here, philosophizing over there, loafing, while simultaneously backgrounded by an infinite colonnade of smoke stacks). Where Marx wants to lead humanity into pragmatic association, neoliberalism, as it imagines itself, has already arrived at that place. As such, Marxist post-capitalism and neoliberalism are both suicidal. In both cases the sacred has either been foreclosed (see Fromm 1973: Chapters 9 and 10)[69] or transposed into the register of the hedonistic social atom.

Marx's theory of the commodity and of the contradictions of the capitalist mode of production as we find them in the *Critique* (1859) and the first volume of *Capital* (1867) are unrivaled in perfection. Beyond the critique of capital and of political economy, however, Marxism runs a deficit with regards to a theory of social ontology and is in need of an historical-comparative anthropology which would reveal that the vicissitudes of exchange-value (real and fictional) are but particular moments, extensions, in a universal human history of consubstantial forces and energies spreading and transforming across the various domains of social life for perhaps 50,000 years. We might conceive of a world without exchange-value and capital but the world of surplus social energies, forces, and sacralization (positive and negative) are permanent and transhistorical features of human life. In my estimation, if critical sociology has a future beyond stale ideology it is synthesizing not only Marx's theory of labor power exploitation with Freud's theory of libido and repression but also an "anthropology" of energy and sacred representations.

Marxists almost uniformly deride the founder of academic sociology as an obscurantist, but the aversion is mutual. Durkheim waved off Marxist socialism as "a cry of grief, sometimes of anger, uttered by men who feel most keenly our collective *malaise*" (Durkheim 1958: 41). In *Elementary Forms* he puts distance between himself and Marxism when he says "the last thing to do is to

---

69   Take for example the Marxist "sociologist" who derails critique with a theory of the pre-
      wired proletariat that does society a great favor with every knee-jerk reaction.

see this theory of religion as merely a refurbishment of historical materialism. That would be a total misunderstanding of my thought" (EFRL: 426). Further

> In pointing out an essentially social thing in religion, I in no way mean to say that religion simply translates the material forms and immediate vital necessities of society into another language. I do indeed take it to be obvious that social life depends on and bears the mark of its material base, just as the mental life of the individual depends on the brain and indeed on the whole body. But collective consciousness is something other than a mere epiphenomenon of its morphological base, just as individual consciousness is something other than a mere product of the nervous system. If collective consciousness is to appear, a *sui generis* synthesis of individual consciousness must occur. The product of this synthesis is a whole world of feelings, ideas, and images that follow their own laws once they are born. They mutually attract one another, repel one another, fuse together, subdivide, and proliferate; and none of these combinations is directly commanded and necessitated by the state of the underlying reality. Indeed, the life thus unleashed enjoys such great independence that it sometimes plays about in forms that have no aim or utility of any kind but only for the pleasure of affirming itself.[70] I have shown that precisely this is often true of ritual activity and mythological thought.
>
>   EFRL: 426

The Karl Marx that writes off religion as a tranquilizer of the masses as well as the Marxism of base and superstructure nonsense are valid targets but the Karl Marx of commodity fetishism is not only far more sophisticated but is, actually, consistent with Durkheim's theory of the totem, or, really, to be fair to Marx. Durkheim's social realist theory of the totem conforms, in a broad sense, not to textbook distortions of historical materialism but the actual historical or dialectical materialism found in *Capital*. When a labor product "emerges as a commodity" says Marx, "it changes into a thing which transcends sensuousness."

> It not only stands with its feet on the ground, but, in relation to all other commodities, it stands on its head, and evolves out of its wooden brain grotesque ideas, far more wonderful than if it were to begin dancing of

---

70   "The Prussian war theoretician Clausewitz, in Napoleonic times, famously said, 'Sometimes war dreams of itself'" (Herzog, in House 2016). The sheer beauty of this statement resides not only in its truth but also in the fact that Clausewitz never said this ("famously") but was attributed to Clausewitz by a confused Herzog.

its own free will.... The mysterious character of the commodity-form consists therefore simply in the fact that the commodity reflects the social characteristics of men's own labour as objective characteristics of the products of labour themselves, as the socio-natural properties of these things.... In order, therefore, to find an analogy we must take flight into the misty realm of religion. There the products of the human brain appear as autonomous figures endowed with a life of their own, which enter into relations both with each other and with the human race. So it is in the world of commodities with the products of men's hands. I call this the fetishism which attaches itself to the products of labour as soon as they are produced as commodities,[71] and is therefore inseparable from the production of commodities.

> C: 164–5

Here Marx, on the mystical qualities of commodity relations, is not only in league with Durkheim's theory of the totem but some formulations become virtually interchangeable with one another. When Marx says that "the products of the human brain appear as autonomous figures endowed with a life of their own, which enter into relations both with each other and with the human race" this could have been written by Durkheim, who, in the conclusion of *Forms*, says that collective consciousness, in the minds of associated individuals, appears as something external and autonomous, and which even goes so far as to pleasure itself for the sake of nothing more than its own pleasure,[72] while remaining connected to social relations and material practices intertwined with consciousness.[73]

The modern world of capital accumulation is not the world of "dust and dollars" in the way most people might interpret this phrase. The modern world

---

71   This "produced as commodities" is itself a fetish expression, a presupposition that Marx shares with bourgeois political economy, that conflicts with the iron-clad assertion in everything that Marx wrote after 1859, that the "social character" of the commodity always and only emerges or is realized within the *exchange relation* (C: 165, *passim*).

72   Durkheim is closer to Kant (1929: 611–12) and Hegel than Marx who says that "the ideal is nothing but the material world reflected in the mind of man, and translated into forms of thought" (C: 102). Collective consciousness, values, spirit, or what have you, are not reducible to the status of mere reflections. Where Marx finds the a priori construct a product of presentation Durkheim locates the social and organizational ground upon which the a priori actually exists. Society itself is the practically existing synthetic a priori.

73   Like the unconscious (Freud [1913] 1950: 88) the dynamics and processes of collective or impersonal consciousness display a greater liberty and playfulness than we find in personal consciousness. If we wanted to locate a true originator of non-vitalistic "transcendental empiricism" look no further than Durkheim's theory of collective unconsciousness.

of work, consumption, and surplus value is not, even though it is our everyday, the realm of the profane set apart from the sacredness of religion. Indeed, the young Walter Benjamin wondered if capitalism was not actually a religion.

> Capitalism is entirely without precedent, in that it is a religion which offers not the reform of existence but its complete destruction. It is the expansion of despair, until despair becomes a religious state of the world in the hope that this will lead to salvation. God's transcendence is at an end. But he is not dead; he has been incorporated into human existence.
>
> 1996: 289

Benjamin was following Marx's insight, gleaned from Shakespeare, that the commodity world was analogous in many of its structural and substantive features to the world of religion. Not only in the fetishism of the commodity but also in the new role of money as the "visible divinity" of the capitalist world system (MECW, 3: 324). In modernity, it is "the making of profit as the ultimate and the sole purpose of mankind" that is "the 'strange God' who perched himself side by side with the old divinities of Europe on the altar, and one fine day threw them all overboard with a shove and a kick" (C: 918). It is with Marx, in the "Paris Manuscripts" that a fine point is made regarding the inverting, "confounding and distorting of things" due to the power of money. The difference between the sacred and the profane in the premodern world has come undone and assumed weird forms, most features of which remain entirely unconscious to people; under capital, "impossibilities are soldered together" (MECW, 3: 324) in ways that make no sense to everyday consciousness, and, I would hasten to add, the presuppositions of capital force themselves into the minds of even our best critical sociologists such that, unconsciously, their minds are bent in ways that ensure the preservation of capital even as they believe they are diametrically opposed to it. Anti-capitalism is almost always, unbeknownst to itself, a sect in dispute not over the evils of value but over the distribution of value. Anti-gods are, as Durkheim says, still gods and anti-capitalism is still capitalism. Let us now turn to the domain of facts and the facticity of facts as external and constraining things and then, in the second chapter, map out the genetic procession of the career of any fact as it emerges, reigns, and finally washes up on the shores of the future in some twisted and disfigured form.

CHAPTER 1

The Facticity of the Social

In societies laid low by chronic anomie (S: 254–57) and where "All that is solid melts into air" (MECW, 6: 514) we can be sure that a new fatalism has enslaved us. Everything in society is a construct, that is true as far as it goes, but even if social things are constructs most of them are nonetheless constraining things. "No matter how sophisticated we may be as to the constructed and arbitrary character of our practices, including our practices of representation, our practice of practices is one of actively forgetting such mischief each time we open our mouths to ask for something or to make a statement" (Taussig 1993: xviii).[1] In this chapter and the one that follows I argue that the facticity of the social, preserved from the wellspring of classical sociology, is indispensable for articulating a coherent ontological ground from which critical sociology may advance as it reconstructs and enriches its theoretical matrix, in part, by exploring the essence of the social fact and then, in the following chapter, decompressing the moments of facticity within a processional constellation of ideal-types. If we fail to recenter critical sociology on the ground of a coherent, consistent, and self-conscious critical social realism, with an eye toward the necessary function of the absolute based on a reconsideration of the structure of reason and the relevance of a dialectical method,[2] we are doomed to subjectivism or the kind of pseudo-gnostic immediacy that plagues the current progressive mentality.

1   Social Facts

According to Durkheim, social facts are "things" and for many thinkers this assertion is a grievous error. For example, Alpert says that "Durkheim's use of the word '*chose*' [thing] is extremely unfortunate."

---

1   "We dissimulate. We act and have to act as if mischief were not afoot in the kingdom of the real and that all around the ground lay firm. That is what the public secret, the facticity of the social fact, being a social being, is all about" (Taussig 1993: xvii). One of my students declared in class that money is a social construct. I agreed with her in principle but wondered out loud if money was aware of its constructed status? I don't think it knows.

2   There can be no dialectical method in the absence of a universal dimension that exceeds the abstract universal of ordinary understanding (Adorno 1973: 199).

It necessitated a good deal of explanation and reinterpretation that would have been obviated had he chosen a different term. Things are concrete, specific entities presenting in their empirical completeness such an infinity of aspects that a thorough study of them is, humanly speaking, inexhaustible. Science, rather, studies phenomena, i.e., processes, or, to use a much abused word, behavior. It is concerned not with things as such but with relations between, and aspects of, things as such but with relations between, and aspects of, things.

> 1939: 132

There is practically no end to Alpert's lamentations over Durkheim's terminology. "Thing" is wrong, "fact" is misleading, "mechanical" is bad, "individual" is unfortunate, etc. For Alpert, though, the terminological misfortunes mask an ultimately salvageable theory of society. For others, however, not only is the terminology bad but the theory of social facts is nothing less than totalitarian. Agger, for example, has harsh words for Durkheim and his ontology of social facts.

Evoking and thus provoking domination, sociology repeats Durkheims dreary ontology; "social facts" turn history into ontology. Freedom is equivalent to obedience; laws govern the advance of hierarchy, patriarchy, capital. Following Durkheim, sociology freezes powerless subjectivity into ontology, thus freezing it politically.[3]

> 1989: 6

From this angle the Durkheimian program amounts to little more than submission to fate and the valorization of obedience.[4] The number of like-minded critics who gang up on Durkheim's terminology, concepts, and theories is truly staggering but if we launch into a formal survey of the past and extant criticisms we will derail our project. If we clear up what Durkheim means by a social fact being a "thing" we might save ourselves a lot of trouble.

---

3   We can detect an underlying pragmatic thread here that, without a lot of extrapolation, we can see how it reduces facts to personal experiences or psychological facts. When pragmatism attempts to build up anything from these kinds of facts it faces the problem of building on top of "drifting sand" (Santayana 1913: 126).

4   "In general, one says that society, according to Riesman's expression, is 'controlled from the outside,' i.e., it is heteronomous; and it is often insinuated that ... individuals fundamentally accept without resistance whatever almighty facticity places before them and inculcates into them, as if what now exists must continue as such" (Adorno, in Adorno and Becker 1983: 107) "Marx recognizes the fact of unreason, but he refuses to transform the fact into fate" (Lichtman 1982: 50).

Durkheimian "things" are really no different than the elementary Marxist "thing" from the standpoint of social ontology. For example, in Marx's analysis of the commodity we find that the thing,[5] the commodity, is comprehensible only if we see that the commodity is not this or that object but a *relation*.[6] "Relations are facts too" (Carus [1900] 1996: 452).[7] The commodity relation is generically comparable in some ways to the totem relation – these relations, and a thousand others, are objectified representations of an enigmatic and ethereal moral "substance" that appears to ordinary consciousness as dwelling within the core of things.[8] The commodity relation is not merely a simple ratio or abstract judgment about universals and particularities (following the jargon of ordinary understanding) but an authority relation (in other words, a "real abstraction") whereby qualitatively unique things are forced to become equivalent to one another.[9] The exchange relation is based on a system of property and alienation. Where Marx and Durkheim diverge concerns the morality of property and the inevitability of alienation. We know Marx's stance: property is theft and alienation is suicide. However, Durkheim was not exactly resigned to theft and suicide.

Of importance is that even if the state, the commodity, or any other "fact" is indeed a "fact" "it is no ultimate empirical datum, to be accepted and built into our world-picture willy-nilly. Its force has no claim on our approval merely because it exists: we prefer the attitude of Carlyle's Teufelsdröckh, holding these and all other facts in "everlasting defiance" until we do approve them because we discover some value in them" (Hocking 1926: 74–75). In other words, something may be a fact but it may not be right and a thought may be socially valid but also absurd (C: 169). Just because something exists does not make it valid

---

5 "A commodity is, in the first place, an object outside us, a thing that by its properties satisfies human wants of some sort or another" (MECW, 35: 55).

6 This relation is concealed beneath a material shell and appears to be an unsolvable riddle to ordinary consciousness (C: 149).

7 "In the same way, the relativity of knowledge does not prove (as some agnostic philosophers claim) the impossibility of knowledge. Concrete things, such as stones and other material bodies, are not the only realities; relations, too, are actual ..." (Carus [1900] 1996: 452).

8 When we say that facts are *substances* we are with both Durkheim and Marx who deny the *material* substantiality of moral things (no ordinary reified ontology can be attributed to either of these authors) but both also insist on the material *effects* produced by collective representations.

9 To say that a relation is a thing is to recognize the realist proposition that some representations go beyond the categories of the mere understanding and impinge upon "hidden potentialities" (Bergson 1920: 248) and expressions of authority. A commodity, like a churinga, etc., is a thing (relation) that is set apart, defended, sacrosanct and inviolable by all but the legally or religiously qualified.

(PR: 13). If a fact is absurd it should be rationally criticized and abolished.[10] We abolish by getting to the bottom of things and then disobeying if we feel the need to. "It is necessary to gain an understanding of what the facts are grounded on, and then do away with that" (Eduard Gans, in Bienenstock 2011: 171). Some facts can be abolished while others may only be open to modification. Other facts are *really* factual and we have to simply genuflect to these "ascertained facts" (Neumann 1944: 463)[11] and go on our way with the knowledge that life is seldom fair and hope that Hegel is correct regarding the cunning of reason.

Reconciliation is difficult for critical and romantic types to accept but f the facticity of the social is rejected on principle then we have abandoned principles altogether. A world without social or moral facts is a world without morality and freedom (DOL: xxviii, xxxiii). Without moral facts, obligations, necessities, duties, and so on, we allow individuals to rise to the level of gods and simultaneously fall below the rank of animal – no facticity means no humanity (Comte-Sponville 2004: 128–29). The negation of a fact does not entail what first comes to mind. The negation of a fact does not mean that it merely vanishes but, in a word, is *socialized* or perhaps made rational. For sure, facticity is generally speaking excessive, and far too many people treat the "facts" of bourgeois society as if they are unalterable "aspects of the natural order of things" (Paul Baran, in Lichtman 1982: 2), but the bad news that radicals (anarchists) do not want to hear is that "facticity" is going nowhere and even in the imagined utopias of the future we will still be subjected to facts (C: 173). The facticity of the social as it will be defined below is a central problem for

---

10   Lichtman says that "when Durkheim advised social theorists to 'consider social facts as things,' he was articulating a methodology that reflected the reification of bourgeois society" (1982: 5). Two things stand out with regards to this statement: first, it would be absurd to believe that only bourgeois society suffers from reified and fetishized relations when in fact (no pun intended) there has probably never been (or ever will be) a human society that is free of reification and some degree of fetishism, or, better, mystification – and that, and this may be hard to believe, not every instance of fetishism is necessarily evil; secondly, reflection is not submission. Durkheim's method appears to reflect social reification but Durkheim most definitely identified many facts and features of bourgeois life that needed to be reconstructed or negated. In a nutshell, what Durkheim most wanted to see return with more force and with more crystallized efficaciousness was a clear and definite professional morality in an organic matrix of vocations that would strengthen the individual and their place in the world. Let it once and for all be eliminated from the sociological imagination that Durkheim was an apologist for the status quo. We are always free to disobey (S: 325).

11   It would be folly to not yield a great deal of the time to "the force of things as they are" (Bloch 1953: 15). However, we will never know just how things truly "are" unless we pick our battles from time to time. Things are frequently not what they appear to be.

sociology and represents different modalities of negation: in Weber's work, for example, the social fact is, at least from the standpoint of individuals, simply "unalterable" and something we are forced to heroically submit to;[12] the critical and deconstructionist traditions seek to annihilate social facts root and branch, marking a transition to human freedom (positively and negatively) where we are finally free of alienation in all its forms;[13] and from the perspective of the Durkheimians, facts are neither destinies nor pernicious excesses. If a thing exists it does so for a reason (ERFL: 77). The real is rational (PR: 21). For Durkheim, civilization is impossible without some rudimentary facts or moral necessities. It would be infantile to believe that we can simply live without some "facticities" that bond individuals to others and stabilize institutions. "Axioms are absolutely necessary for human communication" (Bakker 2009: 243).[14]

Social facts may appear to the individual as fates and furies but necessity is nonetheless alloyed with free will. Indeed, we will never free ourselves from capitalist hegemony until a critical mass of the subjugated comprehends the

---

12 "What is most significant about Weber's consciousness of degradation is not merely that he records the atrophy of alienation – the cage, the loss of spirit, mechanized petrification, the ascendancy of material goods. What is most significant is the alienated voice in which he speaks. Weber does not merely describe the decay of bourgeois life; he participates in it. The mode of his consciousness is isomorphic with the world process upon which he reflects" (Lichtman 1982: 6). No doubt, Weber does reflect the fate of the individual under the powers of capital. However, this does not tell the whole story. Weber makes clear that as far as the individual is concerned, yes, the social order is unalterable (PESC: 19) but collective or class action is another thing altogether. Indeed, Weber worried about the growing power of the politically organized working class and he searched the world over for the spiritual constellation that had made the bourgeoisie a heroic and revolutionary class before succumbing to insipidness.

13 Of course, *orthodox* Marxism embraces the unalterable facticity of historical necessity and Marx has more than enough to say about the inexorable laws of history to satisfy those who view history as a brutal but ultimately progressive march toward freedom (see Lichtman 1982: 7).

14 'Axiom' comes from the Greek *axios* – worthy – related to *axia*, for 'worth' or 'value.' If we wish to preserve 'communication' (literally, the act of communing, of forming communities) then we are forced to embrace a world of values which are, of course, wholly irrational from a scientific-materialist standpoint. Something enjoying maximum value does so on the basis of being unchallenged. Sociologists usually operate in one of two modes: challenging everything (critical devaluation) or blindly wishing that sociology does not meddle in values. However, sociology is a science *of* values and is in no way 'value free.' Sociology cannot tell a person what to do or what is of value but merely that if they desire to achieve such and such objective, there are means by which such and such is possible (or impossible) and, importantly, that there are unintended and unforeseen consequences in pursuing each and every goal. Another service that sociology can provide is insisting that ends do not justify any and all means. Worthy ends deserve and can only succeed with worthy means.

necessity of revolution and that liberation is a requirement for human free-dom (Lichtman 1982: 9). Durkheim makes perfectly clear the commingling of fact and freedom: facticity does not extinguish free will but proves its actual existence (S: 325)[15] and real freedom is not only compatible with rules and regulations, but only made possible on the basis of rules and regulations. An-other way to think of this paradox is that necessity enables the subjectification of facts (and the objectivity of the purely subjective) as well as a functioning reality principle. If millions of people who are capable of rational thought not only act and think irrationally, but also revel in their irrational self-destruction, it is because the social ground of reality, truth, and reason has been eroded by social disorganization and opportunistic demagogues.[16] Without a com-mitment to social facts critical sociology cannot even function in a coherent and rational manner – it will fail to move beyond identity politics, tribal cults, and fanaticism (which is unfortunately fine with many self-identifying critical sociologists).

Social facts are sociological facts – to run down the concept of social facts would be tantamount to denying the existence or relevance of sociology itself as a distinct field (Alpert 1939: 132). Some people do consider sociology extra-neous, a field for leftovers (both problems and personnel) but we hardly have to justify our existence. Though he never thought of himself as a sociologist Marx's critique of political economy and the commodity is sociological to its very core. Marx did not deny the facticity of the commodity but subjected it to a withering dialectical critique and arrived at an objective sociological com-prehension of the thing; and there is no way "beyond" surplus value until we figure out what value is, what kind of authority we are up against, and what we might like to replace value with. But make no mistake, we might imagine a world free of surplus value and the excess labor that it rests on, but a world without surplus moral energies in the most general sense would be synony-mous with human extinction. We might liberate ourselves from labor exploita-tion but the day humans fail to augment physical existence with moral forces via association, and crystallize those forces in authoritative or valid represen-tations, is the day Spirit is extinguished.

Durkheim has long been portrayed as an arch villain of positivistic and con-servative social thought and, for no better reason than having a bad reputation and being reduced to stereotypes, virtually no effort of any kind has been made

15   In would be incorrect, then, to see individuals as completely or universally powerless in the face of social compulsion (Vincent 1897: 14).
16   "Americans believe in facts, but not in facticity" (Baudrillard 1988: 85). This is another way of saying that what passes for facts, in the absence of facticity, are subjective rationaliza-tions. "They do not know that [their] facts are factitious, as their name suggests" (Ibid.).

to forge an alloy of Marxist and Durkheimian thought. Durkheim did share things in common with classical *philosophical* positivism, for example the principle that a whole possess qualities that are different from those found in its parts,[17] but he rejected the notion that we cannot obtain objective and positive knowledge of the substantial core of things.[18] The irony of classical positivism is that the self-evident veracity of sensibility paving the way for objective knowledge (what you see is what you get) actually obliterates the possibility of universal objectivity altogether.[19] Positivism is like hunting for white rhinos at the North Pole. We do not have to fear what Durkheim would call "positive" knowledge because negation without a corresponding positivity is meaningless[20] and, as for his conservatism, only an anarchist or juvenile delinquent would be enticed by the prospects of the total revolutionary annihilation of the existent.[21] Due to a raft of misconceptions (political, ontological, etc.) the artificers of a "Marxheimian" sociology are few and, in that one fact, we missed an opportunity to build a better sociology. One of the things I hope to convey in this volume is that social facts are usually "'necessities of thought'" as far as

---

17   Note, we are making a distinction between positive *philosophy* (the whole and the concrete) and positive *science* which is dedicated to the parts and the abstract (Bosanquet 1912: 33).

18   For more on classical positivism see Spaulding (1918: 248).

19   One cannot locate the universal 'in' the singular just as we cannot find majesty 'in' the body of the king.

20   In a sense, the positive is merely the portion of the negative that we feign ignorance of, the piece of the negative that we set aside, make untouchable and preserve as something inviolable. The positive is ironic negative. It would be nice if the Enlightenment dream of eliminating ignorance from the world was plausible but, in its own way, ignorance is a value. Our capacity to love others is based to a degree on simply 'not knowing' everything there is about them, to *ignore* certain aspects of their being. To ignore something about a person or a group means that they have multiple dimensions of existence and that what they do in private is their business and does not impinge on the values that determine public life. Ignorance, then, is in a way an anti-magical technique. The magical-minded fantasize that what goes on in private life of the other is not good, that the profane (private) side of life is actually contaminated with the impure and that their actions might conjure a whirlwind of evil. Ignorance is even a necessity and virtue of collaborative life. "As people invented new tools for new ways of living, they simultaneously created new realms of ignorance; if everyone had insisted on, say, mastering the principles of metalworking before picking up a knife, the Bronze Age wouldn't have amounted to much. When it comes to new technologies, incomplete understanding is empowering" (Kolbert 2017: n.p.).

21   We do not build the good on the "ruins of the past. [For Durkheim] [t]he revolutionary shock demolished the traditional frameworks of social life, dissolved the bonds joining men together, shattered the familial and religious constraints to which men were subject and which structured their daily life and representations, and left a void which has still not been filled" (Jankélévitch 2012: 34).

individuals go (Vincent 1897: 14)[22] but not exactly fate, that a theory of alien-ation is incomplete without a theory of reconciliation, and that, while life is often an unhappy state of affairs and filled with evils, society is in the final analysis not only inescapable without embracing sacrifice (Hardimon 1994: 20) but a "positive evil" that we should embrace even as we criticise it (S: 212). It's one thing to criticize in order to repudiate or disown something or someone and another to criticize so that we can draw closer. After Hegel, the gateway to a noumenal dimension is barred and we cannot flee from this world into another. We cannot liquidate society and hope to survive the liquidation. We will have to face the facts.

Social facts (*faits social*) are ways of collectively acting, thinking, and feeling (either fixed or fluid) that are external, coercive, and irreducible or *sui generis* (RSM: 50–9; EFRL: 15; also C: 1054; Cassirer 1946: 36; Lukács 1971: 47, 133; Mauss 2005: 7; Simmel 1950: 10; Weber [1930] 2001: 19). The boundaries between act-ing, thinking, and feeling are fluid.

> In fact, what the great philosophers meant by thought, the highest pos-sible phase of realisation, is much what most people mean ... when they speak of feeling. For if we admit thought to be in part intuitive, a unity asserted through diversity, there is no longer anything to prevent it from reproducing the character of feeling in the sense of immediate appre-hension; an immediate apprehension which is the totality of a mediate discourse. This is the sort of apprehension, which a name, familiar and adored, awakes in us.
>
> BOSANQUET 1912: 65

While we normally think of action and thought to be two separate things, and, indeed, while thought and action may be radically alienated from one another in one sense (Bakhtin 1993: 54–55) it is also possible to see thinking as a kind of proto-action. Freud referred to thinking as "experimental action, a kind of groping forward, involving only a small expenditure of energy in the way of discharge" ([1925] 1959: 184).[23] But I think that we must still enforce an analytic separation between individual thoughts which are mere reflections and action

---

22   We are reminded of Weber who does not say that capitalism is simply an "unalterable or-der" but is "unalterable" insofar as it confronts the individual (PESC: 19). With association and solidarity we depart, at least potentially, the domain of inevitability.

23   "The agent endowed with reason does not behave like a thing of which the activity can be reduced to a system of reflexes. He hesitates, feels his way, deliberates, and by that dis-tinguishing mark he is recognized. External stimulation, instead of resulting immediately in [physical] movements, is halted in its progress and is subjected to a *sui generis* elabo-ration; a more or less long period of time elapses before the expression in movement

proper (S: 279).[24] Where we find thought crossing most freely into the domain of action is in pragmatic currents and among those sympathetic to the pragmatic tradition (e.g., Peirce [1878] 1992: 129; Royce 1982: 137). We find this thought-action unity emerge most clearly in Fichte's positing of an Absolute Ego that "acts by thinking and thinks by acting" (Kroner 1961: 241). However, the coordinates of Fichte's thought-action unity are within the realm of the transcendental absolute and are radically different from the unity of either revolutionary praxis or the garden reveries of alienated intellectuals – both suffering in their own ways from what Durkheim would call the "disease of the infinite" (S: 287). It is most productive to conceive of thinking, acting, and feeling as entangled but nonetheless analytically separate moments in the unity of human expression as a whole (Volosinov 1973: 84) if by that we mean that the mediating substance for both thought and action, where they are sublated into a sui generis compound, is human association and collective action.[25]

> The intercourse of men does not arise from their essence; it is their real essence and is indeed not only their theoretical essence, their real life-consciousness, but also their practical, their real life-activity. Thinking and doing only arise from the intercourse, the collaboration of individuals, and what is called the mystical "Spirit" is just this life-air, this workplace, this collaboration of ours.
>
> HESS 1845: n.p.

The fact of association transforms abstract concerns over thought and action into nullities. Perhaps the most powerful expression of this assemblage unity of thought and action is found in *Elementary Forms* where Durkheim says that in religious ceremonies what the participants ultimately offer up to the collective representations are their thoughts (EFRL: 345–54).[26]

---

appears. It would appear, then, that the reason ... is not as inert as has been supposed. Indeed, how could it be otherwise?" (Durkheim 1974: 3).

24 One place thought and action blend together indissolubly and are no longer distinct is in the totalitarian social order ruled by a brutal dictator (Arendt 1968: 325–26).

25 In other words, we have to abandon the atomistic assumptions of contemporary sociology that authorizes the reduction of sociological research down to surveys of individual attitudes. What individuals think about this or that is not unimportant but it is also not sociology which focuses on collective action historically and comparatively. The mind that completes a survey is a far cry from the syntheses of united consciousnesses bent by authoritative imperatives (Bouglé, in ESS, 5: 291).

26 "The true raison d'être of even those cults that are most materialistic in appearance is not to be sought in the actions they prescribe but in the inward and moral renewal that the actions help to bring about. What the worshipper in reality gives his god is not the food

Using the phrase "social fact" segregates a distinct class of things from those studied in other areas such as "ideal facts" (Bosanquet [1923] 1965: 32) and bio-logical facts, etc., (S: 325). If we contort Bosanquet a little we can say that the totality of society is "not exhausted in the facts" but the social "is at every mo-ment embodied in the facts" ([1923] 1965: 33). These facts are crystallizations of social life partially "fixed on material supports" (S: 314; cf. Hegel 1975a: 88). The term "fact" sounds unbearably quaint,[27] however, when we examine its etymology the concept is a veritable mansion and is far more intriguing than we might first suspect.

"Fact" is derived from the Latin *factum* and the range of possible meanings includes "deed, action, event, occurrence, achievement, misdeed, real happen-ing, result of doing, something done, in post-classical Latin [a] thing that has really occurred or is actually the case, thing known to be true ... use as noun of neuter past participle of *facere* to make" (OED). *Facere* is the shared root for both "fact" and "fetish." A *factum* denotes not just an action or thing done but also an "evil deed" by a *malefactor*. A fact is not only believed to be real but is actually real; it is a thing that may preexist our individual existence but it is nonetheless, like human history, made (*manufactured*)[28] through concerted

---

he places on the altar or the blood that he causes to flow from his veins: It is his thought" (EFRL: 350).

27   Perhaps nowhere is this better illustrated than Freud's training in Vienna and in France by hardcore empirical positivists; early on, reflecting his training, he believed that "theory is all very well, but that does not prevent facts from existing. This was the principal lesson Charcot had to impart: the scientist's submissive obedience to facts is not the adversary, but the source and servant, of theory" (Gay 2006: 51). Indeed, the earliest writings with Breuer exhibited a "barely developed theoretical basis" that would, once it departed from physiology and psychiatry, then mushroom into a full-blown philosophy of culture (Vo-loshinov [1927] 2012: 4). The 'facts' of positivism were part of a highly mechanistic and Newtonian reduction of mental illness to chemicals, motion, repulsion, and attraction (Gay 2006: 34–5, 79). While Freud may have started off as a reductionistic materialist his development moved in a more interesting direction. A genuine materialism would find incomplete descriptions of the world as a failure and insist that all mental facts to be regarded as "'ontologically dependent' on physical facts in the straightforward sense of following from them by necessity" (Kripke 1980: 155). This is clearly not the Freud of even 1899.

28   See, e.g., Marx ([1869] 1963: 15; C: 493). Critical terminology usually centers on the notion of *praxis* (practice or practical activity) but it is actually *poiesis* that is of importance with regard to the facticity of moral and social life. The poet (*poeta*) was originally one who created, a maker, and in the Old Occitan language, *poeta* meant authority (OED). Aristotle says that the function of the poet "is to describe, not the thing that has happened, but a kind of thing that might happen, i.e., what is possible as being probably or necessary" (1984: 2322–23).

effort, a fact is a *feat*, in other words, with definite *features*, that normally lead across time and space to *stupefaction* on the part of makers and remakers, the eventual *petrifaction* (hardening or reification) of our creations, and, ultimately when the sun sets for any fact, the *putrefaction* or rotting of the thing and the degeneration into a putrid monstrosity.[29] Society reduced to a mob of rotting monsters is anathema to reason but the dream of anarchy or liquid intersubjectivity without end (life as permanent festival, revolution, and ekstasis) is repellent to the need for solidarity, peace, agape, and collective security. *Facere* leads off into two contrary directions: *facts and fetishes*, just as for example *mimesis*, the proto-cult (EFRL: 391), leads into two antithetical directions simultaneously (cf. ES: 23–24): mindless imitation on one hand and prestigious emulation on the other. But not all "facts" are "fetishes" and the latter can at least in theory be defetishized. Fetishism is detrimental to rational life but facticity in itself is inescapable.[30] The goal of critical sociology is the defetishization (literally the *radicalization*) of society and the transformation of fetishes into rational relations, processes, and regulated forces.[31] A good critical sociology, therefore, is an absolute sociology and not the mediator that vanishes (C: 187) in the ontically flat world of dyadic and socially psychotic relations of "personal autonomy." Authority (the sacred) is permanent, essential, and necessary but tradition must be made to justify itself; charisma must be disenchanted, and law must be made to serve the substantive over technical requirements of social life. It is impossible to conceive of rational collective existence in the absence of sacred forces.[32]

29 "Facticity parallels the reified object in Simmel's and Lukács's formulation; the given situation appears eternal" (Aronowitz 1994: 22).

30 Defetishiation is of course one of our principle goals (the analytic dimension of life has no inherent moral qualities) yet are we sure that we want to relentlessly defetishize every aspect of life right down to the bone? Do we want to send folks to reeducation camps for saying "The sun went behind the clouds" or for enjoying music or art? Should we criminalize the naming of a tree or steadfastly believing that our pet loves us? Absolute disenchantment may not be the realm of freedom and rational cooperation we imagine.

31 As the neo-Hegelian Bosanquet says, if it is a fact, it is a force ([1923] 1965: 36). This is pure Durkheim: social facts are immaterial forces and passions that are expressed in representations and have material effects (S: 307–15; cf. Harvey 1989: 165). Are we really willing to give up on a concept of social forces? Certainly, neither Marx nor contemporary critical sociology can do so without committing intellectual suicide. As Pannekoek says, "The wage-relations between workman and employer, the constitution of the United States, the science of mathematics, although not consisting of physical matter, are quite as real and objective as the factory machine, the Capitol or the Ohio River. Even ideas themselves in their turn act as real, observable facts" (1937: Part I, n.p.).

32 Without the sacred there can be nothing secular and purely individual. The sacred is the foundation of real individuality.

Normal contemporary sociology is terrible at accounting for social facticities in our sense because facts are forms of authority and possess objective
"dignity" (Adorno 1976: 72). The basic problem is that commercial sociology
does not have at its disposal a concept of authority. There are merely equal
subjective attitudes. In other words, what sociology investigates today, and
for the last several generations, is the abstracted person rather than society,
institutions, and forces (S: 212). An abstracted person is not identical with actual individuals which only exist and can be comprehended as singular moments within the life of the social totality. The *methods* of normal sociology
are "objective" but the findings and interpretations are incapable of pointing
beyond alienated subjectivism (Adorno 1976: 72). As Durkheim says, empirical
methods are simply irrational (EFRL: 13) and useless in penetrating the "dignity" of social facts. And where commercial and academic sociology simply
lacks a concept of authority, critical sociology, on the other hand, has gone to
war against anything resembling authority in the good fight against authoritarianism. The goal of critical sociology (and this includes Durkheim) cannot
be social anarchy but the defetishization of society and the transformation of
fetishes into comprehensible relations and processes. The purpose of sociology is not to kill authority per se but to rationalize and transform facts in accordance with biophilic values.

A few examples of social facts include words and language,[33] bodily hexis,[34] gender distinctions, money, gift-giving, commodities, mores, folkways,
proverbs and maxims,[35] temporary mob anger, laws (i.e., "permanent anger"),[36] totems, professional and religious ethics, mythologies,[37] ideologies,[38]

---

33   "The word, like a god ... confronts man not as a creation of his own, but as something exis-
      tent and significant in its own right, as an objective reality" (Cassirer 1946: 36; cf. Agamben
      2004: 36).

34   "Bodily hexis is ... a permanent disposition, a durable way of standing, speaking, walking,
      and thereby of feeling and thinking" (Bourdieu [1980] 1990: 69–70).

35   A proverb "is the concentrated expression of a collective idea or feeling.... Beliefs and
      feelings of this kind cannot even exist without their crystallizing in this form" (DOL: 12c).
      See Smith (2006) and Manders (2006) on the hegemony of proverbs, folk-sayings, and
      common sense.

36   See Bosanquet ([1923] 1965: 36) on the distinction between the simple penal law of the
      small group compared to the permanence of recognized standards of conduct.

37   A myth is a sacred story or tale that functions as a regulating force in society (Malinowski
      1948: 101; see especially EFRL: 379). Myth is the frozen or crystallized remnants of ritual
      possession frenzy – permanent fury, if you will (see Jaynes 1990: 374).

38   "But, inasmuch *as a social ideology changes man's psychic structure, it has not only repro-
      duced itself in man but, what is more significant, has become an active force, a material
      power in man, who in turn has become concretely changed, and, as a consequence thereof,
      acts in a different and contradictory fashion*" (Reich 1970: 18, emphasis in the original).

worldviews,[39] racism, suicide and murder rates, kings, and gods. Even our thinking and reasoning abilities, seemingly just a brain activity on the part of individuals, are social facts: "Reason, which is none other than the fundamental categories taken together, is vested with an authority that we cannot escape at will.[40] When we try to resist it, to free ourselves from some of these fundamental notions, we meet sharp resistance. Hence, far from merely depending upon us, they impose themselves upon us" (EFRL: 13).[41] The ordinary person does not typically think of things like suicide as social facts. Self-destruction is almost universally framed in terms of personal psychology. It was Durkheim's task to bring consciousness around to seeing our most intimate actions, thoughts, and emotional structures as arising and reflecting impersonal social forces as they refract through representations (see Mannheim 1982: 208 ff; Meštrović 1988: 97). In a nutshell, society, its institutions, and its imperative forms of conduct, thought, and emotions are things "above and beyond" a mere collection of interactions and if we want to grasp the social nature of, e.g., money, we will have to consider it not as a material fact or a psychological fact but as something stranger, a social fact.[42]

For sure, we look around and we see only individuals going about their business (S: 310) but things like "Esprit de corps, national sentiment, sym-pathy [sic], are no mere metaphors" (Peirce [1892] 1992: 350). Indeed, nations, "social classes, cities, and even universities are actually real .... Nations, for example, are made up of citizens, but at the same time they have features which cannot be explained in terms of the characteristics of individuals – [i.e., features such

---

39   "World-views are social facts. Great philosophical and artistic works represent the *coherent* and adequate expressions of these world-views. As such, they are *at once individual and social* expressions, their content being determined by the *maximum potential consciousness* of the group, of the social class in general, and their form being determined by the content for which the writer or thinker finds an adequate expression" (Goldmann 1969: 129).

40   "Thinking has a social form.... I do not invent my own language; my thinking depends on forms which have come to me ready-made, from beyond the present moment of consciousness" (Collins 1998: 858).

41   "'As reason is a communal thing, not an inborn property of single individuals, so man, unless he lives in a community, cannot attain to Reason. He comes to Reason not by himself, but through the actual presence of Reason, in the form of a living community'" (Feuerbach, in Wartofsky 1977: 44).

42   We might think that science is a social fact but, ironically, like science in general, the branch of science that studies social facts, sociology, is not itself a social fact. As Weber puts it in his famous "Science as a Vocation" lecture, science does not tell us what we must do. "The concepts of science ... are arbitrary constructions [and are therefore not actual concepts in our sense]; there is not one of them that need be thought" (Collingwood 1946: 197).

as] borders, currencies, languages, states, etc." (Smith 1994: 7; see also Elias [1939] 1994: 389). Even a single word like "liberty" can be a social fact in the way it unifies thought, sentiment, and action. The word "[L]iberty is not just an idea, an abstract principle. It is power, effective power to do specific things" (Dewey 1946: 111). Ontologically, those things which mark the uniqueness of the European Union or the Power Elite are not mysterious emanations from some inaccessible dimension separate from the people that live in what we call the EU but these entities *manifest themselves in the consciousness of individuals as external things* invested with meaning and power rather than just whimsical notions.[43] In other words, the "power elite" is not a puff of air we use to conveniently lump together a group of individuals under a label or category of the understanding, rather, the power elite is a real interlocking network possessing qualities and potentials that cannot be found in any of the individual members of the group,[44] in the same way that, analogically, bronze alloy (RSM: 39) possess qualities (hardness, for example) not found in bronze ingredients: copper, tin, along with trace quantities of silver and arsenic. Durkheim clarifies that "we do not say that social facts are material things, but that they are things just as are material things, although in a different way" (RSM: 35). As he says later, something immaterial or ideal can be nonetheless objectively real and have *physical effects* (EFRL: 369, 390)[45] in the same way that the reduction of, say, concrete labor to an abstraction yields, for Marx, what has been called a *real abstraction* or a "concrete abstraction" (Harvey 1989, *passim*).[46] Nowhere is the power of this kind of abstraction better expressed than in Marx's characterization of the moneyed person:

> Being the external, common medium and faculty for turning an image into reality and reality into a mere image ... money transforms the real essential powers of man and nature into what are merely abstract conceits and therefore imperfections – into tormenting chimeras – just as it transforms real imperfections and chimeras – essential powers which are

---

43 Marx's criticism of nominalism and the way it can oscillate with naive realism is especially useful (C: 677).

44 The power elite's ability to "sympathetically" take the view of others within its own class, not to mention the seemingly occult abilities of its members to slide from one role to another, is made comprehensible to the fool as the result of a conspiracy theory (Mills 1956: 269–97).

45 The issue has less to do with matter per se (versus the immaterial or ideal) and more to do with the "sensory reality" of the immaterial (Hegel 2007: 29).

46 Money "is a *real* or *concrete abstraction* that exists external to us and exercises real power over us" (Harvey 1989: 167).

really impotent, which exist only in the imagination of the individual –
into real powers and faculties.... Money, then, appears as this overturn-
ing power both against the individual and against the bonds of society,
etc., which claim to be essences in themselves. It transforms fidelity into
infidelity, love into hate, hate into love, virtue into vice, vice into virtue,
servant into master, master into servant, idiocy into intelligence, and intelligence into idiocy.[47]

> PM: 168–69

Both Marx and Durkheim would agree, then, that something like capital is not
a thing *per se* but a social relation and an imperative form of thought (C: 169)
that appears or takes the form of a thing and gives it a "specific social character" (C, 3: 953).[48]

Working beyond the dead ends of idealism and materialism Durkheim
notes that "the greater part" of fluid social life lacks materialization (S: 315; also
Bouglé [1926] 1970: 74)[49] leaving only certain elements to crystallize and even
fewer to materialize out all the way (S: 315; cf. Volosinov 1973: 91–92). Materiality in itself is morally inert. Even money sometimes fails to rise above the
threshold of the profane.[50] But this is not an idealism pure and simple.[51] "First,
it is not true that society is make up only of individuals; it also includes material things, which play an essential role in the common life" (S: 313; cf. G: 265).

---

47   We find in Benjamin Franklin's utilitarianism the notion of surplus virtue as waste. The
      appearance of a virtue is just as good as the real thing (PESC: 17). "Of course one ought
      to *express* pity, but one ought to guard against *having* it; for unfortunate people are so
      stupid that they count the expression of pity as the greatest good on earth" (Nietzsche
      2015: 11).

48   There is no such thing as value *per se* or in itself. The attribution of "value *per se*" or the
      idea of intrinsic value is fetishism (Adorno [1975] 2000: 41).

49   "[T]o comprehend that the social phenomena which are among the most solid and un-
      yielding of our experiences, are nevertheless ideal in their nature, and consist of con-
      scious recognitions, by intelligent beings, of the relations in which they stand, is to make
      a great step towards grasping the essential task of science in dealing with society" (Bosan-
      quet [1923] 1965: 33; cf. Bouglé [1926] 1970).

50   For years I have asked students if they bother to pick up pennies they find on the sidewalk
      and less than five percent say they do and, even then, inconsistently. Less than ten percent
      bother with nickels and when I ask about dimes someone invariably asks if the coin is
      heads-up because they don't want bad luck. About half my students will get down for a
      dime. The quantitative threshold (heads-up or not) seems to be the quarter where more
      than 75 percent of the class with pick it up. A greater percentage will chase a dollar bill
      blowing down the street or across a parking lot.

51   Durkheim rejects all the worn categorizations such as materialist and idealist for his so-
      ciology (RSM: 32). There is nothing traditionally materialistic, positivistic, empiricist, or
      idealist about Durkheim's theory of collective representations (Jones [2000] 2006a: 38).

Social life as we know it can never fully dematerialize[52] but Durkheim comprehends, like Marx, that the materiality of a totem or a commodity is only
the passive, contingent, and superficial "envelope" or embodiment for what is
really decisive: the objective *relation* of the clan members or workers within
the overall social process and the representations that emerge from and reflect
back on these relations. Whether money takes the form of metal or paper is
irrelevant because they are all signs of value and have similar effects (Montesquieu 2002: 375). Heed Marx's note: "when Galiani said: Value is a relation
between persons ... he ought to have added: a relation concealed beneath a
material shell" (C: 167). As a social *relation* and a form of collective consciousness (G: 309) value must assume some objective *form* but the important aspect
is not the profane material shell (EFRL: 327).[53] Recall, value is an "abstraction
from" the concrete (C: 127) or an alien[54] way of thinking about the concrete

---

52   Can the economy ever dematerialize? Of course not. Purely imaginary debts, bets, deriva-
      tives, and swaps represent a nearly incomprehensible flow of fictional or semi-fictional
      value (see McNally 2011) but "material consumption takes priority over other forms.... In
      addition, there are very few real forms of non-material production" (Goodchild 2009: 83).
      It bears repeating that material consumption is not value consumption.

53   Social forces may "borrow the outward and physical forms in which they are imagined but
      they own none of their power to those things. They are not held by internal bonds to the
      various supports on which they eventually settle and are not rooted in them" (EFRL: 327).
      Social, moral, or religious things exist only as representations (EFRL: 349). Durkheim says
      that this is true of anything "for things exist only as representations" but this "is doubly
      true" in the case of sacred things. This is a subtle allusion to the double consciousness of
      individuals – the side of the social involves a complex reciprocating intermittent inter-
      change between the thinker and the thought where energies and vitalities ebb and flow
      across time and space. The gods will collapse without our support (EFRL: 349).

54   Alienation, here in the form of quantitative reduction, represents the scaffolding that
      bridges the gulf separating consciousness and matter: "The most heterogeneous objects
      we know, the two poles of the world view which neither metaphysics nor science has
      succeeded in reducing to each other, are the motions of matter and the states of con-
      sciousness. The pure extension of the one and the internality of the other have not so
      far allowed any point to be discovered that could plausibly be regarded as their meeting
      ground.... The logical principle that appeared to make the ability of money to measure
      value dependent upon its own value is thus breached. It is indeed correct that the quanti-
      ties of different objects can be compared only if they are of the same quality; wherever
      measurement is done by direct comparison of two quantities it presupposes identical
      qualities. But wherever a change, a difference or the relation between two quantities is to
      be measured, it is sufficient for their determination that the proportions of the measuring
      objects are reflected by the proportions of those measured; and there need be no qualita-
      tive identity of the objects. Two objects with different qualities cannot be equalized, but
      two proportions between qualitatively different things may be. The two objects m and r
      may have some relationship that has nothing to do with qualitative identity, so that nei-
      ther one can serve directly as a measure for the other. The relation may be one of cause

and as values not an "atom" of concrete usefulness enters into the problem (C: 128).[55] Although it may not know it, what matters to Spirit is not the world of carriers but the system of representations borne by the physical and confused with the perceivable. "Social life" per se is "made up entirely of representations" (RSM: 34)[56] which are crystallizations of abstract yet objectively real "social substance" (C: 128).[57] Relations between singularities give rise to "a third thing, which in itself is neither the one nor the other" (C: 127; S: 209). To the extent that material stuff is relevant it is because it is useful and is swept up in the representational system as carriers or props, the concealing shells.[58] A commodity, for example, loses its *objective* status as a bearer of value when viewed in isolation, outside or abstracted from its *relation* with its social mirror and, when that relation ("purely social") is disregarded, the universal equivalent, that emergent third thing[59] that singulars and equivalents have in common, becomes mystified and incomprehensible.[60]

Everything worthwhile in the classical tradition hinges upon a mostly invisible unity between *dialectical process and structure* (Piaget 1970) whereby the accidental and singular participates in the essential and universal by way of the mediating particularity that appears to vanish under the sign of the

---

and effect, of symbolism, of common relationship to a third factor or anything else. Let us assume as given that an object *a* is known to be a quarter of *m*, and an object *b* is known to be some quantitative part of *n*. If a relation exists between *a* and *b*, corresponding to the relation *m* and *n*, it follows that *b* equals a quarter of *n*. In spite of a qualitative difference and the impossibility of any direct comparison between *a* and *b*, it is nevertheless possible to determine the quantity of one by the quantity of the other" (Simmel [1907] 1990: 132–33).

55 For Marx, this objectivity is "phantom-like" (C: 128), i.e., spectral and horrifying.

56 The term 'representation' is still a useful one compared to many postmodern regressions since it reminds us that the sign is a re-presentation, i.e., an image of spirit but not spirit itself (PS: 273) and that we should never confuse symbols and other signs for the things they signify (S: 315).

57 "All this supra-physical life is built and expanded not because of the demands of the cosmic environment but because of the demands of the social environment" (S: 211).

58 "Sacred images, idols, utensils, clothing, dwellings, buildings, and so on are all characterized by the fact that the natural is used as a means, as medium for realizing a contexture of meaning ... " (Mannheim 1982: 231).

59 "The first commodity's value character emerges here through its own relation to the second commodity" (C: 141–42).

60 The underground tunnel that connects crude materialism and transcendental Realism is short. Abstracted from its necessary exchange *relation* the commodity (not really a commodity at all in this non-relational state, or, perhaps, a presuppositional, imagined commodity) can appear to be *nothing but* a chunk of material devoid of any synthetic qualities (nominalism) or, alternately, as a "store of value" by Realists and materialists. For a recent example see Piketty's blockbuster book on inequality (2014).

universal.[61] What is decisive in this regard is that while Durkheim never dis-
regards the profane life of positive materiality, they are, after all, the base and
supports for social life, his interest in social facts is, like Hegel's, not a positive
one but one rooted in negativity – *negative social facts*[62] are not the empirically
available things we perceive directly but the relations between subjects, intersubjective thought, conceptual culture, surplus moral energies, forces, and
authoritative forms of thinking, reasoning, and rationalizations with regard to
the problem of solidarity and normative regulation.

The creators of classical sociology, though they differed in their problems,
methods and terminologies, all agreed, at least, on what we are calling the
"facticity" of the social as something actually real, something that individuals
are a part of, something that exists independently of our individual selves. Of
course, this does not preclude curators from protesting that their sage is incom-
mensurable and unavailable for such fusions. Even though the factual status of
the commodity, money, and capital in Marx's writings is self-evident, so-called
dialectical materialism has been reluctant, at best, to admit the existence of
anything like a "supra-individual consciousness" (Goldmann 1969: 127). As for
the Weberians, we are told that collective phenomena are incompatible with
a view that finds only individuals and their subjective value orientations and,
by implication, there is no way for interpretive sociology to interact with the
Hegelian, Marxist, or Durkheimian strains without doing irreparable damage
(Kalberg 1994).[63] If we would like to create a powerful contemporary critical
sociology, however, partisanship and cultism will have to give way to synthesis
(Dahms 2011: 85) and synthesis must originate from, and adhere to, the thread
of dialectical analysis that runs, consciously or unconsciously, through the
classical tradition, not, as it is known to us as cardboard ideological cutouts,
but as it emerges when we keep our conceptual eye on the processes of the
social absolute.

2   The Impersonality of Facts

Social facts are *collective* or impersonal in nature as opposed to being
merely subjective or personal, though, we would never deny subjectivity its

---

61   "Structural dialectics does not contradict historical determinism, but rather promotes it
        by giving it a new tool" (Levi-Strauss 1963: 240).
62   On Hegel's negative social facts and negativism see Steinberger (1977).
63   Kalberg separates Weber from the rest by reducing Durkheim, Marx, and Hegel to cari-
        catures. For example, the old worn out textbook version of Durkheim as a positivist and
        functionalist it trotted out to make Weber appear diametrically opposed; Hegel's concept
        of *Geist* is thrown away without explanation; and the dialectic is mumbo jumbo (1994: 25).

importance and depth. The problem with subjectivity is that it is too deep but also too shallow – it misses the social both coming and going (G: 264–65). The idea of "intersubjectivity" at the heart of *Lebensphilosophie*, pragmatism, and phenomenology (*qua* the description of subjective experience) has been used to denote the constructed and shared nature of collective thought and, true, intersubjectivity *is* an an undeniably important aspect of social life and we cannot dispense with a grasp of social life at this scale[64] of organization.[65]

> Every word, every sentence, every gesture, or polite formula, every work of art and every political deed is intelligible because the people who expressed themselves through them and those who understood them have something in common; the individual always experiences, thinks and acts in a common sphere and only there does he understand. Everything that is understood carries, as it were, the hallmark of familiarity derived from such common features. We live in this atmosphere, it surrounds us constantly. We are immersed in it. We are at home everywhere in the historical and understood world; we understand the sense and meaning of it all; we ourselves are woven into this common sphere.
>
> DILTHEY 1976: 191

It sounds like a nice place to live but while we may often feel "at home" and "understand" much about our world, due, mainly to our simplifications (EFRL: 25) and "summary representations" (RSM: 63) there is also a corresponding sense of being a stranger in a strange land and a corresponding lack of understanding when it comes to very basic and primary institutions and processes we confront every day.[66] What hobbles "intersubjectivity" and the perspectives

---

64 "From the fact that science can explain the world although there is so much which we do not know follows that the world must be stratified: its regularities are not anchored in one basic level (elementary particle physics), but it has many levels each of which generates its own regularities. Chemistry cannot explain why dogs bark. Psychology cannot explain why capital must accumulate. Therefore a concept of emergence is necessary ... " (Ehrbar 1998: 1).

65 "Society does not consist of individuals, but expresses the sum of interrelations, the relations within which these individuals stand" (G: 265).

66 "I have called my tiny community a world, and so its isolation made it; and yet there was among us but a half-awakened common consciousness, sprung from common joy and grief, at burial, birth, or wedding; from a common hardship in poverty, poor land, and low wages; and above all, from the sight of the Veil that hung between us and Opportunity. All this caused us to think some thoughts together; but these, when ripe for speech, were spoken in various languages ... fatalism ... indifference ... or reckless bravado" (Du Bois [1903] 1969: 102–03). The double consciousness (of being simultaneously a part of a community while simultaneously being apart from the totality, being marginal) is an interesting phenomenon and does give one a kind of double vision but this can also devolve

that turn on it is the reduction of relations to dialogue or speech acts[67] as well
as intentional actions between two actors, two subjectivities or singularities
such that the essential is reduced to a twinkle in a web of momentary situations and fluid definitions of those situations.[68]

We all know how to use money but how many of us know what money is?
Can two ordinary subjects riddle the thing out through discourse and situa-
tional definitions? The facticity of the social is characterized by an intersubjectivity but also transcends the notion of the interpersonal (S: 309) such that we
have to account for the *reified* and *alien* qualities of social facts, not to mention
their *unconscious* dynamics.

Two things stand out here in juxtaposition: the idea of the "psychological
poverty of groups" (Freud [1930] 1961: 74; SGS: 33) on the one hand and, oppo-
sitely, the notion of collective consciousness[69] constituting nothing less than

---

  into a perspectivalist fetish for the charisma of the margins. The double vision of the oppressed (the within without) is not identical with a dialectics capable of sublating alienated consciousness. The perspective of the oppressed is not a higher truth but a symptom
  of alienation. We must always reject the notion of the charisma of the margins.

67   It is of course true that we are, in Aristotelian terms, *zōon logon echon* (literally "life that
  has speech") but speech and discourse are dependent upon integration in an organized
  community; our status as speakers is inseparable from our 'political' identity and partic-
  pation, *zōon politikon* (Gillespie 2008: 44–45).

68   Symbolic Interactionism, the so-called new social ontology, hard core constructionism,
  feminist theory, Habermasian pragmatism (with debts to Mead) all generally fail to solve
  the problem of the authority of collective consciousness. In a recent chapter Fultner
  (2017: 529) claims a "primacy" of intersubjectivity for the field of critical social theory.
  Nothing could be further from the truth. It is also interesting that the discussion of intersubjectivity leads into a section on cognitive psychology. Wrong way!

69   We typically associate the phrase "collective consciousness" with Durkheim but the
  phraseology originated with Espinas, a Spencerian, who "introduced the idea of *conscience collective* to sociology by assimilating society to a living organism" (Fournier 2006:
  23). Alternative synonyms include social consciousness (CPE: 20), the social mind (PM:
  137), the collective personality, and class consciousness. Class consciousness in its deformed or undeveloped state, lacking the rational insight inculcated by historical materialism, is *false* consciousness (Lukács 1971; cf. Durkheim 1974: 5). When Sweezy and
  Bettelheim write: " ... Marxism-Leninism is the revolutionary theory of the proletariat.
  It is for this reason [?] that it is capable of permeating the working class with lightning
  speed ..." (1971: 67). This charming but apparently ludicrous statement actually makes
  sense (though empirical sightings of this revolutionary permeation are rare compared
  to, say, the effects of authoritarian propaganda) when we take the theory as merely the
  clarified expression of the already existing but confused proletarian collective consciousness (1971: 66). The right theory at the right time 'sparks' the collective mentality and mo-
  tivates alienated individuals into coordinated action. When Absolute Idealists used the
  phrase "Transcendental Ego" they were groping toward Durkheim's subsequent theory
  of collective consciousness, a kind of metaphorical transcendental ego if, taken too far

an embarrassment of riches (SGS: 35).[70] How can the We be so magnificent and yet staggeringly idiotic? If genuine Reason can only emerge from association then we have to make space for the emergence of its inverse, absolute irrationality, as well. The sheer inertia of much of social life dooms a good portion of our conduct to ineffectiveness and unintended consequences. As Hegel put it:

> We learn from their [Greek and Roman] history how common it is, through customs and the limitation of certain representations, to regard the greatest nonsense as rational, disgraceful foolishness as wise. *This will make us aware of our inherited and propagated opinions, to examine even opinions concerning which we never had any doubts, the assumption that they might perhaps be completely false or only half-true never entering our mind.* We shall be awakened from our slumber and idleness which often make us indifferent toward the most important truths. – If these experiences have taught us to think it possible, indeed probable, that many of our convictions are perhaps errors and that many of those of another who thinks differently are perhaps truths, we will not hate him, not judge him unkindly. We know how easy it is to commit errors and therefore will seldom attribute these to malice and ignorance and thus become more just and more charitable toward others.
>
> 2002: 12–13

---

leads to reification and mystification. Frequently, we find assertions that the Freudian Over-I (superego) or Mead's 'generalized other' are equivalents to the concept of collective consciousness, yet, to conflate these concepts would be to disregard the *sui generis* quality of collective consciousness as an autonomous and absolute subject-substance (in the Hegelian-Marxist sense; cf. Simmel [1907] 1990: 452). Indeed, the superego is precisely the opposite of a collective consciousness in some respects or, perhaps better, it is only *part of or one contradictory aspect of collective conscience*. The superego or ego ideal is "the heir of the Oedipus complex" and subjugated to the id. The ego represents the external world, the superego represents "the internal world of the id" (Freud [1923] 1960: 26). And as Žižek says somewhere (or everywhere) the superego is not an ethical agency at all but an obscenity. Freud is helpful when we want to know about society in its individuated and tormented moments (subjectivity) and Mead may (or may not) be of assistance when dealing with intersubjective concerns, but absolute or social subjectivity should never be confused with, or boiled down to the merely subjective or intersubjective scales of life. For an amplification of my point, see Obeyesekere (1990: 93). Not even Freud's "cultural super ego" gets us where we want to go.

70   "It is said that truth does not love crowds. But why lend it this aristocratic disdain?" (Durkheim 1973: 28). Freud does not neglect this: "even the group mind is capable of creative genius in the field of intelligence, as is shown above all by language itself, as well as by folk-song, folklore and the like" ([1921]1959: 20).

We have all experienced the famous group effect whereby the "We" develops a course of action that appears to be the work of idiots.[71] As Simmel says, "The best authority on British trade unions notes that their mass assemblies often result in very stupid and pernicious resolutions ..." (SGS: 33).[72] "People talk about the wisdom of crowds, but crowds are only wise when the group has access to everyone's individual information. Aggregating these pieces can lead to better decisions than any person could have made alone. But if everyone just follows everyone else, or keeps their information to themselves, the value of the group is lost" (Berger 2016: 58). Here, the model is one based on the flow of information from individuals to the group and that "wisdom" is the sum total of individual "information." However, reality is much more complicated than this model suggests.

The problem is that collective consciousness, says Durkheim, "is independent of the particular conditions in which individuals find themselves." Further:

> Individuals pass on, but it abides [it is external]. It is the same in north and south, in large towns and in small, and in different professions. Likewise it does not change with every generation but, on the contrary, links successive generations to one another [it is fixed and durable rather than fluid and temporary]. Thus it is something totally different from the consciousness of individuals, although it is only realized in individuals [irreducible but not "out there" behind the world]. It is the psychological type of society, one which has its properties, conditions for existence and mode of development, just as individual types do ....
>
> DOL: 39

Although Durkheim does say that the search for real laws means forgetting the individual (S: 299) it is nonetheless not true that he discards individuals. The socialized person is, indeed, "the masterpiece of existence" (S: 213). Durkheim

---

71   One of my colleagues used to have a sign on their office door that read: "Committees None of us are as Dumb as all of us." Charitably, in relation to the mediocrity that plagues academia and university life, Weber says that: "It would be unfair to hold the personal inferiority of the faculty ... responsible .... The predominance of mediocrity is rather due to the laws of human co-operation, especially of the co-operation of several bodies ..." (FMW: 132).

72   Per Veblen: "human culture in all ages presents too many imbecile usages and principles of conduct to let anyone overlook the fact that disserviceable institutions easily arise and continue to hold their place in spite of the disapproval of native common sense.... Wide even extravagant, departures from the simple dictates of this native common sense occur even within the narrow range of the domestic and minor civil institutions ..." (1914: 49).

conceives of sociology as a variety of psychology (social psychology) with "its own laws" (S: 312) and "that specific psyches can be analyzed psychologically, but that the 'synthesis' of psyches requires sociology for its explanation" (Smith 1988: 67).

An early sociological prototype of a theory of collective consciousness, apparently unbeknownst to Durkheim, is located in Hegel's *Phenomenology* where we find moral or sacred consciousness of duties and obligations existing in another form of consciousness distinct from individual consciousness – i.e., a theory of multi-mindedness or a complex system of minds within the socialized individual (cf. DOL: 67; Hesse 1963). The universal and the singular are unified within one consciousness. When the individual fulfills the demands of social or moral conscience the result is a harmonization of the various spheres of the mind. The moral person is a happy person because they have "another being" within them. The moral person is a "master" no longer at war with their passions and egoistic drives (PS: 370–73). Ego and other are sublated into a state of grace; externality is an enveloping power that reconciles the will and raises the individual to the apex of actual individuality within the community.

Collective consciousness, because we as individuals fail to realize the totality of it within ourselves, is both the *external* absolute[73] of practically infinite richness[74] (but often appearing horrifyingly simplistic)[75] while at the same time it is a *force* that pushes us around, takes possession of us,[76] setting up

---

[73]   "'All the interconnections of man to man such as love and friendship are limited, particular, finite, in nature…. There must therefore be some way in the depths of man in which the yearning for the Thou can be fulfilled: where the *I* and the *Thou* are no longer counterposed, where this unity is not only a virtual one, not only a mere connection, but is absolute, unconditional, fully realized. And such a unity exists only in thought'" (Feuerbach, in Wartofsky 1977: 45).

[74]   "'The individual is an ass, and yet the whole is the voice of God'" (Carl Maria von Weber in SGS: 35).

[75]   Collective consciousness is simultaneously greater than and less than individual consciousness if we take both *absolute* and *relative* points of view and always *different* than individual consciousness. We can see how each individual represents an inaccessible and abysmal infinity at the level of the psyche (the depths of each psyche are bottomless and can never be known in their totalities) while also recognizing that collective consciousness, while also *practically* infinite as far as individuals go, stands a better chance of being circled and grasped by science (systematic thinking). If consciousness is, as Bloch says, the true "subject-matter of history" (1953: 151) it is not consciousness per se but collective consciousness in the Hegelian, Marxist, and Durkheimian sense.

[76]   "Intelligence is not a private endowment that the individual possesses, but rather a living principle which possesses him, a universal capacity which expresses through him the nature of a larger whole in which he is a member…. In a very real sense we must admit that we have received all that we have; our wisdom is not our own, but has come to us from without" (Creighton 1925: 57).

contradictions and tensions such that individuals who want to do good end up, with the best of intentions, defeating themselves.[77] In any society, "good rubs shoulders with evil, injustice is ever on the throne, and truth is continually darkened by error" (EFRL: 422).[78] Instead of the social conscience[79] being experienced as a universal third to enjoy we end up being the playthings of the reified third that enjoys at our expense (Worrell 2008: 181). It is not only the commodity that is, in Marx's terms, an "automatic subject" with "occult" capacities (C: 255; cf. Horkheimer 1972: 200) but all objective manifestations of value, the Spirit of the modern world. This is a good place to clarify the notion of the absolute.

In simple terms, the first humans to create a name for their group and to crystalize that name in some objective symbolic form (and be willing to spill their blood and guts for that name) can be thought of as having given birth to the first absolute. Sometime between the departure from Africa and the earliest known beadwork (roughly 100,000 BCE) and the oldest known European graphical systems (approximately 40,000 BCE) is the rather large window in time in which this absolutizing occurred.[80] The substance of the absolute, in a very crude sense, is the intuition that humans have universally had that *there*

---

77   We will never free ourselves entirely of contradictions. If we set out to never contradict ourselves we will never do anything (Singer 1983: 44). "Do I contradict myself? / Very well then I contradict myself, / (I am large, I contain multitudes)" (Whitman [1892] 1992: 68).

78   "Sir, in life we never know what we should be cheering and what we should be grieving over. Good leads to evil and evil to good. We stumble along in the dark beneath what is written on high, as crazily yoked to our desires as to our joys and our sorrows" (Diderot 1999: 69).

79   Here we have an opportunity to reflect with Freud on the relationship between conscience and consciousness: "On the evidence of language it [conscience] is related to that which one is 'most certainly conscious'. Indeed, in some languages [French] the words for 'conscience' and 'conscious' can scarcely be distinguished. Conscience is the internal perception of the rejection of a particular wish operating within us. The stress, however, is upon the fact that this rejection has no need to appeal to anything else for support, that it is quite 'certain of itself'" (Freud [1913] 1950: 85). So, taboo and categorical imperatives, etc., are experienced as authoritative commands issued, it is felt, by a thing greater than and different than, the individual's own consciousness. Here Freud and Durkheim are in agreement with regard to the 'externality' of social facts (e.g., taboo or ethical imperative) and the conflict-ridden split between individual and collective mental dimensions (Freud [1913] 1950: 86). With respect to the conflation of 'conscience' and 'consciousness' in Romance languages, compared to German and English, for example, see Damasio (1999: 232–33). Additionally, Parsons (1978: 218) makes a strong distinction between conscience and consciousness.

80   The creative explosion of the European Upper Paleolithic around 40,000 BCE may have been an outgrowth of changes in behavior already enacted in Africa 5000 years earlier (Klein with Edgar 2002: 261–64).

seems to be something else here besides us, that, in other words, we are not alone.
As we will see in the second chapter, when humans associate they create an effervescence that adds another "dimension" to mental reality; we might think of
this as surplus or alien consciousness based on surplus praxis (hyper-praxis).[81]
The individual perceives physical reality, has a sense of self and others, but
there is in addition to this some weird surplus, some It or Thing, a supplement
or remainder that goes beyond what is given. Of course, as Durkheim says, this
something is not literally some extra thing apart from us but the emergence of
a new species of psychical being (RSM: 129) that evades comprehension. When
that shared feeling and intuition of some Other passes the threshold into
symbolization, we have something new in the world.[82] The vague Thing has a
name and a life of its own. All religions utilize rituals to generate and replen-
ish this surplus in a variety of forms from totemic proto-gods, ancestor spirits,
full-fledged deities, etc. We find the first philosophers attempting to nail down
this enigmatic surplus in elemental, natural forms but being continuously perplexed by their reflections back into the mind and the entanglement of gods
with matter and the fate of humans.

Through the European Middle Ages philosophy, dominated as it was by the
Church, was incapable of liberating itself from god as the unconditioned and
unlimited absolute. The Church as "heaven on earth" was supposed to mediate
the community's relation to god and manage terrestrial creation but ultimately it came to displace god as a kind of bad practical absolute or apotheosis
(G: 331–32). Working in the name of god the Church became the god substitute
and a worldly end in itself. The name for this process is "corruption" and was the
engine that powered reformism and the eventual 16th Century breach that created Protestant Christianity with the aim of restoring god to the coordinates of

---

81 On the connection between surplus and the alien see Marx (C: 988). Also, if we are ca-
    pable of hyper-praxis we have to leave open the fact that we are also prone to hypo-praxis;
    surplus is meaningless without a corresponding lack or insufficiency. We should be a little
    more insistent, in fact, and state that the capacity for hyper-praxis *depends* upon hypo-
    praxis at another coordinate and that they are dynamically linked: "An individual worker
    can be *industrious* above the average, more than he has to be in order to live as a worker,
    only because another lies below the average, is lazier" (G: 286). I worked in a factory with
    a record-breaking Scotsman who so overproduced that he created problems of underpro-
    duction for the workers on the next shift. They encouraged him to moderate his zeal by
    threatening to break his legs but, rather than being deterred by the threats, he earned a
    black belt in tae kwon do in order to defend not only his lower torso but also his ability to
    to continue breaking production records.

82 In the following chapter I will be more specific as to the dynamogenesis of this surplus
    as a kind of 'overdoing it' (in the real as well as the ideal) that we find only in the human
    world.

the absolute.[83] Renaissance Humanism and the Enlightenment witnessed an increasing confidence in human reason, the growth of science, and an erosion of god's absolute position in the universe. By the time we arrive at Spinoza, the absolute is a mono-substance from which everything we experience spills forth; Spinoza's substance is the philosophical equivalent of a god. Kantianism turned the absolute into whatever the "ultimate reality" is. In Schelling we find the absolute is a "pre-reflective orientation necessarily coming before even the division into subjective and objective points of view.... In Hegel's treatment, that 'absolute' became the 'space of reasons,' which itself requires articulation in terms of a 'logic' that tries to make sense of the way in which we can be the authors of the 'law' to which we are bound" (Pinkard 2002: 362). This process is one where "our own thought" becomes "the other of itself'" (Ibid.). Hegel's renovations transformed the absolute into the conditioned but unlimited unity of nature and knowledge, with science being the coming-to-know the absolute in its developmental journey or *Bildungsroman*.[84] Marx strikes us as a bit of the religious reformer: where the protesters within the Church were dedicated to the negation of corruption and establishing direct relations with the word of god, Marx perceives capital as a vast, global, absolute monstrosity that has to be overturned through the revolutionary praxis of the proletariat. Where Marx envisions a day in which humanity is free of delusions regarding absolutes reigning in the negative heaven of capitalist civilization (communist association is free of the absolute and the domination associated with "society") Durkheim, starting from another view of the negative heaven of capitalist hyper-civilization, rendered dysfunctional due to deregulation (anomie) and egoism, seeks not the revolutionary overthrow of the existing order but the reformation of the existing and the restoration of a kind of "positive hell" of social existence where the absolute, society, knows itself transparently and rationally as the absolute.

About as well as anyone can, O'Connor situates the divided theoretical "houses" of bourgeois sociology and the radical theory of capitalism in terms that we have been pursuing. Durkheim's

> obsession with solidarity and social bonds, or what holds society together, is explicable only because capitalism deeply divided society. Marx's

---

83   The Church was perhaps not as corrupt as it is normally portrayed. See Ryrie (2017: 16) on why the Church may have appeared to be more corrupt than it was.

84   See Inwood (1992: 27) for insights into the trajectory of the absolute but especially Pinkard (2002: passim).

obsession with what divides society is explicable only because there were powerful forces uniting capitalist society, i.e., nationalism, patriotism, and above all capitalist ideology, or the ideology of equal exchange of equivalents. Marx wanted to show that these "solidarities" were ideological and illusory. Durkheim wanted to show that social conflicts and divisions were illusory. If you only look in the right place, Durkheim argues, you will find the moral bonds that hold society together. If you look in another place, Marx argues, you will find what divides society, namely, capital and capitalist classes. Durkheim is concerned with morality, Marx with exploitation and power. Durkheim finally becomes a "Marxist" when he states that the working class is establishing commitments and solidarity in the course of its development, i.e., with his recognition that morality is class-based. Hence, it is the working class which will hold society together. Marx found that working class solidarity would destroy society and reconstruct it materially; Durkheim suggests that the working class will reform society and reconstruct it morally.

    1980: 67

Where, for Marx, "Man" in free and spontaneous praxis is the thing that is sacred for Durkheim it is Society that makes the person what it is and is the only source of the sacred and genuine freedom. In that sense, both Marx (the spontaneously free "Man") and Durkheim (the regulated and rational society) construct visions of the absolute that have yet to materialize because, at bottom, the shared program of defetishizing social relations, processes, and institutions, has yet to work itself out and, usually appears to be working in the opposite direction.

    For now what is important is that the absolute may confront ordinary individual consciousness as an enigmatic *Thing* of seemingly and practically transcendental powers or it may appear to recede from view entirely (leaving what seems like a void or dispersed field of unrelated variables and plastic networks). Yet, even when the absolute seems to be on hiatus and minds have seemingly lost touch with social reality, one never knows when the absolute will suddenly come storming back. The liberal psychology professor Jonathan Haidt says that in the immediate aftermath of the 9/11 terror attacks:

> I felt an urge so primitive I was embarrassed to admit it to my friends: I wanted to put an American flag decal on my car. The urge seemed to come out of nowhere, with no connection to anything I'd ever done.... I had an overwhelming sense of being an American. I wanted to do something,

anything, to support my team…. But I was a professor, and professors don't do such things. Flag waving and nationalism are for conservatives.[35]
2012: 220

After three days, Haidt solved his "dilemma" by installing flags for both the United States and the United Nations on his car. We see in this solution national particularity as the most pressing concern for the individual but "impossible" without the universal signifier. For liberal professors the universal is the world (or, for some, their ego) and the nation is the embarrassing and repressed middle thing that, though we do not spend much time thinking about it, actually connects the individual to the universal dimension. Then, the repressed returns as an irresistible force that imposes itself. Haidt did not just have an idea. No, it was "three days and a welter of feelings I'd never felt before" (2012: 220).

Social theorists, especially in the US and England, are prone to falling prey to pragmatic and hyper-constructivist interpretations of the social world where we find autonomous individuals engage in "happy go lucky" (Durkheim 1983: 57) language games, speech acts, negotiated discourse, simulations and constructions, where situations are subject to provisional definitions, where the truth merges with what is useful to individuals or their momentary dyadic relations, or where the strength of the "man of action" attempts to reshape reality through sheer force of will. Reification? What reification? It seems like an outdated notion (see Vandenberghe 2013).[86] "Pragmatists believe," says Durkheim, "that it is we who construct both the world and the representations which express it. We 'make' truth in conformity with our needs. How then could it resist us?" (1983: 74). As we will see later, toward the end of his career Durkheim identifies this drive as "will mania" (1915) and is not unrelated to Freud's notion of "megalomania" where the oversized will continuously collides with reality (Freud 2002: 38; cf. Jones 2001: 60) dreaming that with enough willpower it can prevail (see also Freud [1913] 1950 on omnipotent thought). One way to think about the problem of pragmatism and representation is that the paradigm fails to account for the normative aspect of any representation

---

85   Durkheim says that "beneath the moral indifference that pervades the surface of our collective life, there are sources of commitment that our societies contain within themselves" (in Lukes 1973: 517). We cannot know in advance what historical contingency will release these forces and in what form they will assume but "an intense life is growing and seeking outlets, which it will eventually find" (Ibid.).

86   When postmodern theory and feminism came to the fore, Marxism and the otherwise critical mapping of the commodity world were relegated to the margins because, at the end of the day, both radical modernists and postmodernists interested in power discourses and civil society, as well as feminists interested in identities, no longer took as much interest in capitalism (Dahms 2011: 93–98).

as a figure of authority. As such, it breaks sharply from the Hegelian model of social thought.[87] Pragmatism, in the final analysis, is an egocentric bourgeois ideology that champions the rugged individual (the constructor) over and against the rest of the world, terminating with self-serving utilitarianism where personal greed (rational self interest) supposedly benefits the remainders of society. In short, pragmatism fails to live up to the meaning of *pragma*: the collective deeds and actions that give rise to factual life and long-standing love between committed individuals. However, even as one-sided and rotten as it is, we cannot dispose of the intersubjective fixation and experiential grounding of pragmatism; each individual does contribute to the making of their world, and we do engage in acts that build and rebuild reality every day, but there is also the crucial fact that individuals are also *made by* society. As Durkheim says, we are more the handiwork of society than the conscious creators of it (S: 214).[88] Subjective experience and action are grounded in "social territory" (Volosinov 1973: 90). Durkheim was very much in line with Marx when it came to the power of history and society over the individual:

> Men make their own history, but they do not make it as they please;[89] they do not make it under self-selected circumstances, but under circumstances existing already, given and transmitted from the past.[90] The tradition of all dead generations weighs like a nightmare on the brains of the living. And just as they seem to be occupied with revolutionizing themselves and things, creating something that did not exist before, precisely in such epochs of revolutionary crisis they anxiously conjure up the spirits of the past to their service, borrowing from them names, battle slogans, and costumes in order to present this new scene in world history in time-honored disguise and borrowed language.
>
> MARX [1869] 1963: 15

With this, however, we should not conclude that even though we are the product of society that we are, at the end of the day, merely cogs or drones that

---

87   "Hegel learns from Kant to think about representation in *normative* terms. What is represented exercises a distinctive kind of *authority* over representings. Representings are *responsible* to what they represent" (Brandom 2013: 15).

88   "Thus the personality of the speaker, taken from within, so to speak, turns out to be wholly a product of social interrelations" (Volosinov 1973: 90).

89   Cf. Luxemburg's variation: "Men do not make history just as they please, *but they make their own history*" (in Jacoby 1981: 67). "*Social structures shape us (Foucault) even as we remain responsible for their shape (Kant)*" (Cladis 2012: 99).

90   When it comes to social action we are "authors" but not usually "inventors" (S: 128).

possess only an illusory free will and a lot of id impulses, that we are simultaneously doomed to oscillations between anarchy and necessity. Durkheim made
the excellent point that the authority of social facts flows *from the bottom up*,
that the leader, even the charismatic leader,[91] is a product of the followers
(S:126).[92] The personal qualities of the leader matter not – what counts is *belief*
on the part of followers (FMW: 295–96).[93]

> It was not Jesus himself who elevated his religious doctrine into a pecu-
> liar sect distinguished by practices of its own; this result depended on
> the zeal of his friends, on the manner in which they preached and propa-
> gated it, on the claims they made for it, and on the arguments by which
> they sought to uphold it.[94]
>
> HEGEL 1948: 80

It's good to have friends. As we will discover more fully in the next chapter,
though, to ordinary consciousness the flow of energy and authority appears to
run in the opposite direction. In reporting on Trump rallies, Saunders gives us
a good image of this inversion:

---

91   For the best analysis of charismatic authority available consult Smith (2013).
92   "It is not because he is a leader of industry that a man is a capitalist; on the contrary, he is
     a leader of industry because he is a capitalist" (C: 450). Compare the sociological theory
     of charisma with the contradictory explanation of Freud where he cannot make up his
     mind whether charisma flows from the people or from the personality of the so-called
     great man (1939: 138–39). Ultimately, however, Freud leans toward the mass wish and im-
     personal aspects over leader personality when it comes to charisma. If the 'bottom-up'
     dynamics of authority fail to make sense to you it is probably because you are a liberal
     who votes Democratic and who cannot fathom how Trump was installed in the White
     House. Conservatives, oligarchs, and right-wing demagogues have known all along that
     winning the base is the winning strategy. Lincoln knew that winning popular sentiment
     was the key to political mastery: "'Public sentiment is everything. With it, nothing can fail;
     against it, nothing can succeed'" (in Lilla 2017: 5). Lilla continues: "The American right un-
     derstands in its bones this basic law of democratic politics, which is why it has effectively
     controlled the political agenda of this country for two generations. Liberals have for just
     as long refused to accept it" (2017: 6).
93   "The capitalist possesses ... power, not on account of his personal or human qualities, but
     inasmuch as he is an *owner* of capital" (PM: 78). Recall that, for Weber, the rise of capital-
     ism hinges on more than the entrepreneur which is only a potentiality actualized by the
     formation of an ascetic and conscientious *working class* that broke from traditional labor
     ethics (PESC: 26).
94   "To describe Wat Tyler and Pugachev as individuals in revolt against society is a mislead-
     ing simplification. If they had been merely that, the historian would never have heard of
     them. They owe their role in history to the mass of their followers, and are significant as a
     social phenomena, or not at all" (Carr 1961: 65).

And make energy [Trump] does. It flows out of him, as if channelled in thousands of micro wires, enters the minds of his followers: their cheers go ragged and hoarse, chanting erupts, a look of religious zeal may flash across the face of some non-chanter, who is finally getting, in response to a question long nursed in private, exactly the answer he's been craving.

2016

You cannot get more anti-sociological than this description.[95] In reality, the excitement flows in the opposite direction. As Michael Wolff notes regarding the current between Trump and his rally fans: "He sucked in the energy from the crowds" (2018: n.p.). If the followers were to withdraw their support or disobey in some manner, there would be no energy for the leader and, in this case, Trump would no longer enjoy the status of a leader for his millions of enthusiasts. There is nothing in Trump's personal qualities or language that determines his leadership principle (e.g., S: 142). The subordination of the "little man" to the "Big Man" is certainly not based on metaphorical wires flowing from the master to the hapless slaves. If anything, Trump himself is the slave. We are always free to disobey (S: 325) and a person incapable of disobedience, what Wilde calls our "original virtue" ([1891] 2003: 1176), is nothing more than a slave (Fromm 1981: 18).[96] It is true that a given *quantity* of individuals are predetermined (S: 325) to lose life or liberty but for those who enjoy the *qualities* of social attachment and discipline that comes from a sufficiently vibrant group life, their individuality and personal weaknesses will not be the source of their misfortune. It was for this reason that Marx did not conceive of personal defects of workers as an impediment to the inevitability of proletarian revolution. At one level, Marx suffered no illusions: the workers were dehumanized, dull, deformed, etc., but they were mechanically destined to rise up in unison due to the contradictions of the "laws" of capitalist accumulation to overthrow the production for exchange system. It was the fate of the revolutionary subject-object of history to perform this deed and it was *inevitable*.[97]

---

95   Ideology and fetishism cohere like Peter and Paul or pizza and beer. The inversions and reversals of the latter mean that the active constructors of the fact have no idea that they are responsible for the product, believing, instead, that they are the product of the fact.

96   We should not exclude *hyper-obedience* ("malicious obedience" or "malicious conformity") as a form of active disobedience. A command issued by an authority depends on not on adherence to the letter of the law but the spirit of the law (Bendix [1956] 1974: xlv). Doing the job 'perfectly' is just as good as not doing the job at all as far as disobedience goes. Žižek makes this point: ultra-conformism and strict rule-following will lead to bureaucratic and institutional breakdown.

97   "To call the proletariat a revolutionary class is a condensation: it means a class with the historical potential of making a revolution; it is a label for a social drive; it is not a

However, this inevitability transformed the proletariat from a collectivity actually plagued by ambivalence and contradictory conduct into an abstraction
and myth that moved according to external laws.

3   Collective Conduct

The word "behavior" is sometimes used in sociology to depict our ways of acting but it carries with it unfortunate connotations such as people reduced to
automatons reacting mindlessly to external stimuli as well as the idea that
humans are just another kind of animal. However, a person is "not simply an
animal plus certain qualities" (EFRL: 62) or "developed ape" (G: 251) or a Gou-
da cow wearing pants (Carlyle [1836] 1987: 51). Humans are, if you will, *weird
nature* – "a kind of prosthetic God" (Freud [1930] 1961: 44)[98] or the "freak of the
universe" (Fromm 1973: 225; cf. Haidt 2012: 229). Hence, any statement regarding a "natural" way of living is by definition invalid when it comes to people.
"Human nature is the product of a recasting, so to speak, of animal nature.
There have been gains as well as losses in the course of the intricate operations
of which this recasting is the result" (Freud [1930] 1961: 44).[99] "What a chimera
man is, what a strange monster, what a chaos, what a bundle of contradictions, what a prodigy! Judge of all things, and a miserable worm; a depository
of truth, and a sink of uncertainty and error; at once the glory and the scum of
the universe!" (Pascal, in Levy-Bruhl 1899: 94).[100]
   It was not so long ago that scientists by and large subscribed to the idea of
"genetic determinism" whereby people are simply born with a certain organic
structure and ruled by their genes. Problems such as intelligence, violence,
and poverty were reducible to genetic and biological defects. Opposed to this
determinism stands a voluminous body of research that emphasizes the quality of childcare and socialization processes as being responsible for shaping

---

description of current events. This revolutionary class begins, like everybody else, by being filled with 'reactionary cravings' and prejudices: otherwise the proletarian revolution
would always be around the corner. Marx's theory looks on the proletariat as an objective
agency of social revolution in the process of becoming. In this respect his conception of
the proletariat as the historically revolutionary class is similar to his reiterated view that
the bourgeoisie was such a revolutionary class in a previous era, in spite of its well-known
timidity and narrow-mindedness" (Draper 1978: 51).

98   In capitalism we find a reversal: "the proposition that tools are prolongations of human
organs can be inverted to state that the organs are also prolongations of the tools" (Horkheimer 1972: 201).

99   The human is, in a sense, a "compromised animal" (Cioran 1974: 76).

100   I prefer this translation to Trotter's, see Pascal (1941: 143).

intelligence, dispositions toward violence, and social adaptability. This old "Nature Vs. Nurture" debate has, in the last couple of decades, finally been put to rest: "the nature–nurture dichotomy that has long pitted biological and sociological approaches to understanding violence has not merely been resolved; it has been superseded…. Biology is *not* destiny" (Niehoff 1999: x).

People are not simply stuck with an unchanging, static set of genes. Instead, the genetic makeup of infants and young children, along with propensities for violence and emotional happiness, are dynamic. Genes are characterized, in other words, by a great deal of plasticity.[101] "Advances in our understanding of brain development emphasize how the environment begins to shape the nervous system even before birth and, conversely, how the innate features of the brain begin the process of defining the way in which each of us perceives and reacts to the environment" (Niehoff 1999: x).

How your brain is "wired," the size of your brain, the balance of chemicals in your brain (such as serotonin and adrenalin etc.), the distribution of electrical energy throughout the brain, the density of your neural network, gene activation, and, among other things, the physical temperature of your brain are all factors that are shaped, to a great extent, by the quality of care given to you during your earliest years of development.[102] Kids need an environment rich in hugs, kisses, language, music, colors, etc. But, just as genetic determinism is flawed, so to is the belief that all you need is love – that caregiving alone determines whether or not a child grows up to be an emotional nightmare and plague on society. Parenting and environment go a long way in explaining the brain but they cannot account for everything. Some children are born to mothers who abused drugs or experienced high levels of stress during pregnancy and are born with defective "raw materials" that subsequent parenting

---

101 "One of the most profound [of the recent findings is] that environmental stress can activate genes linked to depression and other mental problems…. stress or drugs of abuse, like cocaine and alcohol, can turn on a gene called C-fos. The protein made by the C-fos gene attaches to a brain cell's DNA, turning on other genes that make receptors or more connections to other cells…. The problem is that these new connections and receptors are abnormal. They cause a short circuit in the brain's communication networks that can give rise to seizures, depression, manic-depressive episodes, and a host of other mental problems." In short, "When it comes to building the human brain, nature supplies the construction materials and nurture serves as the architect that puts them together" (Kotulak 1997: 42–46).

102 Mothers in industrial and post-industrial societies are giving up breastfeeding their infants with noticeable differences in physical and emotional health. "To be sure, breast milk contains lots of biochemical compounds that have the power to change behavior, including prolactin, cortisol, and oxytocin. But the psychological benefits of nursing seem to have less to do with breast milk as a magic elixir and more to do with how much time is spent engaging the baby in affectionate repartee" (Pinker 2014: 125).

or intervention will not overcome. But, obviously, if we could eliminate drug abuse, violence, and increase support for mothers, fewer children would be born with debilitations.[103] Further complicating the notion of "human nature" is the rise of the biogenetics industry.

> Biogenetics, with its reduction of the human psyche itself to an object of technological manipulation, is therefore effectively a kind of empirical instantiation of what Heidegger perceived as the "danger" inherent in modern technology. Crucial here is the interdependence of man and nature: by reducing man to just another natural object whose properties can be manipulated, what we lose is not (only) humanity but *nature itself*. In this sense ... humanity relies on some notion of "human nature" as what we have inherited, as something that has simply been given to us, the impenetrable dimension in/of ourselves into which we are born / thrown. The paradox is thus that ... there is man only insofar as there is impenetrable inhuman nature (Heidegger's "earth"): with the prospect of biogenetic interventions opened up by the access to the genome, the species freely changes/redefines *itself*, its own coordinates; this prospect effectively emancipates [potentially and at a price] humankind from the constraints of a finite species, from its enslavement to "selfish genes."
>
> ŽIŽEK 2008: 435

4   Collective Consciousness

Our thoughts are not strictly speaking our own. Hyperion laments: "We speak of our hearts, our plans, as if they were ours, and yet there is an alien power that flings us about and lays us in the grave as it pleases, and of which we know neither whence it came nor where it is going" (Hölderlin 2008: 52). If our ideas were purely subjective they would be completely arbitrary or contingent (Hegel 1969: 756) and there would be no basis for collective life, shared meaning,[104] or any kind of coordination. Psychology is important but the psyche considered in isolation disappears into "infinity" and sociology is unprepared to grapple with the infinite.[105] Of course, the uniqueness of individual representations

---

103   For more on the relationship between socialization and genetics see Karr-Morse and Wiley (1997).
104   To enjoy shared meaning already implies a reason to do so. For people to share anything means a voluntary loss or alienation of subjective and perhaps idiosyncratic meanings.
105   This is also why bottom-up descriptions of societies or institutions and so on are a dead end. No society, no group, no relation, can ever be thoroughly described in a way that

and ideas cannot be denied or trivialized but the mind alone, says Bosanquet, cannot produce a synthetic reality if our world is not already synthetic. "But again; no world can be synthetic in itself, that is, can possess universals[106] as part of its own nature, if its elements have not, pervading them, the living *nexus* and endeavour towards a whole which indicates participation in the nature of minds" (1913: 35). The key is not mind but associated minds enmeshed in common elements and conveyed through the medium of common language. The ideas we have, our concepts, judgements, the way we infer things, deductions, etc., are not merely subjective (S: 36) but are part of a living, self-moving "process that forms the passage from subjectivity to objectivity" (Hegel [1830] 1991: 257).

This "self-moving" process is not hidden behind empirical reality but, rather, addresses our double state as both *private* individuals entangled within interpersonal relations with others and as members of an impersonal *public*.[107] *Homo duplex* means that the self has *two sides*: the personal and the collective, being and becoming.[108] In the *Symposium*, Plato transmits a myth of the initial splitting of humans:

----

leads to worthwhile generalizations. "Every individual is an infinity, and infinity cannot be exhausted" (RSM: 110).

106   Bosanquet "universals" are not the lifeless categories of the understanding but substantive vitalities – think not Bergson but Durkheim's collective representations seemingly vibrating with collective effervescence.

107   "But apart from this contemporary mood, the ideas of economists and political philosophers, both when they are right and when they are wrong, are more powerful than is commonly understood. Indeed the world is ruled by little else. Practical men, who believe themselves to be quite exempt from any intellectual influences, are usually the slaves of some defunct economist. Madmen in authority, who hear voices in the air, are distilling their frenzy from some academic scribbler of a few years back. I am sure that the power of vested interests is vastly exaggerated compared with the gradual encroachment of ideas. Not, indeed, immediately, but after a certain interval; for in the field of economic and political philosophy there are not many who are influenced by new theories after they are twenty-five or thirty years of age, so that the ideas which civil servants and politicians and even agitators apply to current events are not likely to be the newest. But, soon or late, it is ideas, not vested interests, which are dangerous for good or evil" (Keynes 1953: 383–84).

108   The first form of *Homo duplex*, as far as we know, is the doubling of the person in the form of of the totemic species (Halbwachs 1962: 53). For a somewhat sceptical view of the personal-public dualism see Barthes (1982: 63–65). Durkheim frequently alludes to the double nature of the person as that between the natural and the spiritual, e.g., a mind-body dualism, but what he really is getting at is the division between the individual and the social, the profane and the sacred. See Verheggen (1996: 207) for more on *Homo duplex*. Freud, too, sees the person as a kind of duplex: "The individual does actually carry on a double existence: one designed to serve his own purposes and another as a link in a chain, in which he serves against, or at any rate without volition of his own" ([1914] 1959: 35). Each aspect is involved in a unique economy of energies all its own. On one side,

... primeval man was round and had four hands and four feet, back and sides forming a circle, one had with two faces, looking opposite ways ... When he had a mind he could walk as men now do, and he could also roll over and over at a great rate. Terrible was their might and strength, and the thoughts of their hearts were great, and they made an attack upon the gods ... .

    1945: 315–16

Zeus solved the problem by cutting these primeval men in half, diminishing their powers.

After the division of the two parts of man, each desiring his other half, came together, and threw their arms about one another eager to grow into one.... [S]o ancient is the desire of one another which is implanted in us, reuniting our original nature, making one of two, and healing the state of man. Each of us when separated is but the indenture of a man, having one side only like a flat fish, and he is always looking for his other half.

    PLATO 1945: 316–17

The kernel of this myth is that, anthropologically, we probably lost our original, instinctual unity (if we ever had an instinctual unity) as we shifted from animalistic behavior to symbolically-mediated normative conduct. As we will see in the next chapter, the concept of "instinct" is an extraneous problem for the social sciences; instinct "explains nothing. It's a sort of conventional agreement between scientists to stop trying to explain things at a certain point" (Bateson 1972: 39).

Our anatomical history goes back roughly 200,000 years but the moral history of our species extends roughly 50,000 years into the past – at least this is the current consensus among anthropologists. It is plausible that our ancestors were doing weird things like making art (e.g., necklaces) tens of thousands of years earlier. Aside from dates, Plato gets to something profound: alone, we are weak and born incomplete whereas united we not only enjoy a heightened capacity but develop into a new species of life characterized, as Marx put it, by an "omnipresence" and hands everywhere (Antonio 2003: 16). We were physically "terrible" in our primeval state but combined, we moderns are capable of not merely *threatening* the "gods" but, especially in the nuclear era, rising

---

interestingly, Freud says that we are "the mortal vehicle of a (possibly) immortal substance – like the inheritor of an entailed property who is only the temporary holder of an estate which survives him" (Ibid: 36).

to the scale of a *threatening god*. The original cutting, however, was not Zeus's sword but the signifer.

Language, ritual conduct, and relations of authority separate moral life from our prehistoric ancestors who no doubt communicated and vocalized with *signals* but the emergence of authoritative language, the paradoxical source of our greatest solidarities and hostilities,[109] represents a fundamental breach in the natural life of the species. Every society has, at bottom, to deal with the unification of the individual and the collective, the personal and the public, made troublesome by the inherent ambivalence introduced by the proliferation of minds within the brains of individuals (collective, personal, unconscious). No doubt animals experience "perplexity" but doubt and ambivalence belong to our socialized species (Lacan 2014: 57–68).[110] We learn how to cultivate and value relations. Collective consciousness is surplus or "excess" consciousness, the cultivation of a surplus self or supplemental being joined to our originary being as we develop and flourish in the lap of society.[111] To the extent that we develop and embrace our second self, a process of subjectification, we are recognized as valid and embraced as members of society. If we run away from a society that cares, and all functioning societies care, we are punished and reduced to a taboo entity.

The unity of the subjective and the objective would yield an "absolute" form of consciousness in which, as Hegel would say, spirit knows itself as spirit. This is the essence of "Absolute Idealism" in a nutshell: idealism is bogged down in subjectivity and cannot lift itself above conflict between competing egos, their perceptions, interpretations, and opinions, whereas the sociological absolute is the ground upon which we can view ourselves from an imagined impersonal perspective and share in common projects. In a disaggregated society it appears that the absolute has come undone and that society has dissolved

---

109   Language is the "bond of identification and recognition. Those who speak the language with the right tone and inflection ... are kinsmen, neighbors, fellows: people to trust. Those who do not are outsiders and enemies: at best, ridiculous creatures.... So the deepest bonds became in time one of the greatest barriers between the tribes and races of man; and man's most universal artifact, the spoken word, because it is so deeply steeped in the individuality of experience, became an obstacle to the union of mankind" (Mumford 1973: 416–17).

110   "Don't let yourselves be taken in by appearances. Just because anxiety's link to doubt, to hesitation, to the obsessional's so-called ambivalent game, may strike you as clinically tangible, this doesn't mean that they are the same thing. Anxiety is not doubt, anxiety is the cause of doubt.... The effort that doubt expends is exerted merely to combat anxiety..." (Lacan 2014: 76–7).

111   "[T]o the spontaneously egoist natural being education 'adds' a being 'capable of leading a moral and social life'" (Durkheim, in Jankélévitch 2012: 46).

back into a war of all against all, where anomie reigns supreme. However, this is an illusion. Our postmodern absolute assumes a different shape from the modern one but it exists nonetheless. One of Durkheim's most interesting comments on collective consciousness is relegated to a footnote in which he specifies that to refer to a collective consciousness is to "simplify" what is in reality much more complex: "In fact we form a part of several groups and there exist in us several collective consciousnesses" (DOL: 67). This is reminiscent of the Hegelian universal undergoing a process of determination and *doubling* as reason moves across the threshold from subjectivity to objectivity (Worrell and Krier 2018).

Each particular group affiliation brings with it the possibility of conflicting with the expectations and demands of other groups. Modern life and the multiplicity of group identity magnifies the importance of ambivalence experienced daily. Feeling at odds with the world, feeling dis-eased and out of sorts, is the norm. Just as the communications between the I (ego), the over – I (superego), and the It (id) are subject to processes of distortion, inversion, reversal, fragmentation, transformation, condensation, etc., (Freud [1900] 1965) the relationship between the I and the We (Hegel [1807] 1977: 110) is fraught with non-linear and irrational communions.[112] At times we are ill due to our loss of contact with the We whereas other times it is the over-presence of the We that causes illness.

> This way, that way
> I do not know
> what to do: I
> am of two minds.
>   SAPPHO 1986: 69

As Jones says, "there is a tension not only between the internal and the external, but also between individuated and collective forms of thinking – between the two consciences within us, the *particulière* and the *collective* (2001: 139–40). It can be said that social facts are "phenomena of consciousness, without being also [only] phenomena of the individual consciousness."

Social facts exist in the individual as representations but the "impression of social things on the individual is altered by the particular state of the consciousness which receives them." Society "exists only in the individual, but each

---

112   This distortion in the relationship between the We and the I is troubling because the subjective I only exists on the basis of a We; the subjective is always "backgrounded" by the objective and social (Voloshinov [1927] 2012: 165).

individual has only a particle of it" (Mauss 2005: 18, 19). Here we are dealing not with a transcendental subject but a "transindividual" subject or modality of consciousness that prevents social theory from devolving back into either subjectivism (leading to mystified idealism and transcendentalism) or reductionistic materialism (Goldmann 1976: 104; cf. Vincent 1897: 68–69). Made all the more difficult is the *unconscious* aspects of social facts.[113] When speaking of "social facts" we are dealing, as we will see in the section on externality, with a problem not merely of collective consciousness but also collective, historical *unconsciousness*.[114]

> The thoughts and aims of an active man are considered by him as the cause of his deeds; he does not ask where these thoughts come from. This is especially true because thoughts, ideas and aims are not as a rule derived from the impressions by conscious reasoning, but are the product

---

113   Our conscious thoughts are determined "at every moment" by our unconscious thoughts (Durkheim 1974: 21). I think Durkheim would agree with Freud that consciousness, in relation to the unconscious, is only the "surface" of the mental system ([1923] 1960: 9). "[T]he whole of cognitive life is linked to structures which are just as unconscious as the Freudian Id ..." (Piaget 1970: 131). The "relation of a commodity to the *law of its value* is an *unconscious* relation" (Goux 1990: 53).

114   (Cf. Braudel 1980: 39). At all cost, we want to avoid connecting with Jung at this point. The collective unconscious, for Jung, was an hereditary *a priori* or "patterns of instinctual behavior" (1969: 44). Even though Jung explicitly deploys the language of "collective representations" and cites Levy-Bruhl and Mauss positively, his theory of archetypes is where sociology goes to die. What we can agree with is the assertion that archaism haunts the modern world (we've never not been primitive) and that social phenomena cannot be reduced to the dynamics of the personal psyche (1969: 47). "Durkheim had argued on several occasions early in his career that representations are never totally obliterated. Rather, they combine and associate with other representations to form new myths, legends, and folklore. Freud, Jung, and Durkheim took the extreme position that nothing from the past, collective or individual, is ever lost, even though it is reconstructed in the process of retrieval" (Meštrović 1988: 100). Actually, the problem of representational survival might be very different between Freud and Durkheim (I recall Lichtman having good insight into this when contrasting Freud with Marx). Whatever the case with Freud, for Durkheim, the past is never carried over into the future without undergoing radical transformations and changes of meaning. The modern commodity-lover and totem-worshipper are both fetishists, for sure, but there is a gulf separating clan rites and capitalist production and the delusions of the clan member are radically different than those that plague the contemporary laborer. The greatest and most obvious difference lies in the sense of omnipotence and mastery of forces among the wielder of totemic instruments compared to the utter impotence of the modern worker subjected to the colossal forces of production and market dynamics. If economists don't know anything what chance does the 'average' person have?

of subconscious spontaneous processes in our minds. For the members of a social class, life's daily experiences condition, and the needs of the class mold, the mind into a definite line of feeling and thinking, to produce definite ideas about what is useful and what is good or bad.

PANNEKOEK 1937: Part II, n.p.

Perhaps we would be more attuned to reality if we think of *Homo duplex* as itself *doubled* again into four mental domains: consciousness, collective consciousness, unconsciousness, and collective unconsciousness, or, more precisely, consciousnesses (plural).[115]

---

115   "It is ... wrong to consider society as a single subject, for this is a speculative approach" (CPE: 199). It is best to follow Durkheim and say that in us are two beings (EFRL: 15) and that each being, the personal and the public, each possess, and are possessed by, a multiplicity of minds. An example of simple duality is offered by Fadiman: "As is all too often the case these days, I find my peace as a reader and writer rent by a war between two opposing semantic selves, one feminist and one reactionary" (1998: 73). But as we will see later, Durkheim's use of the *Homo duplex* concept veils what is more accurately portrayed as a theory of *Homo quadriplex*. We have not two but four dimensions relevant for grasping the divide between individuals and society: consciousness (the domain of products and their representations), unconsciousness (the home of the It), collective consciousness (the realm of objects), and collective unconsciousness (the asylum of the Thing). As such, what commonly goes by the name of critical realism seems close to Durkheim's realistic and rationalistic sociology but it is actually a regression from the latter (cf. Ehrbar 1998). This multiplex model is also different from Meštrović's notion of a *Homo duplex* within *Homo duplex* (a kind of simple doubling) where we have individual and collective representations in both domains of individual and collective consciousness (see Verheggen 1996: 208). Philippe Périer says that we have six selves "fused into a single being: physiological, psychological, logical, metaphysical, moral, socio-political" (Barzun 1964: 306). For Buber, the picture is more complicated because, when two interact, six more figures appear (1965: 77). Two, four, six, eight? As we will see in volume two, perhaps the reality of the late imperial epoch is such that we are now eight-sided beings – *Homo octaplex*. With each new 'fold' or expansion of the mind, the moral foundation becomes more precarious, reduced, and lopsided. Mental expansion may be accompanied by moral contraction, or, rather, simplification. Remember, however, this kind of 'moral geometry' is a theoretical construct and a radical simplification. No person, "not even an idiot ... is so conveniently simple that his being can be explained as the sum to two or three principal elements; and to explain so complex a man as Harry by the artless division into wolf and man is a hopelessly childish attempt. Harry consists of a hundred or a thousand selves, not of two. His life oscillates, as everyone's does, not merely between two poles, such as the body and the spirit, the saint and the sinner, but between thousands, between innumerable poles" (Hesse 1963: 63). Maybe "identity is less a matter of binary oppositions, the contemptuous or the kindly, the father or the husband, the father or the son, than it is of kaleidoscopic perspective. Maybe it's a question of which section of the circle, the loop you happen to be in a position to see" (Mendelsohn 2017: 149).

Social facts like money and kings are obviously located in the minds of individuals as representations,[116] yet, when we inquire into the origins, causes,
and logic of things like money or kings our understanding fails. In the case of
suicide attempts, for example, people quite often are "unable to understand
what they did or why they did it; they do not seem able to make any particular
'sense' of it – i.e., to give an 'adequate' meaning from their own standpoint"
(Douglas 1967: 249). It is not simply a matter of ignorance that we are oblivious
to all but parts and effects of social facts (S: 315), rather, the dilemma resides
in the fact that the causes and logic of social facts are, as Durkheim says, absolutely *unconscious* (RSM: 212–13)[117] and operate behind the backs of individuals
(Durkheim 1974: 18–19).[118] In the 1908 essay "'The Unknown and the Unconscious in History" Durkheim says that for both individual and collective events
"the causes escape the consciousness of the individual'" (in Meštrović 1988:
95). Human nature, that is, "weird nature" has a complexity that approaches
infinity and "has, buried within it, hidden depths whose existence ordinary
people never suspect; we know that the way in which it presents itself to itself is deceptive ..." (Durkheim 1977: 280). The logic of repression and anxiety
in Freud's work around the time of *Totem and Taboo* is apropo. "The psychology of the neuroses has taught us that, if wishful impulses are repressed, their
libido is transformed into anxiety. And this reminds us that there is something
unknown and unconscious in connection with the sense of guilt, namely the
reasons for the act of repudiation. The character of anxiety that is inherent in
the sense of guilt corresponds to this unknown factor" ([1913] 1950: 87).

Importantly, given that causes are unconscious to ordinary thinking and
that, additionally, ordinary thinking often confuses effects for causes (RSM: 131)
and that effects can turn into causes, engendering new effects, even leaving
aside the nonlinear nature of the cause-effect relation (RSM: 124), both cause
and effect can easily be pushed into the domain of the inaccessible. We should
be wary of interpreting unconscious actions as thoughtless behavior. Goffman
says "most actions which are guided by rules of conduct are performed un-
thinkingly, the questioned actor saying he performs "for no reason" or because

---

116 What needs to be said about "representations" will not be exhausted in this chapter but
distributed principally between the first two chapters working in tandem.

117 According to Freud, we are capable of communicating knowledge that we do not exactly
possess ourselves (1963: 47). Rather, the knowledge, or some fragment of knowledge, possesses us so to speak (symptoms). As with many artists, they don't know what they are
doing, but they are doing it all the same.

118 That's just the way things are! "[S]ome mysterious law of decorum required that the newly affianced should always be regarded as being also newly known to each other. In the
southern states things were differently conducted ..." (Wharton 1924: 164).

he "felt like doing so." Only when his routines are blocked may he discover that his neutral little actions have all along been consonant with the proprieties of his group and that his failure to perform them can become a matter of shame and humiliation" (1967: 49). We may not produce a good reason for the things we do on a routine basis, at least without some reflection, but routinization is not necessarily unthinking. The real is rational, in a manner of speaking (FR: 20; Durkheim 1961: 4).[119] Routines are profane everyday actions that have simply crystallized into automatic conduct ("habit") that allows for a forgetting and ease of operation until such a time as they become ineffective. What is routine today was yesterday's war of wills and a mortal struggle between reason and infantile irrationality.

Ignorance certainly plays its part in sinking logic into the unconscious but training and repression also play a role. It is literally taboo[120] in many cases to even inquire into the 'machinery' of social process and, perhaps, the (fetishistic) denial of facts and facticities of postmodern society is one way that academia has of not only expressing, symptomatically, some truth about reality but also a defence against its sheer ignorance due to the chase for money and the corresponding paradigmatic regressions necessary for the commodification of thought, fads, and simple conceptual poverty vis-a-vis the enigma of contemporary processes and structures.[121] However, there is something else going on beyond just ignorance or repression.

---

119 An "institution cannot rest upon error and falsehood. If it did, it could not endure. If it had not been grounded in the nature of things, in those very things it would have met resistance that it could not have overcome.... [T]hey are grounded in and express the real.... No doubt, when all we do is consider the formulas literally, these religious beliefs and practices appear disconcerting, and our inclination might be to write them off to some sort of inborn aberration. But we must know how to reach beneath the symbol to grasp the reality it represents and that gives the symbol its true meaning. The most bizarre or barbarous rites and the strangest myths translate some human need and some aspect of life, whether social or individual. The reasons [i.e., rationalizations] the faithful settle for in justifying those rites and myths may be mistaken and most often are; but the true reasons exist nonetheless, and it is the business of science to uncover them" (EFRL: 2). "A representation or image ... has its actual existence in something other than itself" (PS: 273).

120 "The idea of forces not readily identifiable in everyday lives appears to remain anathema to most people, and for good reason. It is chilling and initially insulting to face the possibility that control, so precious and fundamental in the pictures most people entertain of themselves, is not subject simply to the whims of unjust others and one's personal decisions but resonates to entire societal structures and inner processes that people are trained to overlook or simply to ignore" (Fellman 1998: 35).

121 It almost goes without saying that it is for this reason that the 'masses' of ordinary people are left, in the wake of their incomprehension, to follow demagogues and populist heroes. "When the people feel that they are unable actually to determine their own fate ... when they are disillusioned about the authenticity and effectiveness of democratic political

For years I have asked my students in an undergraduate sociological theory course to close their eyes and imagine an apple. The results are amazing: better than 80 percent conjure up an image of a perfect, symmetrical, red apple and three or four students imagine a green or yellow apple. None have ever reported rotten, partially eaten, or worm-infested fruit. Also, while the overwhelming majority of students report owning an electronic device from the Apple corporation, only two have so far reported imagining either the corporate emblem or a device bearing the firm's logo. Let us exclude the possibility that I am a magician that makes people see what I want them to see and, further, that my students coordinated their responses in advance. What is communicating with these students?

We experience the unconsciousness of social facts on a daily basis when we use and are used by language and representations.[122] And it is not as if we are consulting a rulebook. According to Wittgenstein, "in general we don't use language according to strict rules – it hasn't been taught to us by means of strict rules, either.... In practice we very rarely use language as ... a calculus." Wittgenstein continues:

> For not only do we not think of the rules of usage – of definitions, etc. – while using language, but when we are asked to give such rules, in most cases we aren't able to do so. We are unable clearly to circumscribe the concepts we use; not because we don't know their real definition, but because there is no real 'definition' to them. To suppose that there *must* be would be like supposing that whenever children play with a ball they play a game according to strict rules.... Let's not imagine the meaning as an occult connection the mind makes between a word and a thing....[123]
>
> 1958: 25, 73–74

---

122   We both use language and are used by it. As Žižek says, "language is not a neutral medium of designation, but a practice embedded in a life world: we do things with it, we accomplish specific acts ... Is it not time to turn this cliche around: who is it that, today, claims that language is a neutral medium of designation? So, perhaps, one should emphasize how language is not a mere moment of the life world, a practice within it: the true miracle of language is that it can also serve as a neutral medium which just designates conceptual/ideal content. In other words, the true task is not to locate language as a neutral medium within a life-world practice, but to show how, within this life world, a neutral medium of designation can nonetheless emerge" (2012: 7).

123   Elsewhere: "... A meaning of a word is a kind of employment of it. For it is what we learn when the word is incorporated into our language.... When language-games change, then

processes, they are tempted to surrender the substance of democratic self-determination and to cast their lot with those whom they consider at least powerful: their leaders" (Adorno 1950: 419).

Wittgenstein clearly illustrates the split between being a conscious user of language but having no recourse to the logic that somehow cannot be raised into consciousness.[124] When everyday consciousness attempts to delve into the causes, drivers, and logic of social facts it is entering into what Hegel called the "night of the world" (1983) where we find a phantasmagoria of disconcerting images. How many holiday dinners were ruined by ethnomethodological experiments? We see in all this, then, the weird identity of rule-bound conduct and what appears to be the exact opposite. Ultimately, Wittgenstein was simultaneously correct and incorrect as to the nature of language and that paradox hinges on the concept of *autonomy*: on the one hand, language is not "chained to the world of object" but, rather, "runs free." Language is autonomous. We are the creators of language and are free to do whatever we want with it (Edmonds and Eidinow 2001: 230) but, there is the other side to linguistic autonomy: if we wish to communicate with others we are forced to use language according to grammar and convention. The language we use is, in a way, less important than the grammar that a particular language imposes upon us because each grammar (English, German, etc.) has built into a different set of obligations regarding what must or should be included in any communication (Boas 1938: 132–33). For example, an English-speaking person may make a reference to a neighbor without revealing their gender whereas a French or German-speaking person does not "have the privilege to equivocate, because [they are] obliged by the language to choose…" (Deutscher 2010: 151). Here, language is autonomous vis-a-vis its users.[125] To commune with others means submitting to the rules of communication that we did not invent. Pure personal autonomy or self-absorption is incoherent. "Thus the idea of a private language – a language that only one person can understand – is incoherent" (Edmonds and

---

there is a change in concepts, and with the concepts the meanings of words change" (Wittgenstein 1969: 10).

124 "The child learns to believe a host of things…. Bit by bit there forms a system of what is believed, and in that system some things stand unshakably fast and some are more or less liable to shift. What stands fast does so, not because it is intrinsically obvious or convincing; it is rather held fast by what lies around it" (1969: 21). His fundamental problem was profound: "'What is your aim in philosophy? – To show the fly the way out of the fly-bottle'; 'An *image* held us imprisoned. And we could not get out, for it lay in our language which merely seemed to repeat it to us, inexorably'" (in Kaufmann 1958: 57). Then why regard 'ordinary language' sufficient if it imprisons the user? Kaufmann is perhaps justified in saying that Wittgenstein was "too respectful before the wisdom of simple people" (1958: 60). Bertrand Russell "accused Wittgenstein of debasing himself before common sense" (Edmonds and Eidinow 2001: 238).

125 As Žižek says, "autonomy and receptivity coincide" (2000b: 46).

Eidinow 2001: 230).[126] Just as language is autonomous it is also, at its limit, heteronomous or other to us as well as domineering. Rather than searching behind language, trying to "penetrate phenomena and reach an immaterial core" the aim is to "battle against the bewitchment of our language" (Edmonds and Eidinow 2001: 230–31). Yet languages, like our laws, *are* mirrors or "visible symbols" that do reflect on an immaterial core: solidarity, shared sacrifice, and collective consciousness, i.e., society (DOL: 24–25).

Our trained inclination is to look around when asked to think about society as if "society" were an ensemble of material things, active individuals, visible signs, and so forth, but, if we examine the etymology of the word we find that the essence of society is simply the *relations* between companions, the relations that emerge from association. As Marx makes perfectly clear, any *relation* is an *abstraction* and can only be represented in the domain of ideas (MECW, 28: 101). Animals do not have relations. Relations, like consciousness, are a product of human society (MECW, 5: 44). However, even though the "heart" of society is immaterial, relational, a form of consciousness and a whirlwind of ideas and representations (RSM: 253), it rises from action and objectivations and produces physical effects (money, totems, etc.) and patterns of collective conduct. This is why, for example, Durkheim turns to changes in the rate of suicide across time and space as indices of social disintegration. Has the emotional "atmosphere" of the collective changed? We should expect to find that alteration expressed in various indices of collective self-destruction or collective self-preservation. Central to Hegel, Marx, and Durkheim is the absolute substantiality of social consciousness and feelings – our relations, unlike the relations between inorganic physical objects, do not peter out at the dyadic level but spawn not only triadic forms but, more importantly, a normative order as well as as panoply of other supplements.[127] Qualities may emerge from material combinations, e.g., the hardness of bronze (to use Durkheim's analogy) but there is nothing like an emergent categorical imperative when it

---

126 Consider the turmoil the Voynich manuscript, a 'language' *no one understands*, has stirred up over the last 100 years. The attempt to decode the text is driven not by a collective excitement but by the fascination and consternation of cryptological experts.

127 "To commune is to share without dividing. This may sound paradoxical. Where material goods are concerned, it is indeed impossible." However, at the level of group 'consumption' (e.g., enjoying a cake at a party) "the enjoyments of each is enhanced by the enjoyment of all! True, their stomachs will receive smaller portions, but their mental enjoyment will be increased, paradoxically enough, by the very fact of sharing. This is why we talk about communion of minds – because only the mind knows how to share without dividing" (Comte-Sponville 2007: 15–16).

comes to the hardness of metal. Of course, if "bronze" were to be swept up into a set of signifying practices it could become a sign of some moral sentiment—expressing no longer the toughness and durability of an alloy but the resilience and lustre of a Nation, e.g., or some other social aggregate. But almost everywhere we find positivistic, pragmatic, or hyper-constructionist impulses decked out with a disconcerting mysticism as an ever-present supplement that is not only antithetical to rational comprehension but also rational solidarity; constructionism of the "hot" kind and pragmatic ideologies are exciting and creative but also corrosive to rational energetic bondings between individuals and groups.[128] They also promote a feeling of rebellion ("Down with the Absolute!") toward reason, society, and authority, but far from demystifying the social domain, they actually render it more opaque and mysterious to individuals. Pragmatic types may *feel* free while simultaneously being more externally determined than most.

5   Collective Emotions and Sentiments

Social facts are, in addition to forms of conduct and consciousness, also ways of feeling. Nothing would seem more personal than our emotional lives, yet, the way we feel at any given moment is determined by our socialization, coordinates, and ideology.[129] "The emotions always have a quite definite class basis; the form they take at any time is historical, restricted and limited in specific ways. The emotions are in no sense universally human and timeless" (Brecht, in Willett 1992: 145). For example, the early English settlers to America came in different waves and originated from different regions of England. Each "wave" varied greatly in its customs, ethics, and religious beliefs. And the emotional structure of each group was distinctly different. Every group thinks of itself as representing a certain "type" or kind of people and that certain emotions are appropriate while others are wrong for that type. For example, some people grieve openly and flamboyantly at the death of a loved one but the English who settled Virginia expected mourners to have a stiff upper lip and take

---

128   Wittgenstein's own asceticism, destructive guruism, irrational mysticism, and suicidal inclinations, correlate with the pragmatic conception of human association as flat, plastic, and agitated. Literally, the history of pragmatism in England and the US is a spectacle of mentally unstable mystics with a propensity for self-destruction. One need not be a theologian to see the folly of exclaiming "Damn the Absolute!" (see Kaag 2016: 8; Goodman 2002: 179; Myers 2001: 293).

129   *"Emotion is not a psychic internal fact but rather a variation in our relations with others and the world"* (Merleau-Ponty, in Lichtman 1982: 73).

misfortunes in stride, with a stoic and fatalistic resignation. "Here was a way of thinking about mortality that was far removed from the cultivated death-obsessions of Calvinist New England. The Virginia attitude of stoic fatalism rested upon a belief that people were not personally responsible for their misfortunes, and that they must accept what fate might bring" (Fischer 1989: 331). This fatalism toward death was different than the "nescient fatalism" found in the "backcountry" where lawlessness, vigilante justice, and frequent wars created a feeling of powerlessness and anger toward a mysterious and "illimitable" world "where sudden, violent and senseless death was a constant fact of life" (Fischer 1989: 699). The best countermeasure was courage in the face of capriciousness (Ibid.). Puritan fatalism was entirely different from the preceding two in that the mourning of deceased loved ones triggered the total loosening of restraints and manic levels of alcohol consumption among adults and children. "Entire communities became intoxicated. Even little children went reeling and staggering through the bleak burying grounds. There are descriptions of infants so intoxicated that they slipped into the yawning grave" (Fischer 1989: 115). This was no orgiastic sublimation (Weber) nor a Dionysian cult frenzy (Nietzsche) but a plunge into desublimation. This puritanical obliteration of the embattled ego, drowning anxiety in the face of mortality, was very different from Quaker fatalism that promoted an optimistic glorification and "apotheosis" of death as a welcomed end of physical life and the doorway to eternal life. The "Quakers cultivated an attitude not merely of resignation, but confident expectation" (Fischer 1989: 520). In sociological terms we see the four distinct, fatalistic emotional orientations toward death flowing out along neat conceptual lines: fatalistic egoism (Virginia); fatalistic altruism (Quakers); fatalism *alternating* with anomie (Puritans); and, finally, fatalism *blending* with anomie (backcountry).

The actions, thoughts, and emotions that sociology is interested in are the forms that are shared and constraining. Take the notion of obligation, for example. The feeling of obligation means nothing in the abstract. The idea has to have value to a society and impart that value or virtue onto the individual. When a person does something approved by others that action is said to fall in line with virtuous conduct. We learn to value obligations and ultimately we arrive at a point where not only do we acquire a sense of duty but a duty toward duty itself, we value the sense of obligation toward the idea of obligation in general so that we know it when we see it (Shand 1914: 114).[130] Knowing what

---

130   "How often is it said that a man must have a family himself to realise fully the duties of the
      family-life. But he will not realise them any the more if he does not acquire the sentiment
      of the family" (Shand 1914: 114).

is obligatory, optional, or irrelevant to the system of vices and virtues is part of the long and difficult process of socialization and much of what we imagine to be irrelevant from the standpoint of obligations masks an unconscious system of compliance that is simply in the "social atmosphere around us" (Shand 1914: 114). Emotional life is organized around the requirements of the groups or circles we belong to into a system of sentiments or patterned feelings. Social organization is also *emotional* organization and the articulation of sentimental life or coerced and necessary feelings.[131]

Even though we fancy ourselves as totally unique most of us follow rather conventional and characteristic patterns of action: we cry when we are expected to cry, we laugh at jokes that are not funny to avoid embarrassing the joke-teller, we tell people we know exactly what they are talking about when in fact we do not, we feel sad when our team loses and angry when somebody disrespects some holy object. Attire conforms to certain styles (uniform-like in many cases), we follow stereotypical speech patterns, use formulaic gesturing and are unaware of how others shape the formation of bodily *hexis*. We are taught at an early age how to make our thoughts and feelings conform to expectations – we literally have to be taught when and how to act sad, when to put on that happy face, even how to "correctly" respond to things like changes in weather or how a "normal" person should respond to a "beautiful" sunset. Of course, when a person has been more or less socialized, ways of acting, thinking, and feeling, appear to be quite natural, as if no reflection at all is required to function as a member of society. This "naturalness" is not at all natural but actually social. Effective socialization results in the development of our *second nature* (personality and the underlying character structure)[132] such that how we act, think, and feel normally happens nearly automatically and more or less trouble-free. Sentiments crystallize into character. "The qualities that

---

131   Social facts are necessities. Our greatest moral necessity is the fact of periodic communion or association. "Without it, no society can develop, or even subsist. Law is not enough. Repression is not enough.... Democracy and public order are all well and good, but neither can replace communion; both are rooted in it" (Comte-Sponville 2007: 17).

132   "We come into the world as individuals, achieve character, and become persons" (Park 1950: 250). "*Character structure*, in our vocabulary, is the most inclusive term for the individual as a whole entity. It refers to the relatively stabilized integration of the organism's psychic structure linked with the social roles of the person" (Gerth and Mills 1953: 22; C. Shand 1914). Character "is the congealed sociological process of a given epoch. A society's ideologies can become a material force only on condition that they actually change the character structures of the people" (Reich [1933] 1972: xxvi). The problem of character will be taken up more fully in the next chapter. On the emergence of the concept of 'character' and personal conscience in Egyptian society see James Breasted (1933: 396, 398).

a sentiment acquires for its own needs in becoming fixed, tend to qualify the character as a whole" (Shand 1914: 121).

6   Currents and Crystallizations

Some social facts are said to be fixed, "crystallized," or relatively permanent "ways of being" (RSM: 57–58). As Simmel says,

> The large systems and the super-individual organization that customarily come to mind when we think of society, are nothing but immediate in-teractions that occur among men constantly, every minute, but that have become crystallized as permanent fields, as autonomous phenomena. As they crystallize, they attain their own existence and their own laws, and may even confront or oppose spontaneous interaction itself. At the same time, society, as it's constantly being realized, always signifies that indi-viduals are connected by mutual influence and determination.[133]
>
> 1950: 10

Much of reality is a tempest of words, images, and ideas, whirling around, gen-erating copies and alterations, almost an autonomous being[134] entertaining it-self for no reason other than entertainment, but also surging toward durability then reliquidation, alternating through the "spiral helix" of devaluations and revaluations.

> The social world is at all times filled with countless spiritual [*geistige*] forces or entities that one can simply call ideas.[135] Political, social, and artistic movements embodying specific contents of some sort arise one day and run their course. What these ideas have in common is that they all want to penetrate the extant world; they all want to become reality themselves. They appear within human society as a concrete, material should-being [*Sollen*] and have an inborn drive to realize themselves. It is

---

133 "'The musical conventions today destroyed were not always so objective, so objectively imposed. They were crystallizations of living experiences and as such long performed an office of vital importance: the task of organization. Organization is everything. Without it there is nothing, least of all art'" (Mann 1948: 190).

134 Images "have, so to speak, a life of their own ... " (Tonnies 1988: 115).

135 "Many old gods ascend from their graves; they are disenchanted and hence take the form of impersonal forces. They strive to gain power over our lives and again they resume their eternal struggle with one another" (FMW: 149).

only once they cease being mere chimera without influence on reality
and begin to have an effect on the social world, bringing it to a boil, that
they take on sociological significance.

KRACAUER 1995: 143

The impersonal rules of a bureaucracy are slow to change and endure sometimes for decades before being revised whereas other social facts are highly
"fluid" ("currents") that undergo rapid change, such as fashion trends, fads, or
charismatic social movements that, though potentially very powerful, are here
today and gone tomorrow; from year to year the public gets carried away by
one random thing or another – yesterday the coconut, today cocaine, tomorrow popcorn (Kracht 2015: 117). "At every point in time, societies are producing
novelties, from the almost daily variations in style to the great political and
moral revolutions. All these changes, however, are always varying degrees of
modifications of existing institutions" (Mauss 2005: 11). Religious dogma and
related ceremonies approach ideal-typical rigidity whereas economic practices, still fairly rigid are characterized by relatively more plasticity.[136] While it is
true that religious "innovation and reform" lead to fatalities and are considered
abhorrent, we find an almost incomprehensible amount of change, especially
where authority weakens and throws the individual back upon him or herself
for the seeking of answers (S: 157–59).

There is no such thing as a social fact that is absolutely fixed or uncea-
singly fluid; they are merely "forms of life at varying stages of crystallization"
(RSM: 58).[137] Social facts are alloys of both fixed and fluid elements under constant metamorphosis. Tonnies approaches this continuum with the termino-
ogy of congealed forces in contrast to fluid will; "The relation between the two
is comparable to that between potential and kinetic energy" (1988: 118). With
the capitalist system of production, for example, we find labor power being absorbed by the means of production (fixed or constant capital) creating a "jelly"
(the commodity) of objectified human labor (Marx 1978). Any large institution, like a university for example, offers insights into the interdigitated nature
of the fixed and the fluid: the impersonal rules and regulations, bureaucratic structures, aesthetic totality, and so on are fairly static and change slowly,

---

136   "Virtually no variation is allowed in the moral and religious domain where innovation and
       reform are fatally viewed as crimes and sacrilege; while rather more is permitted in the
       realm of economic phenomena. But sooner or later there is, nonetheless, a limit beyond
       which we cannot go. This is why the characteristic of social phenomena is entirely found
       in the ascendancy which it exercises over particular [individual] minds" (Durkheim 1982:
       1065).
137   We would want to add to this statement, the opposite: they are also forms of life at varying
       stages of *liquidation*.

followed by the university faculty and administrators who occupy their offices for extended periods of time, sometimes decades. Then we come to the students and adjunct instructors – some of whom endure only a semester or two, a few who hang on for years, but most arrive and depart right on cue. We can imagine the student population of a university as a flowing current moving through a crystallized matrix of rules and offices, etc. The entire scale of normative life illustrates the distinction between the fixed and the fluid. Laws are routinized and "frozen" whereas, at the other extreme of the scale, folkways are more fluid and variable with eddies and currents, turbulent and dynamic. If laws are like "ice" and folkways are like water, mores are the ambiguous middle dimension between the frozen and the liquid; mores are metaphorically akin to slush, which is reminiscent to Marx's portrayal of the commodity as a "jelly" (1978; Worrell 2014).[138] Marx's phenomenology of the value form in chapter one of *Capital* (as well as the second chapter on the exchange process) provides us with a good representation of the development of a fact as it emerges from accidental and transient exchanges, where the universal equivalent "comes and goes" (C: 183),[139] to the fully crystallized money form where the externality of thought *becomes* (S: 39) sanctified and obligatory.

7   Externality

The externality (C: 381) of social facts means, among other things, that they are experienced by individuals as preexisting,[140] objective realities as opposed to merely subjective or fluid consensus realities.

> When the world does not change very much, when the same phenomena and the same experiences always return, the habits of acting and thinking become fixed with great rigidity; the new impressions of the mind fit into the image formed by former experience and intensify it. These habits and these concepts are not personal but collective property; they are not lost with the death of the individual. They are intensified by the mutual intercourse of the members of the community, who all are living in the

---

138   As both a "jelly" and a monstrosity the commodity is akin to the central 'character' (?) in the film *The Blob* (Yeaworth 1958) that is described on its promotional poster as "*Indescribable ... Indestructible! Nothing can stop it!*"

139   Spirit is "here and there" but only accidentally; when will humanity itself begin to reflect? (Novalis 1997: 29). Novalis (von Hardenberg) should not have worried.

140   "'Thus God [i.e., the imagined collective symbolic big third] knows the world, because He conceived it in His mind, as if from the outside, before it was created, and we do not know its rule, because we live inside it, having found it already made'" (Eco 1983: 247).

> same world, and they are transferred to the next generation as a system of
> ideas and beliefs ... the mental store of the community.[141]
>
> PANNEKOEK 1937: Part III, n.p.

According to Eagleton, our ultimate social fact, language, is "less a personal possession than a medium into which we are born.... So we are faced with the materialist paradox that the human is born of the non-human. Of course language is in some sense a human invention. But it bears in upon us with a certain implacable force. It is as much a fatality as an arena of creativity" (2015: 20). Individuals do not come into existence under their own power. "It would be the highest absurdity to suppose that I was before I came into existence, in order to bring myself into existence" (Fichte 1848: 27). Yet, what is absurd for the individual, autogenesis, is true for social facts and collective consciousness.[142] No individual or single group, for example, can really be identified as the inventor or creator of, for example, capitalism. Capitalism was not born out of capitalistic intentions and, far from being its creators, we are born into that econo-spiritual system where we will conform or find ourselves "thrown into the streets" (PESC: 20).

> There is no principle for which we have received more criticism; but none
> is more fundamental. Indubitably for sociology to be possible, it must
> above all have an object all its own. It must take cognizance of a reality
> which is not in the domain of other sciences. But if no reality exists out-
> side of individual consciousness, it wholly lacks any material of its own.
> In that case, the only possible subject of observation is the mental states
> of the individual, since nothing else exists.
>
> S: 37–38

Nota bene: "individual consciousness" in contrast to consciousness per se.[143]
As Haidt says "Durkheim focused on social facts – things that exist outside of

---

141 "Even if ethics are human and relative ... they do not result from decisions ... We all find
     them in ourselves to the extent that we have received them ... and we can criticize one
     of their facets only by invoking another. For instance, we can invoke individual freedom
     to condemn the morals governing sexual behavior, or invoke justice to restrain freedom.
     All ethics come down to us from the past: For society, they are rooted in history, and for
     individuals, in childhood" (Comte-Sponville 2007: 24).

142 "In an individual, a God-man, the properties and functions which the church ascribes to
     Christ contradict themselves; in the idea of the race, they perfectly agree" (Strauss 1892:
     780).

143 "[W]e can and must speak of a collective consciousness distinct from individual con-
     sciousness. To justify this distinction there is no need to hypostatise the collective con-
     sciousness; it is something special and must be designated by a special term, simply

any individual mind ..." (2012: 314).[144] This statement in all its bluntness sounds absurd but it is true: social facts are in minds but as we will see later we can look high and low and never find the *totality* of the fact in any mind or in any assembled group of minds (see Mannheim 1982: 209).[145] Think of this problem of externality from the standpoint of Marx's discussion of the simple value form: in the exchange relation between two commodities, the relative and the equivalent moments or poles of the social relation are predicated on their identical nature as metaphorical *crystals of a third thing they both have in common but which neither actually possess*, namely, abstract labor as the substance of exchange-value. To say that abstract labor is "in" the commodity would be an absurdity even though value is not only real but *really real* (external, coercive, and irreducible). This imperative form of thinking is rooted, in the final analysis, on negation and alienation. Let us take for example the wish to exchange quantities of two non-identical objects, say, slices of pizza and bottles of beer. As the owner of pizza who would also like a drink with my food I am forced out of necessity to negate my possession by setting aside what it is and to render it abstractly, i.e., regard it from a point of view that is alien to its qualitative and profane nature. I will need to alienate it (signified by the lowercase "a" in the expression below) and thereby transpose it to a different register altogether such that my pizza is no longer qualitatively what it is in isolation (a simple and tasty *objectification* of labor and an *object* of utility that could be consumed) but, instead, a relative (R) moment in the quantitative exchange relation whereby, as an *objectivity*,[146] it seeks its moral equivalent (E) in the form of some quantity of beer.

$$xR = yE$$
$$\underline{\hspace{4cm}} (a) \underline{\hspace{4cm}}$$
$$\text{Pizza} \neq \text{Beer}$$

because the states which constitute it differ specifically from those which make up individual consciousnesses. This specificity arises because they are not formed from the same elements" (RSM: 145). See also Marx's positing value as a form of consciousness ("in their heads") but not reducible to individual subjectivity (C: 189).

144   Despite possessing a sub-optimal grasp of Durkheim's sociology Haidt's book on moral psychology is nonetheless a valuable, though fatally flawed, work.

145   Without getting into the nitty-gritty details here I would like to point readers in the direction of Kant's critique of the second paralogism of transcendental psychology (1929: 335).

146   "The value of the linen as a congealed mass of human labor can be expressed only as an 'objectivity' [*Gegenständlichkeit*], a thing which is materially different from the linen itself and yet common to the linen and all other commodities. The problem is already solved" (C: 142).

We may twist and turn the physical bodies[147] of the relative (pizza) and its equivalent (beer) for as long as we like and we will never locate the third thing they have in common: the *emergent*,[148] non-physical, social substance exchange-value. The "transcendental" third thing here in the simple, isolated, or accidental value form "comes and goes" with every transaction (C: 183) but this plastic, ephemeral, and somewhat straightforward construction is not the kind of fact we see operating in a developed capitalist economy, yet, this simple form is nonetheless the key to everything. "The whole mystery of the form of value lies hidden in this simple form" (C: 139). Again: "The whole mystery..." is laid bare right here.[149] The gateway between the concrete infraliminal dimension of use and the abstract supraliminal domain of the sacred is *reduction*: setting aside, forgetting, lacking, separating, reducing, ratiocination, ratio-producing, abstinence, withdrawal – in other words, *negation* (see EFRL: 303–29). Negation (here, reckoning and regarding) as a form of thought determines the ways objects are treated – something functioning as a "bearer" or a physical husk that carries value is always a matter of a "point of view" with respect to a kind of social relation (C: 143; see especially DOL: 56).[150] However, this "point of view" is not merely subjective or intersubjective (a form of "understanding where the I and the We figuratively stand under the abstract expression) but also an absolute necessity for survival in a capitalist order. In a way, since we have arrived at a common form of thought that is both universal but also necessary for the interactors, we can say that Spirit has, at this point, raised itself up to a "philosophical" shape (cf. Collingwood 1946: 335).[151] What once merely came and went with every exchange now "fixes itself firmly and exclusively onto particular kinds of commodity, i.e., it crystallizes out into the money-form" (C: 183). Once the permanent money form emerges it is here to stay which means that the merely temporary representations in the minds operative at the subjective "level" and within the intersubjective exchange matrix

---

147   Within the exchange relation the contradiction of the *use* of the body and the simultaneous *non-use* of it by the 'relator' which makes it available for some equivalent others unified in the concept of the bearer.

148   The "value character emerges here through its own relation to the second commodity" (C: 142).

149   Do not forget that "In a certain sense, a man is in the same situation as a commodity" (C: 144).

150   Social forces of whatever kind (religious, economic, etc.) are super-additions or "super-added" to the world (EFRL: 327). Spirit is excessive in relation to its supporting material (Origen, in Strauss 1892: 42). "Spirit itself is the real miracle in the operations of nature" (LHP, 1: 72).

151   Here, to be 'philosophical' means to enjoy intimate contact with the wisdom (right judgment) of divinity.

of the expanded form, become permanent and omnipresent authoritative representations filling out the social space, not limited to the exchange relations in which they were born. What was once perpetrated is now perpetual. Once capitalism emerges it grows into what Weber calls "an immense cosmos" (PESC: 19). This logic could be avoided outside of market relationships and "capitalistic rules of action" (Ibid.). However, once almost all labor becomes social labor, the division of labor becomes a social division of labor, and almost all products confront subjects as commodities that, even after the exchange of goods for money has been completed, seem to live on in the imagination not merely as useful objects but as carriers of an aura or some moral surplus even after the exchange relation has collapsed (i.e., the fetishism of the commodity in all its meanings). The commodity world is a superstitious landscape populated with ghosts and spectral remains – our critical objectivity is not shared by the mystical objectivity of the commodity fetishizers.

Critical sociology as a socially-realistic enterprise cannot tag along in the confusion between the social (sacred) with the material (profane). Value is "purely social" (C: 139) and "only within the limits of this relation" (C: 148) does the one thing appear "to be endowed with its ... property of direct exchangeability, by nature" (C: 149). Neither Marx nor Durkheim can be considered guilty of this confusion of intrinsicality. The intrinsicality of mana, value, and other moral forces, is an "illusion" or a "mirage" but one that is also "universal" and "necessary" and, therefore, "inevitable" for alienated Spirit (DOL: 56). But neither Marx nor Durkheim are naive realists or vulgar materialists. Alexander says "Because he did not yet understand the process by which social order could be outside the isolated individual and still be subjective, or "inside," at the same time, Durkheim was compelled at this early point to turn to the notion that order could be stable only if it were external in an ontological sense" (1986: 95; cf. DOL: 56). Alexander goes on to provide a flawed interpretation of the externality of social facts by rendering them and society as essentially "physical" in the final analysis (1986: 95). Right here we need to separate the notion of *physical* externality with *psychical* externality.

Knowledge can be objectified or externalized in machines, e.g., where they confront people as alien and external powers over and against individuals (G: 695) and the entire history of graphical representation stretching back perhaps 40,000 years, enabling a durability and transmissibility of symbolic material, is also an externalization (Alperovitz and Daly 2008: 44–49).[152] But this concept of physical externalization (which will be pursued further in the next chapter)

---

152   Alperovitz and Daly reporting on the work of Merlin Donald.

is different from our concept of external consciousness as it pertains to social facts. No doubt, Durkheim does not neglect the "role" that physical objects play in society but that "role" is one of providing profane and singular "supports" for the essentially "psychical" reality of society (S: 310–16; see especially RSM: 120; Bouglé [1926] 1970: 74). There is a materialization process and material things are involved in society just as physical individualities are obviously involved. But we cannot fall into a naive materialism any more than we can regress to ordinary idealism.

A church needs a temple or other holy place-thing for ritualizing and the "administration of the sacred" (Caillois 1959: 20) but the essence of a church is non-physical.[153] A church is not a place or a physical thing but a group unified by a set of representations that transform the imaginary into regulated and creative praxis (EFRL: 41). In short, a church as a kind of institution, is a "spiritual reality" (Mannheim 1982: 231). Of course, it is difficult for us to imagine society without material things, property, etc., and this stuff has to be taken into consideration as playing a "part" in the life of a society but the material eye leads only to negative conclusions when we fail to see how material things become avatars of social relations and dynamics (DOL: 72–73). The non-physical essence of society is imagined in a physical form (EFRL: 208). This needs to be expressed as strenuously as possible: *society itself is not physical but has physical effects*[154] and is imagined and experienced to be a physical thing by naive consciousness.[155]

To repeat, "society" is derived from the Latin *societas* for a friendly association or relation between companions. *Associations and relations are abstractions, products of thought* and must assume the form of ideas for us (G: 164). Strictly speaking, the notion of ideal expressions of "material relations" is

---

153 "As we pulled out onto the road again, I thought about how affecting the simple flame of the memorial had been. It had rendered the forest ancient, and on the dead soldiers it had conferred a sort of immortality, drawing them into the eternal ranks of the fallen. In reality, death was small and dirty, nothing to aspire to, nothing to celebrate. But with the aid of this memorial, death had been elevated from the real world into the ideal. The flame was the agent of this elevation; it was bound to grimy materiality but reached up into the pure ether; it moved as if alive, but it was dead" (Knausgaard 2018: n.p.).

154 "Thus we can repeat about society what was previously said about the deity: It has reality only to the extent that it has a place in human consciousness ... " (EFRL: 351).

155 "For many centuries, philosophers, artists, and psychologists have studied modern art to learn the truth about beauty and popularity. For understandable reasons, many focused on the paintings themselves. But studying the patches of Monet and the brushstrokes of Caillebotte won't tell you why one is famous and the other is not.... Famous paintings, hit songs, and blockbusters that seem to float effortlessly on the cultural consciousness have a hidden genesis; even water lilies have roots" (Thompson 2017: 20–21).

incoherent (G: 164; MECW, 5: 59).[156] Social facts are objectively existing things but, once we get behind appearances, they are not of a physical or material kind and this is in sympathy with Marx's insistence that value is a thing of collective thought *realized* in the exchange *relation* and *only* in the exchange relation.

> The price or money-form of commodities is, like their form of value generally, quite distinct from their palpable and real bodily form; it is therefore a purely ideal or notional form. Although invisible, the value of iron, linen and corn exists in these very articles: it is signified through their equality with gold, even though this relation with gold exists only in their heads, so to speak.[157]
>
> C: 189

Value is socially real – a real way of thinking imposed upon us by the imperatives of the system of production, exchange, consumption, and accumulation. Even if I wanted to wish value away I find that I cannot. I know that value is "in my head" but even with things that are no longer useful to me, things that I paid money for in the past, I nonetheless treat and regard them *as if* value continued to reside within them. I know very well that they are not actually crystals of value but I still act in accordance with the (apparently obligatory) delusion that they are somehow greater than and different than the sum of their parts. Consequently, value as a form of consciousness acquires an independent existence (C: 255) as a "self-moving substance" (C: 256) or automatic subject that acts on its own accord (PESC: 20.[158] When Marx says that value 'exists in these very articles" (C: 189) we should not make a wrong turn by imagining that this substance is of a material variety.[159] The value of the commodity

---

156   In this particular case the expression "*materiellen Verhältnisse*" would be better translated as "material conditions." See the original German text: (Marx 1969: n.p.).

157   We must be precise. When Marx says "the value ... exists in these very articles" we must always remember that what appears to be intrinsic or inherent "in" the body of the commodity is imagined, an ideal product of thought. 'Article' (from *artus*) means a *joint* relation or connection. As such, what is really intrinsic is not the moral substance "in" a material object but the form of thinking that is inherent to the institutionalized exchange relation. When we say 'commodity' we always mean a *relation* in contrast with the bodies of utilities in the relation.

158   Marx rejects both naive realism and nominalism (C: 677) and situates his 'materialism' alongside the ontological alternatives (C: 493–94, 683).

159   Likewise, when Durkheim says that the totem is wakan he is expressing the point of view of the totemist. When Marx makes analogous statements, he too is expressing the point of view of the capitalist. In the third volume of the present work we will pay careful attention to how Marx shuttles back and forth from one perspective to another in *Capital*.

is here the "soul of the concrete which it indwells [transference via projection] ..
in the manifoldness and diversity of the concrete" (SL: 602) but this value substance is nonetheless ideal. The material world seems to the ordinary mind to
be entangled with moral energy and, since it has no dialectical method from
which is can perform an analytical "dissection" (G: 704) consciousness cannot
find a way to disentangle the real from the ideal.[160] Matter does "embody" and
mediate social life (Durkheim 1974: 15–18; Pickering [2000] 2006a: 13) and, to
ordinary consciousness, it appears that vitality flows from what are really just
material props.[161] But sociology commits intellectual suicide when it capitu-
lates to everyday thinking – and it does so routinely. Matter itself "has no truth"
(Hegel 2007: 30). We therefore cannot, for example, confuse the "envelope" or
the body of the totem with the totemic principle itself, the thing signified; nor
should we confuse the "bearer" or "carrier" aspect of the commodity for its
value (C, chapter 1).[162] Likewise, the physical body of the neighbor is not itself
the enemy of god – the body comes "bearing the signs of eternal damnation"
(PESC: 75) – but if we want to rid ourselves of evil we tend to run the sign-
bearers out of town.

A perfect example of ambiguity over the ontic status of a social fact is provided by Sennett who says about authority that "In ordinary life, authority is
not a thing. It is an interpretive process which seeks for itself the solidity of
a thing. Faith, sin, and despair transformed into stone churches" (1980: 19).
On the surface this statement seems correct and most social realists would
find nothing to rebuke, however, it is ambiguous. Ordinary thinking does in
fact confront authority as a thing and precisely not as a process. Moreover,
what is meant by sin being "transformed into" stone? Is the moral (sin) being

---

160   It is too long to quote here entirely, but one should read the description of projective en-
       tanglement offered by Proust, pertaining to the manner in which we construct represen-
       tations of things and people. We would want to qualify his description by replacing the "in
       part" with "wholly." "Even the very simple act that we call "seeing a person we know" is in
       part an intellectual one. We fill the physical appearance of the individual we see with all
       the notions we have about him, and of the total picture that we form for ourselves, these
       notions certainly occupy the greater part.... ([1913] 2002: 19–20).

161   "The sentiments experienced fix themselves upon it [the physical thing], for it is the only
       concrete object upon which they can fix themselves. It continues to bring them to mind
       and to evoke them even after the assembly has dissolved, for it survives the assembly, be-
       ing carved upon the instruments of the cult, upon the sides of rocks, upon buckler, etc. By
       it, the emotions experienced are perpetually sustained and revived. Everything happens
       just as if they inspired them directly. It is still more natural to attribute them to it for, since
       they are common to the group, they can be associated only with something that is equally
       common to all" (Durkheim [1912] 1915: 252).

162   "[H]ow should one be inclined to boast overmuch about being an embodiment!" (Mann
       1951: 9).

conflated with the material effect of the social subjects who feel sinful? This is the problem of what normally goes by the name "objectification" that will consume much of our time in volume three where we tackle the problem of labor products and commodities. If we refuse to go along with normal realism are we simply trapped, then, in an idealism? Not in any traditional sense of the word. Durkheim rejects idealism that raises "psychic life into a sort of absolute, derived from nothing and unattached to the rest of the universe" (1974: 23) yet this negation of the old Absolute Ego does not refute the idea of society as a "mental absolute" produced through the synthesis of interacting and instituted individuals (1974: 24).

It would be no doubt absurd to imagine minds without brains or society without the existence of physical individuals (Verheggen 1996: 204) but brains and individuals are not "society." Durkheim does *not* have an "ontology" as such (S: 319) but he does have a *social* ontology, and therein lies a world of difference. It bears reiterating: the physical aspects of a building that "embodies" a "definite type of architecture" (S: 313–14) is not itself the social fact. On the one hand the building is a physical thing that satisfies some physical and profane need and, on the other, a representational prop that satisfies not a physical need but a psychical and social need. In a way, a building that is sociologically interesting (property, monument, etc.) would, like any "normal" person, exist in two dimensions: the analytic and the synthetic, the concrete and the abstract, the profane and the sacred. Beyond the stark contrast between these two dimensions, the physical layout of a building will determine how and when people relate to one another, determining to a certain extent the forms of association that are made possible and impossible (see Durkheim [1901] 2006: 31).[163]

It is normal for us to reify the profane building, the material thing, the stone, and misplace its precise ontic coordinates – i.e., confuse expressions for essences. This amounts to obedience to the norms of ordinary or vulgar realism. But if our ultimate project is to defetishize the domain of the social and demystify the nature of our own authority, it can never be achieved so long as we fail to master the dialectical gaze and the paradox of *Homo duplex* and sociological externality. Perhaps at this point in our history the notion of *Homo duplex* seems trivial, overly simplistic, or just plain wrong-headed but the stakes are high. There can be no human society without human duality raised to the point of sanctification. Under totalitarian regimes, it is the aspect of personal life that is obliterated; there are no individuals, merely "atoms in a huge rolling

---

163 Authoritarian regimes are known for designing public spaces that inhibit spontaneous public interactions and mass gatherings.

block of stone" (Klemperer [1957] 2000: 23).[164] Likewise, under the regime of neoliberalism, there is no public, just a bunch of atoms (minus the block). Before collapsing into identity politics America was a land of duality – nowhere better expressed than in the separation between church and state (Lilla 2017: 62). Between these two limits established by totalitarianism and anarchy rises the spectre of our onrushing future, what Durkheim calls a "sociological monstrosity" (DOL: liv) whereby the state has to forcefully solve the problem of millions of irrelevant, impoverished, unproductive, and anarchic lives gumming up the works. The extent to which we avoid the cataclysm of a future civil war can be measured in terms of our commitments to the duality of the person and the facticity of society and a universal moral dimension that can humble the derangements of particularities (e.g., fundamentalist evangelicals, identitarian professionals, movementism, taboo-values, etc.) that confuse personal interests, group ethics and values for morality itself. The problem of consciousness and collective consciousness, mapped across the political landscape, is a matter of life and death.

The reality "outside" of *individual* consciousness is located in *collective* consciousness, which is a distinct form of consciousness within the mind[165] of the *individual* (we have one brain and at least two minds and myriad forms of consciousness and unconsciousness in contact and in conflict with one another).[166] This may sound weird but it is all too common and can be found in anyone who holds contradictory beliefs. For example, many scientists believe in gods and see no conflict between the two systems of representations because they do not subject one another to criticism and they are capable of keeping "their scientific views and their religious views in separate idea-tight

---

164 "We admitted no private sphere, not even inside a man's skull. We lived under the compulsion of working things out to their final conclusions. Our minds were so tensely charged that the slightest collision caused a mortal short-circuit. Thus we were fated to mutual destruction" (Koestler [1941] 1968: 100; italics omitted).

165 The twin modalities of consciousness "are not regions of ourselves that are 'geographically' distinct, for they interpenetrate each other at every point" (DOL: 86).

166 Such is the difference between having an opinion and the state of public opinion. "Opinions are individual, but the attitudes upon which they are based are collective" (Park 1950: 232). We all have opinions but deviating too far from received wisdom "is invariably shocking, and frequently quite unintelligible" (Ibid.). As we will see in the chapters on suicide in the next volume, what I have in mind (no pun intended) is an elaboration of the *Homo duplex* idea such that consciousness, parted out into its individual and collective dimensions, conscious and unconscious aspects, yields not a duality of consciousness but a mental quadratus that is itself doubled. As indicated elsewhere, it is important to recall that, for Durkheim, we have a collective consciousness for each group we belong to. Consequently, individuals not entangled in and 'consumed' by a sufficiently large number of affiliations suffer from a preponderance of individual consciousness.

compartments" (Otto 1924: 201). For these people, their religion is a private matter whereas science is their professional vocation. Science deals with matter and things and religion deals in the sacred. Life is divided and in conflict with itself along this axis of matter and spirit and that conflict is reflected in our divided minds. Being of two minds is normal; it is the single-minded people that we distrust. Social antagonism and divisions are reflected in the minds of individuals, however, no single individual possesses the totality of society within their consciousness. Durkheim's argument on the exteriority of social facts hinges on this statement: "*It is external to each average individual taken singly*" (S: 316, emphasis in the original). As far a I have been able to ascertain, only a handful of writers have ever reproduced this passage *in totum* regarding the externality or exteriority of facts. If we interrogate any individual we will never find the totality of society within them. The single person is just a fragment.[167] Perhaps the best way to illustrate the mystery of the externality of a collective and therefore authoritative representation is to consider, for example, the totality of the federal legal code or some other legal monstrosity.

The Code of Laws of the United States is a massive compilation of statutes that is, practically speaking, unknowable in its entirety by an individual and, in a sense, is therefore not "in them." We can add attorneys and judges, etc., until the cows come home and, still, the code is not entirely represented in any individual nor the collection of individuals taken together. We could bring the combined legal giants of America together for a weekend and still they would never be able to reproduce the totality of the code; there would be many gaps and holes in the construction. On top of the code's existing totality is the fact that it evolves and changes over time. In a way, then, it is entirely correct to say that the code is not in the individual or individuals (it is possessed by neither any subject nor even at the level of the intersubjective web) and, really, *as a totality* it is in no one per se. The code is real and has an autonomous existence apart from the individuals and groups who make it their business to know and work with it. We reside in the house of law but we do not possess it.[168] I have

---

167 Each person "contains only a spark" (S: 316) of collective consciousness and, even if we 'add up' all the individuals in a group, the totality will still have gaps and lacunae.

168 "If we presuppose [for example] that Newton's discovery was only preserved in a book which no one knew, it would still be part of the objectified mind and a potential possession of society, but no longer a cultural value. Since this extreme case can occur on countless levels, it follows that in society at large only a certain proportion of objective cultural values become subjective values. If one looks at society as a whole, that is if one arranges the objectified intellectuality in a temporal-objective complex, then the whole cultural development, assuming it has a uniform representative, is richer in content than each of its elements. For the achievement of each element is incorporated in the total heritage, but this heritage does not permeate each element" (Simmel [1907] 1990: 453).

internalized some laws but there is no Law within me. I am possessed by Law but I do not possess Law. "You might as well seek to sum up the successive tongues of flame in your fireplace as to find the sum of the ever-moving, up-springing, and dying contents of restless human conscious life" (Royce 1969: 251). A language like English is an even more radical example.

Nobody can inhabit (live in) or be possessed (lived by) the totality of a language (Fink 1997: 87). Wielding a vocabulary of only 30,000 words constitutes a kind of linguistic virtuosity for the individual. Counting the current words, obsolescences, and derivatives, the Oxford English Dictionary contains roughly 230,000 entries, spread out over its 20 volumes. Of course, this does not include an ocean of vernacular jargon and gibberish produced daily by interlocutors.[169] Even our physically externalized compendium of the English language is lacking and will never catch all the words or their meanings. But then, on top of the lexiconical finite structure of language as it exists at any given moment we have metaphor with its ability to "stretch out over an infinite set of circumstances, even ... creating new circumstances" (Jaynes 1990: 52).[170] Collective representations are of this nature: as totalities they are not in me and, moreover, they are not in anyone taken singly or even collectively. As a whole, any social fact is excessive – it exceeds me, you, and practically (as well as literally) everyone. This is why both subjectivism and intersubjectivist perspectives are important but nonetheless inadequate to the task of theorizing society. Even though the person is fashioned in the image of society (S: 212) and represents an individuation of general causes (S: 151) the individual is not actually an adequate microcosmic reflection of the social macrocosm in the sense that society reproduces itself in each person. In totemism the part may be as good as the whole,[171] as Durkheim says, but in capitalism the hundredaire is not as good as the millionaire. In this sense, it is *not* true that each person is really a "spark of the divine" in the conventional sense because the "spark" of the divine and the totality of that divine substance would be qualitatively identical in all respects, varying only in magnitude. This is why, when Durkheim says of the single person they are "*only* a spark" of the totality (S: 316, emphasis added) he means that they are lacking both qualitatively and quantitatively in comparison to the absolute. The individual, compared to the totality of society, is

169   The online 'Urban Dictionary' contains more than 1.6 million entries.
170   As soon as we move beyond the object in hand, metaphor begins to govern the mind (Alain [1934] 1974: 116).
171   "Mythically, the name is never taken as a merely conventional *sign* for a thing, but as a real *part* of it – and a part that, according to the mythical-magical principle of 'pars pro toto' ... not only represents the whole but actually 'is' the whole" (Cassirer 2013: 22).

rather threadbare and impoverished, "almost a nothing" as Hegel says, both quantitatively and qualitatively.[172] We should not waste our time investigating individual consciousness (S: 149) because the individual can never tell us what we want to know. Now, collective *action* is different – this is where individuals actually represent society incarnate, society individualized (S: 212).

A good context in which to see the difference between personal and collective consciousness in bold contrast to one another is the political rally.

> There was a rhythm to these references, and, in the course of the forty-odd-minute speech, they served a purpose. Most of the time, Trump ranted about Clinton or Obama, and the crowd responded in set ways. They booed any reference to Obamacare; the e-mail scandal prompted chants of "Lock her up! Lock her up!" People seemed to enjoy venting, but these targets were distant and somewhat abstract, and I sensed that the routine would have become boring without the more immediate presence of the media. We were available at a lower level of abstraction: all of us were right there, with faces and expressions clearly visible, but, once the rally began, the barrier meant that we weren't quite close enough to touch or talk to. And Trump worked the rhythm brilliantly: he made a media reference every few minutes, pausing to give the crowd time to react. Eventually, people started leaning over the barrier to shout, "Crooked press! Crooked press!," and at one point a man on crutches became so frenzied that he tried to squeeze through a gap. He banged his crutches against the metal, shouting angrily; finally, a policeman escorted him away. After the rally was finished, a nice-looking blond woman made her way down the fence, shouting, "Journalism is dead! Journalism is dead!" But, when I stepped forward and asked her to explain what she meant, she immediately calmed down, and we had a pleasant conversation.

> This reminded me somewhat of public events in Egypt during the difficult years after the revolution began on Tahrir Square, in 2011. At Islamist

---

172 Empirical sociology, in the way it is ordinarily practiced, is an absurdity because it literally attempts to generate enlightenment (or, more likely dollars) by asking individuals to reveal the things that they don't know and that they don't know that they don't know. Consult Marx (CPE: 205 ff.) for more on the methods appropriate for the critical sciences as well as Durkheim's assessment of empiricism as irrationalism (EFRL: 13). How can one make contact with society through the doorway of the individual? "Human deliberations ... so far as reflective consciousness affects them are often only purely formal, with no object but confirmation of a resolve previously formed for reasons unknown to consciousness" (S: 297). Necessity or facticity is observable in action and conduct of groups not in the things *individuals* think or merely say.

> rallies, I had seen effective speakers who shifted between targets that
> were distant and targets that were nearby, working the audience into a
> frenzy. And I had always been struck by how, even in the most tense situ-
> ations, with the most violent rhetoric floating around, it was still surpris-
> ingly easy to talk to people on a personal level. It took no time at all for
> most individuals to snap out of the trance. I had seen young men scream
> anti-American slogans with a look of absolute fury on their faces, and
> then it was as if somebody threw a switch: they showed no negative re-
> action to my identification card, which listed my nationality, and they
> politely answered my questions.
>
> HESSLER 2016

Durkheim makes a similar observation with regard to mourning rituals where
the most violent self-mutilations of the group members easily alternated with
personal indifference and calm interpersonal interactions (EFRL: 400–12). Participants can instantaneously and effortlessly snap back and forth between
collective obligations and private and dyadic concerns. The dramatic example
of the mob or the crowd might lead us to conclude that the difference between
individual and collective consciousness is a binary one where people switch
between the two modalities or different systems as if they were not intimately connected. However, the line of demarcation (RSM: 145) between the two
systems is a theoretical artificiality. Obeyesekere (1990: 85) says that collective
consciousness emerges when we interact with others, and this is true, however, even in our private moments we usually continue to mentally interact
with others. This consciousness, as an emergent fact, is something that rises
up, comes forth out of obscurity and submersion, and becomes a thing observable. Every moment of emergence is one where being is spurred along into
becoming.

Collective consciousness is different than personal consciousness, a different way of thinking with its own logic and materials but the two systems
are mutually dependent upon one another; individuality and personality
depend upon social consciousness. The person is society individuated, at its
"molecular" level and if each person were not unique in his or her personal
ways of acting, thinking, and feeling, they would fail to create a society; their
association would amount to little more than a herd gathering for the benefit
of "bovine warmth" (Mann 1948: 67).

Hegel holds the same basic assumptions as Durkheim on collective consciousness. With regards to deities (collective representations in contrast to
the representations peculiar to a given individual) he says:

I may have ideas of objects which are wholly fictitious and fanciful; what constitutes the idea here is in such a case my own, but only my own; it exists merely as an idea; I am at the same time aware that the content here has no existence. In dreams, too, I exist as consciousness, I have objects in my mind, but they have no existence. But we so conceive of the consciousness of God that the content is our idea, and at the same time exists; that is, the content is not merely mine, is not merely in the subject, in myself, in my idea and knowledge, but has an absolute existence of its own, exists in and for itself. This is essentially involved in the content itself in this case. God is this Universality which has an absolute [i.e., moral or social] existence of its own, and does not exist merely for me; it is outside of me, independent of me. There are thus two points bound up together here. This content is at once independent and at the same time inseparable from me; that is, it is mine, and yet it is just as much not mine.[173]

[1840] 1974: 116

Another dimension that separates individual and collective representations, a point that will taken up more completely later, is that of obligation and force.

If I walk to my kitchen and observe a *red* apple I am in no way compelled to eat the apple or treat it with respect. The redness tells me nothing about the edibility, taste, or condition of the apple. Red does not mean good apple or bad apple and it does not demand to be eaten nor does it prohibit me from consuming it. This red is a "profane" red – it is the red of individual and common understanding. However, if while driving my automobile, I observe an identical hue of *red* on a sign of a certain shape (even without the word "STOP" on it) I will feel compelled to bring my vehicle to a stop. I probably ought to stop. Even if the sign were to take an unfamiliar form, say in the shape of an apple, so long as it is red and located at an intersection I will probably stop my car – even though the situation is ambiguous I think I *should* do something. This red sign has an authority that the red of the apple in my kitchen lacks even though the physical colors may correspond exactly. One red is a mirror whereas the other is a reflection; one red is a thought while the other thinks. My kitchen is ordinarily a place of everyday, prosaic activities but out in public crisscrossed with intersecting webs of laws and regulations, I am operating in a public space. Individual representations and categories of the understanding

---

173   The basic social theory of religion is essentially identical in the writings of both Hegel and Durkheim (Westphal 1990: 196–201). A god is but the personification of the moral energy (Whitehead 1978: 343) of a community.

lack the degree of authority or prestige that collective representations enjoy (EFRL: 214; Gilbert 1989: 249).[174] If I were to describe my everyday kitchen life as one that includes a "whirlwind of organic and psychological phenomena" (DOL: 53) as well as a fount of moral energies and amelior?tory sacrifices we would be forced to conclude that my kitchen is remarkably different than normal kitchens. Moral energies, however, come in various flavors.

We express dismay when people vote against their own personal and material interests as if everyone were utilitarians or rational actors calculating costs and benefits at all times. Yes, to put it bluntly, millions of Americans screw themselves time and time again at the ballot box in ways that are mind-boggling to observing reason. This problem of self-defeat runs in many directions, and we will follow several lines of inquiry in the next volume dealing with suicide, but the bulk of the problem lies in obedience to external power. When we witness a frenzied mob of apparently drooling morons screaming "More taxes! Less bread!" it is easy to dismiss them as authoritarian imbeciles, and perhaps many of them are just that, but the sociology of such circumstances points to the dynamics of mental pressures, the contagious nature of moral power, and the respect people have for representations of some current or crystallization (positive, pure, holy) or immoral (negative, impure, demonic).[175] "We are then moved not by the advantages or disadvantages of the conduct that is recommended to us or demanded of us but by the way we conceive of the one who recommends or demands that conduct" (EFRL: 209). In other words we are not witnessing the work of authority but alienation. Take, for example, the slogan "Make America Great Again." The term "Great" is not a concept

---

174   Of course, since the apple in my kitchen is part of not only my reality but a larger or shared reality the categories, classifications, and words I use are to some extent obligatory or, at least, are accompanied by a sense that I 'should' think and speak in certain ways. The optional is a road that leads in two directions: on the one hand, down and out, away from society and, on the other, to greater heights of prestige or, at least, the restoration of one's standing in the eyes of others.

175   The idea of the *respect* we hold for something is not settled in advance. We respect legitimate authority but we also respect something that has no authoritative hold over us. Respect comes from the Latin *respectus* which simply means to look back – we usually connect the idea of *admiration* to this looking but people can admire the legitimate as well as the illegitimate. To admire something is not identical with a recognition of its claims as authoritative. To admire something is merely to wonder at it (from the Latin *admirari*, from *ad-* 'at' + *mirari* 'wonder'). The authoritarian demagogue plays the part of being a marvel. Admiration and the marvelous share the same house. 'Marvel' comes from the Old French *merveille*, from late Latin *mirabilia*, neuter plural of Latin *mirabilis* which means 'wonderful,' derived from *mirari* 'wonder at.' We often obey things where authority is lacking, where the truth is on hiatus, and logical plausibility is held together with absurd rationalizations.

of pure understanding, it is not a sense intuition, and "just as little is [it] a concept of reason, because it brings with it no principle of cognition" (Kant 1951: 86). The notion of making anything Great again moves in the domain of the sublime and submission to the simultaneously attractive and repulsive representation. When Americans witnessed the first televised debate between Clinton and Trump they received a crash course in what Durkheim calls "moral influence" (EFRL: 209). Clinton opened by blabbering on the way establishment politicians do while Trump responded with one word: "Wrong!" For millions of Americans raised in authoritarian households by domineering fathers, this was the image of strong leadership: rigid, binary, simple, punitive, and outraged. The Trump campaign team took a page from the authoritarian playbook: signify succinctly. "This is why a command [Wrong! Make It Great! Lock Her Up!] generally takes on short, sharp forms of address that leave no room for hesitation" (EFRL: 209). Just do it. Whatever Trump is, the whole platform was based on creating the image of a powerful leader who would deliver punishment to those who *deserve* to be in the grip of pain and suffering. When folks got behind Trump it was not their individual, calculating egos that were acting but mob consciousness that obeyed the call issued by an energized image. The price may be high but he might "Lock her up!" and, really, that would be priceless for the Trumpsters. There is no price too high for sweet revenge. "To the last, I grapple with thee; From Hell's heart, I stab at thee; For hate's sake, I spit my last breath at thee" (Melville 1892: 532). Whether we are interested in demagogues or stop signs they both point to the "externality" of a social fact qua representation.

The standard and erroneous criticism against the concept of externality revolves around the notion that a thing cannot be known while simultaneously being outside of the mind. We know nothing if we lack an experience of it (PS: 487). True, but again, being outside "individual consciousness" is not identical with being outside consciousness.[176] Collective consciousness "is something totally different from the consciousness of the individuals, although it is only realised in individuals" (DOL: 39; EFRL: 435). "The whole social world seems populated with forces that in reality exist only in our minds" (EFRL: 228). As Bosanquet says, the coordinates of the external are not contrary to the internal (1912: 75). The internal and the external are "entwined" (Durkheim 1961: 216). Some representation being "external" to the mind of the individual has to be grasped with the etymology of the term.

---

176 Peter Berger gives us this classic pratfall: "The concept of dialectics, in Hegel as elsewhere, refers to a reciprocal relation between a subject and its object, a 'conversation' between consciousness and whatever is outside consciousness" (1969: 51).

"External" comes from the Latin *exterus* which means that a thing is *foreign*. This bears upon Marx's theory of estrangement (alienation). The cooperation of individuals within the division of labor yields products and results that appear to the mind of individual as a constellation of alien forces "existing outside them, of the origin and goal of which they are ignorant, which they thus are no longer able to control" (MECW, 5: 48). We see in Freud's essay on negation the distinction between the internal and the external in regards to *pleasure* is that between a representation (*Vorstellung*) which is embraced by or taken into the ego ("inside me") and one that is rejected by the ego and held at bay ("outside me"). In terms of reality the issue comes down to the rediscovery of a representation that is subjective and internal in the perception of the external world ([1925] 1959: 183). It is a mistake to think of things as being merely external in the sense of being disconnected from the mind when, in fact, what people do is externalize thoughts and representations, that is, experience their own thoughts as alien commands and powers.

> We are contingent beings and, according to Cartesianism, finite beings. As limited beings, we are subject to foreign influences; our thought is not pure and master of itself, it is dominated occasionally by exterior circumstances which dictate our judgments, to which, from that time onwards, it remains only an appearance of rationality and therefore they can be fundamentally irrational. The [Cartesian] evil spirit is nothing other than a personification of the violence to which the possibly irrational nature of the universe perhaps subjects the mind.
>
> HAMELIN, in RAMP 2012: 120

The vulgar materialist view is responsible for mistaking objective and external for matter over and against a passive receptor of sensations (S: 313, 315).[177] "Viewed from the outside, that which in reflecting upon the mind appears specifically as not mental, as an object, is material" (Adorno 1973: 193). This is the same delusion that "speculative realism" falls into: trying to think away the mind leaving behind the material residue all the while doing so from *within* the mind.[178] But unlike philosophical realists, ordinary consciousness

---

177 Externality is better thought of as "consecrated" (S: 314) and, as such, a force that is difficult to evade, though, some do in fact evade it as non-binding (S: 316–17). As it turns out no social fact can impinge upon the life of every single person in a given society.

178 A transcendental materialism of this kind would have to presuppose an empirical idealism, which simply means, that this kind of materialism is by and for egoists attempting in vain, to locate the origins of their free-floating egos, and attempting to construct a

confuses moral facts in the mind (specifically in collective consciousness) as being somehow outside of the mind and physically real even though the inverse is true. For sure, consciousness, both personal and collective, may be mounted on or "attached to" (EFRL: 202)[179] material props, fashioned through artifice but, as Hegel knew, externality as it pertains to collective consciousness, is *immaterial* (SL: 759; cf. EFRL: 351).[180] My *family*, for example, is not reducible to materiality in any way yet our house is *included* (cf. S: 313) in our conception of the family. "Hegel never denies that there is an external material world, nor that there are fundamental ways in which this world is independent of our cognitive and linguistic activities.... While ... [objects] ... must be conceptualized, and in this sense be 'constituted' by consciousness, in order for it to have significance, it is not created *ex nihilo* by the mind" (Berthold-Bond 1995: 65).

The ordinary or mundane conception of externality is that of material stuff "out there" independent of thought, however, social externality, the externality of social facts, are "given an external existence" and anything "out there" in the mundane, material sense is only known through our representations of them in the dimension of the ideal – what we experience and know as reality is not merely dumb matter as it is passively perceived and neither is it a mere subjective construct or a simple projection actively built up by the isolated psyche (and it is certainly more than a web of intersubjective agreements and practical definitions) but nonetheless, the externality of social facts resides in the dimension of collective and *sui generis* ideality (Hegel 1975a: 247–48).

No doubt, the mind organizes matter (Lichtheim 1967: 13) but it would only be *metaphorically* true to conceive of the products of human labor *as*

---

ground for egoistic survival in an imagined world populated mainly by academic egoists – remember that all these discourses are developed *almost* exclusively by and for over-educated, Anglo, white males). Note well: transcendental materialism is anathema to reason (Fichte 1847: 19).

179 Ritual "energy alone is the real object of the cult" (EFRL: 191) not the contingent and accidental material shapes it assumes for individual perception. The material realm, e.g., animals in the totemic system, "receive only a reflection" of the mana ascribed to the totemic emblems (EFRL: 208).

180 'Society" includes the physical environment and profane satisfactions but in Durkheim's sociology the essence of the "*milieu social*" and the *sui generis* reality of society is "distinguished from the predominantly physical environment which was the focus of the Cartesian tradition" (Parsons 1978: 219). The idea that a social fact is a "material fact" is a common mistake we find nearly everywhere in the education of sociologists. The usual blunder is to confuse the notion of "materialization" (the mounting of moral subject-substance to the infraliminal prop) with something like moral matter (e.g., Ritzer and Stepnisky 2018: 82). Remember, mana in its organized form is the essence of society (e.g., Kracht 2015: 50).

crystallized mind (to take it literally true would be to slide into the errors of naive realism where the moral and the material are identical or confused). The Hegelian-Marxist and Durkheimian conception of the externality of social facts that I am advancing here is difficult to keep consistently centered for those burdened with ordinary realist presuppositions (e.g., common sense, mindless empiricism, etc.). Jones indicates that, for Durkheim, externality refers to a "logical point, and does not mean" that a fact is "literally outside of as external in the sense of the material world" though it does not exclude external materialization (Jones 2001: 138; S: 314–15; see also Boutroux 1914: 198 ff.). *Externalization* encompasses the ideal and the material. "For example, a primitive tribe externalizes its collective attitudes by certain behavior, certain gestures, certain patterns, signs and symbols, weapons, ornaments, clothes, emblems, masks, cries, songs, dances, [and so on]" (Gurvitch 1964: 3–4). Both "dialectical materialism" and Durkheim's "qualified idealism" (EFRL: 229) sublate the old dualisms of matter and the immaterial with the focus shifted to collective ritual practices, collective representations, and relations of material production and ideologies. In other words, social relations and stereotyped collective conduct structure the minds of individuals and, in so doing, carve out a dimension of externality. "Externality" has less to do, I think, with a "logical" point *per se*, (Jones) and more to do with psyche[181] and morality (RSM: 41; Weber 1949: 96).[182] Though Durkheim was rightfully critical of transcendental idealism, Kant's excursus on rational psychology and the pitfalls of materialism do intersect with Durkheim's thesis:

> There may well be something outside us to which this appearance, which we call matter, corresponds; in its character of appearance it is not, however, outside us, but is only a thought in us, although this thought, through the above-mentioned outer sense, represents it as existing outside us.... They have, indeed, this deceptive property that, representing objects in space, they detach themselves as it were from the soul and appear to hover outside of it.... As long as we take inner and outer appearances together as mere representations in experience, we find nothing absurd and strange in the association of the two kinds of senses. But as soon as

---

181   Durkheim says of collective consciousness that it is "the psychological type of society" that possesses its own qualities distinct from individuals (DOL: 39). Bouglé amplifies this point when he says that "the true reality of societies is psychical" ([1926] 1970: 74).

182   Social categories "do not present themselves to the individual consciousness so much as logical necessities but as moral necessities" (Degré 1985: 88). For Weber, "empirical historical events occurring in men's minds must be understood as primarily *psychologically* and not logically conditioned" (1949: 96).

we hypostatise outer appearances and come to regard them not as representations but as things existing by themselves outside us, with the same quality as that with which they exist in us, and as bringing to bear on our thinking subject they activities which they exhibit as appearances in relation to each other, then the efficient causes outside us assume a character which is irreconcilable with their effects in us.

KANT 1929: 355–56

Freud is often in glaring contradiction with the basics of sociology, yet, with regard to objective subjectivity or the externality of the subjective, Freud has something to offer.[183]

Freud argues that, "originally the ego includes everything, later it separates off an external world from itself" ([1930] 1961: 15).[184] Ego separation or "disengagement" and the formation of the "objective" world within the ego "is provided by the frequent, manifold and unavoidable sensations of pain and unpleasure the removal and avoidance of which is enjoined by the pleasure principle, in the exercise of its unrestricted domination. A tendency arises to separate from the ego everything that can become a source of such unpleasure, to throw it outside and to create a pure pleasure-ego which is confronted by a strange and threatening outside" ([1930] 1961: 14). What we have, then, is the situation where "perceptions, thoughts and feelings ... appear alien" to the individual "and as not belonging to his ego; there are other cases in which he ascribes to the external world things that clearly originate in his own ego and that ought to be acknowledged by it" ([1930] 1961: 13; also Freud [1923] 1960: 13; [1926] 1959: 18). In simple terms we have conflicts between id wishes and superego injunctions (subjugated to the id) and the reality principle and we are disturbed by the experience of some other bearing down on us "as if" it were an autonomous reality existing somewhere outside of our minds. The upside to this rudimentary alienation is that, at least, this externalization constitutes a relation between the internal and the external (Buber 1965: 63) that can be surmounted and spiritualized.

---

183   I find value in Freud's work and cite him frequently but I disagree vehemently with Kushner that "Sociology without psychology, Durkheim without Freud, seems unable to uncover a satisfactory answer to the question that sociology was founded to answer" (1989: 149). What Kushner fails to realize is that Durkheimian sociology is actually an absolute psychology, the psychology not of the mind *per se* or individual minds but group processes.

184   The ego or self is "an external view or image of the subject which is internalized or interjected. The ego is thus an object, and consciousness may adopt it as an object to be observed like any other object" (Fink 1997: 86).

"We say for instance that 'the group says,' the group feels,' 'the group thinks.' But these are all psychological activities that actually pertain only to individual human beings.... [T]he group has no brain" (Harding 1947: 47–8). No doubt, there is no such thing as a group brain, however, for a thing to be in *consciousness* is less a personal experience and more collective:

> My idea is ... that consciousness does not really belong to man's indi-
> vidual existence but rather to his social or herd nature.... Our thoughts
> themselves are continually governed by the character of consciousness –
> by the "genius of the species" that commands it – and translated back
> into the perspective of the herd. Fundamentally, all our actions are al-
> together incomparably personal, unique, and infinitely individual; there
> is no doubt of that. But as soon as we translate them into consciousness
> *they no longer seem to be.*
>
> NIETZSCHE [1887] 1974: 299

Of course, as Kant suspected, there is a real out there, over and against us, but we do not have access to something as an experience outside of thought and signs. To repeat, "nothing is *known* that is not in *experience*" (Hegel [1807] 2008: 727; PS: 487) and nothing is experienced that has failed to take up residence as a representation in the mind.[185] The words on a page or the colors of vegetation appear to be physical marks and qualities existing in front of the reader holding onto the book or gazing out the window but the experience is based on a constructed or synthesized image in the mind. The standard model of visible light that ruled until recently states that "the brain works up the light waves into an image, identifies it as Sally, and puts that up on the stage or film screen of consciousness" (Baumeister 2010: 33).[186] Colors in this model are imagined as being in light itself and that, e.g., green was the result of a filtering in the

---

185   "For experience consists in precisely this, namely, that the content – and the content is
      spirit – exists *in itself*, is substance and therefore the *object* of *consciousness*. However, this
      substance, which is spirit, is its *coming-to-be* what it, the substance, is *in itself*; and it is as
      this coming-to-be which is taking a reflective turn into itself that spirit is truly in itself
      spirit. Spirit is in itself the movement which is cognition – the transformation of that
      former *in-itself* into *for-itself*, of *substance* into *subject*, of the object of *consciousness*, i.e.,
      into an object that is just as much sublated, that is, into the *concept*. This transformation
      is the circle returning back into itself, which presupposes its beginning and reaches its
      beginning only at the end" (Hegel [1807] 2008: 728).
186   "We say of course that music 'addresses itself to the ear'; but it does so only in a qualified
      way, only in so far, namely, as the hearing, like the other senses, is the deputy, the instru-
      ment, and the receiver of the mind" (Mann 1948: 61).

visual apparatus and operations in the brain.[187] But the leading edge of theories of consciousness and perception, returning to Galileo, are telling us that there is no color "out there" at all – not in the material things and not in light. Nor is color in the brain: "when scientists look inside the brain to see what's going on, they find only billions of neurons exchanging electrical impulses and releasing chemical substances. They find what they call correlates of consciousness, not consciousness itself; or in this case, they find correlates of color, but not color itself. There is no yellow banana in the head, just the grey stuff" (Manzotti and Parks 2016). "We don't *see* anything directly" (Ornstein 2003: 71).[188] As Hegel insists, perception is always thinking and our thoughts are the product of society.[189] This insight does not lead to the aporias of idealism nor to the reductions of psychology but to the weirder domain of socialization and collective life where matter appears to be intertwined with spirit or collective consciousness[190] and where minds are multiple. "There is a sense of course, in which our representation of the external world is itself nothing but a fabric of hallucinations. The odors, tastes, and colors that we palace in bodies are not there, or at least are not there in the way we perceive them" (EFRL: 229).[191] If color is not

---

187 "That is the other traditional claim, still widely taught in school, that colors exist *in light*, or that different colors are different *wavelengths of light*. And of course the colors of the rainbow immediately come to mind. But that explanation doesn't work 100 percent.... The same wavelength, for example, will give rise to different colors if the surrounding environment is different. To his credit, Newton himself, who actually introduced the word 'spectrum' into the English language to refer to the range of possible colors, eventually dismissed the idea that colors are literally contained in the light. 'For the Rays, to speak properly, are not coloured. In them there is nothing else than a certain Power and Disposition to stir up a Sensation of this or that Colour.' Three hundred years on, what and where colors actually *are* remains a mystery" (Manzotti and Parks 2016).

188 Ornstein proceeds to blow it: "In these [data-processing] modules [of the brain], extraction of meaning from converted sounds takes place..." (2003: 72). Extracting meaning from sound! It is *in* the sound itself; meaningful matter. Data-processing (sic) is like sucking value from the earth. "I turn my head; new colors come into sight, even the whole of the sky, with no difficulty; but we also know very well that vision alone gives us no knowledge of anything" (Alain [1934] 1974: 41).

189 "Even the objects of the simplest 'sensory certainty' are only given [to the person] through social development ..." (MECW, 5: 39).

190 André Lalande "who was Durkheim's colleague in the French Philosophical Society, claims that Durkheim used the term *conscience collective* more as 'soul' (*âme*) or 'spirit' (*esprit*) than as the Anglo Saxon 'consciousness" (Verheggen 1996: 205; Meštrović 1985).

191 In the section on commodity fetishism in volume one of *Capital*, Marx says "Through ... substitution, the products of labour become commodities, sensuous things which are at the same time supra-sensible or social. In the same way, the impression made by a thing on the optic nerve is perceived not as a subjective excitation of that nerve but as the objective form of a thing outside the eye" (C: 165).

"out there" and not in the physical brain and not reducible to *subjective* or in-dividual consciousness that leaves only signification and socialization. Indeed, people only 'see' colors that they have names for. The word "blue" is, without exception, the last color category to emerge in world languages and does not pop up until the Egyptians learned how to produce blue dye and paint ("blue" does not appear in ancient Greek texts nor in the Hebrew bible, for example). We need the word, the label, the category in order to perceive what is right in front of us (Deutscher 2010). If we could return to the antiquities with our modern minds *we* would see the blue sky but the locals would have no idea what we were talking about, not because they would lack the *physical* ability to perceive just as we do, but because of a lack in their language and the social setup.

In terms of basic psychology, the formulations by Kant and Freud sharpen our understanding of how something that is constructed in the mind can *appear* to be going on *outside* of the mind (EFRL: 369), hovering over us, to use Kant's imagery. Two aspects should to be delineated here: one, love is the condition whereby the ego blends with the external world; the biophilic character (Fromm 1973) or Sartre's "starfish world" (1948: 56) is one of omnierotic, Whitmanesque love for the totality of existence; a non-diseased society populated by well-adjusted individuals would not be experienced as a system of alien and dominating entities on the part of its members. Secondly, we need to avoid the notion of some transcendental ego or coagulated group mind,[192] which is made all the more difficult when Durkheim says, following Post, that "'it is not we who think, but the world which thinks in us'" (RSM: 201).[193] This is

---

192   We need to remain wary when we read: "The individuals are the brain cells of the collective mind, as it were. Again, the collective thoughts, ideas, images and so forth are partially independent of their substratum. They exist in a totally unique domain" (Verheggen 1996: 197; cf. Harding 1947: 47–8). This is untroubling as a metaphor so long as stress is placed on the "as it were." Also, note that the independence is partial and not total and the "domain" of the collective is "unique" and not separate. Verheggen walks a fine line but does not fall into error.

193   "It was not *he* who was thinking of the insurrection, it was the insurrection, living in so many brains like sleep in so many others, which weighed upon him to such a point that there was nothing left in him but anxiety and expectation" (Malraux 1961: 41). "[T]he performers not so much played the little phrase as executed the rites necessary for it to appear'" (Proust, in Žižek 2012: 213). "It is not I who think, ... it is my ideas that think for me'" (Lamartine, in Jaynes 1990: 376). "Bastian had in 1868 stated, 'we do not think, but it thinks in us' referring to the autonomy of the psychic processes or of idea system ...'" (Koepping 1983: 148). "She had half an idea, she had a seed of a plan, though perhaps it was untrue to say that she had it, for she felt rather as if it had her" (Hardinge 2012: 26). Being a person is complicated. We have the world thinking through us (the Big Thing) as well as our personal "It" that rages against the ego. Groddeck says: "I hold the view that man is animated by the Unknown, that there is within him an "Es," an "It," some wondrous

simply a way of presenting the idea that the self is, in addition to a "me" also a
"we" (Durkheim 1973: 13) submerged in the "organic" totality of life. Universal,
general, or absolute concepts exist only in the minds of socialized individuals
(EFRL: 434). Kant's idealist representationalism is, by comparison, more or less
autistic in its isolationism (see RSM: 40–41). We need to know how people get
back simultaneously more than and less than they put into the world (e.g.,
EFRL: 345) but from Kant's perspective we can only get back out of the world
what we put into it (Holzner 1968).

The mind is almost completely detached and estranged from society in Kantian philosophy: "thought has through its reasoning got so far as to grasp itself
not as contingent but rather as in itself the absolute ultimate" (LHP, 3: 424).
With Hegel, then, Durkheim rejects the Kantian supposition that the framework of reason is innately part of the physical makeup: "We have no justification for supposing that our mind bears within it at birth, completely formed,
the prototype of this elementary framework of all classification" (Durkheim
and Mauss [1903] 1963: 8). We are surely "with" Kant (against Hume) in the
belief that synthetic propositions and judgments are not meaningless (Körner
1955: 17–18) but we have to go further, with Durkheim, beyond the "Protestant"
and egoistic line of thinking whereby "the *a priori*, the distinguishing characteristics of which are universality and necessity, is not given in sense but is
imposed by the mind" (Smith 1992: xxxiii). The status of the synthetic a priori
in sociology is unique.

In his *Philosophy Lectures* of 1883/1884 Durkheim unequivocally embraces
the synthetic a priori: "'Are there synthetic, a priori judgments, and, if so, how
is this possible?' But this is a question we already answered by showing that the
mind – by its very nature – requires such judgments. In reasoning, the mind
brings together two previous judgments to form a new one" (DPL: 137). The key,
here, is the difference in logical propositions and judgments: "Kant's [system
of] classification is, first of all, not of propositions, but of judgments, i.e. of
propositions asserted by somebody. He is concerned not with the proposition
that the cat is on the mat but with the judgment by some person to that effect. This is in many ways an advantage, since judgments are personal events,
and the manner in which they exist is less problematic than the manner of
existence of propositions" (Körner 1955: 18). But judgments are not merely
"personal events" but, rather, social and herein lies the basis for Durkheim's
reformulation of the synthetic a priori.

force which directs both what he himself does, and what happens to him. The affirmation
"I live" is only conditionally correct, it expresses only a small and superficial part of the
fundamental principle, 'Man is lived by the It'" ([1949] 1961: 11).

Judgments can be classified in various ways. It's common to distinguish
between particular and universal judgments – the latter affirm that the
attribute pertains to the entire subject while the former affirm that
the attribute pertains to only one part of it. Another distinction is sometimes made between positive and negative judgments. But the most important is Kant's distinction between analytic and synthetic judgments.
The former are those in which the attribute is included in the subject, so
that when we think of the subject, we immediately think of the attribute.
In analytic judgments, therefore, the attribute can be deduced from the
subject (for example, 2 + 2 = 4). In synthetic judgments, by contrast, the
attribute is added to the subject (for example, all bodies fall vertically).
Here the property of falling vertically goes beyond what's included in the
subject.

        DURKHEIM 2004: 136

Durkheim's example of an analytic judgment is incorrect from Kant's perspective.[194] The synthetic a priori is a dead end from the standpoint of logic and
psychology (EFRL: 12) but in sociological terms the idea makes sense, the same
way the concept of "vitality" does (RSM: 136) if, that is, we view it as a *social* a
priori that points back to the "externality" of representations (the mysterious
nature of our conscious representations sunk in the operational ground of the
unconsciousness) as an independent "organic" system or "skeleton of thought"
(EFRL: 9).[195]

    Durkheim was an "organicist" but it was not the organicism of Rousseau or
Spencer (cf. Lasch 1977: 24; C: 93). The notion of an organicism of forces and
representations, according to Durkheim, came from Espinas. "If societies are
organisms, they are distinguished from purely physical organisms in that they
are essentially consciousnesses (*consciences*). They are nothing if not systems
of representations. One has not, therefore, sufficiently characterized them

---

194   Durkheim's "2 + 2 = 4" example is not, from Kant's point of view, analytic at all but is an
       a priori judgment: "if a judgment is to be a priori it must be logically independent of all
       judgments which describe experiences or even impressions of senses. Examples are the
       judgment that 2 + 2 = 4.... Kant holds that there are [synthetic a priori judgments and]
       that almost the whole of mathematics consists of them and that they constitute the fun-
       damental presuppositions of the natural sciences and of moral thought.... Consider ... the
       arithmetical judgment that the addition of 5 to 7 yields 12. That this proposition is *a priori*
       would be readily agreed. Kant, however, regards it as at the same time *synthetic* [emphasis
       added] since 'the concept of a sum of 7 and 5 contains nothing over and above the uniting
       of both these numbers into a single one'" (Körner 1955: 20–21).
195   The transcendental deduction, the condition necessary for thinking in terms of a priori
       categories, is grounded in society and socialization.

when one has said that they are living beings; one must add that 'they are living consciousnesses, organisms of ideas'" (1973: 13). As Durkheim says, these
representations as organic systems are "real, living, active forces" (S: 39).[196]
Collective consciousness and our system of representations have lives of their
own in the same way that, in Marx's terms, value is a self-moving substance-
subject (C: 256).[197] Kantian representations, then, were not identical with
Durkheimian (nor Marxist) representations and cannot be reduced to psychological dynamics. But the connection to "rationalism" was, if not a curtsy
to Kantianism, the same cannot be said about neo-Kantianism. Some have
claimed that, basically, Durkheim was a neo-Kantian (e.g., Gillian Rose 2009);
I do not believe this to be the case but that also does not mean that Durkheim
was not influenced by the neo-Kantian program to a certain extent (see Jones
[2000] 2006).

Far from portraying institutions as a set of organs functioning for a common
goal free of conflict, Durkheim's organicism represented a sublation of materialism and idealism where socially generated systems of countervailing and
contradictory forces (DOL: 5) and representations appear to "consume" the
material substratum of life in their interactions, reminiscent of the imagery
Hegel deployed in his lectures on religion ([1840] 1974: 109–10) where nature is
sacrificed as the burnt offering to Psyche,[198] and tended toward what Bouglé
referred to as a "spiritualism" (in SP: xl–xli). Durkheim also compared his anti-
materialism to "spiritualism" but, ultimately, noted that "neither designation"
(that between materialism and spiritualism) "fits us precisely; the only one we
accept is that of *rationalist*.... What has been termed our positivism is merely
a consequence of this rationalism" (RSM: 33).[199] In other words, Durkheim's
rationalism was non-sectarian (see Brinton 1963: 84). The label "rationalist"
was chosen to not only connect sociology to the enduring prestige of the Cartesian heritage (Durkheim 1977: 278) but, also, to set sociology off from, and in

---

196   Durkheim's universal organicism bears a family resemblance to the neo-Hegelianism of
       John Caird (1880).
197   Importantly, Marx likens the substance-subject of value to the powers of a god that "dif-
       ferentiates himself from himself as God the Son, although both are of the same age and
       form..." (C: 256).
198   "She was not there now, and 'the embroidery of the imagination upon the stuff of nature'
       so depicted her past presence that a void was in his heart which nothing could fill" (Hardy
       [1894–95] 2006: 33).
199   Both Marx and Durkheim thought of their projects as falling within the tradition of "posi-
       tive science" (e.g., MECW, 5: 37; EFRL: 1) but they are not positivists. Positive science is no
       more positivistic than science is scientistic. Both Marx and Durkheim reveal that appear-
       ances are contrary to underlying realities and that the empirically observable sign is not
       the essential aspect but veils undisclosed social dynamics.

opposition to, the *irrationalism* of empiricism[200] and mystical transcendentalism (EFRL: 13).[201] This was exactly how Marx situated his own work. Marx
"never uses the formula 'materialist dialectic', but calls it 'rational' as opposed
to 'mystical', which gives the term 'rational' a quite precise meaning" (Gramsci
1971: 456–7; cf. Rosen 1996: 271). Gramsci references Marx's qualified and quite
unexpected defense of Hegel whereby the dialectic "must be inverted, in order
to discover the rational kernel within the mystical shell" (C: 103). Weber also
stands in this broad tradition of rationalism (FMW: 138) as does his intimate
colleague, Troeltsch (see Liebersohn 1988: 44). An additional word on "rationalism" is in order because it is here that Durkheim makes a monumental contribution to social thought.

Durkheimian "rationalism" is inextricably bound to the theory of *Homo duplex*, the duality of the human being, and bridges the domains of the private
and the public, individual and collectivity. Constructionism and subjectivism
are insufficient in themselves. For the subjectivist social categories are, from
one angle, "purely artificial constructs" or "works of art" and, from the standpoint of the transcendentalism, they are a priori and "natural" or reified, in
other words (EFRL: 17). "Rationalism" the way Durkheim employs the idea,
"stands between empiricism and classical apriorism" (EFRL: 17; cf. Murphy
1971: 166). But his "rationalism" is not actually situated "between" these two
moments but sublates both poles. Levy-Bruhl writes that Kant was slighted in
France because it was believed that Kant's critical philosophy terminated in
skepticism but that with Lachelier, Boutroux, and Renouvier, Kant was given a
fresh hearing (1899: 444–45) and Durkheim's debt to Renouvier and *Criticisme*
(1899: 447) has been documented (Jones 2001). Gone was the Thing-in-itself
but the inseparability of object and mind was retained. In other words, empirical realism was still in play but there was no grasping the world of things
outside of the constructive and synthesizing powers of the mind. Intersecting
with Espinas and the organicism of ideas was Fouillée's theory of "idées-forces"

---

200 Experience does not "reform reason" says Kant. Those that would subjugate reason to
     empirical observations believe that they "can penetrate further and more clearly with ...
     mole-like eyes fixed on experience than with eyes belonging to a being created to stand
     erect and gaze at the heavens" (1983: 62). "So long then as this sensible sphere is and con-
     tinues to be for Empiricism a mere datum, we have a doctrine of bondage; for we become
     free, when we are confronted by no absolutely alien world, but by a fact which is our
     second self" (Hegel in Dunayevskaya 1961).

201 The hegemony of Cartesian rationalism did not give way until the early years of the 20th
     Century in France (see Clark 1973: 199, 215). In his lectures on secondary education in
     France, Durkheim says Cartesianism, as a philosophy of "clear ideas … has remained, and
     which in a new form ought to remain, as the basis of our national mentality" (1977: 278)

whereby the idea is not simply a representation but additionally "a force work-ing for its own realization" (Levy-Bruhl 1899: 453).

> For instance, liberty is not a reality given objectively, of which we have an idea because we perceive it; but, on the contrary, it is because we have an idea of our own liberty, because we believe in it, because we adapt our conduct to this belief, that we are actually free, and that our freedom is effectual in the world of phenomena. Our ideas and feelings are conditions of real internal change, and consequently factors in men-tal evolution, not mere signs of an of an evolution wrought independent-ly of them by exclusively physical causes. Furthermore, every internal change, being inseparable from an external change or motion, produces effects upon inwardly, at the same time find outward expression with all the resulting consequences. Thus the internal and the external efficacy of mental states are inseparable, because of the fundamental unity between the physical and the mental.
>
>   LEVY-BRUHL 1899: 453

Fouillée was not arguing for an hypostatic conception of ideas operating tran-scendentally above and beyond society and its members (Platonic transcen-dental materialism) but a unity of thought and action in praxis.

French post-materialism was not subordinate to German thought, yet, the influence of Hegel, Schelling, the Romantics, and, later, Kant was profound as Levy-Bruhl indicates (1899; see also Strenski 2006 for insights into various German–French connections). Durkheim's sociology represented, arguably, the most refined synthesis of European social thought and, with respect to the status and logic of representations, we can see it clearly even in his earlier writ-ings where representations of the collectivity were not reducible to individual representations (cf. Mauss 2005: 18), he left open the possibility of a "formal psychology" as a bridge to a nascent "social psychology" where the generic na-ture of representations could be worked out (RSM: 41).

Swinging back to a comparison with Kant, we are now in a position to see how collective representations are simultaneously in the minds of social-ized members of society but experienced as if they are autonomous physical realities:

> A thing is any object of knowledge which is not naturally penetrable by the understanding. It is all that which we cannot conceptualize ad-equately as an idea by the simple process of intellectual analysis. It is all that which the mind cannot understand without going outside itself,

proceeding progressively by way of observation and experimentation from those features which are the most external and the most immediately accessible to those which are the least visible and the most profound. To treat facts of a certain order as things is therefore not to place them in this or that category of reality; it is to observe towards them a certain attitude of mind. It is to embark upon the study of them by adopting the principle that one is entirely ignorant of what they are, that their characteristic properties, like the unknown causes upon which they depend, cannot be discovered by even the most careful form of introspection.

RSM: 35–36; see CLARK 1973: 171

Conscience is experienced in the mind of the person *as if* it were originating from somewhere outside of the mind.[202] This "as if" logic is rooted in our sociality but our sociality is not something eternal and unchanging. Each historical epoch has its own form of externality. If we follow Hegel we discover that Greek externality[203] was radically different from and represented a marked advancement of freedom over Persian externality (Singer 1983: 18–21).

Persian: where one is free the external command is experienced as something external;
Greek: where some are free the external command is experienced as something internal;
Modern: where all are (subjectively) free the internalized command is experienced as something external.

---

202   "[B]ecause of their *collective* genesis and operation" norms and representations "exercise a *constraint* over the actions (both physical and mental) of *particular* individuals, and, consequently, appear to the individuals involved to impose themselves *from without* in some form of rational and moral compulsion" (Degré 1985: 85). In Hegelian terms, our moral drivers seem to be alien powers imposing themselves upon us from without but, in reality, the "otherness" is within ourselves, our being driven is actually a process of recognition and self-movement in relation to the expectations and desires of others (PS: 34).

203   Per Singer: "the readiness of the Greeks to do what is best for the community as a whole comes from within. This would suggest that the Greeks were free in a way in which the Orientals were not. They did as they themselves wished to do, not as some external decree required them to do. Yet Hegel says that this is an incomplete form of freedom just because the motivation comes so naturally. Whatever is the result of the habits and customs in which one was brought up is not the result of the use of one's reason. If I do something from habit, I have not deliberately chosen to do it. My actions, it might be said, are still governed by forces external to my will – the social forces that gave me my habits – even though there is no despot telling me what to do, and the motivation for the action appears to come from within" (1983: 20). The ultimate irony is that the Greeks were ordered to stop thinking externally by an external decree issued by Apollo (Singer 1983: 21).

Left open is the final condition of universal objective freedom where the internal is experienced as arising from within the individual. The notion of epochal stages has something to stand on but the collapse of external authority in a hyper-autonomy terminates not in universal objective freedom but social anarchy. If the "internal-internal" means anything sociologically coherent it means that what is currently experienced as an enigmatic or alien thing over and against the individual is de-reified and made consciously transparent, i.e., "socialized" – Spirit knows itself as Spirit.

If we return to Marx's theory of the value form, commodities have something in common (value) that neither commodity actually possesses. Our social conscience is likewise something we have in common with others but not something that we "possess" in any simple or straightforward manner. This collective form of thought is a necessary illusion and inevitable mirage (DOL: 56) that emerges through our interactions and varies with our degree of integration. This consciousness becomes fixed or crystallized but subject to diffusion and diminution if we fail to periodically "recharge" the representations that tell us how we must or should act, think, and feel in the presence of others and in the performance of our duties. No, we do not "possess" this consciousness, rather, we are possessed by an echo of an alien force that we project outside of ourselves (DOL: 56). The "rationalization" of collective representations, their "subversion" in other words, is not synonymous with disenchantment per se but the voluntary and transparent sub-mission to the enchantment of reason.

Somehow it got into the heads of sociologists that Durkheim shifts from a theory of social facts in *Rules* to one of representations in his later work but the reality is that our collective representations *are* social facts (Pickering ([2000] 2006a: 19). "Because social pressure makes itself felt through mental channels, it was bound to give man the idea that outside him there are one or several powers, moral yet mighty, to which he is subject" (EFRL: 211).[204] Our psychological defense mechanisms (*Abwehrmechanismen*) serve to transform internal processes into "external events" to be responded to by the psyche (Bettelheim 1982: 92).[205] Pushed to the extreme such that the experience of language is felt

---

204 Our representations "appear to us to exist outside of ourselves, but ... they can only be located in [the] mind" (Verheggen 1996: 202).

205 "What is worst about using the word 'defense' [for *Abwehr*] is that it permits, even encourages, the impression that inner processes, such as reaction formations or denials, are something alien – something outside oneself. While one may think or wish this were so, the task of psychoanalysis is to show that it is not. Psychoanalysis tries to make us see that what we thought of as something alien that we need to deny or parry is really a very significant part of ourselves, and that it is to our advantage to recognize what it is and to integrate it into our personality" (Bettelheim 1982: 92–93).

to be completely external and alien to the subject – the previously quoted passage by Holderlin (who did go insane) leans in this direction – we have a more or less psychotic situation where the subject feels as though they do not participate in language but are possessed by language and used like a tool or conductor. Of course, the "normal" level of linguistic alienation leaves most people most of the time feeling as if they are subjectively effective users of language more than they are used by language (see Fink 1997: 87). Nonetheless, people experience many thoughts and feelings as if they were somehow other than thoughts and feelings, confusing the real external with the ideal external.[206] This does not signify anything like mass mental disorder but is the precondition and starting point for normal collective life and also the precondition for social analysis that operates above the level of methodological individualism and reductionism.

As Bourdieu puts it, "social science cannot 'treat social realities as things', in accordance with Durkheim's famous precept, without neglecting all that these realities owe to the fact that they are objects of cognition ..." ([1980] 1990: 135; cf. Bourdieu 1977: 203; cf. EFRL: 369). For Hegel, externality means that what is known in the mind seems "to have come by things, by what is different from itself, and by the difference of a variety of things, *without comprehending how and whence they came*" (PS: 489–90, emphasis added). For Marx, this externality was quintessentially modern because the premodern world lacked the degree of alienation that modernity introduced into life. Marx, says Lefebvre,

> shows that the period of civilization known as bourgeois (capitalist) society is characterized by extreme separation, scission and duality; as man emerges from material nature, everything which makes him a species-being (his essence) becomes externalized as if it were a material thing. Man and the human do not disappear; but whatever stands in their way still comes from within themselves. It is their "other" self, their double: their alienation.
>
> 1995: 169–70

---

206   A simplistic duality of internal and external is not productive. "Freud's 1938 distinction between repression as related to the internal world and disavowal as related to the external world is reminiscent of his 1924 distinction between 'neurotic anxiety' and 'realistic anxiety.' Neurotic anxiety stems from an internal danger – that is, an impulse within the patient that is considered inappropriate by the patient's own ego or superego – whereas realistic anxiety (which Freud also refers to as 'fear') stems from a real external danger... Insofar, however, as disavowal clearly involves a *thought* related to a perception – that is something generally considered to be *inside* the subject, part of his or her *psychical* reality – not a perception alone, the internal-versus-external distinction breaks down. Both repression and disavowal involve thoughts, not perceptions" (Fink 1997: 168).

At the level of personal psychology the injunctions of, say, the maternal superego are experienced as emanating from somewhere "out there," yet, the injunction is actually in the mind of the person. It can be said that social facts are "phenomena of consciousness, without being also [only] phenomena of the individual consciousness." Social facts exist in the individual as representations but the "impression of social things on the individual is altered by the particular state of the consciousness which receives them." A social fact like the sacredness of a holy object is, sociologically, not to be found in the physical object itself (no physical examination of the object will ever detect its sacredness) so it must be in the minds of people who regard the object as sacred (EFRL: 214). An objection may be raised here: do we not sometimes buck the system and think wild and original ideas that are ours alone? Does Durkheim not impose upon us the idea of a transcendental Subject that is unwarranted in the face of such apparently subjective facts? This is certainly the objection leveled by Adorno (2000: 44) who proffers an alternative view of social dynamics such that "the totality of society is maintained not by solidarity but by the antagonistic interests of human beings, by its antitheses..." (2000: 44). This is reminiscent of Sartre's view that "if we do not wish the dialectic to become a divine law again, a metaphysical fate, it must proceed *from individuals* and not from some kind of supra-individual ensemble" (2004: 36; cf. FMW: 155). Durkheim's position was similar to Simmel's with respect to the external and coercive nature of social facts:

> The real, practical problem of society arises from its inherent powers and forms in relation to the individual lives of its members. It is true that society lives only through individuals. But that does not exclude a multiplicity of antagonisms and conflicts. For on the one hand, the individuals form this society out of elements which crystallize into this particular form of "society"; society in turn evokes its own representatives and organs, confronting the individual with demands and orders as if it were an extraneous party. On the other hand, conflict accrues from the invasions of the individual by society. For man's faculty of splitting himself into parts and then experiencing a particular part as his very ego, which collides with other parts and struggles to make a decision to act – this faculty of man often puts him, insofar as he is a social being and so recognizes himself, into an antagonistic relation with the impulses and interests of his ego which are not part of his social character. The conflict between individual and society is transposed in the individual himself into a struggle between the antinomies of his nature.
>
> SIMMEL 1959: 47–48; see GANE 1992: 66

It is certainly true that Durkheim was prone to phrases such as "collective personality" and society as a "sentient being" and so on, however, a careful reading of *Suicide*, for example, reveals that any conception of a solidified substance ruling over people separate from people, is to misconstrue Durkheim's theory of social dynamics. Alpert claims that Durkheim is thankfully not actually a social realist because he has no theory of *substance* but Alpert makes the mistake of seeing "substance" and substantiality as pertaining only to a transcendentalism that is anti-sociological (1939: 151–53). Both Durkheim and Marx have a theory of what we can call, following Marx, a subject-substance reproduced every day by individuals. Social substance is not a transcendental fact but one of immanence. Durkheim does not neglect individuals. In fact, it is none other than Durkheim who insists, like Hegel, that the *only* active elements in society are in fact individuals and nothing more than individuals (S: 310; EFRL: 351; see also PS: 66; Hegel [1807] 1967: 160).[207] History is driven by individual passions, corrupt "private aims," and the "satisfaction of selfish desires" (Hegel 1956: 20).[208] The Absolute is not some unfathomable thing but is nothing other than "a people" going about its business (1948: 41). Of course, as an absolute, it is not just any assemblage of individuals but a people that has worked itself up to "a higher representation of itself" (PS: 426) such that Spirit knows itself *as* Spirit rather than confronting itself in the guise of a distorted, alien thing (DOL: 14). Hegel, Marx, Durkheim, and Weber diverge in important ways but are in concert on at least this aspect: the active agent in society is the individual, not the abstracted individual, but actual people in definite acts of cooperation and conflict (MECW, 5: 35–36).[209] Nonetheless, and all would agree on this as well, we are born into a world already constituted and even ideas of individuality and indifference, or even hostility to customs, tradition, and so on, are themselves, social forces – both effects of class and status antagonisms, social disintegration and, later, causes of further social disintegration by championing the individual ego over the collectivity, battling, says Durkheim, in its own name (S: 209–15). For example, early modern sentimentalism

---

207 "Society is a society of individuals and the individual is always a social individual. He has no existence by himself. He lives in, for and by society, just as society has no existence excepting in and through the individuals who constitute it" (Dewey 1903: 8). So long as social mediation holds out, individuals are universalized and universals are individuated (SL: 683). The "species is actual only as a free concrete individual" (Hegel 1975a: 144).

208 "Yet though 'needs, passions, and interests' are the evident agents of the historical process, their activity presupposes – and obscures – the progress of Reason in history" (Henderson and Davis 1991: 200).

209 "For Durkheim the notion of 'society' itself is a *Vorstellung* [representation]. There is no society in itself. It only exists *in* and *through* individuals" (Verheggen 1996: 203).

held that it had discovered the "laws of the 'heart'" and that "in acting on our genuine and natural feelings, we are acting on something that is *within* us and part of us, not *external* and alien to us; we are no longer caught in the throes of a blind necessity but are *expressing* ourselves and are therefore free" (Pinkard 1996: 99).

Two points regarding freedom need to be raised. First, the idea of personal autonomy and individual freedom are social ideas that circulate, looking for adherents to recognize their claims. Secondly, just when we think we are acting freely and on our own accord is when we come to find out that our supposed autonomy is grounded in the opposite, *heteronomy*.[210] As Žižek says, we are always free to choose so long as we make the right choice (*passim*). Or, some things we take to be optional are really obligatory: you *should* because you *must* (Nietzsche) and, of course, some things we consider obligatory are actually optional. Consider a hyper-nomic religious ethic that emerges in response to a pessimistic doctrine of one's fate: pushed to the extreme realization that none of my ways of acting, thinking, or feeling will have any determination upon my fate can lead a person to the direct opposite moral domain, antinomianism, where I follow my own heart and intuition because it cannot have any effect whatsoever on what was always already going to happen anyways. If, with Lacan, I think that "what is going to happen has already happened" then I might as well just compartmentalize destiny and live without regard for the future punishments or rewards I will receive regardless of the course taken. We can see that the hyper-regulation of life is always already "identical" with practical and spiritual *anarchy*.[211] Is this not, though, a case of personal autonomy and pure subjectivity vis-a-vis external authority? Not exactly: "it is not we who think, but the world which thinks in us'" (RSM: 201). Even something as seemingly intimate and personal as mental illness is actually social, where money, cultural currents, markets, and pharmacology converge.

There is no depression per se. Residents of the modern West would consider depression a normal and apparently universal feature of life but depression is not an inherent human condition. Neither is, for example, suicide. Some societies know neither depression nor suicide. The linguist Daniel Everett recounts how the Pirahã people laughed in his face when he told them the story of his stepmother's suicide and his embrace of evangelical Protestantism.

---

210 "Belonging to a society" says Žižek, "involves a paradoxical point at which each of us is ordered to embrace freely, as the result of our choice, what is anyway imposed on us (we all *must* love our country, our parents, our religion)" and so on (2006a: 12).

211 The attempt made by Marxism to leave behind Hegel's identity of opposites for a theory of overdetermination was a mistake (see Piaget 1970: 126). Indeed, it should be read as a form of repression productive of ideological symptoms.

When I concluded, the Pirahãs burst into laughter. This was unexpected, to put it mildly. I was used to reactions like "Praise God!" with my audience genuinely impressed by the great hardships I had been through and how God had pulled me out of them.

"Why are you laughing?" I asked.

"She killed herself? Ha ha ha. How stupid. Pirahãs don't kill themselves," they answered.

They were utterly unimpressed (2008: 265).

Depression is a culturally bounded experience and wildly variable across time and space. What most people in the United States would consider being depressed was, returning to the Japanese, just being Japanese.[212] Before major pharmaceutical marketing efforts, depression in Japan was a rare and extreme disorder and, importantly, the Japanese were not interested in being diagnosed with depression.[213] They did not want that disease because it lacked what Weber might call a psychological "premium" or reward – that is, symptom value.[214] This is a problem, not for the Japanese, but for the company who wants to sell billions of dollars worth of Paxil where there is no demand. As such, like much of the pharmaceutical industry, the reality is one of not finding cures for existing problems but creating the disease to fit the medicine (Watters 2010: 193). Where there had been no "depression" there is now "GlaxoSmithKlein Depression" and Paxil is the remedy (Watters 2010: 249). The American mental health system is built on a set of paradigmatic assumptions: "hyper-introspection," "hyper-individualism," and chemical reductionism (Watters 2010: 254). It also assumes that the Japanese "empire of signs" is no different than any other national system (Barthes 1982: 9). In sociological terms, we are in the domain of

---

212   When 80 people committed suicide in the Indian village of Badi in just the first few months of 2016, the inhabitants, not attuned to concepts such as social isolation, depression, underdevelopment, or chemically-induced neuropathology chalked it up to demon possession (Kotwal 2016).

213   "Japanese people in sad isolation may feel limited by *gaman*, the ideal of suffering through tough times without complaint, keeping a stiff upper lip. Similarly, the society has traditionally rejected the American trend toward medicalizing mental illness and mood disorders, spurning talk therapy and antidepressants long after they became commonplace in the West" (Zeeberg 2016).

214   Freud offers us a glimpse of the use, value, and profit motive of symptoms ([1926] 1959: 19–20). Weber indicates that obedience to god through adherence to the covenant led to the expectation of "wages for obedience" (AJ: 121). The 19th Century German view of the artist was one where sickness was a sign of aristocracy, genius, and "a mark of the sensitive few" (Harrington 1965: 56). In just one generation, the meaning of sickness changed entirely to "an infection of society and of the times themselves" (Ibid.).

stoic egoism and its intersection with materialism. Mental illness (sometimes a surplus of sanity and, as such, a form of waste) is not a "me" problem in itself but one of abstract and impersonal social dynamics individuated. In the case of Japanese depression (i.e., the GlaxoSmithKlein variety) the marketing was hitched to "that country's lengthy and painful recession. Ongoing economic upheaval can be particularly unsettling because the unrelenting threat to one's status, security, and future seems to come from everywhere and nowhere at the same time" (Watters 2010: 249). But give the pharmaceutical firm some credit for paving the way for a full-blown depression industry complete with its own, cute collective representation. In 2015, Sanrio, the company behind Hello Kitty, introduced a new mascot to signify the new depression premium: a misanthropic egg named Gudetama.

> But is it possible to market malaise? In Japan at least, the answer is yes. Meet Gudetama, the anthropomorphic embodiment of severe depression. Gudetama is a cartoon egg yolk that feels existence is almost unbearable. It shivers with sadness. It clings to a strip of bacon as a security blanket. Rather than engage in society, it jams its face into an eggshell and mutters the words, "Cold world. What can we do about it?"
> WINN 2016: n.p.

Japan not only has pharmaceutical depression now but also the worship of depression. Depression "evolved" from a personal problem to a transcendental force (complete with an anthropomorphized "totem") in one generation.

It is possible to speak of a kind of "transcendence" without sliding off into the Kantian synthetic a priori, the reintroduction of a virtually inaccessible noumenal realm, or a hypostatized substance. Here we merely insist that authoritative representations are not *merely* projections (although they *are* projected) and that objectivities are permeated with subjectivity and, likewise, subjectivities are objective (Mounier 1952: 65–70; S: 310). For example, money and the entire commercial system do not rely on the lone individual for its existence, but our existence as lone individuals does rely on access to money and jobs, etc. Marx agrees: even if you are a member of the master class, "Under free competition, the immanent laws of capitalist production confront the individual capitalist as a coercive force external to him" (C: 381). The capitalist rules over labor but capital itself rules over the capitalist (PM: 78). Weber would concur with Marx (see PESC: 19–20). Ideas, for Weber, were not merely subjectively real at the level of the individual but also objectively real (e.g., there is a big difference between Calvin and Calvinism): active *forces* at work in the world, sweeping people up and carrying them along, converting people into "carriers" much the same way that a labor product that is priced and ready for exchange is converted into a "bearer" of a moral surplus that it lacks as a mere utility or use-value. We see, then, in his most famous essay on the Protestant ethic that capitalism is portrayed as an immense and "monstrous cosmos" that "forces on the individual ... the norms of its economic activity."[215] Capitalism is something greater and different than the sum of its parts and, as a subject-substance or automatic subject, as Marx calls it, "selects" for itself "the economic subjects – entrepreneurs and workers – that it needs." This "selection" process "had first to come into being, and not just in individuals, but as an attitude held in common by groups of people" (Weber [1905] 2002: 13). This group "attitude" or ethos is the sociological meaning of "spirit" or *Geist*. The main objective of any society, the alpha and omega, is the inculcation of *spirit* in its young (Durkheim 1961: 103).[216] Of course, if *we all* (or some critical mass of society) stopped using money then it would cease to function as a social fact but those cases are rare, and, historically, when societies are shaken to the ground and its members come to the realization that it is "just us" here (reality having undergone a radical process of derealization) they are quick to rebuild the absolute dimension. This brings us to the heart of the matter: the social nature of authority.

8   Coercion and Authority

Everyday social reality is only ultimately possible on the basis of the externality of social facts because communication and thinking on the basis of signs would otherwise lose coherence. "Because language itself is a necessary condition of reflection, because philosophical awareness arises only in and through language, the human spirit always finds language present as a given reality, comparable and equal in stature to physical reality" (Cassirer 1955a: 117; cf. Piaget 1970: 74–75). A well-known metaphor such as the lion being the king of the jungle "implies the existence of both /king/ and /lion/ as functives of two previously codified sign-functions. If signs (expressions and content) did not preexist the text, every metaphor would be equivalent simply to saying that something is something. But a metaphor says that *that* (linguistic) thing is a

---

215   Cf. Durkheim's imagery of the crushing Leviathan of modern societies compared to the spontaneity of clan and tribal life (EFRL: 226).

216   Hegel's "Spirit" was not some kind of "soul thing" that was "out there" in the great beyond but self-conscious social relations, a self-reflecting moment whereby actors determine if their forms of thought and actions correspond with their self-conceptions and reasons (Pinkard 1996: 9).

the same time *something else*" (Eco 1984: 25). Not only, though, does a fact (like language or a metaphor) confront the individual as a pre-existing reality but these facts have the power to impose themselves over personal inclinations (Fink 1987: 86–87; EFRL: 209). For social organization to exist, the development of our linguistic and conceptual "apparatus" cannot be left up to us: "society cannot leave the categories up to the free choice of individuals without abandoning itself" (EFRL: 16).

> To live, it requires not only a minimum moral consensus but also a mini-mum logical consensus that it cannot do without either. Thus, in order to prevent dissidence, society weighs on its members with all its authority. Does a mind seek to free itself from these norms of thought? Society no longer considers this a human mind in the full sense, and treats it ac-cordingly. This is why it is that when we try, even deep down inside, to get away from these fundamental notions, we feel that we are not fully free; something resists us, from inside and outside ourselves. Outside us, it is opinion that judges us more than that, because society is represented inside us as well, it resists these revolutionary impulses from within.
>   EFRL: 16

As such, many of our most cherished beliefs, those that we find to be "practi-cally irresistible" and even compulsory, are simultaneously lacking in the area of rational truth (Bradley 1916: 151). This is especially so in the domain of reli-gious beliefs which, frankly, admit to absurd levels of irrational incoherence, but also in the formal and technically rational domains of capitalist enterpris-es and in the theoretical reflections of economists and, unfortunately, critical anti-economists as well. The "laws" of society usually have more than enough power to overwhelm or at least confound rational comprehension.

In a capitalist society, for example, "Under free competition, the immanent laws of capitalist production confront the individual capitalist as a coercive force external to him" (C: 381). We may be forced to comply with a law, e.g., out of simple fear of punishment and the desire to avoid the pain or inconve-nience associated with the violation of a prohibition. Social facts exert simple domination over us (comply or die). Indeed, as people are subjected to nothing but *force*, they approach the limit of thinghood (Weil 1965: 6). For Marx, the original fact producing class exploitation rests primarily on sheer coercion: "In actual history, it is a notorious fact that conquest, enslavement, robbery, mur-der, in short, force, play the greatest part" (C: 874). The "greatest part" perhaps but raw power is not the whole story. As Plutarch says, "Necessity is unmusical, Persuasion musical" (in Barnes 2001: 137).

During the 20th Century, Marx's followers came to realize that much more was involved in the command of capital. Seduction and indifference are also powerful forces. People sometimes bow to brute force but typically there is more involved than compliance simply due to fear.[217] "Even in the most oppressive and cruel cases of subordination, there is still a considerable measure of personal freedom.... Even where authority seems to 'crush' him, it is based not only on coercion or compulsion to yield to it" (Simmel 1950: 182–83). Likewise, "No regime, however fanatical, can act without accepting any overt moral restraints.... [N]aked power is bound to support – and at the same time to limit – itself by the exercise of persuasion" (Polanyi 1962: 233; see also Arendt 1968: 325).

We should never forget the role of brute necessity and force: "The silent compulsion of economic relations sets the seal on the domination of the capitalist over the worker" (C: 899) but it is "silent." To really work the working class must conceive of the requirements of the mode of production as "self-evident" and the work of "natural laws" instead of sociohistorical contingencies. This is the work of "education, training, and habit" (C: 899). The ruling class, in other words, has to create a population that either loves or at least respects, even grudgingly, the prevailing system of work, accumulation, and the distribution of goods because once a power is no longer "worthy of love" it does not generally inspire indifference but "dislike and resistance" (Kant 1983: 103).[218] Raw power is definitely insufficient. Rather, what is "peculiar to social constraint" says Durkheim, is the "prestige with which certain representations are endowed" (RSM: 44; see also Dewey 1946: 96).[219]

---

217   "Might! Might! Who can't defy might? What's called might is nothing: seduction is the only real might" (Lessing [1772] 1979: 80). As in the case of the heretical Cathari, brutalized during the Albigensian Crusades, "force alone scarcely sufficed" in solidifying Church legitimacy and authority (McNeill 1963: 554).

218   "An individual or collective subject is said to inspire respect when the representation that expresses it in consciousness has such power that it calls forth or inhibits conduct automatically, *irrespective of any utilitarian calculation of helpful or harmful results.* When we obey someone out of respect for the moral authority that we have accorded to him, we do not follow his instructions because they seem wise but because a certain psychic energy intrinsic to the idea we have of that person bends our will and turns it in the direction indicated" (EFRL: 209).

219   Prestige can be of either a pure or impure variety – a god (positive devil) is good but the negative god is also prestigious. We "must recognize the prestige of the Devil. The pedigree of the evil One is older than the oldest European aristocracy and royal families; it antedates the Bible and is more ancient than the Pyramids" (Carus [1900] 1996: 445–46).

The coercive power that we attribute to the social fact represents so small a part of its totality that it can equally well display the opposite character- istic. For, while institutions bear down upon us, we nevertheless cling to them; they impose obligations upon us, and yet we love them; they place constraints upon us, and yet we find satisfaction in the way they function, and in that very constraint.[220]

> RSM: 47

We "love" our subordination because we consider our institutions to be legiti- mate and have a "genuine respect" for them (EFRL: 209). A life of compliance in the absence of love or respect for the object of obligation would dissolve the conscience of the individual (Shand 1914: 120). Submission without love would engender little more than "resignation to a fatality" (Carid 1885: 26). There is no other explanation for, say, the exploitation of millions or even billions of peo- ple by a handful of elites as we find under capitalism. Sheer force of quantity lies on the side of the oppressed (Bendix 1978: 16–17). True, the elites control military, police, and legal institutions but the entire system could be brought to its knees almost immediately through a coordinated passive revolt. Why can- not the toiling masses just sit down and stop cooperating with their enslavers? In a word, the system of command is deemed legitimate (lawful, hence fixed). Where "power is vigorously pursued and exercised, ideas of legitimacy tend to develop to give meaning, reinforcement, and justification to that power" (Bendix 1978: 17).

> Pannekoek posed some elementary questions: Given its numerical and economic superiority [as the producers], why had not the proletariat at- tained power? How did a smaller exploiting minority, the bourgeoisie, dominate a larger mass? The conventional answer of the political and military muscle of the bourgeoisie did not suffice. On a raw empirical level the working class possessed the greater power. Yet the cultural su- periority of the bourgeoisie compensated for its material weakness. The bourgeois minority controlled the vehicles of culture and education: schools, churches, newspapers. By these means bourgeois values and perspectives infected the masses. "This intellectual dependence ... on the bourgeoisie is one of the major causes of the weakness of the proletariat."

---

220   Today, we hear the word "constraint" and we shudder. Oh, to be constrained, what a pity. Sometimes the constrained are more free than those who drift untethered. "Socrates died in prison, but he died more free than his judges" (Comte-Sponville 2004: 1). "Ah Bartleby! Ah humanity!"

The cultural atmosphere mediated and sustained the exercise of power.
"Cultural power [*Geistige Macht*] is the most powerful force in the human
world." Yet the technical reason for the reign of the bourgeoisie is not to
be forgotten: It also wielded a superior organization, the state.

JACOBY 1981: 73–74

The state represents a technical and organizational instrumentality but *Geistige Macht* (better translated as "spiritual power") is the real driving force that
makes people obey norms that reduce them to the status of tools while making
them feel that they are acting autonomously and enjoying positive freedoms.
When we obey according to our "own free will ... coercion is not felt or felt
hardly at all..." (RSM: 51). Recall that domination that has been legitimated is
synonymous with authority; yet, there are various forms of authority and the
kinds of claims that correspond with them.

Simple coercion is domination pure and simple. Imagine a person or utopian
group that renounces money or, by extension, any form of material exchange:
they are subject to being tracked down by money and unmercifully executed.
And most people would say that such "lazy" or "crazy" people, in renouncing
money, work, exchange, etc., get what they deserve. In a way, modern social life
flows along three possible channels of existence: we can work, parasitically live
off others who work and support us, or we can die. Work, suck, or die, these are
our options, apparently. Even the act of messing around with our common language has implications. Mauss alludes to the "intellectual death" resulting from,
for example, the person who attempts to invent and use his or her own private
language[221] in place of the official language of the group or society. There can
be no private language (MacCabe 1985: 2). The privatization effort will come
to naught. Even in cases where running afoul of a social fact does not lead to
biological death, the transgression can lead to a social death whereby the individual is treated as an unwanted thing. And once we reach our social death it
is only a matter of waiting for our second death that reduces us, finally, to dust
and ashes. But the vast and overwhelming majority of people do not want to
evade money or work but cling to it as if they were routes to the sacred. The
pursuit of material wealth, as idea and practice, enjoys an authority (legitimate

221   "I realized Salvatore spoke all languages, and no language. Or, rather, he had invented
        for himself a language which used the sinews of the languages to which he had been
        exposed – and once I thought that his was, not the Adamic language that a happy man-
        kind had spoken, all united by a single tongue from the origin of the world to the Tower
        of Babel, or one of the languages that arose after the dire event of their division, but pre-
        cisely the Babelish language of the first day after the divine chastisement, the language of
        primeval confusion" (Eco 1983: 59).

domination) denied simple domination.[222] Following Weber, we will concentrate on three types of authority: legal, traditional, and charismatic (FMW: 79). Legal authority[223] is predicated "on a belief in the legality of enacted rules and

---

222 Things that are today considered more or less legitimate, such as the state for example, are sometimes born from pure domination and bondage. Scott provides a clear depiction of force in the building of the first states in Mesopotamia (2017: 152–54). However, while millions of Americans still cling to the state as a necessity and as a potential force for good, it also seems self-evidently true that contemporary neoliberal states are losing the battle of maintaining legitimacy as democracies and democratic institutions disintegrate into authoritarian oligarchy and mass immiseration. Not that fascist oligarchy is America's fate but, at the current rate of devolution, full-scale collapse and mass death seem plausible by some point between 2030 and 2050 in the absence of a radically new course.

223 It is common to see legal authority or legal domination referred to as *legal-rational* or *rational-legal* (e.g., Kalberg 1985; in contrast see Mommsen 1989: 21 or Bendix 1960: 297) but either formulation ("legal-rational" or "rational-legal") is a misstep because things social, including laws, are never *inherently* rational from either a formal or substantive standpoint. Rationality, as Weber says, is always *perspectival* and what is rational from one point of view can be, and usually is, completely irrational from another standpoint. Weber's famous essay on the Protestant ethic is normally regarded as a work driven by a concern for the problem of rationalism but, as he informs us, it is the completely *irrational* aspects (especially those dealing with the idea of a calling) that interests him as the inverse to processes of rationality (PESC: 37). Weber's "economy of forces" (PESC: 65) is one in which positives and negatives are intermingled. Where there is rationality there must be a corresponding "quantum" of irrationality (Mannheim 1982: 175 ff.). Likewise, for Marx, the purely rational acts of the individual entrepreneur, for example, seeking to maximize profits are irrational from the standpoint of the collective well being of society – where profits thrive, humanity is imperiled (see Aron 1965: 173). Halbwachs tells us that "there is no connexion between the methods of industrial production and what is commonly called rationalism. The latin Countries are in enlightened by the philosophy of Voltaire, but it is not in France and Italy that the industrial revolution started. And even if the methods of modern industry are rational, there is something quite irrational about the abnegation of men who devote themselves utterly to a lucrative profession not for love of gain or the useful goods money can procure for them, but out of a sense of duty" (1958: 55). This polarity of rationality and irrationality also applies to all forms of legitimate domination. For the Calvinist, for example, ascetic labor in a calling was a way to rationalize everyday life but, from other standpoints, including the scientific, is totally irrational. As Le Bon says, "The theological doctrines which aroused men's passions so violently, and notably those of Calvin, are not even worthy of examination in the light of rational logic" (1913: 37). Per legal authority, a law from one angle can be viewed as rational but many laws are absurdly irrational from many other angles of vision. Legal processes may be "rationalized" or subject to "rationality" (this is the "formal" rationality of bureaucracy and bureaucratic processes) but that does not mean they are rational at all. The rational can always transform into something else. As Smith says, "anything can be fetishized. That includes laws. An example would be the "strict constructionism" of fundamentalist jurists who regard the Constitution as quite literally sacred, beyond change

the right of those elevated to authority under such rules to issue commands...";
traditional authority is rooted in "established belief in the sanctity of immemorial traditions[224] and the legitimacy of those exercising authority under
them...."; and charismatic authority[225] rests "on devotion to the exceptional
sanctity, heroism or exemplary character of an individual person, and of the
normative patterns or order revealed or ordained by him" (1978: 215).[226] When

---

or challenge. Ceding the authority of all future generations to the will of the "founding
fathers" is alienation to the *Nth* degree. The irony is that, in this doctrine, rationally constituted law acquires a new kind of traditional authority, and hence becomes an object of
fetishism" (2016: 23–4). The distinction between rational and irrational authority is a good
one to make, however. As Fromm says: "Rational authority is the recognition of authority
based on critical evaluation of competences. When a student recognizes the teacher's authority to know more than him, then this a reasonable evaluation of his competence. The
same is the case, when I as the passenger of a ship recognize the authority of the captain
to make the right and necessary decisions if in danger. Rational authority is not based on
excluding my reason and critique but rather assumes it as a prerequisite. This does not
make me small and the authority great but allows authority to be superior where and as
long it possesses competence. Irrational authority is different. It is based on emotional
submission of my person to another person: I believe in him being right, not because he
is, objectively speaking, competent nor because I rationally recognize his competence.
In the bonds to the irrational authority, there exists a masochistic submission by making
myself small and the authority great. I have to make it great, so that I can – as one of its
particles – can also become great. The rational authority tends to negate itself, because
the more I understand the smaller the distance to the authority becomes. The irrational
authority tends to deepen and to prolong itself. The longer and the more dependent I am
the weaker I will become and the more I will need to cling to the irrational authority and
submit" (1957: n.p.).

224   Weber famously characterized the traditional form as the "eternal yesterday" (FMW: 78).
"'We do it that way,' he says, 'and that is how it is. The same as the sun rising in the east and
setting in the west'" (Murakami 1991: 15).

225   If we could summarize charismatic authority it would reside in the notion that "Though
it is written, I say unto thee." We find in the gospel of Matthew the following inversion of
political norms: "But Jesus called them unto him, and said, Ye know that the princes of
the Gentiles exercise dominion over them, and they that are great exercise authority upon
them. But it shall not be so among you: but whosoever will be great among you, let him
be your minister; And whosoever will be chief among you, let him be your servant" (20:
25–27).

226   The translation and phraseology centered on charismatic authority in the "Politics as a
Vocation" address by Weber is troublesome. First, the term "extraordinary" is used when
a better representation lies in the notion of "otherworldly" and, secondly, charisma is
turned into a "personal *gift of grace*" (FMW: 79) when, in fact, charisma is not a personal
quality or gift at all but a social quality bestowed upon the charismatic by the public.
The charismatic leader does not personally embody the social gifts they are imagined to
possess – the "image is purely phantastic." The image is projected onto the person (Cohn
1970: 84). People who create and then attach themselves to a charismatic savior bask in
their own reflected glories. They transfer to the sacred image a bit of the substance they

we examine any social fact it will have validity[227] or legitimacy on the basis of one of these forms of authority, or, sometimes, an amalgamation of forms, or composites in transition. But a social fact is not authoritative unless it is recognized as such by those who subjugate themselves to it – and become *subjects* as a result. As things invested with authority, social facts (1) make *claims*, (2) provide implicit or explicit *proof*,[228] and, (3) when *recognized*, are retroactively constituted as a legitimate power to make ways of acting, thinking, and feeling fall into line with expectations.[229] Being "retroactively constituted" just means that it is the last step in this sequence, recognition, that actually confers the authority status – it is "accorded" or "conferred" (EFRL: 209, 328).[230] "For instance, one man is king only because other men stand in relation of subjects to him. They, on the other hand, imagine that they are subjects because he is king" (C: 149). Note carefully that the problem here according to Marx is not one of simple domination or authoritarianism (neither fall properly within the domain of authority) but one of subordinate imagination.[231] Acclaim is what

---

receive from it and they get back from the image all that they project into it (EFRL: 345). This transference process is drawn out more clearly in ES but readers are encouraged to consult Smith (2013) for a tour de force explanation of the charisma concept.

227   "Valid" and "value" share the same root in the Latin *valere* ("be strong"). Legitimacy embodies the moments of legality, rightfulness, and validity.

228   "If authority wishes to be respected it must of course show itself worthy of respect..." (Sabatier 1909: 140). "The *credibility* of a discourse is what first makes believers act in accord with it" (Certeau 1984: 148). In many cases no proof is required because a thing is felt by subjects to be necessary. Necessity requires no proof: "An idea is said to be necessary when due to some sort of internal property, it enjoys credence without the support of any proof" (EFRL: 16). In other words, some things are treated as being self-evidently true. And as far as "proof" goes, there is no such thing as proof per se – what qualifies as proof for one person or group falls short for others. The miracle worker has no signs or proofs capable of inherently convincing sceptics and enemies of the ministry (Strauss 1892: 413ff.). Lacking belief nothing counts as proof.

229   Cf. Brentano's modalities of intentionality: representation, judgement, and either reception or rejection (Safouan 1981: 78).

230   Bourdieu consistently emphasizes this point that authority flows from the process of recognition (see for example 1991: 72) but more importantly the simultaneous *misrecognition* – a point of linkage, perhaps, between the Weberian and Lacanian perspectives. "The endless reconversion of economic capital into symbolic capital, at the cost of a wastage of social energy which is the condition for the permanence of domination, cannot succeed without the complicity of the whole group: the work of denial which is the source of social alchemy is, like magic, a collective undertaking.... The collective misrecognition which is the basis of the ethic of honor ... is only possible because, when the group lies to itself in this way, there is neither deceiver nor deceived..." (Bourdieu 1977: 195–96).

231   Cf. Screpanti (2007: 89): "According to Marx a master is a master not because he is recognized as such by a subordinate worker.... He is a master not for subjective or spiritual motives, but for solidly objective reasons attaining to the distribution of wealth and power."

converts a claim into a valid or authoritative command that one should or must obey. To common sense it appears that we obey because someone or an institution *has* authority (we obey because he *is* the king) but the truth is actually the inverse: a thing is invested with authority only because we recognize it (Man 1985: 103) and lend our consent (Wesep 1920: 129).[232] In other words, mana "is in the eyes of the beholder" (Becker 1973: 128) rather than an quality of the thing worshiped.[233] It is our consent that keeps society together. "The strongest and most effective force in guaranteeing the long-term maintenance of power is not violence in all the forms deployed by the dominant to control the dominated, but consent in all the forms in which the dominated acquiesce in their own domination" (Robert Frost, in Clegg and Pitsis 2012: 72).

Recognition, however, is more complicated than simple acceptance or rejection.[234] The act of "misrecognition" is always bound tightly to recognition. For example, a speech-maker may be unexpectedly laughed at by their audience (the "place of the Other") and – voilà – the statement is a joke. The "public has the power to determine what someone has said" (Fink 1997: 43). However, if the speaker reacts badly (fails to follow the followers) then the interaction order suffers embarrassment and a slippage into sub-rituals designed to repair parapraxis (a problem we will take up later). The act of recognition alters

---

The point is well taken but here nothing more is stated other than the master rules because the master rules – here we have analysis escorting the subjected back to subjection.

232   This logic is most obvious at the "molecular" level of action: "When an event is taking place people express their opinions and wishes about it, and as the event results from the collective activity of many people, some one of the opinions or wishes expressed is sure to be fulfilled if but approximately. When one of the opinions expressed is fulfilled, that opinion gets connected with the event as a command preceding it. Men are hauling a log. Each of them expresses his own opinion as to how and where to haul it. They haul the leg away, and it happens that this is done as one of them said. He ordered it" (Tolstoy [1869] 1992: 504).

233   "An image is made sacred not by its creator but by its worshiper" (Gracián [1647] 2015: 2). We should qualify this notion of mana because it cannot be reduced to pure subjectivity, interests, or intersubjective agreements. Mana and charisma, etc., are irreducible and superior, not merely phantasmatic fictions; charisma is a real force rooted in the beliefs and actions of millions (Neumann 1944: 85). Yet, if *all eyes* (or at least a critical mass) behold nothing more than a piece of wood or a rock, the churinga (the thing invested with mana) decomposes and falls back into the domain of the infraliminal (rocks, wood, and so forth).

234   At the level of face-to-face interactions we can make a distinction between simple *cognitive recognition* as a "process through which we socially or personally identify the other" and *social recognition* which is a "ceremonial gesture" whereby we agree to treat the other as worthy of interaction (Goffman 1963: 113). Weberian recognition, if we can call it that, is the process in which we accept a command as valid, confer power to the claimant, and get with the program.

the world, adds something to it, opens up a third point of "transcendental-ity" (see Frisby 1983: 89) to the flatness of the dyadic world of face-to-face in-teractions.[235] It is recognition, in other words, that concretizes and socializes the isolated and abstract determinations (PR: 229). Although, the lack of rec-ognition does not entail an automatic withdrawal of respect and obedience, especially in the case of long-established institutions. We have to leave room for inertia. For example, it was thought that French and English kings had the miraculous power to heal the sick with their "royal touch." If the touch resulted in the cure, it was proof that the king's touch was indeed royal. However, if the expected cure was not forthcoming, it did not prove that the king was lack-ing but that another go at it was necessary (Bloch 1961: 238–43; cf. EFRL: 337, 365).[236] Obviously, royal magic is not something observable in the physical body of the king, it is not a property or quality of the individual serving as the king, and it is also not reducible to the subjective expectations of the person on the receiving end of the touch. But in a culture that believes in magic and expects magic to work, failure does not lead to an automatic loss of authority for the king, the practice, the institution, or the collective belief (see Davis 1985 on the dialectic of culture and pharmacology when it comes to the belief in zombies).[237] Although, continued failure exposes the practice of, e.g., the royal touch to a withdrawal of recognition and the search, at least, for a new king.[238] And something taken for granted can undergo sudden devaluation, fall out of the supraliminal dimension of life, and then spring right back to occupy its place of honor.

Exceptional crises can reveal this decomposition and recomposition pro-cess, as, for example, when money was suddenly rendered worthless as a

---

235   The "magic" of authority is that even though authority always flows from the bottom up it appears from the standpoint of befuddled consciousness that it always "operates from the top to the bottom and never inversely" (Neumann 1944: 83).

236   "It is well known that nothing is more difficult to prove than the failure of a magical activ-ity. To explain why the woman on whom a spell has been cast remains alive, or why the charmed animal escapes the hunters, the sorcerer never runs short of reasons; a badly conducted operation, ritual conditions poorly observed, lack of faith on the part of the assistant or the interested parties [i.e., dyspraxia]" (Bouglé [1926] 1970: 164).

237   "The real problem, then, will be to understand how people believed in their wonder-working power when they did not in fact heal" (Bloch 1961: 238). In the wake of an "un-equivocal disconfirmation of a belief" people do not in general simply abandon a belief, as if the revelation of the truth through disconfirmation releases them from a spell once and for all. The process of disconfirmation is dynamic and can lead to a doubling down on proselytizing and a desperate search for clues to failed predictions and guidance on how to proceed (Festinger, Riecken, and Schachter 1956: 208–16).

238   If there were sufficient time and space, a discussion of the consolidating influence of condescension on consent would be in order (e.g., Twain 1872: 271–77).

medium of exchange during Hurricane Katrina or during the interwar period when Germans fueled their furnaces with paper currency.[239] The idea of
"retroactivity" throws into light the non-linear and reciprocal nature of cause
and effect relations in society. "Undoubtedly the effect cannot exist without
its cause, but the latter, in turn, requires its effect. It is from the cause that the
effect derives its energy, but on occasion it also restores energy to the cause
and consequently cannot disappear without the cause being affected" (RSM:
124). Likewise, there really is no claim *per se* until the receivers challenge it,
demand proofs and justifications which transform a statement into a claim or
a command proper that may or may not be recognized.[240] This non-linear, ret-
roactive nature of authority relations is good news for those that wish to enact
civil disobedience and social change. If I personally fail to obey, no longer recognizing the claims of some powerful authority, I will undoubtedly be crushed
(again, try not using money) but if *we*[241] agree to ignore it, the authority object
will no longer be able to push us around. Here, we would be interested in what
constitutes a critical mass. "*If we all downed tools and joined hands for ten min-
utes and stopped believing in money, then money would no longer exist*" (Amis
1984: 354).[242] Of course, many claims are recognized and obeyed without any
proof offered or demanded. In such cases, the category of necessity was overbearing, negating any demand for proof (EFRL: 16). Reason is important but
one should not overlook simple foolishness on the part of millions of ignora-
muses (Pascal 1941: 111).

   In other scenarios, proof may be lacking but obedience based neither on admiration nor brute force may be forthcoming simply on the basis of rewards or
offsets, however, this bribery leaves open the very real problem that the supply

---

239   "As Marx said, in times of crisis, people still want money suddenly, going back to bullion-
      ists" (Karatani 2001: 13). This may be true for market "crises" but people trapped on a roof
      want food, suddenly going back to pork and beanists.
240   "No fact ... can evade the question of its justification, least of all a fact of human will"
      (Hocking 1926: 76).
241   Note Weber's comment (PESC: 19) that it is as *individuals* that we confront the inalter-
      ability of capitalism. It is otherwise with the organized class. Solidarity is the cure for
      inevitability.
242   "We need do no more than recognise the surrounding light of freedom, no more than
      dismiss the nightwatchman, so as to be able to all clasp hands joyously" (Hess 1845: n.p.).
      Easy! "The "fundamental fact is that so long as the generality of mankind deem gold to be
      wealth, then it is wealth; and as soon as this opinion passes, gold then becomes a metal
      of subsidiary importance" (Whitehead [1933] 1955: 77–78). But of course, this kind of hard
      constructionism (Whitehead is a relational-subjectivist) underappreciates the power of
      instituted practices that undergird the authority of any social fact. In general, though, he
      is correct: when public opinion gives up on a thing, it undergoes a desublimation and falls
      into the space of profane utility.

of offsets cannot keep pace with the demand (Habermas 1973: 73). "Offsets" do not have to be strictly material rewards and privileges[243] but can also take the form of ideal escapes such as "culturally approved fantasy" (Riesman, Glazer, and Denney [1950] 1953: 107)[244] and other adjustments made possible by myths and ideologies that bind the disaffected to a social system that fails to work for them. The presence of "soothsayers" of various forms, agitators, demagogues, etc., are valuable in misdirecting collective anxieties in such a way that the status quo is preserved, for the most part, while dishing out emotional compensations. At least in the "democratic" West, lacking a formal caste system, genuine progressive revolution has always been a remote possibility – even the "loudest agitation is no more than a breeze ruffling the surface of deep waters. Dominated by the habits which it has generated, we all of us, even the agitators, uphold the existing order without knowing it" (Cooley [1909] 1962: 276).[245] To further complicate matters, the whole process of legitimation (including proceduralism designed to lend the appearance of legitimacy) may run in a purely negative direction, for example, voting not for the candidate one wants but against the candidate one hates the most – the "winner" being reduced to an unloved thing that is nonetheless somehow "better" than the thing perceived to be even more horrifying (e.g., former Sanders enthusiasts "holding their noses" as they cast ballots for Clinton; being "for" Clinton = negation of Trump, the greater of two evils).[246] Finally, some authorities make no claim at all, or, at least, did not

---

243   However, it must be said, a dominating power can hang on to power for longer than it should when it is in a position to grant privileges to strivers. "On the whole, possessed of one great privilege and eager to gain others, [the ambitious] are not so close in spirit to the unprivileged classes as might be imagined" (Cooley [1909] 1962: 274). If a subaltern group causes trouble for a political regime it does not have to capitulate to the down and out in order to cool them out but, on the contrary, lure away sympathetic and idealistic supporters from the more privileged segments of society. "Thus it is possible to have freedom to rise and yet have at the same time a miserable and perhaps degraded lower class ..." (Cooley [1909] 1962: 275). Shades of Machiavelli.

244   Fantasy in itself has neither revolutionary nor reactionary power. There is nothing in the way of inevitability or necessity connecting fantasy either (approved or vilified) to social action (Weinstein and Platt 1969: 23).

245   The relationship between "habit" and social stability is interesting. As Dewey says, when people are acting most habitually, externality and coercion are not experienced by the individual acting in accordance with norms; authority is, in this case, absolute and perceived attacks on norms generate resentment toward those who would rebel against the prevailing order (1946: 97).

246   A lifelong Republican, my father voted for Johnson in 1964 because he was convinced that Goldwater would get us all killed in a nuclear war. Voting for Johnson made him so physically ill that he vomited in the parking lot of the polling station after casting his ballot. He was not alone among conservatives. Goldwater failed to receive even 40 percent of the vote and only carried five southern states in addition to his home state of Arizona.

know they were claims-makers to begin with or, perhaps the claims were modest but blown out of proportion by followers – and the inverse is also possible. Sometimes the "leader" gets more or less than they imagined they had coming to them or wanted nothing at all. Leadership is sometimes a reward and sometimes a punishment. Some people have leadership accidentally foisted upon them when they neither seek it nor want it (Blackmar 1905: 58) or come into authority simply by virtue of the office they inhabit (Wach 1944: 337–38). Here, we are miles away from rational choice theory and the Rawlsian "community of fair-minded deciders" (Romano 2012: 584).[247]

9   Irreducibility

"The whole of social reality" says Gurvitch, "which cannot be broken down, always takes precedence over all of its particular manifestations; it is ontologically present before all its expressions, works and crystallizations and is never entirely alienated by any of them" (1964: 1; see especially CPE: 205 ff.). Everyday consciousness combines paradigmatic opposites: the naive realism of using money because it "has value" is combined with the perplexed, reductionistic nominalism that consciousness falls back into when asked to articulate the reality of things social.[248] Asked if society is real, assuming this person is not a lady of iron, they will reply that, of course, society is real. But when asked to conceptualize society they will be reduced to pointing to some people or sensible objects.[249]

---

247 Beware those who preach "consensus." Consensus is the transformation of "phantasy into reality ... and not based on reason or critical examination" (Fromm 1973: 203). To repeat myself, consensus is the rationale provided by authorities when you are assigned to a gulag. "For the sake of consensus, comrade, board the train."
248 The naive have faith in the inherent value of things. From this standpoint, value is a property of a material thing. Supposedly, we want things because they have value in themselves. Why else would we dig up gold unless it is valuable? Subjectivism and psychological reductionism of the Austrian variety (of whichever generation: Menger, Ehrenfels, etc.) claim that things have value because we desire them and value is merely a structure of desirability; this perspective is insufficient not only because it can alternate between itself and materialism on the hinge of inherency, but also because value cannot be reduced to personal psychology and individual desires. We would have to sublate both the theory of preexisting value and subjectivism to arrive at the sociological point of view where value is a pre-existing (external) form of collective consciousness – and mere *intersubjectivity* does not suffice. Beyond the subjective and the intersubjective lies the reality of absolute subjectivity.
249 In his criticism of Durkheim's *Suicide*, Simiand flatly rejected the whole reality of the social: "'[S]cience does not need to work with "realities." He rejected what he deemed a "metaphysics of sociology," a "sociological realism'" (Besnard 2000: 101; Lukes 1973: 314.

The natural attitude is led down a blind alley in assuming that the individual is ontologically prior to the totality of society. "Society precedes the subject. That the subject mistakes itself for an antecedent of society is its necessary delusion, a mere negative statement about society" (Adorno 1973: 126).

When we look around we see only individuals going about their lives but the "interweaving" of individual lives results in the emergence of something new, a "higher" unified being. *E pluribus unum*, in other words. As Elias says, the examination of social dynamics reveals "plans and actions, the emotional and rational impulses of individual people, constantly interweaving in a friendly or hostile way.

> *This basic tissue resulting from many single plans and actions of men can give rise to changes and patterns that no individual person has planned or created. From this interdependence of people arises an order sui generis, an order more compelling and stronger than the will and reason of the individual people composing it.*
>
> [1939] 1994: 444, emphasis in the original

The *sui generis* nature of social facts (*sui generis* is a Latin phrase that translates literally as "of its own kind") means, for us, that the social whole or totality is *greater than and different than the sum of its parts*.[250] Durkheim's final word on the matter was that "above the individual there is society and that society is a system of active forces – not a nominal being, and not a creation of the mind" (EFRL: 448; cf. G: 99; SGS: 129).[251]

> Just as the offensive power of a squadron of cavalry, or the defensive power of an infantry regiment, is essentially different from the sum of the offensive or defensive powers of the individual soldiers taken separately, so

---

Many critics accused Durkheim of dabbling in "metaphysics" (Lukes 1973: 314). It is worth pointing out, with Bosanquet, that French sociology was decidedly psychological except for those who adhered closely to the guiding principles laid down by Durkheim. It is also worth noting that Simiand, while a student of Durkheim and linked to *Année Sociologique*, was also a student of Bergson, the famous vitalist, who Durkheim considered to be an irrationalist and threat to the field of sociology (Lukes 1973: 75).

250   "A people is more than a horde. A society is more, and better, than a multitude" (Comte-Sponville 2007: 15). For the Romans, *genus* and *generis* signified a "charm" (Wagenvoort [1947] 1976: 82). *Genitus* (begotten, engendered, or produced) means that a thing is "'endowed with charm.'" The "tus" in *genitus* means that its own activity raises it to the status of a *numen* (mana) or the sacred (Ibid.).

251   For a good discussion of Marx's social realism, the ontological assumption that capitalist society is a *sui generis* totality, see Lichtman (1982: 50 ff.).

the sum total of the mechanical forces exerted by isolated workers differs from the social force that is developed when many hands co-operate in the same undivided operation, such as raising a heavy weight, turning a winch or getting an obstacle out of the way. In such cases the effect of the individual labour could either not be produced at all by isolated individual labour, or it could be produced only by a great expenditure of time, or on a very dwarf-like scale. Not only do we have here an increase in he productive power of the individual, by means of co-operation, but the creation of a new productive power, which is intrinsically a collective one

    C: 443

Society "has its own characteristics that are either not found in the rest of the universe or are not found there in the same form" (EFRL: 15). In our creative and productive lives, where nature and matter are swept up in the cultural lives of humans, ontologically distinct things emerge that cannot be located in the parts that constitute them. "The house is just as material an existence as the stone, wood, etc., of which it is constructed. Yet the teleological positing gives rise to an objectivity which is completely different from that of its elements.... What is necessary for the house is the power of human thought and will, to arrange these properties materially and actually in an essentially quite new connection" (Lukács 1978c: 10–11). Bits become parts and parts are integrated into totalities that mean something totally different than the bits and pieces. What is crucial to keep in mind here, and it is something that seldom gets noticed, is that *the sui generis nature of social facts refers not to that which is observably existent but the underlying (or overarching) essence.* The underlying essence, hidden behind a veil of signs, is enduring relations or associations between individuals – the durability or enduring aspect (institutionalization) points to the quality of collective consciousness as a morally superior or supreme being, if you will, that guarantees solidarity and regulation, at least ideal-typically (Durkheim 1961: 59–61, 92). The German absolute idealists laid the groundwork for this conceiving the *relationship* between wholes and parts.

    Parts, said Hegel, "have their self-subsistence only in the reflected unity which is both this unity and also the existent manifoldness; that is to say, they have self-subsistence only *in the whole*, but at the same time, the whole is a self-subsistent other to the parts" ([1812] 1969: 515). Concerning the "parts" themselves, Hegel's formulation was even more interesting: "the parts ... are the whole relation. They are immediate, *as against* reflected, self-subsistence and do not subsist in the whole but on their own account. Further, they have this whole as their moment within themselves; it constitutes their relation, for without a whole there are no parts" ([1812] 1969: 515). The common sense assertion that "*the whole is equal to the parts and the parts to the whole*" ([1812]

1969: 515) conceals a contradictory tendency toward indifference and "self de-struction" between the separate moments of "part" and "whole" – and that the truth of the relation lies not simply in parts and wholes but the dialectical "passing over" "into the relation of *force and its expression*" ([1812] 1969: 517). "*Force* is the negative unity into which the contradiction of whole and parts has resolved itself; the truth of that first relation. The whole and the parts is the thoughtless relation which ordinary thinking first happens to think of ..." Again, "*Force* is the negative unity into which the contradiction of whole and parts has resolved itself; the truth of that first relation. The whole and the parts is the thoughtless relation which ordinary thinking first happens to think of ..." (SL: 518).[252] Where Durkheim and Marx go further, arguably, is in the specific-ity of how forces do not descend from on high or simply exist but emerge from patterns, memorized obligations, of human interaction and their institution-alizations. Adorno was critical of what he perceived of as Durkheim's hypos-tatization of society but, even here, we find that Adorno conceived of social dynamics in much the same way as Durkheim: as a "field of forces." An idea such as "field of forces" is incomprehensible outside of an "emergence" and dynamogenetic model of social relations where currents are generated and un-dergo a process of reification (S: 312).[253] Indeed, the concept of emergence that

---

252 Durkheim's insistence that sociology is really "collective psychology" and that all social facts, either fixed or fluid, are irreducible situates him in near proximity with Gestalt psychology that emerged in Germany around the same time Durkheim was active. The early pioneers of the Gestalt school were Wertheimer and Ehrenfels who concerned themselves with the ontic nature of forms: "With Ehrenfels's formulation, it was believed that the whole is *more* than the sum of its parts – the whole equals the sum of its parts *plus* another element, the Gestalt quality. But for Wertheimer, the new Gestalt theory was founded upon the position that the whole is entirely *different* from a sum of the parts, in-deed is *prior to* the parts; wholes are integrated, segregated systems that have an inherent structure of their own, and the structure of the whole in fact determines the nature of the parts" (King and Wertheimer 2005: 96–97). With all the talk of "externalities," "wholes," and "things," it would seem that Durkheim had given up on the mind but this misses the fact that, as he puts it, sociology is a "qualified idealism" (EFRL: 229) and, as such, the social mind (not the mind *per se*) is the locus of interest. Durkheim's starting point is the "external" (in the sense of the real) "but only to reach the interior" (S: 315). Dur-kheim's "qualified idealism" overlaps perfectly with Marx's mature *qualified* materialism. Mana and value are both ideal forms that have material effects. If you need help getting over the terminological hurdle of "qualified idealism" think of it as "hyper-materialism." Durkheim would agree completely with Marx and Engels that "The phantoms formed in the brains of men are also, necessarily, sublimates of their material life process, which is empirically verifiable and bound to material premises" (MECW, 5: 36). Of course, for us, mana and value are non-material realities but for the deluded worshiper or exchanger, the material things have value (EFRL: 198; ES, 1: 401). There is a world of difference be-tween realism and sociological realism.

253 Durkheim's "theory of emergent levels" was inspired by Boutroux (Clark 1973: 171).

we find with Durkheim[254] varies not at all with Marx's theory of value-bearing commodities: "The first commodity's value character emerges here through its own relation to the second commodity" (C: 141–42).

Durkheim's theory of social facts has been framed as a theory of "emergence" (Sawyer 2001, 2002; Lefebvre [1968] 2009: 130).[255]

> The concept of social emergence did not originate with Durkheim, but rather was an active current in nineteenth-century French intellectual thought. From Renouvier, Durkheim borrowed the axiom that the whole is greater than the sum of its parts; from Boutroux, the idea that each level of analysis is irreducible to the lower levels, because of the "contingency" of natural laws.... Durkheim was also influenced by an early year spent in Germany, where organicism was dominant; this experience cautioned Durkheim to avoid the metaphysical assumptions and the excessive biological analogies of organicism.... Perhaps more than any other source, Durkheim was influenced by Comte's anti-reductionism. Comte also struggled with social emergence, and is as often misunderstood on this point as is Durkheim. Durkheim's theory of emergence contains several components, including most of his key theoretical concepts.... Durkheim never used the term "emergence";[256] rather, his phrase sui generis was used in a sense synonymous with contemporary uses of the term "emergent." Following common usage in the nineteenth century, Durkheim also used the terms "synthesis" and "association" when referring to emergent systemic phenomena that resulted from nonadditive combinations of elements.
>
> SAWYER 2002: 232

An "emergent" property is the result of the synthesis of elements, the result of which, is the creation of something qualitatively different from the sum of its parts. The analogy Durkheim uses is that of bronze: "The hardness of bronze lies neither in the copper, nor in the tin, nor in the lead which have been used to form it, which are all soft or malleable bodies. The hardness arises from the mixing of them.... Let us apply this principle to sociology." Further, "If ... this synthesis sui generis, which constitutes every society, gives rise to

---

254 "Of course the elementary qualities of which the social fact consists are present in germ in individual minds. But the social fact emerges from them only when they have been transformed by association since it is only then that it appears" (S: 310).

255 For an alternate take on emergence see Bhaskar (2008: 49–50).

256 Sawyer is incorrect, e.g., see Durkheim (S: 310; 1961: 61).

new phenomena, different from those which occur in consciousness in isolation, one is forced to admit that these specific facts reside in the society itself that produces them and no in the parts – namely its members" (RSM: 39–40). Another example is provided by the musical chord. The combination of three acoustic tones (440, 523.25, and 659.26 cycles per second) results in an A minor triad, when played expertly for the enjoyment of civilized adults, can create feelings unattributable to physical vibrations. Separately, these tones mean nothing. Played simultaneously (a chord) or in a sequence (a melody), the resulting pitch relations are no longer just vibrations of air but "... living things; powerful engines ..." (Webb 1998: 13).

The power of money "emerges" from its circulation and use but is irreducible to the concepts of circulation. Likewise, society itself is not just a bunch of people added up with the sum equaling "society." A university is not just the sum total of students and buildings and diplomas are not just pieces of paper.[257] Any material object that is caught up in the web of social meanings and collective practices functions[258] as a carrier of a shared moral surplus – a diploma is a piece of paper and then some. Ask a student why they want a diploma and they will tell you that a diploma "shows" or "says" something important to the rest of the world or that it "opens doors." How can an inanimate piece of paper possess active properties that "show" and "say" anything or accomplish actions? Of course, it is not the paper (the profane carrier, prop, bearer, or envelope) that does the "work" but spirit.[259] A diploma is a symbol

---

257   Neither the mind nor consciousness are reducible to brains. The brain is profane; the mind is divine. The ultimate critique offered by zombie horror is that our rabid consumption of commodities, the chase for the *agalma* hidden at the core of the thing (Žižek) is nothing more than the futile destruction of profane matter. There is no consumption without disenchantment and dissatisfaction. And trophy logic (I have in mind the work of Dan Krier) is dependent upon a network of public display and recognition. I buy X not in order to derive enjoyment from the thing itself but for its display value and the quantification of up-votes it receives from evaluating others. I obtain the X not for X itself but for the expected nod or knowing wink offered by the other-supposed-to-know.

258   "Surplus" is a weird concept when connected to the domain of the moral. The domain of the sacred and "of religious things is partly an imaginary world ... and, for this reason, one that lends itself more readily to the free creations of the mind. Moreover, because the intellectual forces that serve in making it are intense and tumultuous, the mere task of expressing the real with the help of proper symbols is insufficient to occupy them. A surplus remains generally available that seeks to busy itself with supplementary and superfluous works of luxury ..." (EFRL: 385). But any surplus has to come, in the final analysis from a surplus or "excess of energy" (EFRL: 405) that is produced in ritual "nervous overexcitement" (EFRL: 411) or labor context (C: 293–306) where labor (L) is carried beyond what is necessary and into excess labor (L+ΔL).

259   Like the law of gravity, this power "resides neither in objective things themselves nor in the subjective mind, but in that sphere of the objective spirit which, stage by stage, is

of sacrifice, commitment, and proof that you can indulge like a maniac and still crawl to the finish line. Undeniably, the concept of "emergence" is a crucial moment in social processes.

To summarize and conclude let us briefly examine language as a "total" social fact.[260] As Piaget says, "Its rules are imposed on individuals. One generation coercively transmits it to the next ...." The rules of language are things we must submit to if we wish to communicate and even think to ourselves and language and its rules exist independently "of the decisions of individuals it is the bearer of multi-millennial traditions; and it is every man's indispensable instrument of thought" (1970: 74–5). It is impossible to overestimate the decisive social power of language because it is in language that "religion, morality, economy, aesthetics, and technology are crystallized.... They are transmitted more or less entirely in language even though this latter has a certain autonomy towards them" (Mauss 2005: 46; cf. Cohen [1950] 1970). "Language is the highest power possessed by mankind. Adam, it is said, gave to everything (animals) its name. Language is the destruction ... of the sensuous world in its immediate existence, the sublating of it into an existence which is a summons that echoes in every thinking being" (Hegel 1986: 157; cf. Nietzsche [1887] 1974: 218). Indeed, to be human is to use language; to lack it is to fall into inhumanity: "Do not imagine that man invented language. You're not sure about that, you have no proof, and you've seen no human animal become *Homo sapiens* just like that, in front of your eyes. When he is *Homo sapiens*, he already has that language" (Lacan 2008: 33; cf. Wolfe 2016: 169).[261]

Language embodies both fluid and fixed elements (some words have been around "forever" while others come and go with fads and some words are suddenly the coin of the realm while others languish in obscurity. Language is not merely a psychological fact but is an intersubjective fact (Cassirer 1955a: 117) as well as an absolute and external fact above and beyond individuals and dyadic relations. Language is invested with authority, especially the written

---

condensed into reality by our sense of truth. Once this has been accomplished by Newton with respect to the law [of gravity] ..., that law has been incorporated into the objective historical mind, and its ideal significance within that mind is now, in its turn, basically independent of its reproduction by particular individuals" (Simmel [1907] 1990: 452).

260   Total or *general* social facts are those that "involve the totality of society and its institutions ... and in other cases only a very large number of institutions" (Mauss 1990: 78). Things like gifts, contracts, languages, etc., permeate the whole of a society and embody religious, political, economic, and aesthetic dimensions (Ibid.).

261   "My teaching is in fact quite simply language, and absolutely nothing else" (Lacan 2008: 26).

(crystallized) word, which enjoys a special prestige (Saussure [1916] 1983: 25–26) in relation to vocal (fluid) utterances. We are not free to disregard language; we must use it if we are to qualify as normal members of society and, as individuals, we are not free to alter language just as we wish (Saussure [1916] 1983: 68). Finally, we cannot reduce language to just some molecules moving through the air or some marks on paper. Language is a sui generis or irreducible reality that, while only found in the minds of people, survives the transitory existence of the individual. Language seems to take on a life of its own.[262] Even the elementary units of language, single words, are themselves irreducible and powerful forces, the building blocks of our selves and character structure that transforms general social energy into its specific manifestations (Fromm 1970: 27).[263] "The word, like a god or a daemon, confronts man not as a creation of his own, but as something existent and significant in its own right, as an objective reality.... Here one can trace directly how humanity really attains its insight into objective reality only through the medium of its own activity and the progressive differentiation of that activity" (Cassirer 1946: 36–37).[264] The further we move back into the premodern world the more we find that the word is more or less synonymous with mana and authority (Leenhardt 1979: 127–44). But words, by no means all of them, still push us around. Words are not merely tools we use to our advantage. Words have the capacity to divide what is whole, merge what are separate entities, and put us under a spell.[265] Bacon says "Men believe that their reason governs words; but it is also true that words react on the understanding" (in Creighton 1925: 256). Without the word, or, really, the signifying process in general, there could be no projection and no objective powers circulating in the social sphere. "The master's word alone imparts his might" (Goethe 1976: 292).

---

262   Language constitutes an autonomous domain; language plays with itself when we try to deploy it instrumentally. Language wants to be poetic not instrumental. Writing and speaking that lacks poetry is working against language. When we attempt to convey meaning and communicate with others language plays mischief through us; we can and often are outwitted by language – we have to open ourselves up and let language playfully work through us unimpeded (Novalis 1997: 84).

263   "Words not only affect us temporarily; they change us, they socialize or unsocialize us" (Riesman, Glazer, and Denney [1950] 1953: 112).

264   "The word and the meaning that attaches to it is truly a collective reality. The slightest nuance in the total system of thought reverberates in the individual world and the shades of meaning it carries" (Mannheim 1936: 83).

265   Nietzsche attributes to language the power of division and the creation of a counter-world juxtaposed to the real – one so powerful that it feels as if "it could lift the rest of the world off its hinges and make itself master of it" (1986: 16). Of course, for Nietzsche, this is an illusion. See Antonio's discussion of this passage (1995: 12).

Social facts like language appear to have a life of their own (we cannot simply wish them away even though we are their creators)[266] but language, even though it is a *total* social fact, is itself dependent upon a larger social absolute for its existence. "Language is not only more than the sum of its parts (words and sounds and sentences) – it is by itself insufficient for full communication and understanding without knowledge of an enveloping culture" (Everett 2008: 202). Given the "weird" nature of social facts as created creators and alien powers, sociology needs an interpretive framework for comprehending the facticity that avoids reducing them to either hyper-fluid constructions or transcendental crystals that reduce subjects to powerless automatons, as structuralism can and often does. This framework cannot take the form of a theoretical model that attempts to explain how a fact is simultaneously fluid, gelatinous, or crystallized but one that lays out a procession in the career of any fact. In the next chapter I will try to construct a *sociogony* of social facts and, hopefully, what appears as a clash of interpretive angles or perspectives will be made coherent in such a way that cooperation between multiple spheres of sociological inquiry, and their eventual sublation into something that might be construed as an absolute-in-process.

------

266   Social facts, in other words, are hypostatic phenomenon (S: 312).

CHAPTER 2

The Sociogony

Perhaps the material regarding the crystallization of social facts in the preceding chapter could be partially summarized by Marx:

> In fact *collective* unity in co-operation, combination in the division of labor, the use of forces of nature and the sciences, of the products of labour, as *machinery* – all these confront the individual workers as something *alien, objective, ready-made*, existing without their intervention, and frequently even hostile to them. They all appear quite simply as the prevailing forms of the instruments of labor. As objects they are independent of the workers whom they *dominate*.
>
> C: 1054

A truer statement has never been made, however, while Marx devotes roughly 1000 pages to the development of the commodity world, those who followed in his wake, presupposing the commodity form and production for exchange, lost the aspect of the *becoming* of the commodity through the reification and compression of concepts. The product of human effort is rendered inhuman, suddenly fixed, autonomous, alien, coercive, and productive of feelings of estrangement and dehumanization (Lukács 1971: 87; C: 1054).[1] Of course, Marx himself sometimes confounds us as he does in the opening of the second chapter on the exchange process in *Capital*. "Commodities are things, and therefore lack the power to resist man. If they are unwilling, he can use force; in other words, he can take possession of them. In order that these objects may enter into relation with each other as commodities, their guardians must place themselves in relation to one another as persons whose will resides in those objects ...." (C: 178). In this chapter I will make the case that small terminological distinctions make big differences. Left unaddressed, tiny errors multiply at higher scales of synthesis and reduce theory to ideological condensations. Marxism is filled with condensations that, while appearing to be self-evidently true (e.g., the phrases "commodity production" or the "labor theory of value")

---

1 At times, radical critique becomes aware of and even playful with compressions and decompressions but in a way that does not clarify things but leads to another layer of mystification. "He is driven ... to awaken congealed life in petrified objects. Thus, Benjamin, in addressing the fetish character of objecthood under capitalism, demystifying and reenchanting, out-fetishizing the fetish" (Taussig 1993: 1).

actually impede comprehension rather than sharpen and refine thought.[2]
Conceptual distortions of these kinds are analogous to the processes found
in dream work, i.e., psychotic breaks (Freud [1900] 1965) and are at odds with
the professed goal of critical social theory.[3] The allusion to psychosis is not
polemical but points to the inevitable "death struggles" that we associate with
the psychotic imaginary where symbolic authority has failed to intervene
in the dance of dyads. To better grasp the logic of social facts it is important
to situate them within a genetic[4] process whereby they emerge, crystallize,
reign sublime, and eventually disintegrate while spawning new social facticities and countervailing energies. In other words, we need to see the *career* of
any given social fact from its origins in collective ekstasis to its termination in
derealization.[5]

Jones says that what is needed is a "dialectic of reality, conscience,
representation and thing" (2001: 134) but the seemingly odd juxtapositions of
"dialectic," "thing," and "process" has long been a point of contention within
critical theory where we are told that dialectical processes dissolve things
and structures such that these concepts are mutually exclusive (Wood 1993).

---

2   The compressions of Marxism are legion but one of the worst is the conflation of price and
    value. What we have here with the identification of price and value is precisely analogous to
    primitive sign magic; these Marxists, on the basis of their susceptibility to word magic, should
    be classified under the heading of cultists (cf. S: 129). For a hostile analysis that nonetheless
    raises some inconvenient facts for critical sociology see Kolnai (1922: 139–66). And when
    Marxists are not compressing concepts they are often splitting (alienating and fetishizing)
    them, for example, the value vs. exchange-value doubling or the classic splitting of capital
    into productive capital and finance capital (e.g., Hilferding [1910] 1981; for a critique of capital
    compartmentalization see Massing 1949 and Worrell 2008). The reason academic Marxism
    fails to live up to its potential is due to the fact that it often shares the same presuppositions
    as capitalists and that many "Marxists" are not really historical or dialectical materialists at
    all but, on the contrary, simple materialists or crypto-theologists (Worrell 2009a). There also
    exists the related problem that solidarity often necessitates intellectual suicide and personal
    corruption for the sake of continued association. This brings to mind the famous quip by
    Freud that it is better to have friends than good translations.
3   "The reform of consciousness consists *only* in making the world aware of its own conscious-
    ness, in awakening it out of its dream about itself, in *explaining* to it the meaning of its own
    actions. Our whole object can only be – as is also the case in Feuerbach's criticism of reli-
    gion – to give religious and philosophical questions the form corresponding to man who has
    become conscious of himself" (MECW, 3: 144).
4   "Genesis" is a coming-into-being, development, the movement of active and passive
    oppositions, and the passing of one contrary into another (Peters 1967: 67–71).
5   Social facts are independent and domineering but only because individuals combine their
    efforts and minds to enter into the lives of these "facts" as the active elements. Their associa-
    tion gives rise to moral currents that eventually provide authoritative guidance "once they
    are formed" (S: 39).

A well-known expression of this is contained in Fromm's assertion that structure, hierarchy, development, growth, are at odds with oppositional conflict and the production of new facts from this conflict (1970: 35). However, at the outset we should avoid the impression that what we have here is an organic model of growth as a conflict-free process of spontaneous development – perhaps the notion of a phenomenological *procession* of dialectical transformations is a preferable metaphor.[6] Hegel's *Phenomenology* represents a procession of conflict-ridden or otherwise defective ideal-typical constructs, leaping one to another, from the contradictions and dead end of sense certainty to the final apotheosis of absolute spirit that knows itself *as* spirit. Anyone who claims that Hegel's dialectical odyssey of the concept lacks structure is simply not paying attention. Critical sociology, as a distinct current within the broader field of critical social theory, must in my estimation, resolve among a good many things the impasse between dialectics and structure by demonstrating how dialectics (literally split reasoning) is itself a feature of society at odds with itself, i.e., *normal society*, that reified products of human activity emerge out of a process, that the process is driven by contradictions, and that the process and procession has a structure (even a society plagued by anomic fluidity has a structure and a "moral geometry") and, lastly, that dialectics represents not only a feature of contradictory life but also the way out of alienated life as an essential intellectual method.

In order to carry out this task we need to keep foregrounded the knowledge that social facts are always in a state of crystallization and liquidation, changing and being reconstructed at every moment. *However*, we should not fall for the lure of a constructionism that comes at things from a one-sided perspective that overesteems the interactionist and negotiated nature of social facts. There is always a reified aspect that is never subject to negotiation and without a

---

6   "Phenomenological" in the qualified Hegelian sense of an articulated procession of ideal-typical constructs or models mapping the temporal development of collective consciousness or "Spirit" as it appears to consciousness as entangled in material reality and social practices. This procession of ideal-types may emphasize discontinuity, abstract singularities, and breaks between processes and structures but they may also be welded together to form concatenated structures that reveal continuity across theoretical-sociological time and space. This kind of phenomenology is a unique stance toward history. Sociological time, compared to historical time, is free to chop things up, freeze the flow of time, and set things into motion at will (Braudel 1980: 48). Hegel's *Phenomenology of Spirit* has been seen as both fundamentally non-historical, e.g., Robert Solomon, and fundamentally historical, e.g., Lukács, (Forster 1998: 292–93). But when we frame the Hegelian method in terms of a procession of ideal-typical models developing out of one another through conflict I think we are looking at a new conception of social and historical time. Procession: "As it moves changing, a kaleidoscope divine it moves changing / before us" (Whitman [1892] 1992: 185).

grasp of this "side" of the equation we can never hope to achieve sociological objectivity. Cassano provides us a perfect opening to this problem:

> Bonilla-Silva (1999) defines race as both a social fact and a social construction. Race is a social fact, in that it presses upon the socialized subject like the invisible weight of the atmosphere.... And like any social fact, race is a social construction, collectively elaborated over time and space. That Bonilla-Silva's definition is useful has been proven in scientific practice. But even a sensitive structuralism can sometimes reify the everyday interactions that produce race as active, lived, and shifting, identities. Metaphors are important scientific tools. But beneath metaphors like "structures" are interactive, realities, dissolving and reconstituting in transformed patterns. Thus, beneath race, as a social structure, there is race-making as a dynamic process of social exchange.
> 2016: 218

Cassano is right but only partially. How a thing can be a construct and also a structure cannot be answered by the martyrs of liquefaction. Since Cassano deploys the language of "social exchange" let us rely on Marx for the answer: in the exchange relation between two commodities what is at the center of the dynamic negotiation process is the *magnitude* of value expressed as a price (index). However, what is non-negotiable is the underlying *social substance* that the commodities have in common – that "transcendental" third *thing* that seems to live beyond the limits of the exchange *relation*.[7] Yes, value "comes and goes" in the simple value form (C: 183) but, in a developed capitalist society, value is no Daylily but *die Seele der Welt*. I know as well as the partisan pragmatists that exchange-value is, ultimately, a construct and eventually it will reveal its constructed and historically contingent nature to everybody but by that point it will be supplanted by some other unified fact. The bad news for subjectivists, pragmatists, constructionists, and even the perspectival tightrope walkers attempting to keep both structure and process in focus with alternating points of view, is that beyond the purely contingent (singular) categories, for example "white" as it functions in Alabama or Kentucky, and beyond the *particular* "principle of social organization" (Bonilla-Silva 1999: 899) that operates factually in a given society for a duration, there is, at the end of the day, another dimension, let us call it for now the really real substance

---

7 Bonilla-Silva (1999: 901) does not seem to appreciate that a social fact qua *thing* is always already a *relation*.

that grounds all human association and control: that eternal, anonymous, universal and protean energy that assumes particular forms across the millennia: mana, logos, charisma, exchange-value, *jouissance*, and, tomorrow, "– whether finally, who knows? – "[8]

$$\frac{\text{Mana} = \text{Charisma} = \text{Value}}{\text{Collective Ebullience}} \, (s)$$

This non-signified substance of all substances, the fount of the social nimbus, is evidently the fact that is forever non-negotiable.[9] Some dimensions and aspects of human association are indestructible and "destined to outlive all mythologies and all dogmas" (EFRL: 321).

Grasping the logic of a social fact must, in my estimation, draw from a wide array of sources. I am not advocating perspectivalism, rather, I want to put forward the articulation of a *sociogony* (see Gane 2006: 119; Turner 1989). This sociogony is not a heaven for all theories.[10] I think most explanations at our disposal are one-sided and do more harm than good but while Simmel is wrong on the nature of value, for example, and Marx is right, and where the pragmatists are wrong, as Durkheim says, for representing the world as a "happy go lucky" place where we just make everything up as we go, we *should want* to live in a world where the past does not weigh upon us like a nightmare and where we are free to act spontaneously but also rationally. One important but flawed attempt to map out a processional logic of the sort I am advocating is located in the work of Peter Berger with Stanley Pullberg and, more famously with Thomas Luckmann where four broad moments in the construction

---

8   Reading the introduction of Hegel's *Philosophy of History* (1956) we find the destiny of this infinite spiritual energy is to raise itself from its own ruins to the apex of systematic Reason.

9   Structuralism has an affinity with disillusioned resignation whereas constructionism and pragmatism wind up in a makeshift world of relativism and ecstatic self-dissolution. These are the twin poles of the domain of the famous *unhappy consciousness* where people cannot *reconcile* with, on the one hand, human freedom and, on the other, the durability of the absolute.

10   Hans Bakker says that "we need to find a way for ... radically different perspectives to find some common ground" (2009: 233). Why? Common ground in social theory is a dream that will never be realized; and even if it could be realized it would vanish just as quickly as it appeared. This, as well as the consensus dream, has long plagued perspectivalism that imagined one could weave together different strands to create a sui generis explanation of society.

of social reality are identified.[11] Their work is a good starting point from which we can rework the notion of "objectivation" (*Versachlichung*) in our own way.[12]

Sociogony will for now consist of eight distinct moments: (1) *LARD* or lack, assemblage, repression, and desideration as a complex we might simply refer to as *weird nature*; (2) ebullience or effervescence; (3) projection and externalization; (4) objectification and internalization; (5) estrangement and fetishistic inversion; (6) reification; (7) alienation and domination; and finally (8) desublimation and myriad possible consequences flowing from the process of derealization. The eight moments are not arbitrary but neither are they inflexible. Right away readers may intuit another way of separating things by negating every copula and expanding the chain out to nearly 15 distinct moments. Have it your way. One way to think of the sociogony is to picture a spiraling of negations, inversions, reversals, and the continuous return of spectral residues that haunt psyche.

---

11   Berger was himself extending the kind of stage thinking we find in Mary Douglas where the "intelligibility" of social facts is gradually lost over time and are no longer justifiable (see MacIntyre 1984: 112).

12   A few major problems with Berger and Luckmann, as I see it, are the limits imposed by adherence to phenomenological description, no concern with genesis and procession, no concern for social ontology, no conception of unconscious processes, the hysterical rejection of psychoanalysis and the valorization of Mead and symbolic interaction over Freudian currents (1966: 20). The Mead thing is peculiar to say the least because the whole line of thought, in the final analysis, leads into a "strange combination of pragmatism and rationalism" that "does not take into account, to any extent, the variability of social frameworks and their effective reality, or the many aspects of the Other and variations in the character of knowledge of the Other.... Mead based his ideas on sports teams and children's play groups, where the roles are effectively interchangeable..." (Gurvitch 1971: 232). Scheler's brand of "radical" phenomenological empiricism and positivism (see Schneck 1987: 33) bolted onto a transcendental metaphysics, forming much of the backdrop for Berger's phenomenological sociology, is highly problematic and, frankly, absurd. "One of my principal theses is that in every case the nature of a being ... can, in principle, be immanent to and truly inherent in knowledge and reflexive consciousness as it is outside of consciousness, and therefore not only as it is represented by some image, perception, idea [*Vorstellung*], or thought.... Existence, however, can never be immanent to consciousness. Rather, existence necessarily transcends knowledge and consciousness and is alien to them. Existence is essentially transcendent and remains independent of them ... (Scheler 1973: 289). This is where sociology goes to die. For more on this "grey dawn" of "mental entropy" in the history of the sociology of knowledge see Remmling (1967: 199–203; Gurvitch 1971: 231–33). Perhaps Scheler's own words regarding Freudian theory help explain the phenomenological horror of the unconscious (see Scheler 1973: 83). The terror of psychoanalysis for phenomenology can be traced back to a fear of castration found in Heidegger's existentialism an aesthetic "cult of the word itself" (Jaspers 1986: 510) that blocks deep inquiry; curiosity is taboo (Adorno [1964] 1973: 110).

Moments 1–4 have traditionally been the object of scrutiny for psychology, interactionism, constructionism, and pragmatism[13] (relations, intersubjectivity, etc.) whereas moments 5–7 reflect aspects of social life privileged by structuralist and power perspectives (domination, reification, dehumanization, etc.). The final moment represents a return or collapse into the purely, disillusioned, infraliminal domain. The point of a sociogony is to move beyond the usual split between interaction and structure to show how structures are merely crystallized interactions and that interactions are fluid structures.[14] This approach was perhaps nowhere better expressed than in the idea of an "interweaving" of interdependent social actors and the autonomous "figurations" that emerge from this interweaving (Elias [1939] 1994: 444). Despite the appearance of a "diachronic profile" (Turner [1969] 1995: 13) or temporal linearity, the sociogony presented here is equally synchronic and nonlinear, i.e., things can and do happen retroactively. As such, it is important to keep in mind that while "alienation" proper is situated toward the end of the procession, in actuality, alienation (in one form or another) is present from the very beginning in is decisive at every "stage" or moment along the way. Another aspect to bear in mind is that once one arrives at a limit, for example, the hyper-reified or over-crystallized condition of heteronomy or absolute inevitability and bondage, one has, already, arrived at its opposite, complete and pathological autonomy, absolute anarchy, etc., such that, in the terms of our sociogony, once we arrive at a world of monsters and magicians, for example, one has come full circle, the return to a world of fluidity, contingency, and reconstruction; but here we are a long way from the consummation of world

---

13   Carey provides a succinct, if incomplete vignette of what awaits us in these first moments: "Man, the molecule of society, is the subject of social science. In common with all other animals he must eat, drink, and sleep, but his greatest need is that of association with his fellow-men. Born the weakest and most dependent of animals, he requires the largest care in infancy and to be clothed by others, whereas to birds and beasts clothing is supplied by nature. Capable of acquiring the highest degree of knowledge, he appears in the world destitute even of that instinct which teaches the bee, the spider, the bird, and the beaver to construct their habitations, and to supply themselves with food. Dependent upon the experience of himself and others for all his knowledge, he requires language to enable him either to record the results of his own observation, or to profit by those of others; and of language there can be none without association" ([1872] 1967: 77).

14   I think it was the great jazz guitarist Howard Roberts who once, somewhere, characterized melody and harmony in the following way: scales are liquid chords whereas chords are frozen scales. They are all made from the same materials but have radically different effects and differ totally in their degrees of rationalization. As we will see later, for Max Weber, harmony is extremely rationalized in the West whereas melodies are the epitome of the irrational.

spirit and the closing of that circle in upon itself as a scientific triumph over self-concealment (Hegel [1807] 2008: 728).

It is also important to keep in mind that whether we are examining the ritual production of totems, the mass manufacturing of commodities, the veneration of some charismatic leader, or unpacking things like jouissance, prestige, or aura, we are dealing in the final analysis with some facet or another of what Marx called the "productive functions" of human beings. Marx confined himself chiefly to the critique of political economy and a theory of the commodity but, ultimately, Marx was a theorist of *poetikai technai*, human creativity and the alienated products of human creativity. I therefore dispute the notion that everything comes down in the final analysis to labor or labor derivatives. Lukács, guided by Engels, says:

> ... Marx's understanding of labour teleology already goes far beyond the attempted solutions of even such great predecessors as Aristotle and Hegel, since for Marx labour is not one of the many phenomenal forms of teleology in general, but rather the only point at which a teleological positing can be ontologically established as a real moment of material actuality.
>
>   1978c: 8

This time-honored labor fetish neglects or devalues other modalities of creation and has left Marxists, generally lacking an anthropology of religion, dumbfounded when confronting non-labor forms of alienated energy.

1   LARD (Lack, Assemblage, Repression, and Desideration, or, Weird Nature)

Human assemblage, our "first alliance" (PS: 440) occurs not only the basis of *positive* qualities ("values") relative to the rest of animal life (we *could be* portrayed as chimpanzees with tools, laughing animals, primates in pants, reasoning apes,[15] and so on) but also on the purely *negative* basis of what humans lack in relation to the rest of animal life.[16] Nobody theorizes *lack* quite like

---

15   "This ridiculous reason is what sets me in opposition to all creation" (Camus 1955: 51. "Instinct and reason, marks of two natures" (Pascal 1941: 116).

16   Not that we should diminish reason, indeed, reason is the only remedy we have to our "defective" nature (Fichte 1847: 40), however, it is not as if reason is generic, spread evenly across a given society. Durkheim (EFRL: 8–18) and Brown (1959: 273) both demonstrate that the Kantian notion of reason as an immutable schema or thing-in-itself was in error in that it absolutized something that is culturally relative and historically plastic. Neither

the French but *manque* compresses the positive and the negative at multiple scales of reality in a confusing way. According to Deleuze and Guattari, "Desire is not bolstered by needs, but rather the contrary; needs are derived from desire: they are counterproducts within the real that desire produces" (1983: 27). What we want to draw out is that while we have positive needs we also lack nothing, in a sense – our lack is a non-thing. As Dewey says, lack and desire are usually taken as signs of an "imperfection of Being" (1929: 35) but our lack is not deficiency, so to speak, but part of our species "perfection" and necessitates not merely intentionality, interaction, and transactional relations but durable association.[17] As individuals we are born incomplete and "defective" but as a species we lack nothing. One thing we want to derail at the outset is the notion that since the ego lacks it must find *completion* in an empirical other, an alter ego that will complete it or supply a critical missing component. The Cowardly Lion, for example, did not discover that he possessed courage all along nor did he borrow courage from his comrades who were seeking brains, a heart, and a way back to Kansas. Rather, the fusion of individuals in action creates a new psychical being (RSM: 129; S: 310) that is greater than and different than the sum of its parts (*sui generis*). Courage, in this particular case, is not a positive quality individuals who set out to destroy evil possess, but is something that is emergent in the context of collective problem-solving, and then retroactively conferred in the crystallized "phallus" or symbolic substitute – i.e., the failed wizard (a third point external and indifferent to the desire nexus) bestows a symbol onto a demanding lion who steps forward into society, transformed

---

is reason everything that separates us from the rest of nature. "Man distinguishes himself from the animals not only by thinking. His whole being, rather, constitutes his distinction from the animals" (Feuerbach 1986: 69). "The Aristotelian definition of man is 'rational animal.' Now, individual men vary in their gifts: some are possessed of great intellectual gifts, others not. Some guide their lives according to reason: others surrender without thought to instinct' and passing impulse. Some men do not enjoy the unhampered use of their reason, whether because they are asleep or because they are 'mentally defective.' But all animals who possess the gift of reason – whether they are actually using it or not, whether they can use it freely or are prevented by some organic defect – are men: the definition of man is fulfilled in them, and this definition remains constant, holding good for all" (Copleston 1946: 104). The sociological inadequacies of this definition are obvious: essentialism, retrojected functionalism, and so on (see Worrell 1995).

17   Our original sin, our corruption, is merely this lacking what other animals possess. "Corrupt" comes from the Latin *corruptus*, past participle of *corrumpere* and literally means *cor-* "altogether" combined with *rumpere* "to break." Where other animals are not participants in a moral domain except as innocent bystanders and hapless victims, we, the guilty, are capable of deviation from norms. Indeed, our "guilt" presses in from all sides; relaxing the "system of repression" automatically generates crime and punishments (S: 362–63, 371).

from a dandy into a subject capable of enjoying the vocation of city manager. Perhaps a better example is provided by the scarecrow, who suddenly possesses mathematical knowledge in the denouement. It was neither the case that the knowledge was in his head all along nor that he acquired said knowledge. We have the unmistakable impression that the knowledge suddenly possesses him from another dimension, speaking through what could be nothing more than an animated straw hat.[18]

We do not need to speculate about an original act of repression,[19] dwell on first causes, or create a myth about how a lack develops into a surplus. The problem is put to rest quite simply in the fact that "A part of us becomes *other* to ourselves and independent of our control, because we are dependent upon *another* who is independent of our control, and who exercises critical power over the constitution of our selves" (Lichtman 1982: 27). More specifically, ego development involves overcoming primary narcissism via an idealization or valuation of objects and others[20] as standards external to the self. In order to maintain "erotic" relations, self-repression (self-negation) is necessary.[21]

Repression is "our natural substitute for instinct" (Becker 1973: 178). As such, repression is not a matter of convenience or utility for humans, which leads no further than personal interests, mutual agreements, understandings, and moral anarchy, but is a necessity and marks a shift from the relative to the absolute (Kaye 1924: xli). To live is to live "up to" something valid (strong, binding, and providing of a universal ground for reasons) and that "something" imposes "severe" restrictions "upon the gratification of libido through objects, for, by means of its censorship, it rejects some of them as incompatible with itself" (Freud [1914] 1959: 58). Indeed, the restriction of consciousness by external and superior force is the basis of social life (S: 311). In order to rise above nature,

---

18   "He had not even thought of saying this, but it was suddenly said of itself" (Dostoyevsky 1994: 66).

19   In *Civilization and its Discontents*, Freud says that anxiety is "the cause of instinctual renunciation to begin with..." (in Lichtman 1982: 28). I think, however, it is more instructive to shift from anxiety per se to what Freud calls in the same work "'social anxiety" or a fear of loss of eros with others ([1930] 1961: 85). Humans have numerous "reasons" to cohabitate in terms of physical life and biological processes, etc., but what interests us are the emotional and psychical reasons they stick together.

20   Freud uses the term "overestimation" of the object where I use *valuation*. Estimation means literally an appraisal or valuation of an object, from the Latin *aestimatio(n)* (valuing), from *aestimare* (determine or appraise).

21   "The development of the ego consists in a departure from the primary narcissism and results in a vigorous attempt to recover it. This departure is brought about by means of the displacement of libido to an ego-ideal imposed from without, while gratification is derived from the attainment of this ideal" (Freud [1914] 1959: 57).

repressions, abnegations, and ascetic practices are necessary (EFRL: 320). "Society ... is possible only at that price" and it has been this way "since the beginning of time" (EFRL: 321; see also Solovyov 1918). This necessity of restriction and constitutive repression is keeping in line with perspectives that find compulsion behind every form of surplus: economic, religious, political, and cultural.[22] What is interesting, from the sociological standpoint, is not compulsion per se but the transformation of compulsions into valid forms of conduct – the negations of negations.

While, positively, some people are more reasonable than others and trousers and tools abound everywhere, we should not look to the positive side of things but to the negativity of human life. Negatively, all modern people without exception lack instincts, including a language instinct,[23] and, therefore, also

---

22   For instance, Scott says that "a peasantry – assuming that it has enough to meet its basic needs – will not automatically produce a surplus that elites might appropriate, but must be compelled to produce it. Under the demographic conditions of early state formation, when the means of traditional production were still plentiful and not monopolized, only through one form of another of unfree, coerced labor ... was a surplus brought into being" (2017: 152).

23   Wolfe's popular and provocative book makes a number of valid points: first, the theory of evolution has fallen into an unthinking, knee-jerk cosmogonism or "Theory of Everything" (2016: 20) in which every social question is answered, simply: "because evolution!" This is scientism (the religion of science) at its worst and most obnoxious. See Fromm (1973: 30 ff.) on the "idolatry of evolution" and how evolution can function as a substitute for gods. Secondly, any explanation of social problems, organization, norms, social facts, history, etc., that makes as its first principle the notion that humans are nothing but animals has gone off the rails because it reduces normative life to either (a) the realm of nature and is therefore plagued with mysticism or (b) negates norms and morals altogether, reducing humanity to nothing but crude matter: "Religion? You have but to observe *my dog*" (Wolfe 2016: 73). The greatest irony, here, is that atheists would be lower than dogs for not adhering to religion. Max Müller was correct when he says that "'Language is our Rubicon, and no brute will dare to cross it'" (in Wolfe 2016: 54). Alfred Wallace was also correct that something "is infinitely more important than mere natural selection" when it comes to humans – and though his intuition led him astray into spiritualism, he was correct that, metaphorically, there is a "'superior intelligence'" or "'a controlling intelligence'" or a "'power of definite character'" operating 'above' and through the individual mind (Wolfe 2016: 62–63). Wallace ran off into supernaturalism but he was on to something. "In fact, Wallace was attributing to supernatural powers something as natural as breathing to human beings, everywhere – and *only* to human beings – namely, speech, language, the Word" (Wolfe 2016: 64). An an aside, apropos the preceding statement from Wolfe, we would do well to note that it is the "miracle" of speech to singularize the universality of words (Mannheim 1982: 197). Of course, Wolfe falls short himself; language is a social fact, and the chief fact among all others, but the thing that Wallace intuited was not merely language or the word but collective consciousness, social organization, society. After fifty years of dominating (and degrading) the field of linguistics, the "language instinct" (Steven Pinker) and "Universal Grammar" (Noam Chomsky) strains appear exhausted.

lack the capacity for autonomous self-regulation.[24] It is probably the case that we trudged along for millennia with instincts like other animals but the "cultural explosion" and hearth-life we find in the Upper Paleolithic would have been impossible for a species hemmed in by instinctual inflexibilities. At some point humans got "weird" in comparison with other animals: "no Creature was more miserable than man, for that all other Creatures are content with those bounds that Nature set them, only Man endeavours to exceed them" (Erasmus [1509] 1913: 67). Contra the reductionism (intellectual and moral suicide) dominant today I think it is still imperative to cast the difference between animal and human as a "chasm."

> The intellectual life of man, his culture and history and religion and science, is different from anything else we know of in the universe. This is fact. It is as if all life evolved to a certain point, and then in ourselves turned at a right angle and simply exploded in a different direction.
> JAYNES 1990: 9

It is not possible to conceptually regress to a point of origins where we grasp the emergence of moral association *in statu nascendi* and we do not require a creation myth to account for the foundations of human association. All that is necessary is to emphasize the fact that we assemble, associate, divide, and differentiate on a fundamentally different and more abstract basis (FR: 228–29) compared to instinctual life. Some creatures form what we conventionally refer to as "societies" and are considered "social" however, humans are not merely social or even ultra social, but moral beings with spiritual values and that morality emerges from a surplus of sociality (hyper-sociality) that

---

Biolinguistics cannot replace structural and social linguistics for anyone still interested in society and history. For a non-technical overview see Ibbotson and Tomasello (2016). For an extended critique of Universal Grammar and the language instinct myth, see Evans (2014).

24   Liberal autonomy theory misses the irony of the notion of self-regulation, namely, that we are allowed to act *as if* we are autonomous so long as we make correct choices. Instincts "regress instead of extending as general life becomes more widespread, the cause lies in the greater importance of the social factor. Thus the great difference that separates man from the animals, viz., the greater development of his psychological life, comes down to this: his greater sociability" (DOL: 284). It is this negativity that impels humans toward cooperative associations and is the wellspring of our "vital forces" (RSM: 136). Animals also "do not sweat and whine about their condition, They do not lie awake in the dark and weep for their sins, They do not make me sick discussing their duty to God. Not one is dissatisfied, not one is demented with the mania of owning things. Not one kneels to another, or to his kind that lived thousands of years ago" (Whitman [1892] 1992: 45).

corresponds on the other side of the equation to a lack in the area of instincts, i.e., hypoinstinctualism. The concept of *lack* runs in multiple directions.

On the material side, "Life begins as feeling, and it moves because the primitive feeling is one of lack. Consumption of some particular in nature produces enjoyment and finally satiation" (Harris 1993: 37).[25] For Plotinus, privation or lack (*steresis*) was equated with evil but, as we can see, lack opens the way for both evil (the negative good) and good (the positive evil), neither of which are found in nature. But the natural rhythms of *kenosis* (depletion) and *anaplerosis* (refilling), are unremarkable from the sociological standpoint. Animals "most probably feel pleasurable excitement when anticipating the consummation of a need" but humans possess a more complex form of "consciousness which involve neural structures that we do *not* share with other mammals" (Solms and Turnbull 2002: 95).[26] And where animal excitation is fleeting (nutrition and reproduction) human excitement is "universal" – at least at the points where it crystallizes into institutions and durable associations (MECW, 4: 504–05). Contra garden variety Marxism, material needs and satisfactions are insufficient (yet still necessary) sociological bases for durable moral relations because there is a difference between needs (like food) and demands, which are needs "addressed to another person" (Fink 1997: 235). An economistic needs-orientation cannot explain one of the central contradictions pertaining to exploitation regardless of the regime of production and accumulation, namely, the will and stratagems of the few almost always negate the needs of the many. The logic that applies to nuts and bolts problems like use-value production is different from the logic of human demands and desires. As Fink says, the logic of human desire is unlike any other logic (1997: 26). Further, capitalism certainly cannot be explained on the basis of needs or needs-satisfaction since the system as a whole is based just as much on non-use or *uselessness-value* as it is use or use-value. Hegel clearly has the upper hand on this point by conceiving of need as basic yet secondary to desire and the plasticity of human becoming. Animals get excited, satisfy their biological needs, and their one "world of Being, the order of perceptions collapses again" (Cassirer 1946: 38). Animal equilibrium is automatic (S: 246). Bataille put the difference between humans and animals succinctly when he

---

25   From the standpoint of biology and environment, "No closed circles and no repetitive pattern exist to define the adjustments of inner and outer reality. They evolve in curves, never repeating themselves" (Giedion 1975: 720).

26   Monkeys lack a "theory of mind" in that they "cannot distinguish between their own knowledge and somebody else's .... [E]ven calls that serve a referential function may be based on mental mechanisms that differ fundamentally from those found in human speech" (Cheney and Seyfarth 2008: 244).

described the later as existing "in the world like water in water" (1989: 24).[27] And for Kojeve, "'man is a fatal disease of the animal'" (in Agamben 2004: 12).[28]

Like animals we are driven out of necessity to secure food, water, rest, and so on, (so-called "biological values") but humans, unlike other animals, do not have a "biologically fixed ... relationship to the environment .... By contrast, man's relationship to his environment is characterized by world-openness" (Berger and Luckmann 1966: 47; see also Linton 1936; Mead [1934] 1962: 19; Ortega y Gasset [1941] 1961: 204)[29] and an *artistic* bent to many formative activities (Malabou [1996] 2005: 63).[30] "To be human is to be required, by the very absence of a fixed, instinctual disposition, to create one's own nature.

---

27   "If I did not exceed nature, in a leap beyond 'the static and the given,' I would be defined by laws. But nature plays me, casting me further than herself, beyond the laws ..." (Bataille [1962] 1991: 157, italics withdrawn). "In the behavior of the most highly formed groups of anthropoid apes, in the strongest and most permanent animal herds, in the most highly developed insect societies, we do not, I claim, find general wills or the pressure of the consciousness of the ones on the consciousness of the others, communications of ideas, language, practical and aesthetic arts, groupings and religions – in a word the institutions which are the characteristic of our life in common.... When someone shows me even re-mote equivalents to institutions in animal societies I shall give way and say that sociology must consider animal societies" (Mauss 1979: 6).

28   Bataille echoes a similar feeling but overstates the universality of shame for any connec-tion between person and nature ([1976] 1991: 62–63). For example, the horror of bodily functions varies greatly between, say, Eastern European peasants and Massachusetts Puritans.

29   Recall Marx's oft-quoted passage from *Capital*: "A spider conducts operations which re-semble those of the weaver, and a bee would put many a human architect to shame by the construction of its honeycomb cells. But what distinguishes the worst architect from the best of bees is that the architect builds the cell in his mind before he constructs it in wax. At the end of every labor process, a result emerges which had already been conceived by the worker at the beginning, hence already existed ideally" (C: 284). Unlike anything found in nature, the product of the architect is, to borrow a line from Hegel, "*born of the spirit and born again*" (1975a: 2). Animals, according to Aristotle, have no share in praxis because they do not desire the way humans desire; human desire is unique (Salkever 2014: 67). And when we arrive at human desire we are in essence dealing with human self-consciousness (Warminski 1998: 177).

30   "Biology reverts to the mean; civilization does not. The mind is a fabulator. It is designed (by natural selection, if you like) to dream up ideas and experiences *away from* the mean. Its overriding instinct is to be counter-instinctual; otherwise, we could put consciousness to sleep at an early age. The mind has no steady state; it is (as Wallace Stevens said) never satisfied. And it induces the organism to go to fantastic lengths to develop capacities that have no biological necessity. The more defiant something is of the instinctive, the typical, and the sufficient, the more highly it is prized. This is why we have the 'Guinness Book of World Records,' the Gautama Buddha, and the Museum of Modern Art. They represent the repudiation of the norm" (Menand 2002: n.p.).

But we are not predetermined by that requirement to realize ourselves or even to strive in any predefined direction" (Lichtman 1982: 61). But there are "requirements" nonetheless. In other words, it is *necessary* that we *seek* – that is the literal meaning of requirement. And what is required is not falling into animality. We are animals, that is true, but that is not all – when we live at all we live for ideals (Santayana 1913: 6). Humans may develop in any number of concrete ways but, in the final analysis, it comes down to working their way "up" to sociability and living up to common ideals, descent into monstrosity, or regression to defective brutality.

In any event, anything we possess that falls under the heading of drives and impulses, etc., are inextricably connected with and mediated by meanings, culture complex, the unconscious, and the form of society (S: 62). "Animals live in peace[31] with themselves and their surroundings, but in the spiritual nature of man duality and inner conflict burgeon, and in their contradiction he is tossed about" by "strife" and "longing" in the "battle" between the individual against others (Hegel 1975a: 97). The road to understanding human societies does not run through biology or human nature.[32] "By resetting in sociology the social concepts that biology has devised for its own needs, one exposes oneself, therefore, to committing grave contradiction" (Sorel 1950: 252).

In the first half of the 20th Century it was still a common presupposition that humans were instinctual creatures determined by nature. William James was famous for stating that not only did humans have instincts but, in contrast to Darwin, that they had even *more* instincts than other animals (Kuo 1921: 645).[33] In the field of sociology around the same time, Bogardus provides us with a sterling example:

---

31   Animals also do not have a conception of time (EFRL: 10) nor looming mortality. Hegel says that in comparison to humans, animals live in relative comfort (PR: 229).

32   "[P]erhaps a natural residue would have to be conceded; one should not be puritanical about this" (Adorno, in Adorno and Becker 1983: 104). "The heart of Marx's contribution to our understanding of human nature lies in his conviction that *we are neither wholly formed nor wholly unformed at birth*. We form ourselves in the process of social-historical production. We are simultaneously the impediments that prevent our self-realization, and beings capable of transcending these limitations" (Lichtman 1982: 61). I have no doubt this is Lichtman's conviction (and one that many of us share) – and the Western "spin" on Marx supports this reading – yet, I have my doubts about Marx's actual philosophical anthropology. Post-capitalist utopia would either be "pragmatic" or "instinctual" and either would be troublesome from the standpoint of rational society.

33   In *The Descent of Man*, Darwin speculates that the human being "perhaps, has somewhat fewer instincts than those possessed by the animals which come next to him in the series" (1897: 66).

Even the psychic equipment of man can be traced in its origins to the primates with their individual and social instincts. The instinctive bases of human conduct are hundreds of thousands of years old. They are so intrinsically a part of human nature that no discussion of current social problems will neglect the imperiousness of the ancient instinct heritage of the human race.[34]

1922: 302

A weaker version of this instinctivism can be found a decade later with White-head who portrays humanity as an intensely plastic form of nature but still bogged down with instincts ([1933] 1955: 85; also Malinowski 1955: 196—98, 206). There may still be a few holdouts and unfortunate regressions from time to time (biological psychoanalysis, Bell Curves, biocriminology, and so on) but credible sociologists more or less agree with the likes of Montesquieu, de Maistre, and Herder that humans are free to deviate from their nature (see also Becker 1973: 177; Durkheim 1960: 44; Fromm 1941: 34; Fromm 1968: 46).[35] As the heterodox Marxist Pannekoek says "The world for man is society" (1937: Part I, n.p.). Within the orthodox Marxist tradition, on the other hand, there still exists some ambiguity on the matter because "At a deeper level, the theory

---

34   Here we see a reflection of the standard bourgeois liberal notion that humans are natu-
      rally egoistic and rapacious toward their fellow human beings (see Collins 1982: 115—16).
      The debate over instincts was vigorous in the 1920s. For a miniature glimpse see McDou-
      gall (1924) but by all means read Hollingworth's review of McDougall's *Outline of Psychol-
      ogy* where portions of it are described as a "new demonology" (1923: 680). By the 30s,
      rival behaviorism would move psychology away from instinct theory and into another box
      canyon.

35   Montesquieu "ascribes to human societies some sort of ability to deviate from their own
      nature. To his mind, men do not observe the natural laws inherent in their makeup with
      the same necessity as inanimate things, and can at times shake off their yoke" (Durkheim
      1960: 44). Even if one could make the case for individual instincts one would have greater
      difficulty defending a *social* instinct. "Man is not an ant, conveniently equipped with an
      inborn pattern of social instincts. On the contrary, he seems to be stubbornly endowed
      with a fiercely self-centered nature. If his relatively weak physique forces him to seek
      cooperation, his untamed inner drives constantly threaten to disrupt his social working
      partnerships" (Heilbroner 1972: 16). All of this (the necessity of external control for hu-
      mans because they are deprived of instincts) may well be a "philosophical commonplace"
      (Gabriel and Žižek 2009: 98) but this also does not make it not true. And holding out for
      an epoch of mass self-limitation (mass autonomy) is ludicrous. Reflecting the identity of
      autonomy and heteronomy, naturalism can be used to absolve humanity of responsibility
      for the development of "moral superstructures." "Some look to it for permission to be vir-
      tually anything, since man is nothing but an effect of nature and since, driven by external
      causes, he cannot claim responsibility or impose it on himself" (Merleau-Ponty 1973: 72).
      My anomie is my fate!

of alienation expresses a concept of human nature" (Collins 1982: 117).[36] Marx does say in the *Critique* that the evolution of the value forms to the universal form proceeds *instinctively*.

> Da das Geld nicht Produkt der Reflexion oder der Verabredung ist, sondern instinktartig im Austauschprozeß gebildet wird, haben sehr verschiedene, mehr oder minder unpassende Waren abwechselnd die Funktion des Geldes verrichtet (1859: 35).
>
> Since money is not a product of [subjective] reflection or [intersubjective] agreement, but is formed instinctively in the exchange process, very different, more or less incongruous goods have alternately performed the function of money (my translation).

The standard translation by Ryazanskaya turns "formed instinctively" into "spontaneously" (CPE: 49). This is quite a pirouette to say the least.[37]

Being generous, we might see that in the *Critique* Marx probably meant something like "unconsciously" or "non-reflexively" rather than *instinctively* (cf. C: 421). Still, we cannot be certain and it seems to me that instinct plays a considerable role in Marx's theory of modernity, both positively and negatively. In *Capital*, we find animal-like forms of instinctive labor being "cast off" by humans who are forced to sell labor power as a commodity (C: 283). In the original German text, however, we do not find workers casting off their instincts but, rather, being *stripped* of them by the superior power of the employer class – a kind of negative yoga in reverse (Freud [1930] 1961: 28–29).[38]

---

36   "The incorporation of the theory of alienation into Marxism is highly controversial. One problem encountered by Marxists who endorse this concept is that any such fixed notion of human nature appears to run contrary to the principles of historical materialism. If man's consciousness depends in the end upon the material circumstances of life, then there seems no scope for positing some eternal attributes of mankind such as selfishness, altruism or a capacity for love" (Collins 1982: 118).

37   The only way this translation can be justified is if one treats "spontaneous" in the ancient Greek sense of *automaton* where we find action in the absence of any deliberation, in contrast to *proairesis* where we have at least some rational deliberation (see Peters 1967: 199). This interpretation would be a stretch, however, and not without some obvious predicaments.

38   "Er entwickelt die in ihr schlummernden Potenzen und unterwirft das Spiel ihrer Kräfte seiner eignen Botmäßigkeit. Wir haben es hier nicht mit den ersten tierartig instinktmäßigen Formen der Arbeit zu tun. Dem Zustand, worin der Arbeiter als Verkäufer seiner eignen Arbeitskraft auf dem Warenmarkt auftritt, ist in urzeitlichen Hintergrund der Zustand entrückt, worin die menschliche Arbeit ihre erste instinktartige Form noch nicht abgestreift hatte. Wir unterstellen die Arbeit in einer Form, worin sie dem Menschen ausschließlich angehört" (1867: n.p.).

Interestingly, if workers have been deprived of their instincts, the bourgeoisie, free from subjection to another class, continue to act instinctively (C: 789, 438). Earlier, we find in the "Paris Manuscripts" alienation qua estrangement entails alienation or forcible separation *from* something essential such as our species-being, general human nature,[39] and our natural drive toward creativity. And this drive, when left to itself, is spontaneous and unregulated (C: 934).[40] Under the capitalist regime of accumulation "man's species nature is estranged from him means that one man is estranged from the other, as each of them is from man's essential nature" (PM: 114).[41] And when we find workers engaged in nearly "instinctive" labor, as in blacksmithing, which is almost a "human art," the labor is deemed "unobjectionable" by Marx (C: 366). Moreover, the development of the labor movement grows "instinctively out of the relations of production themselves ..." (C: 415). It is here, with relations, that Marx's theory of human essence and instinct converge. In the "Theses on Feuerbach" Marx says that his teacher "resolves the religious essence into the human essence. But the human essence is no abstraction inherent in each single individual. In its reality it is the ensemble of the social relations" (Marx, in Marx and Engels 1972: 109). If capitalism dissolves the relations between workers and reduces society to a field of dispersed and combative egos, "human essence" is likewise dissolved and with it the capacity for self-regulation. The main point is that even if humans are somehow inherently instinctual beings, capitalism, where it makes contact with society, deprives humanity of instincts while also not lifting individuals above animal existence.[42] As such, whether Marx believes

---

39   "Marx proposed a concept of 'human nature in general' as distinct from 'human nature as modified in each historical epoch'" (Fromm 1973: 259).

40   This unregulated and spontaneous life could only be made possible, presumably, if workers liberated themselves from their fanatical and self-destructive masters, and returned to an instinctive and free life. Sociology, of course, would condemn this desire for instinctually-governed "autonomy" as not only utopian fantasy but logically incoherent. This kind of autonomy is already a form of deterministic heteronomy. If capitalism was the negation of spontaneous life, the negation of the negation (communism) would restore humanity not to animal-like instincts but some higher form of instinctual freedom and innate cooperativeness. One has to admire the optimism.

41   From Marx's teacher: "Only in human life, however, indeed only in abnormal and unfortunate cases, is being separated from essence; only here does it happen that a person's essence is not where his being is" (Feuerbach 1986: 42). One can assume that being a proletariat or slave counts as one of these "unfortunate cases."

42   According to Engels, it is only after the communist revolution, when the means of production are socialized, will humanity be "finally marked off from the rest of the animal kingdom" and ascend "from the kingdom of necessity to the kingdom of freedom" in Lichtman 1982: 33–34, italics removed).

in instincts or not,[43] the practical results from the standpoint of a critique of the commodity and the capitalist system of production for exchange, are the same. However, if Marx's theory of the commodity is immune from allegations of instinct theory, at least as far as the working class is concerned, the same cannot be said for the theory of communist association. After the Revolution and the unfortunate but necessary phase whereby society is reduced to a labor camp (Sayers 2011: 119) communist utopia would consist of a web of optional interactions backgrounded by hyper-automated industrial production. Due to the elimination of bourgeois repression individuals would return to their natural (profane) state and conflict would subside.[44] If Marx believed that humans could reclaim their "human nature" distorted or suppressed by the monstrous appetites of the bourgeoisie, it would go a long ways in explaining his model of communist association as a world sans exploitation and repression.

Herf says "The idea of a dialectic of progress, of advances in society taking place through repression of individuals, has been a central theme in modern social theory evident in Hegel, Marx, Durkheim, Weber, and Freud" (1984: 33). They each have good reason to focus on the repression thematic. Our existence as cultural beings presupposes repression (Malinowski 1955: 164). In the absence of repression we would not cease to be a contradiction but would multiply contradictions in another direction. "We hold to the profane world with every fiber of our flesh. Our sensuous nature attaches us to it; our [physical] life depends upon it" (EFRL: 317). But social life depends on real violence against our urge to return to nature and this is why systems of repression are practically universal features of social life (RSM: 32).[45] This amounts to nothing less than a "death drive" if we view the individual's uninhibited collapse into the realm of the profane, if generalized, as the death of society, and, by extension

---

43   Sometimes we get the sense that perhaps Marx has not made up his mind. In *The German Ideology* he and Engels say that consciousness "takes the place of instinct" and, alternately, that "his instinct is a conscious one" (MECW, 5: 44; cf. Bergson 1920: 34).

44   Lord Shaftesbury expresses a way of looking at human nature that seems to fit, in my estimation, with Marx's view: "Sense of right and wrong therefore being as natural to us as natural affection itself, and being a first principle in our constitution and make, there is no speculative opinion, persuasion, or belief, which is capable immediately or directly to exclude or destroy it. That which is of original and pure nature, nothing beside contrary habit and custom (a second nature) is able to displace" (Ashley-Cooper 1904: 48).

45   Cf. Everett (2008) for an example of a society virtually devoid of repression and coercion. However, one is reminded of Weber's claim that historical Calvinism, with its doctrine of predestination, would be for us today "the most absolutely unbearable form of ecclesiastical control of the individual which could possibly exist" (PESC: 5). I dare say, aside from a few recovering hyperarchists, the extreme form of "libertarianism" exhibited by the Pirahã indians would be, for us today, incomprehensible and unbearable.

the death of individuality which is predicated on collective existence. But to rise above the threshold of the profane also entails a kind of self-destruction or system of sacrifice. As Hegel says, "Whatever is confined within the limits of a natural life cannot by its own efforts go beyond its immediate existence; but it is driven beyond it by something else, and this uprooting entails its death" (PS: 51). If you want your share of mana you will have to really abuse yourself with gusto. Whatever the case may be for the young Marx and for Marxism, for the mature Marx (Durkheim vigorously concurs) the human being may be an animal[46] but of a nonetheless special kind: a *Zoon politikon* or "social animal ... that can be individualised only within society" (CPE: 189).

Apart from the defense of instinct theory and the corresponding justification for repressive law to counteract an inborn human nature, there really is no "human nature" *per se*, just as there is no such thing as "Man" in the abstract (Sorel 1950: 256). If a theory of "human nature" is possible it cannot stand as a presupposition guiding research but a theory that emerges at the end (Alpert 1939:144) but I think it would never provide anything definitive other than our nature is to be unnatural as far as it means being social. Unlike ordinary animals "*it is the nature of man to become artificial*" (Hocking 1926: 148).[47] Subtract our language, arts, morality, in other words, subtract our artifice, and we collapse into "animality" (EFRL: 351). But even if we lose our status as makers of culture we are still worse off than the other animals in our negative freedom (Everett 2016).[48] Our infinite freedom from instincts is our "bottomless abyss"

---

46   The realization that we are, after all, "large mammals, made in accordance with genetic instructions about which we can do nothing" can lead to a fatalistic outlook" (Blackburn 2001: 44). Although, it is no longer clear that we can "do nothing" about our biological "instructions."

47   Animals produce but only in a one-sided way to satisfy needs of individuals and immediate offspring whereas humans produce universally (PM: 113).

48   "In Schelling, the ultimate figure of Evil is not Spirit as opposed to Nature, but Spirit directly materialized in Nature as un-natural, as a monstrous distortion of natural order, from evil spirits and vampires to monstrous products of technological manipulations (clones, etc.). Nature in itself is Good, in it, the evil ground is by definition always subordinated to the Good: 'at each stage of nature prior to the appearance of man the ground is subordinated to existence; in other words, the self-will of the particular is necessarily subordinated to the universal will of the whole. Hence, the self-will of each individual animal is necessarily subordinated to the will of the species, which contributes to the harmony of the whole of nature.' When, with the emergence of man, the ground of existence is allowed to operate on its own, egotistically asserting itself, this does not only mean that it asserts itself against divine love, the harmony of the whole, the universal (non-egotistic) will – it means that it asserts itself in the very form of its opposite: the horror of man is that, in it, Evil becomes radical: no longer simple egotistic evil, but Evil masked

that is only avoided by the restraints provided by society (S: 247). If it were true that society and human beings were purely determined by the laws of nature why would we be inclined to *discover* them when we could not depart from them in the first place? (Lukács 1978a: 5). Furthermore, instincts provide a poor explanation for the emergence of sociality or human institutions. "Instincts do not as a rule provide the objects that satisfy them. Hunger seeks food, fear seeks a place of safety; but they expect to find these objects, not to make them. It is therefore an anomaly in the theory of instinct that sociability should be credited with producing the group which satisfies it" (Hocking 1926: 269).[49]

Still, it appears that individuals and groups have some kind of "instinct" for reproducing, conflict, self-preservation, and so on. However, we are better off thinking of these as "organic drives" (Fromm 1973: 5)[50] in conjunction with temperament or basic tilt, anthropological constants,[51] and a bundle of reflexes.[52] Most importantly, however, and the thing that probably leads to

---

(appearing) as universality, as is exemplarily the case in political totalitarianism, in which a particular political agent presents itself as the direct embodiment of the universal Will and Freedom of humanity" (Žižek 2012: 12).

49   Following the trends of the day, Hocking does leave space for a "social instinct" but his concept is linked not to instincts *per se* but desire and the desire for desire (1926: 269).

50   The phrase "organic drives" is a compound of the biological and the social. Following Freud, Lacan indicates that 'drives' are representations or symbolizations of what goes on in the Real of the body. There exists a Lacanian matheme for drives whereby the barred or alienated subject stands in relation to the Other's demand (see Fink 1995: 72–74). When reading Freud we are bombarded with the word "instinct." However, the German *Trieb* should be translated as "drive" or "impulse' – not "instinct." Freud used *Instinkt* when referring "to the inborn instincts of animals – and he shunned it when he was speaking of human beings" (Bettelheim 1982: 104). When pursuing food, sex, or ambition, etc., humans are force-propelled beings and these forces are drives but not instincts of the kind possessed (possessing) animals (Ibid.).

51   "Modern man is not a total innovation or a mutation of the species. Thus he shares with any version of archaic man known to us both his intrinsic sociality and the reciprocal process with society through which his various identities are formed, maintained and changed. All the same, within the parameters set by his fundamental constitution, man has considerable leeway in constructing, dismantling and reassembling the worlds in which he lives" (Berger, Berger, and Kellner 1973: 91).

52   Basically, every objection in favor of human instincts runs into glaring contradictions that disprove human instincts. The current fad of degrading humanity to nothing special, nothing really different than any other animal life, is also misguided. We are told of other animals using tools and so forth but tool-use is far less spectacular than the development of technology. Do not mistake me for a beast "reasoning about beasts" (Voltaire 1962: 114). "True dignity does not blush for nature, but only for brute nature" (Schiller, in Adorno [1964] 1973: 165). We do not enhance the "majesty' of nature by degrading our species. Truth be told, as far as we know, humanity represents the first instance of

confused notions such as "social instinct" is the existence of the "character structure" of the socialized individual. Character is a part of the self that functions as the synthetic nucleus fusing the biological, psychological, and social aspects of the self as a durable and relatively fixed set of dispositions. Character is not nature but *second* nature (Fromm 1973: 227). Social character is the key to understanding all those social facts like gender and ethnicity, etc., where individual choice and determinism break down. As we will see in volume two, when it comes to social facts, things could always be otherwise in the domain of qualitative individuality but simultaneously predetermined in the kingdom of quantification. Debates that turn on the belief in being born a certain way or that everything comes down to personal choice are trapped in an intellectual cul de sac.[53]

One approach to character would be to run through the works of Freud, Reich, Horney, *inter alios*, and parse out the various forms and types relevant for grasping pathologies and perversions in the modern world – in the volume on suicides we will examine sadomasochism in particular – but this would take us too far afield and probably not yield the results we want. If character is truly fate[54] the transformation of the living toward potency and enjoyment would be insoluble. Character leads our discussion toward to the energetic underpinnings of society.

The concept of social character is based on the consideration that each form of society (or social class) needs to use human energy in the specific

---

nature becoming self aware in the form of a particular species in a remote corner of an out-of-the-way galaxy.

53   Capitalist society, especially, is plagued by a choice fetish – everything comes down to personal choices from the brand of peanut butter choosy mothers choose to choose all the way out to the conservative fantasy of choosing sexual orientation. "This belief in ... choice arouses hatred, thirst for revenge, spite, the whole deterioration of [the] imagination" (Nietzsche 2015: 27). Once a person has become the object of hatred they are likely to turn away from attempting to reason sociologically with the aggrieved and make recourse to non-social determinism. Of course, this is a risky move (countering psychological reductionism and liberal autonomy with biology and fate) because, as the Nazis and eugenicists demonstrated, once deviance is linked to fate the gates are open to mass extermination. Without a theory of social facts and counterfactuals we are doomed to oscillations of this sort. Only sociology can explain how a group is not born a certain way while also not choosing how they act, think, or feel. We do not choose our desires nor are we free when we act on the basis of desires (Singer 1983: 39).

54   What Heraclitus (2001) literally meant was that an ethos (character) is a person's daimon (Peters 1967: 66). A daimon is an ambiguous and divine entity associated with a person. The central issue for Greek philosophers when it came to daimonion was whether the daimon was inherited at birth, leading to a fatalism, or whether a person chose their daimon.

manner necessary for the functioning of that particular society.... *This process of transforming general psychic energy into specific psychological energy is mediated by the social character....* The means by which social character is formed are essentially cultural. Through the agency of the parents, society transmits to the young its values, prescriptions, commands, etc.

FROMM 1973: 253

Basically, society creates people that are generally either life-affirming and productive (biophiles) or life-negating and destructive (necrophiles). Few individuals represent typological purities, however, with almost everyone exhibiting a syndrome of passions in which the striving for life and the striving for destruction form contradictory alloyed structures (Fromm 1973: 253–54). Most people we consider normal exhibit mildly neurotic symptoms whereas those falling outside the norm, if we neglect perverts for the time being, are neurotics that cannot fully enjoy their fantasies or are psychotics that cannot enjoy reality (MacCabe 2002: xvi) and, rather than being engrossed in a life project, move around imitating others (Fink 1997: 89).

Apart from psychotics and parrots, imitation is not a sociologically relevant explanation; indeed, real imitators do not actually *do* anything (Murakami 1991: 60). Darwin states confidently that "The principle of *Imitation* is strong in man, and especially, as I have myself observed, with savages" (1897: 72). Unless "savages" are psychotics it is not imitation that makes them do what they do. "To tell the truth, imitation of itself cannot even explain anything, for it supposes something other than itself" (DOL: 311; see also ES: 23–24; Fedden 1938: 302; Mauss [1920/1950] 2006: 45; Mead [1934] 1962: 52, 59; Mumford 1973: 418).⁵⁵

---

55   Imitation is unproductive (Kant 1929: 656). The "mere 'imitation' of the actions of others ... will not be considered a case of specifically social action if it is purely reactive so that there is no meaningful orientation to the actor imitated.... The mere fact that a person is found to employ some apparently useful procedure which he learned from someone else does not ... constitute ... social action" (ES: 23–24). At aggregate levels of institutional life, imitation of preceding forms is pointless: "imitation has never produced much good and often bred much sorrow; how absurd the idea is then of borrowing from some dead and gone social structure, a suitable means of controlling a system of production, whose principal characteristic is that every day it must become more and more opposed to a preceding economic system" (Sorel 1950: 248). "Imitation has little place in music or in architecture, nor in a large part of contemporary painting or sculpture" (Comte-Sponville 2004: 100). Even where we find what might be called 'imitation' it is only a means and never the end itself (Ibid: 101).

Imitation may be suicidal (Emerson 1950: 146) but suicide is not explained by recourse to the concept of imitation. Parrots, for example, imitate[56] but people, when they "mimic" others, are engaged in a process of *prestigious emulation* rather than some kind of mindless imitation (S: 125–28) and, as such, mimesis cannot be considered apart from its relation to prestige (Horkheimer and Adorno [1944] 1972). When Wittgenstein's disciples, for example, copied his mannerisms they did so not because crying "*Ja!*" with a hand over their foreheads[57] is inherently charismatic but because they had a *reason* to do so;[58] the "cult totem" (Wittgenstein, a figure of collective adulation) was invested with that gift (Edmonds and Eidinow 2001: 32–33).[59] Human mimesis, unlike simple imitation, is a *creative* act (EFRL: 361–64, 391; see also Adorno 1997: 53; Caillois 2003: 98; Hocart [1936] 1970: 43–45, 48; Levi-Strauss 1963: 181; Taussig 1993: 83–86).[60] Indeed, if we were capable only of imitation we would be psychotics. "The psychotic's discourse is curiously devoid of original metaphors, specifically poetic devices through which most people are able to create new meanings. Thanks to imitation, a psychotic can learn to speak the way other people speak ... but the essential structure of language is not integrated in the same way" (Fink 1997: 90–91). Where psychotics are creative

---

56   Even the parrot that shrieks "Viva Costaguana!" is not, as Conrad would have us believe, very human at all in this respect ([1904] 1961: 56; see also Pascal 1941: 115).

57   Basically, "anything can be sacred" (EFRL: 35).

58   Human mimesis "implies reasoning: one acts like a person possessing one's confidence because his recognised superiority guarantees the propriety of his acts. One has the same reasons to follow him as to respect him" (S: 129).

59   Prestige can be inspiring but it may not be conducive to real education, as Wittgenstein himself realized, because learners are reduced to the role of "acolytes" – with Wittgenstein, his students were just "scruffier versions of Wittgenstein" (Edmonds and Eidinow 2001: 33–34).

60   We are, here, in the domain of erotic identification and moral contagion, or, what Freud calls "mental infection" as well: "The mechanism is that of identification based upon the possibility or desire of putting oneself in the same situation" as another person (Freud [1921] 1959: 49). "The mimetic creative impulse, which can experience no *impression* without at once striving for a living *expression*, and which sees in every beautiful or vast form of nature a challenge to contend with it possesses the great advantage over nature of being able to treat as a major purpose and a totality in itself what nature ... in passing sweeps along with her in pursuit of some more immediate purpose of her own" (Schiller 1966: 211). Berger provides not much beyond a layman's overview of neuroevolutionary mimesis, however, one point worth amplifying concerns mirror neurons and learning: "Mirror neurons help accelerate learning....[but] Learning may also generate mirror neurons in the first place" (2016: 35). While it is undoubtedly true that we engage in copious amounts of unconscious mimesis, made possible by our physical makeup and brain structure, and made necessary by our need for others, we are free to become consciously aware of our modes of conduct and alter them as we see fit. "By understanding why people imitate, we can also learn to be less susceptible to influence ourselves" (Berger 2016: 53).

is in neologisms lacking meaning for anyone but the psychotic and therefore "incommunicable" (Fink 1997: 95).

Far from imitative and behaving creatures we are *conductive* beings.[61] Our ways of acting are conducive to energetic bonding and the creation, conveyance, and interpretations of symbolic meanings; where there is conduct one may find that spark of solidarity whereby we are not merely pushed around by abstract forces and "magnetic" personalities but also unconsciously leading from behind (Reich 1974: 7, 12; Simmel 1950: 185; see also la Boetie [1552–53] 1975; S: 126; Hegel [1821] 1991: 120; Sartre 1976: 382).

> In the abstractions of human relations, the skin becomes a particularly important metaphier.[62] We get or stay 'in touch' with others who may be 'thick-' or 'thin-skinned' or perhaps 'touchy' in which case they have to be 'handled' carefully lest we 'rub' them the wrong way; we may have a 'feeling' for another person with whom we may have a 'touching' experience.
>
> JAYNES 1990: 50

As a species, we are conducive to energetic bonding because we do not simply have primary needs and simple secondary wants, but desire (*epithymia*); and we desire not just this or that,[63] rather, we more importantly desire Desire[64]

---

61   Just as the "instrument of labor" is a "conductor" interposed between the laborer and the "object of labor" (C: 285) the individual is a "conductor" interposed between collective consciousness and his or her particularities. On the prophet as "tool" and divine instrument see Weber (AJ: 293, 298, 299); on the ecstatic as "fool" see Weber (AJ: 101). Nothing was more 'conductive' than the great me myself, the Cosmic Walt of *Leaves of Grass* with "instant conductors all over me ..." (Whitman [1892] 1992: 43). Here, we are far from the dark pessimism of Baudrillard who conceives the "masses" as terrible conductors: "A statistical crystal ball, the masses are 'swirling with currents and flows,' in the image of matter and the natural elements.... They can be 'mesmerized,' the social envelops them, like static electricity; but most of the time, precisely, they form an earth, that is, they absorb all the electricity of the social and political and neutralize it forever. They are neither good conductors of the political, nor good conductors of the social, no good conductors of meaning in general. Everything flows through them, everything magnetises them, but diffuses throughout them without leaving a trace" (1983b: 1–2).

62   "I have coined [the] hybrid term [metaphier] simply to echo multiplication where a multiplier operates on a multiplicand" (Jaynes 1990: 49).

63   Of course, we do desire this and that in particular; desire takes many empirical forms and desires are also colored with love or hate (Greene [1951] 2004: 31) as well as love alloyed with hate.

64   "Thus, in the relationship between man and woman, for example, Desire is human only if the one desires, not the body, but the Desire of the other; if he wants 'to possess' or 'to assimilate' the Desire taken as Desire – that is to say, if he wants to be 'desired' or 'loved,'

itself – often to the point of exhaustion and sometimes to death.[65] As such, I think it is incorrect that obligations toward others, our duties, "takes precedence over desire" (Goodchild 2009: xi). To the contrary, it is our duty *to* desire, not in the abstract, but concretely in others. Without our relations we are as Erasmus put it, "no man but a playne [sic] stone" (in Leites 1985: 122).[66] What appears on the surface to be nothing more than personal, egoistic pleasure-seeking can be deceptive. As we know from Durkheim, our thoughts and desires are social; we want, in a sense, what society wants us to want. Winder says that, according to Simmel, in contrast with Marx's social realism, " ... since value cannot be said to arise from interaction, it [must] first be shown to originate in individual desire rather than social need" (Winder n.d.: 7). However, I think this might get things turned around. We do not associate because we desire to associate – desire is not identical with that initial lack or an expression of individual deficiency. We associate because we have no choice if we wish to live the life of something other than a defective and wounded animal. To sustain those relations means the development of symbolic culture and it is only in the symbolic domain that we desire and learn how to desire (Fink and Žižek make this point in many places). Desire appears in consciousness as a personal desire. "But this personalness ... is illusory: actually the 'I want' is just a personal expression of the fact that life itself 'wants' in me" (Harding 1947: 16; see DOL: 287). Beware, however, "life" is not instinctual drives, as Jungians would have us believe but rather social intercourse.[67] The necessity of association means some pain and suffering.

---

or, rather, 'recognized' in his human value, in his reality as a human individual" (Kojève [1947] 1969: 6).

65   "I want to *deceive* him enough to make him – want me ... Blanche, do you want *him*? I want to *rest*! I want to breathe quietly again! Yes – I want Mitch ... *very badly*!" (Williams 1947: 95). What is the "death drive" but the wish to be put to rest in the face of unrelenting desire? See the section on "drifters" in the suicide chapter.

66   The context for this statement was marriage. "Nothing can be said for the man content with bachelorhood. 'What is more hatefull then the man which (as though he were borne only to hymselfe) lyveth for hymselfe, seketh for hymselfe/spareth for hymselfe/doth cost to hymselfe, loveth no persone, is loved of no persone?'" (in Leites 1985: 122).

67   "No more fiendish punishment could be devised, were such a thing physically possible, than that one should be turned loose in society and remain absolutely unnoticed by all the members thereof. If no one turned round when we entered, answered when we spoke, or minded what we did, but if every person we met 'cut us dead,' and acted as if we were non-existing things, a kind of rage and impotent despair would ere long well up in us, from which the cruelest bodily tortures would be a relief; for these would make us feel that, however bad might be our plight, we had not sunk to such a depth as to be unworthy of attention at all" (James 1918: 293–4).

Secondary ego processes, absent in animals limited only to primary process-es are built on our unique "capacity to inhibit drive energies … [as] the basis of all the ego's rational, reality-constrained, and executive functions" (Solms and Turnbull 2002: 99).[68] We negate our drives and inhibit ourselves in order to cooperatively and competitively relate to others, to live, because for humans it is either desire relations with others and the enjoyment of their regulating effects or die (Williams 1947: 149).[69] The life apart is a life for monsters and the cursed:

> An individual who is aware that he is the object of sorcery is thoroughly convinced that he is doomed according to the most solemn traditions of his group. His friends and relatives share this certainty. From then on the community withdraws. Standing aloof from the accursed, it treats him not only as though he were already dead but as though he were a source of danger to the entire group. On every occasion and by every action, the social body suggests death to the unfortunate victim, who no lon-ger hopes to escape what he considers to be his ineluctable fate. Shortly thereafter, sacred rites are held to dispatch him to the realm of shadows. First brutally torn from all of his family and social ties and excluded from all functions and activities through which he experienced self-awareness,

---

68 Physical damage to the ventromedial quadrant of the frontal lobes can lead to cases where "the demands of the internal world of the drives take precedence over the constraints of external reality, and inner wishes displace outer perceptions" (Solms and Turnbull 2002: 103). Life, here, is like a dream where wishes come true. We are in the domain of psychosis where there is no longer a reality principle operating to check the free reign of the mind. In the domain of politics and ideology we often find psychotic breaks of this kind, where wishes override facts and reality. Believing is seeing, as they say. Two aspects are worth drawing out. In the case of the tightly knit group, where solidarity is well-developed, the pressure of the group imposes its wishes on that of the members who suffer very high levels of inhibition. The Big Other, in other words, makes us see what it wants us to see, but, on the other hand, where a society is falling apart, where anomie and not solidarity runs high, it is the lack of inhibition that results in the loss of reality. This undergirds the difference between monsters on the one hand and freaks on the other. In anomic, late capitalist societies, not only are we free to think whatever we want, we are encouraged to pursue our personal dreams no matter how unreasonable. The superego, collaborating with the id, demands the satisfaction of all wishes.

69 "The individual must subordinate himself to an Existence outside itself in order to find in it the source of his own stability…. The being … who loves nothing outside himself, and really lives for himself alone, is by that very fact condemned to pass his life in a miserable alternation of ignoble torpor and uncontrolled excitement" (Comte 1969: 76). The famous cases of near-instantaneous death among "savages' who accidentally consumed taboo food indicates the inability to live a physical life beyond the social in societies where hyper-individuation had not developed as in modern, egoistic civilization.

then banished by the same forces from the world of the living, the victim yields to the combined effect of intense terror, the sudden total
withdrawal of the multiple reference systems provided by the support
of the group, and, finally, to the group's decisive reversal in proclaiming
him – once a living man, with rights and obligations – dead and an object
of fear, ritual, and taboo. Physical integrity cannot withstand the dissolution of the social personality.

LEVI-STRAUSS 1963: 167–68

To live apart from others, either voluntarily or involuntarily, to try and go it
alone, would relegate us to "bipolar" oscillations between ecstatic and apathet-
ic states. Desire and inhibitions, especially the inhibitions that are produced
through language,[70] are inextricably intertwined; there is no subjectivity, intersubjectivity, or social life without voluntary[71] drive inhibition, without self-
repression, self-restraint, and self-alienation. "Desire does not lack anything;
it does not lack its object. It is, rather, the subject that is missing in desire, or
desire that lacks a fixed subject; there is no fixed subject unless there is repression" (Deleuze and Guattari 1983: 20). It is tempting to believe that something like a rational principle of reality can substitute for repression, however, what we call "reality" is actually the *leftover* that remains after repression
has submerged the vast majority of psychic material below the threshold of
consciousness – "draining the swamp!" When Deleuze and Guattari say "desire produces reality" (1983: 30) they are clearly wrong. Desire is a product of
symbolic assemblage but reality is a product of repression. To lack this aspect of psychic negation would be to stuck in a condition of, as Spinoza says,
"dreaming while awake" (2002: 18). Does this mean that we "normal" people are
doomed to being neurotics? Freud clearly believes that to be the case but what
he actually says is not that we (if I may be so bold) are neurotics *per se* but that
we are *virtual* neurotics and, this distinction is of central importance: "dreams
appear to be the only symptoms which [the normal person] is capable of forming" (Freud [1917] 1966: 568; Fink 1997: 243). "People referred to in common

---

70   "If primitive man was at first almost a neurotic victim of his own excessive image-making
      power, the invention and elaboration of language may have acted as a helpful inhibiting
      agent, which kept him from being overwhelmed. By displacing autonomous images that
      welled up from the unconscious with verbal symbols attached to conscious processes, he
      may have brought his whole life under greater control" (Mumford 1973: 417).

71   Marcuse makes the decisive point that there has to be more than merely external con-
      straint imposed on the individual; sheer coercion or simple domination is a poor founda-
      tion for human association and there has to be some basis for introjected identification
      (1955: 16).

parlance as 'normal' do not have some special structure of their own; they are generally neurotic, clinically speaking – that is, their basic mechanism is repression" (Fink 1997: 77). Generally speaking, however, people do not live in a clinic. Virtual neurosis, i.e., a normal level of repression, is from a sociological standpoint not identical with mental disease; it would be correct to think of normality as mental *unease* but if everyone is neurotic than nobody is neurotic, at least in any pathological sense.

It is neither instincts nor imitation that make us act the way we do but, in radical contrast, "sympathy constraining us not to wound the feelings of our fellows, lest we forfeit their intercourse, and on the other, to the respect we feel for collective ways of acting and thinking and the direct or indirect pressure exerted on us by this collectivity, to avoid dissension and maintain in us this sense of respect" (S: 127).[72] Freud said as much in the *Massenpsychologie*: "love alone acts as the civilizing factor in the sense that it brings a change from egoism to altruism" ([1921] 1959: 44).[73] Freudian and Durkheimian concurrence, however, is fraught with difficulties.

In *Civilization and Its Discontents* we find that humans are naturally and primarily wolves toward their fellow human beings and have to be bribed and coerced into getting along ([1930] 1961: 69). We recognize, obviously, that a society can descend into barbarism[74] and people can be reduced to what would appear to be nothing better than monsters toward their fellow human beings but there is no reason to believe that barbarism is our default condition; "men are not naturally enemies" (Rousseau [1762] 1968: 55) and we normally go to great lengths to prove that we are better than wolves and, as such, good candidates for association. It is undeniably the case that violence is an "integral part" of Western history but it is not a fact of nature that our species is necessarily fated to be aggressive toward one another (Sussman 2013: 99–105). Feuerbach was on the mark when he said that we possess an "'insatiable desire to unite with others from whom ... [we are] divided by nature'" (in Wartofsky 1977: 44). Our basic negative constitutional need for others transforms everybody

---

72   "But very few people have realized that true force lies in limitation and not in expansion, and that more strength belongs to self-denial than to self-indulgence" (Schelling [1813] 1997: 141).

73   It was Saint Paul who said "you have died to the law through the body of Christ, so that you may belong to another, to him who has been raised from the dead ..." (Romans 7: 4). Where there is agape there is no need for nomos. Liberalism expands nomos and diminishes agape; neoliberalism diminishes both agape and nomos.

74   It should be obvious, here, that preliminary inhibitions form one of the bases for later, collective abandonments of inhibitions, the explosions of collective enjoyment and the periodic descent into savagery and infantilism.

into contortionists (Diderot 1966: 120; Worrell 2016) in order to stay connected because "detached from society we become detached from life ..." (S: 212).[75] With repression and renunciation,[76] the launching point into the domain of values (Goux 1990: 53), we arrive at a quite disturbing realization: human society is in a sense the domain of the living dead, between plant and ghost as Nietzsche surmises. Plants and animals (the world of natural determinacy) are either living or dead. However, for the weird ape, the lacking, naturally nature-less desiring animal (Lefebvre 1995: 138) that must associate and collaborate to be what it is, the virtues and morality[77] that emerges from restrictions, negations, deprivations, and renunciations necessary for stable relations, are separated from deadly vices by a matter of degrees. To live in the normative sphere of a good society is to be surrounded on all sides by death – the extension of the normal by degrees, shading off into the pathological. To exist means to sacrifice partially, to die thousands of little deaths over time, for the sake of life with our regulating others.[78]

In a purely negative sense, repression marks the beginning of a splitting and doubling process of the ego (more on this later) that liberates time and energy for poiesis. Actually, here negation is doubled; as Hegel famously put it, humanity is pushed along and educates itself not merely by negation but the continuous *negation of negations*. For example, the plant is the negation of the seed but bringing the matter into the brewing or baking processes is the negation of the negation and the raising up of the natural into the spiritual domain

---

75   "Social belonging is in no case an unmixed good. Every group exerts a pressure upon its members which tends to standardize them and warp them from their own true" (Hocking 1926: 95). Once integrated into the symbolic world, every gesture and movement of the body becomes symbolically expressive (Parkin 2012: 109). "Even walking straight, which appears at first sight man's natural, anatomically innate trait, is in actual fact a result of educating the child within an established society: a child isolated from society à la Mowgli (and such cases are numerous) prefers to run on all fours, and it takes a lot of effort to break him of the habit" (Ilyenkov 1960, Chapter one).

76   Horkheimer and Adorno claim that the "history of civilization is the history of the introversion of sacrifice. In other words: the history of renunciation. Everyone who practices renunciation gives away more of his life than is given back to him: and more than the life that he vindicates" ([1944] 1972: 55).

77   We do not repress ourselves and others because we are moral beings, rather, morality emerges from repression (Reich [1933] 1972: 179). Morality "is no mere phantom of the brain" (Kant 1964: 112) but the product of collective, institutional practices.

78   To theorize is to combat monsters and, as we will see in the volume on the commodity, when the objective dimension of *particular* theoretical space of critical reason is incapable of mediating the *individual's* relation to the social *universal*, or has been abandoned altogether for commercial interests, for example, theory is in danger of being perceived as a social danger, a threat to the sacralized order.

(Lukács 1978a: 42). While self-repression and discipline may indeed be painful to one degree or another,[79] Hegel argues that the rewards, at least logically,[80] amount to at least a fair share of enjoyment for everyone who sacrifices for common ends (see also Durkheim 1961: 241).[81] Lack becomes the foundation for surplus: "'I think the reason our children are so – so fully loved by all of us, is that we never – any of us – have enough of our own'" (Gilman [1915] 1998: 60).[82] For Rousseau, the condition of the "social pact" is one where not only are all losses recovered in equivalence but a surplus of power is gained ([1762] 1968: 61). Restrictions liberate energy. The greater the repression, the more liberated energy available for mobilization; the more torture we have in the basement the more impressive our columns and ceilings (Adorno 1997: 49) and more taboo yields more power (Freud [1913] 1950: 58). The balance between too little and too much repression has to be pretty good, though. The human being, says Sartre,

> ... is revealed as a tension which results from the application of two opposing forces; and at bottom each of these two forces aims at the destruction of the human element because one tries to turn him into an angel and the other into an animal.... According to Baudelaire's conception, man is ... the clash of two opposing movements which are both centrifugal and of which one is directed upwards and the other downwards. They are movements without driving power, mere spouts – two forms of transcendence which, to borrow a distinction of Jean Wahl's, we might call *transascendance* and *transdescendance*.
>
>   1950: 38–39

The theorist par excellence of repression and energy was Freud who located "the ultimate source of the vital energy necessary to drive society in the individual's sexual instinct ('id,' 'libido,' 'Eros')."

---

79   "But terror and pain have turned us into souls. There is something struggling with us. There are moments when something enters into us. Thoughts come upon us which are not of us. We feel what we did not use to feel. We hear voices" (Capek [1923] 1961: 95).

80   And, ideologically, idealism will arise to justify "the renunciation of desire which nature and societal situations have forced upon man" (Horkheimer 1972: 23).

81   Even with Marx, we see labor power being purchased at its value. The exploitation of labor is not located solely at the point of sale (dispossession of means of subsistence) but in the extension of the workday beyond what is necessary for the reproduction of labor power. The 'genius' of the neoliberal regime of capital accumulation consists not only in the expansion of the domain of fictional value (including the ability to price free bio-data) but also the extension of consumer credit in lieu of higher wages as well as offloading wages onto the state in the form of public support.

82   Cf. Dame Eisengrein's "passion" in Mann (1951: 59–60).

All societies can obtain the energy necessary for their operation and en-
hancement only by repressing the individual's sexual instinct to rechan-
nel it from personal pleasure toward social goals. The neuroses produced
by the excessive *sexual repression* in modern society, however, render the
individual less useful to society, actually reducing the amount of instinctual energy available for social purposes.[83]

    1986: 292

The meaning of negation, here, is twofold. On the one hand there is pure,
psychoanalytic repression linked to the unconscious and, on the other, conscious and purposive sociological repression whereby "general human energy
is transformed into specific energy which can be used by the society for its own
proper functioning" (Fromm 1970: 27). In short, not only reason but also the
lack of pure biological determinism along with self-negation and association
results in the permanence of desire through symbolic expressions and crystallizations, beyond the moment of satisfaction, which means that humans are
perpetually dissatisfied and constantly on the prowl for streams and vouchers
of *jouissance*.[84] Naturally, other animals "associate" or hang together in collective life but what they do for 'reasons' of descent (progeny and gene transmission) we do for reasons of ascent (the sublime life of enjoyment).

What is "Desire" but the sublation of these features of human life? Desire is
a plus, a minus, a cut, and a tie. Where our species lacks inherent regulation,
symbolic culture and desire pick up. As Crombez puts it, "… if the subject lacks
nothing then s/he can want for nothing, but it is the initial realization of the
subject's incompleteness, translated as lack, that causes desire to spring forth
and grow alongside the lack instituting their dialectical relationship" (2016).

---

83   Something that will be of great importance in the suicide volume: repression produces a
leftover or a residue of "repressed remainders" (Žižek passim) that will return – the return
of the repressed in the form of the uncanny (Freud [1919] 1959) and possibly terrifying
thing. This return of the repressed will interest us greatly when dealing with the fanatical destruction of self and others. We can take some comfort in the idea that "A proper
comprehension of the relativity of goodness and badness, far from invalidating the objectivity of the moral ideal, will become a great stimulus that will work for the realisation of
goodness, for there ought to be nothing so bad but that it can be judicious management
be turned to good account" (Carus [1900] 1996). Monsters may devour our stars but they
can be seduced and converted (Hugo 1887: 133).

84   The first coins were minted from electrum for ritual purposes by the Lydians and Greeks
and were stamped with symbols of animals (Seaford 2004). "It has been long known that
the first markets were sacred markets, the first banks were temples, the first to issue money were priests or priest-kings" (Brown 1959: 246). See especially Desmonde (1976) on the
sacrificial-religious origins of money.

For survival we rely on a desire for *others* as a precondition for cooperation and the resulting eros and *value* of association (Radcliffe-Brown 1952: 140–41).[85] If desire were to ceases for us we would fall out of our world (Cioran 1974: 78).[86] That constitutive lack (*endeia*) impels us towards our fellow human beings and this drive is what we call *desideration*. This concept combines, from its Latin origins, the ideas of something being missing, longing and desire, and an examining gaze, with a possible connection to the Latin for star and constellation. Like the ancient mariner, we navigate on the basis of external points of reference.[87]

> *This seraph band, each waved his hand,*
> *It was a heavenly sight!*
> *They stood as signals to the land,*
> *Each one a lovely light.*
>   COLERIDGE 1798: n.p.

The "lovely light" of the other forms the basis of association; the soul in love with solitude would banish the stars.[88]

---

85 Objects "can only have a social value for an association of persons. In the simplest possible instance we have a triadic relation; Subject 1 and Subject 2 are both interested in the same way in the Object and each of the Subjects has an interest in the other ..." (Radcliffe-Brown 1952: 140). When Marx says that "The wealth of societies in which the capitalist mode of production prevails appears as an 'immense collection of commodities'" (C: 125) the emphasis should be placed on the word *appearance*, for what the commodity veils are the relations and associations obtaining between people. The "*real ground*" of the commodity and capital are the social relations (Hanzel 2014: 238) of those caught up in the systems of production, consumption, and accumulation, i.e., everybody.

86 "Everything, in the end, comes down to desire or to the absence of desire. The rest is nuance" (Cioran 1974: 108).

87 Unless you are the solitary Thoreau: "I have, as it were, my own sun and moon and stars, and a little world all to myself" ([1854] 1960:91). As a side note, Thoreau lived to the ripe old age of 44, the same, incidentally, as *der Kokovore*, August Engelhardt, the leader of the disastrous *Sonnenorden* cult that worshiped sunshine and the coconut as an imagined *Kraftfrucht*. "At the end, Engelhardt weighed just 66 pounds and became a freak show for tourists. Imprisoned by Australian soldiers during World War I, he returned to Kabakon after his release and was reportedly found dead on the beach in 1919, though ... no one knows for sure when or where he died" (Martyris 2015). In Kracht's novel based on Engelhardt's misadventure we find this pearl of wisdom: "Now, it would probably be overstating things to say that Engelhardt's psyche had drunk from the river Lethe, on whose shores it had long been resting, gazing at its own reflection, sinking into the most profound cosmic forgetfulness about why he had ever come here in the first place. The truth looks much more mundane; the farther he removes himself from the community of man, the more outlandish his behavior and relationship to it grows. He is thrown back into an atavistic mental state that expresses itself in a premonition of total loss of control ..." (2015: 137).

88 "Night! you'd please me more without these stars / which speak a language I know all too well – / I long for darkness, silence, *nothing there* ... " (Baudelaire 1993: 119).

Maybe ... life [is] ... a marvelous array of lenses. We have to look for every glimmer, every pinpoint of light in the vastness and magnify it again and again and again in our effort to truly perceive it. How can we, looking out at a space teeming with stars, call it a Void? And how can we, gazing around us, not be dazzled by the blazing aspirations of humanity?[89]

CHANCE 1992: 123

However, the light of the other needs a third link to not just an array of others but to the Other.[90] "It should be noted that without these rallying points – these stars – society, the synthesis of consciousnesses, would lack an ordering principle. The existence of superior values, exacting universal reverence, is a condition of its very life" (Bouglé [1926] 1970: 35).[91] Lacking the social absolute we chase futility. "Look at the stars! / look up at the skies! / O look at all the fire-folk sitting in the air! / The bright boroughs, the circle-citadels there!" (Hopkins 2015: 2).

After failing to extricate Gretschen from her cell, we find Faust "reclining on a lawn with flowers, weary, restless, seeking twilight sleep." The spirits seek to

Relieve the bitter conflict in his heart,
Remove the burning arrows of remorse ...

Faust must be restored to "the holy light!"

Night succeeds the twilight's glimmer,
Star is linked to holy star,
Brilliant light and faintest shimmer,
Glisten near and gleam afar,
Glisten, in the lake reflected,
Gleam above in the clear night;

---

89   "We moderns may be excused for feeling a little surprise ... by the fact that the stars twin-
      kle. It is because they are ... sorry for us" (Murray 1915: 38).
90   "Marius and Cosette were in the dark as to one another. They did not address each other,
      they did not salute each other, they did not know each other; they saw each other; and like
      stars of heaven which are separated by millions of leagues, they lived by gazing at each
      other" (Hugo 1887: 92).
91   "We said it is impossible for man to feel 'right' in any straight-forward way, and now we
      can see why. He can expand ... self-feeling not only by Agape merger but also by the other
      ontological motive Eros, the urge for more life, for exciting experience, for the develop-
      ment of the self-powers, for developing the uniqueness of the individual creature, the
      impulsion to stick out of nature and shine" (Becker 1973: 153).

> And his deep sleep is perfected
> In the full moon's splendid light.
> GOETHE [1808] 1961: 423–25

All this for the sake of coupling and association. "Association is not," said Durkheim, "a phenomenon infertile ... which consists merely in juxtaposing externally facts already given and properties already constituted.... By aggregating together, by interpenetrating, by fusing together, individuals give birth to a being, psychical if you will, but one which constitutes a psychical individuality of a new kind" (RSM: 128–9; cf. S: 126).[92]

To locate what is essentially human, says Marx, is to seek not for qualities found at the level of the isolated individual but those present within the "ensemble of ... social relations" (in Marx and Engels 1972: 109; see also Feuerbach 1986: 71).[93] To speak, to have a voice, and to give voice to one's self is to presuppose common and taken-for-granted values and the "'choral support'" provided by others (Voloshinov [1927] 2012: 170).[94] The reason association (*synkrisis*) is essential for humans is that assemblage is productive of "special effects" (S: 310)[95] or what Weber calls, in reference to the "apostolic" era, "sacred psychic states" (AJ: 292). The association of humans (the pan-agora or assembly of all) creates a "spark" and, like no other animal, we humans are eager to partake in the enjoyment of this energy.

> I sing the body electric,
> The armies of those I love engirth me and I engirth them,
> They will not let me off till I go with them, respond to them,
> And discorrupt them, and charge them full with the charge of the soul....
> I have perceiv'd that to be with those I like is enough,
> To stop in company with the rest at evening is enough,
> To be surrounded by beautiful, curious, breathing, laughing flesh is enough,

---

92 Here Durkheim is referring to "collective consciousness."

93 "All must have reference to the ensemble of the world, and the compact truth of the world..." (Whitman [1892] 1992).

94 "I hear the sound I love, the sound of the human voice, I hear all sounds running together, combined, fused or following.... I hear the chorus, it is a grand opera" (Whitman [1892] 1992: 42–3).

95 The aggregation of "a certain minimum number" of individuals negates differences, "errors," and variations among individuals and gives rise to the abstraction of the "average" individual, e.g., the "average worker" (C: 440).

To pass among them or touch any one, or rest arm ever so lightly, round
his or her neck for a moment, what is this then?
I do not ask any more delight, I swim in it as in a sea
                WHITMAN [1892] 1992: 72, 74

Assemblage has become a hot topic in the area of social ontology but the
"special effects" we are interested in are missing from the works of, e.g., Deleuze
and Latour.[96] Actor-Network-Theory (ANT) is less a coherent sociological
perspective and more a symptomatic reflection of an unhinged society "where
things are changing fast" (Latour 2005: 142). Latour's networks are "neither objective nor social" (1993: 6) and may not be worth much to the critical sociology
of institutions, or of anything relevant to sociology as it turns out (Latour 2005:
141). ANT is anomic thought for anomic times; subjects reduced to uncertain
descriptions: "uncertainty" and active skepticism are so rampant in Latour's
thought that actual comparisons and explanations are foreclosed resulting in
nothing less than an often interesting intellectual anarchy. For Latour, "society" is a polemical invention, it is not a concept and, along with the word "nature," does "not describe domains of reality" (2005: 110). For network actors, to
believe in the reality of the social is to live in a prison (2005: 114) and ANT is
supposedly the way to break out of prison. Latour concludes *Reassembling the
Social* by claiming:

> Whatever its claims to science and objectivity, critical sociology cannot
> be sociology – in the new sense that I propose – since it has no way to
> retool itself to follow through on the non-social elements. When faced
> with new situations and new objects, it risks simply repeating that they
> are woven out of the same tiny repertoire of already recognized forces:
> power, domination, exploitation, legitimization, fetishization, reifica-
> tion. Law may be socially constructed but so is religion, economics, poli-
> tics, sport, morality, art, and everything else built with the same material;
> only the name of the 'field' changes.
>
>   2005: 249

Constructionism certainly has its limits but ANT is part of a larger current that
includes within it "speculative realism" whereby humanity, society, and the

---

96   "We maintain that the social field is immediately invested by desire, that it is the his-
      torically determined product of desire, and that libido has no need of any mediation
      or sublimation ..." (Deleuze and Guattari 1983: 38). Lacking mediation and sublimation
      "libido" will simply "evaporate" or go to waste. There can be no meaningful crystalliza-
      tion of assemblage (though it may be ecstatic) without repression and projection into
      symbolized material that will function like a totem.

person is negated or devalued. For its part speculative realism is just a long suicide note written by privileged male academics wondering what the universe
would be like without them (You'll miss me when I'm gone!).⁹⁷ We have to
stand with Polanyi who says that "Any attempt rigorously to eliminate our human perspective from our picture of the world must lead to absurdity" (1962: 3).
However, Latour does make a good point about critical sociology: a small
number of concepts are overused in a compressed manner such that, like any
other ideology, "it can never fail to be right" (2005: 249). Ultimately, though,
ANT trails off into the heterogenous infinite because it lacks any unifying social "substance." The reason critical sociology clings to its little ensemble of
concepts is not merely ideological but, additionally, an intuition regarding the
consubstantiality of heterogeneous forms filling out different "fields" of social
reality.⁹⁸ The way out of the impasse is not by abandoning the search for the
absolute⁹⁹ as nothing more than superstition.

Carrying the torch for Deleuze, DeLanda wraps up his study of the human
beehive with the following: "every social entity is shown to emerge from the
interactions among entities operating at a smaller scale. The fact that the
emergent wholes react back on their components to constrain them and enable them does not result in a seamless totality. Each level of scale retains a
relative autonomy and can therefore be a legitimate unit of analysis ..." (2006:
118–19). Fair enough, but this description obscures as much as it reveals. Given
DeLanda's engagement with B-team starters, Goffman and Bourdieu, the absence of Durkheim especially, but also Marx is puzzling until we see that this
theory of assemblage is not only non-dialectical but actively *anti-dialectical*
and incompatible with the main currents of classical (rational) and critical

---

97 Semi-literate, rural, white, middle-aged males are currently killing themselves off with
    guns at historic levels (there goes the GOP base) whereas the hyper-literate, urban, white,
    middle-aged male is committing intellectual suicide at Zero Books.
98 One can see Bourdieu's consubstantial motif in his comments on symbolic capital, cha-
    risma, and power ([1980] 1990: 141). The best work on social energy can be found in Smith's
    exploration of the consubstantiality of mana, charisma, and value (1988). Mana is a hy-
    postatic and transfigured form of clan societies and its alienated operations (EFRL: 351).
    Each species of society has its own name for what is, at bottom, the same thing: surplus
    moral energy. Whether we are examining totems, dollars, or kings, etc., we are in the pres-
    ence of representations of this substance or residue of collective life. Brown made a very
    good point that concepts such as mana are are social universals that transcend locality,
    they are objective absolutes (1977: 62–3). Freud's libido theory also rested on a presup-
    posed consubstantiality (e.g., [1921] 1959: 29).
99 Speculative realism intuits an absolute substance but it is hypostatized as an alienated
    "Substance X" and misplaced by being projected into nature (Harman 2010: 120). This
    brand of voodoo realism (garnished with "magic" and "animism") is carried to an irratio-
    nal highpoint in Morton (2013).

sociology. Indeed, the term "contradiction" is not even in this lexicon along with others important ideas such as sublation, polarities, unities of opposites, etc. The Hegelian dialectic is set up as a "rival" to this theory of assemblage such that "The main difference is that in assemblage theory the fact that a whole possess [sic] synthetic or emergent properties does not preclude the possibility of analysis. In other words, unlike organic totalities,[100] the parts of an assemblage do not form a seamless whole" (2006: 4). To Hegel or not to Hegel? That is the question! First, the idea that a synthetic "Hegelian" totality is in some way seamless is nothing more than textbook stuffing. The whole point is that the sublime object or collective representation is always constitutively prevented from totalization and riddled with contradictions. All social totalities are immensely irrational and ambivalence is woven into their very fabric. Secondly, and as a result of this lack of totalization, analysis and "self-analysis" is necessary and built-in for *Geist* to move beyond deadlock. That's what the Absolute does in Hegel's speculative philosophy. A fatal flaw with the type of "assemblage theory" we have today is that things emerge but what we find are strata of entities externally related and contradictions, if they exist within some entity, can be unplugged from the current location and plugged in at new coordinates or at another scale and made to function. The resulting block functionality[101] is probably not the intended outcome of this theory but there it is. The larger problem is that the *sui generis* nature of emergent properties might (or might not) be greater than the sum of their parts, or not, but certainly not *different* than the sum of their parts (cf. C, 1: 443). Further, any theory of authority is deficient from this point of view. We find a schematic rendering of authority derived from Weber's classic ideal-types (DeLanda 2006: 68–75) but the contradictory *dynamics* needed are absent.[102] We find an emphasis on "rational-legal" processes, contracts, consensus, jurisdiction, obedience, and so on with a lack of interest in the interpenetration and contradictions of multi-form authority and, especially, the *irrationality of the rational*, a point that Weber stresses repeatedly (see also Adorno 1997: 43).

---

100   Indeed there is no organicism here – what we see is mere aggregation (see Kant 1929: 653).

101   It even conjures up a bit of Comte's functionalism: "Conflict indicates radical incompatibility only when it takes place between two elements employed in analogous functions, and when the gradual growth of the one coincides with the continuous decline of the other" (1969: 95).

102   This has been a recurring problem in objectivist structuralism. "It is not at all difficult to determine which functions are compatible and which incompatible with a given social structure. The hard question is, given a systematic ensemble of such structures, how do the modalities of their mutual connections 'induce a *dominant* function within one of the structures so connected'" (Piaget 1970: 127).

Discord and conflict are seen as aberrant rather than constitutive and, perhaps worse, the professed "social realism" of this theory falls into Realist mystifications that are fitting of Mitt Romney or Citizens United where corporations are people: "... the organization itself may be considered a goal-oriented corporate actor. As the sociologist James Coleman puts it, 'these entities, viewed from the outside, may be regarded as actors, no less than individuals are'" (2006: 70). The "special effects" and the dynamics and contradictions we are interested in are entirely missing.[103]

Emergent representations manifest in at least two directions relevant for present discussion: association or assemblage produces not only "special effects" – effervescence and sublimations such as totems and Others (RSM: 129) of various sorts at the social-transcendental scale of life – but also the metamorphosis of the person into a member of an entirely *different* mental species (S: 310).[104] We find precisely the same logic at work in the "stimulation of the 'animal spirits'" in labor gangs and industrial rivalries (C: 443). Metamorphosis falls along a continuum terminating, at its extremities, with the monstrosities (S:126) of disaggregated society (RSM: 131). If one was interested in the "monstrous" quality of the crowd or the brutalization of the labor and valorization processes[105] one must grasp the whole before explaining the parts.

2   Ebullience

In psychoanalytic terms people "get off" on interacting with other humans to produce, maintain, and enrich relations. Desideration alone is not enough

---

103   Keep in mind that all institutions, agencies, departments, and bureaus, pursue multiple goals (some public and others private) at different scales, frequently at odds or in conflict with one another.

104   "Perhaps they will teach that the tenet is wrong which says that a man is the quotient of one million divided by one million, and will introduce a new kind of arithmetic based on multiplication: on the joining of a million individuals to form a new entity which, no longer an amorphous mass, will develop a consciousness and an individuality of its own, with an 'oceanic feeling' increased a millionfold, in unlimited yet self-contained space" (Koestler [1941] 1968: 266).

105   "By turning his money into commodities which serve as the building materials for a new product, and as factors in the labour process, by incorporating living labour into their lifeless objectivity, the capitalist simultaneously transforms value, i.e. past labour in its objectified and lifeless form, into capital, value which can perform its own valorization process, an animated monster which begins to 'work,' 'as if its body were by loved possessed'" (C: 302). "Over the fields of the West those crawling monsters, The human-divine inventions, the labor-saving implements; Beholdest moving in every direction imbued as with life the revolving hay-rakes" (Whitman [1892] 1992: 271).

to produce an enduring moral surplus – beyond assemblage and the level of excitation capable of rising up from the "rubbing of elbows" there has to be something more extreme (e.g., ascetic renunciations, rites, etc.) if we want to generate large currents that can account for conduct and the processes of conduction that gives rise to and "nourishes social forces" (Hubert and Mauss 1964: 102). At bottom, humans are excessive, both in the real and the ideal. The young Marx thought that the ideal was merely a spontaneous reflex spun out of the confrontation between natural forces, material production, and productive relations – ideological, rationalized, etc.[106] Durkheim gives us a related but different way of seeing how the excesses of the ideal are equally as important and exist for no other reason than perpetual excitement, novelty, and self-augmentation.[107] Just as the body enjoys pleasures, the social mind, for no other reason than self-enjoyment, also pleasures itself with new constructions and ensembles (EFRL: 385). Unlike other animals we over do it when it comes to our activities. I have never witnessed an industrious squirrel gathering nuts at midnight in an attempt to corner the acorn market. At dusk the birds retire and will not return to my feeder until dawn. Not so with humans; we have no internal limitations that prevent hyper-praxis. We are excessive at work, play, worship, and argument. We produce surpluses of the real and with each new creation arises new significations, images, references, mobility and the contagious diffusion of thought (EFRL: 327). With each new signification arises new contradictions, subtleties, and fine-grained distinctions. New ideas engender more ideas that may or may not bear directly on the real of their

---

106   In *The German Ideology* Marx and Engels adopt a quais-naturist explanation for the rise of consciousness where animal-like minds are overawed by the "unassailable" forces encountered in the environment (1970: 51). Ultimately, with Marx and Engels we get the sense that consciousness can fool itself in thinking that it enjoys autonomy over the material conditions and relations of life, and that impersonal mind can 'take off' on its own, so to speak, but this flight of Spirit is either a distorted reflection, pure illusion, or, if not merely illusionary and ideological, it is nonetheless "quite immaterial what consciousness starts to do on its own: out of all such muck we get only the one inference that these three moments, the forces of production, the state of society, and consciousness, can and must come into contradiction with one another ..." (Ibid: 52). So, even if consciousness does something on its own, it is trivial. "'The same spirit that builds philosophical systems in the brain of the philosopher,' Marx writes, 'builds railways with the hands of the workman'" (in Eagleton 2016: 93).
107   Having endured the tumult of the "Dreyfus Affair" Durkheim would well-appreciate the idea that "antisemitism has an autonomy, a being distinct from its declared object of hostility, and serves many functions which are unrelated to the actual presence of Jews or Jewish communities" (Wilson 1982: xiv). Durkheim downplayed antisemitism as a "superficial symptom" of capitalist anomie and "social malaise" (Ibid: 635) but his reaction to it suggests that he considered it more than a mere superficiality.

origins.[108] And the more we produce in the real the greater the chasm of the pseudo-noumenal realm, the Real. Some images are direct reflections; some are duplicates; some are echoes; and some are rumors. Ideas take on a life of their own and determine the volume and contours of the real. In order for us to live, the real needs this supplement that keeps us suspended between life and death.[109]

Under the right conditions, two or more people in association will produce some emergent "third thing"[110] to which they may attach to one another – some universal "third term" we address when dealing with particular others.[111] "Two human beings are needed for the generation of man – of the spiritual as well as of the physical man; the community of man with man is the first principle and criterion of truth and generality" (Feuerbach 1986: 59). In Christian theology, for example, we find a savior who says "where two or three are gathered[112] in my name, I am there among them" (Matthew 18: 20).[113] In Marxist theology it was History and "The Worker" that functioned as the transcendental guarantee

---

108 Human "thinking has preserved the liberty of inventing dependencies and connections that have no equivalent in reality. It obviously prizes this gift very highly, since it makes such ample use of it – inside as well as outside of science" (Freud 1939: 137).

109 In the Lacanian terms, the person needs a fantasmatic support to live in the real. The real is never enough on its own (Žižek, passim).

110 Any "third term" functioning as an abstract mediator *at this point* in the sociogony is transitory; as Marx says about the "universal equivalent" in its pre-institutionalized form, it "comes and goes" (C: 183), that is, that it is purely accidental. The "third" will undergo a process of *expansion* and *generalization* before it reaches its *universal* status. See Durkheim's point about emergent or formless (liquid) facts versus the formed (S: 39).

111 See Voloshinov on the heroic third ([1927] 2012: 171–4).

112 "You need two to hope. All laws of large numbers begin with that certainty" (Gary 2017: 75). These interpersonal dyads and emergent triads are certainly interesting and highly relevant for sociology and social psychology but keep Marx in mind when it comes to the gulf that separates the simple and expanded value forms from the general and money forms. "Whatever enables humans to organise mass-cooperation networks, it isn't intimate relations.... [I]t is risky to extrapolate from small-group behaviour to the dynamics of mass societies. A nation of 100 million people functions in a fundamentally different way to a band of a hundred individuals" (Harari 2017: 140). Nonetheless, it is important to remember Marx's point that even if aggregate life is quantitatively and qualitatively distinct from small-scale life, the mystery of the totality is actually contained in the simple or elementary relation. We cannot reduce the aggregate to the elementary but we will also never comprehend the totality if we do not grasp the elementary social relation.

113 It is not to be forgotten that in Judaism the name was a "symbol of power" and that *calling* god by his *name*, a "widely diffused conception ... native to Egypt" was a form of compulsion, compelling the god to appear face-to-face with mortals (AJ: 221). The extension of this god-name in Christianity is important where, especially with forms such as Pietists and Quakers, god is not a tyrant delivering punishments from behind the world but a manageable, non-authoritarian mediator that regulates interpersonal conduct.

of world revolution (Worrell 2008). Here, the third is not grasped in its essential social nature but in a reified and mystical form of the kind we find in Emerson: "In all conversation between two persons tacit reference is made, as to a third party, to a common nature. That third party or common nature is not social; it is impersonal; is God" (1950: 267).[114] Of course, this "God" is merely the alienated name and representation or emblem of society itself. Transitory salutations amount to "filing a report with the Big Other" (Žižek, passim) and maintaining the texture or normalcy in our everyday reality. Negatively, I say "Hello" to you in the hallway to forestall any notion that I am a sociopath. Lack of ritual interactions would result in a de-energizing of the social matrix. Positively, rites regenerate the "spark" of life.[115] Ritual energy is experienced by participants, if they successfully avoid dyspraxia (bad praxis or ritual failure), as a kind of lift, enthusiasm, or all the way out to frenzy and possession that can lead to the splitting of the person[116] and the blurring or melting of one being into another – the transformation of the single members of the congregation into "drops within the Social River" (Huxley [1932] 1946: 54; cf. Koestler [1941] 1968: 260).[117]

There are times when we know for a certainty that all is well. A batsman who has played a fine inning will say afterward that he felt he could not

---

114   The antisemite and Nazi sympathizer Henry Ford was maniacally fixated on the writings of Emerson: "Emerson advocated a 'new, more natural theology' that found religious ecstasy in the manners of everyday life, honored the 'green solitude' of the broad outdoors, and revered the great ideals of Progress with a decidedly capital *P*. Self-reliance diametrically opposed to dependence upon property and government; the exercise of power in motion, never repose; education through experience, not book-learning; focused thought as the key to all other human qualities; trusting your own instincts; beauty found in utilitarianism – such were the fundamental Emersonian principles so attractive to Ford" (Baldwin 2001: 45–46).

115   "Neither interest, nor agreement, nor habit creates the social bond; it is ... holy communion piously accomplished in the presence of the gods ..." (Fustel de Coulanges [1873] 1956: 158). See Durkheim (RSM: 143) on the force of social facts not being reducible to agreements.

116   "Ebullience" comes from the phrase "to boil" – in Stevenson's *Dr. Jekyll and Mr. Hyde* we find the boiling and smoking potion used to split the self called an "ebullition" ([1886] 1992: 62). As we will find out with regard to the creation of collective consciousness in the volume on suicide, it is the energetic relations with others (rituals and so forth) that lead to the successful splitting of the self into separate spheres, e.g., the public and the private.

117   *Interaction Ritual Chains* by Collins (2004) is worth noting here with respect to the energy-seeking drive of humans, yet, his program is held back by its commitments to, and limitations that derive from, the American dramaturgical, interactionist, and constructionist paradigms from which the book is embedded. The Durkheim we find here is a kind of mini-Durkheim (2004: 14) where structures are reduced to interaction and ritual "ingredients" for the production of more excitement (2004: 43). Telling is the avoidance of the Durkheim of *Suicide* but, especially, Durkheim's lectures on pragmatism.

> miss the ball, and a speaker or an actor, on his lucky day, can sense his
> audience carrying him as though he were swimming in miraculous, buoy-
> ant water.
>
> ADAMS [1972] 2000: 199

In anthropological terms, participants are mounted by some unseen, abstract
but nonetheless real power that, unbeknownst to them, they have themselves
created – this force is nothing other than their own surplus energies.[118] To the
extent this surplus is "cognized" is the extent to which surplus consciousness
arises.[119] One consideration that is especially important is the generic quality
or plastic interchangeability (EFRL: 390) when it comes to the production of
collective effervescence via rites that produce this energy. "[J]ust as a single
rite can serve several ends, several rites can be used interchangeably to bring
about the same end" (EFRL: 390). The terminology of force, powers, energies,
and especially the idea of a surplus of energy, is real trouble. In speaking of
"energies" we do not want to fall into Bergsonian mystical vitalism, Reichian
orgone delusions, or Jungian life-force hypostatization, nor conversely do we
wish to conjure the thermodynamic "energism" characteristic of totalitarian
materialism (Weber [1909] 1984) that would reduce social facts like money
and charisma to transfigured sunshine (e.g., Bataille [1967] 1989: 20 ff.; cf.
Bergson 1920: 18–19).[120] Sociology does not begin at the center of the solar system. Worse still would be the attempt to reconcile the moral and physics, "a
universe shot through with signs of mind" (Polkinghorne 2007: 8; cf. Teilhard
de Chardin 1959).[121] Moral or social energy arises from social interactions.[122]

---

118   Only the *unity* of individuals is capable of elevating energy to the plane of *force* (see Hegel
       [1807] 2008: 719).
119   Not just with respect to material possessions, anomie can spread to the intellectual do-
       main as well: "The more he knew, the more he desired to know. He had ... hungers that
       grew more ravenous as he fed them" (Wilde [1890] 1995: 151).
120   Bataille is correct to counter orthodoxy with a "general economy" that corrects a one-
       sided labor ontology, but his treatment of energy is unhelpful. Class struggle and class
       solidarity are not primary concerns in *The Accursed Share*. However, we must leave open
       the continuum that allows for alienation and exploitation to become so extreme that it
       results in the monsterization of the human into a carrier of impure forces or even the
       total desublimation of the human into an atom of *fixed* capital (absorbed into the real of
       production like so much combustible fuel).
121   "Either the whole construction of the world presented here is vain ideology or, some-
       where around us, in one form or another, some excess of personal, extra-human energy
       should be perceptible to us if we look carefully, and should reveal to us the great Presence.
       It is at this point that we see the importance for science of *the Christian phenomenon*"
       (Teilhard de Chardin 1959: 292). It was, unfortunately, vain ideology.
122   "Social energy" means what, exactly? "The term implies something measurable, yet, I can-
       not provide a convenient and reliable formula for isolating a single, stable quantum for

"As rich in emotive power as an idea may be, it cannot add anything to our natural vitality; it can only release emotive forces that are already within us, neither creating nor increasing them" (EFRL: 419).[123] Here is a theory of relative and absolute surplus mana, in other words.

Once a society reaches a point of material development where the satisfaction of basic needs no longer results in physical exhaustion, a surplus of time and exertion becomes available for the creation of "luxuries" that are not required for the maintenance of rudimentary physical existence.

> It seems to be only after the demands of the simpler, more immediately organic functions, such as nutrition, growth and reproduction, have been met in some passably sufficient measure that this vaguer range of instincts which constitutes the spiritual predispositions of man can effectually draw on the energies of the organism and so can go into effect in what is recognized as human conduct. The wider the margin of disposable energy, therefore, the more freely should the characteristically human predispositions assert their sway, and the more nearly this metabolic margin is drained by the elemental needs of the organism the less chance should there be that conduct will be guided by what may properly be called the spiritual needs of man.
>
> VEBLEN 1914: 86

Why go the extra mile when we could lay around like animals? Referring to our earlier discussion, openness to the world and lack of fixed needs automatically spurs cohabitating humans toward lavish expenditures of time and energy. As a species lacking and desiring we tend towards a friskier life. We desire others and act upon those desires, not contingently, but upon a regular and repeated basis (EFRL: 420) and the stage is set for the transformation of individuals into cult members – the cult being the "engine" for the mobilization of free time and energy for the creation of collective effervescence, representations, and a

---

examination. We identify *energia* only indirectly, by its effects: it is manifested in the capacity of certain verbal, aural, and visual traces to produce, shape, and organize collective physical and mental experiences. Hence it is associated with repeatable forms of pleasure and interest, with the capacity to arouse disquiet, pain, fear, the beating of the heart, pity, laughter, tension, relief, wonder. In its aesthetic modes, social energy must have a minimal predictability – enough to make simple repetitions possible – and a minimal range enough to reach out beyond a single creator or consumer to some community, however constricted" (Greenblatt 1988: 6).

123 Representations are "highly charged with mental energy" and mobilize, concentrate, and focus our natural, bodily energy (EFRL: 321).

normative life. So, it is actually not the case that the mobilization of free time and energy is some kind of unnecessary or "optional extra step by which society, being already made, merely adds finishing touches" (EFRL: 425) rather, this is what makes us produce the social realm and thereby our humanity; "it is the act by which society makes itself, and remakes itself, periodically" (EFRL: 425).

Surplus energy makes possible our capacity to externalize our own powers,[124] thoughts, and emotional states[125] and create myriad interlocking symbolic worlds. The quest for a vibrant life shakes us out of contentment, habit, and boredom and makes everything exquisitely chiseled.

> Why do I go into such detail? Because the charged atmosphere made every little thing stand out as a performance, a movement distinct and vastly important. It was one of those hypersensitive moments when all your automatic movements, however long established, however habitual, become separate acts of will.... You take nothing for granted, absolutely nothing at all.
>
> CHANDLER 1995: 439

Externalization, as we saw in the previous chapter, is complicated and counterintuitive. The essence of moral energy and externalization resides in the act of splitting, doubling, or self-alienation. What was ordinary suddenly becomes new and foreign. Classical sociology (and psychoanalysis[126] for that matter)

---

124   Freud's libido theory is ambiguous: on the one hand it is rooted in biological drives within the person, yet, at the same time it is an external, 'transcendent' power that holds together not only groups but "everything in the world" ([1921] 1959: 31). In this sense, libido persists metaphorically beyond the capacities of the body. "Sexual feeling might decline, but I have learned that the libido, like Elvis and jealousy, never dies" (Kureishi 2017: 4). The problem is that 'libido' is rendered equivalent to Plato's 'Eros' and the latter is sociologically untenable in all its fine details. Where Freud and Durkheim make contact is in the idea of the love of the other's love serving as the foundation for our desire for association.

125   Durkheim's dynamogenetic theory of moral energy is not identical with vitalism, now justifiably discredited as crypto-theology. The two ideas are easily confused (e.g., Reiser 1932: 64) but in no way can Durkheim be accused of vitalism.

126   Freud expressed uncertainty as to how best to express the reality of psychic energy: "Here we have approached the still shrouded secret of the nature of the psychical. We assume, as other natural sciences have led us to expect, that in mental life some kind of energy is at work; but we have nothing to go upon which will enable us to come nearer to a knowledge of it by analogies with other forms of energy" ([1940] 1969: 37). "Some kind of energy" but what? According to Boothby, the totality of Freudian psychology is comprehended in the concept of energy and energetics: "The key concept that underlies the whole system of metapsychological ideas is that of psychical energy. The notion of a mobile energy, capable of variable investments or 'cathexes' and susceptible of transfer along

is unimaginable without recourse to energies, forces, and powers[127] but several problems have to be addressed: the problem of interaction between the domains of the natural and social sciences and conceptual compression, such, for example, energy, force, and power tend to be treated as more or less synonymously when, in fact, powers can never come before forces (Tolstoy

---

a chain of associated representations, remained throughout Freud's career his single most important theoretical construction.... It was in terms of the buildup and release of energetic tensions that Freud conceived the nature of pleasure and pain. Moreover, the notion of psychical energy was virtually consubstantial with Freud's concept of libido" (Boothby 2001: 4). Freud was correct to doubt that the energies of the psyche were identical with the energies found operating in the natural universe. Yet, there remains no doubt that as mammals we are bioelectric beings. This observation can be taken to absurd extremes. A good example is the extension of electromagnetic theories to the sphere of sexology, the best example being, arguably, the "Karezza Method' of J. William Lloyd where we find this gem: "At other times – and this is most important – be silent and quiet, but try to feel yourself a magnetic battery, with the Finger of Love as the positive pole, and pour out your vital electricity to her and consciously direct it to her womb, her ovaries, her breasts, lips, limbs, everywhere filling her in every nerve and fiber with your magnetism, your life, love, strength, calmness and peace. This attitude of *magnetation* is the important thing in Karezza, its secret of sweetest success. In proportion as you acquire the habit and power of withdrawing the electric qualities from your sexual stores and giving them out in blessing to your partner from your sex-organs, hands, lips, skin, everywhere; from your eyes and the tones of your voice; will you acquire the power to diffuse and bestow the sex-glory, envelop yourselves in its halo and aura, and to satisfy yourself and satisfy her without an orgasm. Soon you will not even think of self-control, because you will have no desire for the orgasm, nor will she. You will both regard it as an awkward and interrupting accident. And the practice of Magnetation will beautify and strengthen every organ in your body that you thus use to express it, as well as hers. It is the great beautifier. Every look from your eyes, yes, every touch of your hands, and the tones of your voice will become vibrant with magnetic charm" (1931: 31).

127 The idea of "social forces" and "energies" played a central role in the thought of all major theorists in the classical, European tradition of sociology and in the newly emergent field of psychoanalysis. Marx, Simmel, and Freud each operated from more or less a theoretical position that placed the "production" of energies (we are not dealing with an occult ability to break the rules of thermodynamics) and their transformations into objective forces of various forms, at the center of their thought. Even Weber was a theorist of forces and their routinizations and desublimations. However, whereas they each drew variously on language derived from the thermodynamic lexicon (in varying degrees) their sociologies were not centered on physical energy but, rather, bridged the pre-thermodynamic concept of moral energy with language, analogies, and metaphors of the new "science of energy." Nowhere was this more dominant than in the writings of Durkheim. "All the world" he famously said, "is a system of forces" but he also claimed that all the world is a "system of representations" and, further, that from top to bottom the world was "spirit." Either he was an obscurantist, an assessment I would vehemently disagree with, or, like Marx, Durkheim had found the narrow and difficult path between the many fruitless routes ending in theoretical cul-de-sacs.

[1869] 1992: 489) and depend upon organization, direction, discharge, and effectiveness.[128]

The danger associated with the use of terms such as "energy" in the social sciences is the automatic assumption that we can only drag the term in as metaphor or that we reduce sociology to some kind of social physics.[129] It is essential to recall that it was the natural sciences that borrowed ideas such as "energy" and "force" from their prototypes in religious and cultic practices, transferring them to the domain of amoral nature.[130]

---

128 It is tempting to couch ritual bodies in the language of thermodynamics (some anthropologists did just this) but when it comes to representations, like a totem, the idea of surplus energy takes us out of the domain of "mechanical conservative systems" where "energy is equal to the sum of the potential and the kinetic energies..." (Fermi 1936: 11).

129 Moral or social energies are objectively real yet imagined (EFRL: 369, 385). This imagined reality makes no sense from the standpoint of personal psychology, on one side, nor does it register in the domain of nature. Things that are not *literally* true such as a phrase like "the ritual production of surplus moral energy" can be nonetheless practically true in the same way that a god can be not a literal truth but a practical one (EFRL). Invoking the "energy" concept automatically conjures all kinds of misguided attempts to put sociology or the social sciences on a firm, natural scientific foundation. For example, Weber ([1909] 1984) demolished Ostwald's naïve intrusion into the cultural sciences where social relations were reduced to thermodynamics and chemical reactions. With Ostwald and the energetics school, grasping society began with solar outputs. Rosa and Machlis (1983) offer a good chronology and summary of the various attempts to reduce society to a system of natural energies and provide a number of reasons why the reduction of society to natural dynamics is impossible. I would like to add another objection to the energetics school of thought: the brain may be determined by natural laws but minds are routinely capable of a feat that is extraordinary here on earth in the world of reactors and materials: fusion. The mind fuses concepts generating new ideas all the time that inspire people to raise themselves up from thermodynamic indifference; a great idea, a name, or dramatic event quite literally "energizes" a person or group. We give a name to a thing "and now see it 'out there' in the world" (Taussig 2009: 233).

130 The underlying premise of political theology is that all social norms are rooted in the sacred and "all human nomoi are 'nourished' by a single divine nomos" (Schmitt 2003: 70–71). Nomos is inseparable from the notion of boundaries and ritual separations, literally fences separate land and, in the process, what is separated and unapproachable is sacred (Schmitt 2003: 74–5). Nomos is about keeping things compartmentalized, separation, demarcation lines, and the distribution of shares. When hiking in the backcountry of Central New York one finds many old rock walls that used to mark off the boundary lines of small farms. The legal imagination of settlers required things as hefty as rocks to demarcate property lines whereas, today, not even a string is required – a splotch of yellow paint on a tree and, perhaps, at most, a sign indicating private property. Regarding Schmitt, readers familiar with the history of *Telos* will realize that I teach at what amounts to the "scene of the crime" (SUNY Cortland) where back in the late 70s the journal made its "right turn" at the Cortland Conference (Worrell and Dangler 2011).

The 19th and 20th centuries can be encapsulated in what Plenge calls the
"'eruption of energy.' All the forces of the earth are unleashed; the effect is to
overwhelm mankind, to force our society into an incalculable transformation, beyond the control of any insight or of any will ..." (in Löwith 1964: 122).
"From the late nineteenth century onwards, a discourse around energy starts
to appear in economics involving the reading of all transactions as, at base, the
consumption of energy by one party in order to satisfy needs.... The population becomes conceived of in terms of collective *arbeitskraft*, and this itself is
understood in thermodynamic terms as occurring within a bounded system"
(Brown and Capdevila 1999: 37). The major intellectual development that separated Hegel from, say, Durkheim or the other key figures of modern social and
sociological theory, was thermodynamics as a scientific field.[131] Carnot published *Reflections on the Motive Power of Fire* in 1824, just a few years before
Hegel's death, and it wasn't until the 1840s that the term "thermodynamics"
was itself coined by Joule. It would take roughly a decade more for the science
to emerge as a fully identifiable field. As such, for example, the philosophical
and social theoretical use of the term "energy" meant something very different
for thinkers on either side of the thermodynamic divide. Eventually, thermodynamics became an irresistible paradigm for drawing metaphors and analogies but it also spawned whole schools of thought that re-centered society and
history around the notion of thermodynamics. The body was no longer animal
nor mechanism but generator (cf. Mettrie [1748/1912] 1993).[132] "Evidently every
one of us is a dynamo, which produces a measurable electrical current. The
body, moreover, produces heat in measurable quantities; it causes an expense
of heat merely to keep a muscle in an organized condition capable of activity.

---

131 This is a point at which Lacan stumbles when he interposes the steam engine between
     Hegel and Freud – obviously, Lacan lacked a firm grasp of the history of the steam engine –
     but he is partially correct, but only partially, when he focuses on the concept of energy
     (1988: 74–5). What he should have said was that the concept of energy shifts radically from
     the first third of the 19th century (when Hegel was active) to the closing of the century
     due to the rise of the "science of energy."
132 "What is it which is beyond the machine? One answer I gave you is: the field. It does not
     rest simply on the concept of immutable particles of fixed mass with variable velocities.
     The field is a description of the state of affairs, an energetic state of affairs, in a space,
     in all space. Yet every effort to get away from matter, and have the field only, has failed
     also. We must expect not the death of mechanism, but its swallowing up in something
     richer of which mechanism is but one factor. Einstein believes, but cannot prove, that
     matter is but the location of great concentrations of energy in space. He would love to
     have the field swallow up matter. He is still trying hard for a unified field theory which will
     unite the electro-magnetic and gravitational fields, and still produce the atoms of matter
     or electricity naturally (from the mathematics) and in their right indeterminate place"
     (Malisoff 1940: 412).

Evidently there is direct connection between bodily energy and the forces of the inorganic world." The idea here was the dream of precisely measuring "bodily force" and explaining "human behavior in terms of mathematical formulae" (Nichols 1935: 174–75).[133] But it is important to point out, time and again, that the energy concept has ceremonial, religious, and rhetorical (Greenblatt 1988: 6) origins that were carried over into later philosophical systems and scientific discourse. "Energy" lost its meaning as a self-moving, "spiritual" substance and was relocated to the movement of molecules, chemicals, and oxidation.[134]

---

[133] The lure of thermodynamics outlived the classical era. Fairly recently, even, the call has been made to reconfigure theoretical anthropology, for example, around a revised model of thermodynamics. In his Presidential Address at the 1977 meeting of the American Anthropological Association, Richard Adams put it this way: "In conceptualizing a human society as a dissipative structure, we are neither dropping the human individual from sight, nor ignoring his exercise of symbolic abilities or voluntarism. We are seeing him as part of a structure of such individuals whose activities collectively comprise a flow of matter and energy. The individuals themselves are embodiments of this flow. Some of them will additionally be the agents responsible for the channeling of much additional flow from other sources through the society. Everything they do requires matter and energy within some set of limits; if the flow is insufficient or too much, those activities will be disrupted, and will contribute to some future fluctuations of the whole" (1978: 304).

[134] The thermodynamic model of the natural universe was founded upon, and borrowed from, a *social or moral prototype* (EFRL: 17). *Energy is not a metaphor smuggled into sociology from physics. "Energy" is a feature of all domains of nature, including human society.* When asked if he had been influenced by quantum mechanics the author Jorge Luis Borges replied "that although he had not been influenced by work on quantum mechanics, he was not surprised that the laws of physics mirrored ideas from literature. After all, physicists were readers, too.... So if there was influence, it was from literature to physics, not the other way around" (Lloyd 2006: 101). As such, as we will see later, it is not always inappropriate for the social scientist to borrow from the language of the natural sciences insofar as we are reclaiming, at times, what was borrowed from us to begin with. For example, "force" and "energy" (not formally distinguish until the 14th century in Peter Aureoli's *Liber Sententiarum*, see EP, 1: 511) are concepts used in both physics and social sciences. However, the natural sciences borrowed the notions from the world of religion pure and simple and then altered their meanings such that "forces" were cleansed of their social origins. In other words forces ceased to be the measure of moral powers in the world and became a one-sided conceptualization of natural phenomena. Furthermore, if we want to leave questions about "radiation" and "light" and so forth to the appropriate science and interrogate, instead, problems of gods and monies, the natural sciences can provide few answers. Value, mana, charisma, etc., are forms of collective thought that find material expressions but we will never discover a chemical foundation for value, etc. Nevertheless, value and other moral objectivities are energies and forces despite their inability to be reduced to chemicals or materials. Interestingly, much of Marx's critique of capitalism exhibits an affinity with thermodynamics (e.g., labor-power, a term coined by Hermann von Helmholtz) but when it came to "exchange-value" Marx was forced to leave

"Energy" is derived from the Greek *energeia* and makes its first appearance in Aristotelian philosophy.[135] There is no stable, unitary meaning of *energia* that we can locate in Aristotle's work. Chen (1956) identifies no less than ten differentiations but, despite the multiplicity, we find that on the whole *energeia* denotes a vital and dynamic force working itself out (assuming an objective form in the world) toward perfect actuality through the agency (the unity of action and thought) of human beings. "The chief moment in Aristotle's philosophy" says Hegel, "is that the energy of thinking and the object of thought are the same" ([1840] 1995a: 148).

It was the revolutionary dynamism of religious reform in 16th century Europe and ensuing revolutions in the burgeoning global capitalist economy that lay at the bottom of "the new doctrine of energetics" espoused by Helm and Ostwald: for the latter,

> not only was energy the universal currency of physics, but all phenomena of nature were merely manifestations of energy and of its manifold transformations. In 'Lectures on Natural Philosophy' ... [in 1901] he contended that since substance is by definition that which persists under transformations of changes, energy is substance.... From this point of view the totality of nature appears as a series of spatially and temporally changing energies, of which we obtain knowledge in proportion as they impinge on the body, and especially upon the sense organs fashioned for the reception of the appropriate energies ...
>
>   EP, 1: 517

Within classical mechanics, energy was rendered secondary because "all processes [were] reduced to motions of particles and motion [was] the fundamental concept for physical explanation."[136] The decline of the classical tradition came when "energetics," the late 19th century school of thought represented by Rankine, Helm, Zeuner, Mach, Gibbs, Maxwell, Oettingen, and Ostwald, posited the idea that energy was not only "the universal currency of physics,

---

behind naturalistic explanations (and Engels) and revisit his old master, Hegel, and the dialectics of Spirit.

135 "The question of a rhetorical *energeia* is not a linguistic question, but a political one. Aristotle's *Rhetoric* is about a *civic* art of rhetoric" (Garver 1994: 39). As Aristotle says, "liveliness is got by using the proportional type of metaphor and by making our hearers see things.... By 'making them see things' I mean using expressions that represent things as in a state of activity" (1984: 2252). It is that act of creating an objective representation in the minds of hearers that is energeia.

136 See Gay (2006: 79) on the Newtonian positivism that Freud was trained in.

but all phenomena of nature were merely manifestations of energy and of its manifold transformations."

> The discovery of energy as the quintessential element of all experience, both organic and inorganic, made society and nature virtually indistinguishable. Society was assimilated to an image of nature powered by protean energy, perpetually renewed, indestructible, and infinitely malleable. The pioneers of energy conservation viewed the transformation of mechanical energy into heat, and subsequently, the transformation of all natural forces as manifestations of a single *Kraft*.
>
> RABINBACH 1990: 46

By the time we arrive at Einstein's theory of relativity we have something that, as an analog, resembles very much the kind of thinking we find in Durkheim: "Energy was released mass, and mass was frozen energy" (EP, 1: 516–17). This analog applies to Weber as well apropos bureaucracy as *routinized charisma*.[137] The oscillation of fluid energy (charisma), crystallizations (institution – best comprehended in the Latin verb *instituere* just as much as the noun where the former means *in* "in" + *statuere* "set up"), and energetic transformations and creative destruction are continually at play in all realms of society and history and reflected even in literary and artistic careers.[138]

The concept of force, like energy, also has religious origins. Of course, it is true that "the notion in physics of force is an anthropomorphism.[139] It is

---

137 "... Simply by turning this handle, any one of you can produce up to three sonatas per hour. And how much labor such a thing cost your ancestors! They could create only by whipping themselves up to attacks of 'inspiration' – some unknown form of epilepsy" (Zamyatin [1924] 1993: 17–18).

138 "Prior to 1935, his [Shostakovich] scherzos can still be perceived as the explosive expression of new aggressive and grotesque vitality and *joie de vivre* – there is something of the liberating force of the carnival in them, of the madness of the creative power that merrily sweeps away all obstacles and ignores all established rules and hierarchies. After 1935, however, his scherzos had clearly 'lost their innocence': their explosive energy acquires a brutal-threatening quality, there is something mechanical in their energy, like the forced movements of a marionette" (Žižek 2008: 246).

139 The further one recedes into the history of philosophy the clearer this transfer of social logic to nature is evident. Two cases should be sufficient for the purpose of illustration: the declination of the atom in Epicurean materialism and, later, the orbit of heavenly bodies in Boethius. In the former we find atoms with a mind of their own swerving on their own accord, deviating from a straight course: "while the atom frees itself from its relative existence, the straight line, by abstracting from it, by swerving away from it; so the entire Epicurean philosophy swerves away from the restrictive mode of being wherever the concept of abstract individuality, self-sufficiency and negation of all relation to

the result of a projection into nature of our own sense of effort" (Reiser 1932: 67).[140] Vaihinger exposes the projective, psychological nature of "force" as well when he says: "One of the most important fictions that arise through isolatory abstraction is that notorious and frequently dangerous product of the imagi- nation, the concept of *force*.... Force, so far as it is thought of as the cause of motion, is nothing but a disguised outlet for the irresistible tendency to per- sonification" (1924: 197, 198). Whereas "force" possesses no theoretical value to reductionism it nonetheless capable of retaining methodological and utilitary worth due to practicality and convenience – i.e., it is a "useful fiction" (1924: 198).[141] Nominalism has continuously waged a war on what it conceives as

---

other things must be represented in its existence" (MECW, 1: 50). In the *Consolation of Philosophy* Boethius imagined the solar system in such a way that we can easily perceive the original concept of tension between the tight social cohesion associated with a dense moral center and the abstracted individual removed from the social totality and enjoying/ suffering relative independence: "Consider the example of a number of spheres in orbit around the same central point: the innermost moves toward the simplicity of the center and becomes a kind of hinge about which the outer spheres circle; whereas the outer- most, whirling in a wider orbit, tends to increase its orbit in space the farther it moves from the indivisible midpoint of the center. If, however, it is connected to the center it is confined by the simplicity of the center and no longer tends to stray into space. In like manner, whatever strays farthest from the divine mind is most entangled in the nets of Fate; conversely, the freer a thing is from Fate, the nearer it approaches the center of all things. And if it adheres firmly to the divine mind, it is free from motion and overcomes the necessity of Fate" ([524] 1962: 92).

140   Our respect for our ideas are projected onto objects (Kant 1951: 96). "The fetichist [sic] an- imates the forms of things around him, all the material objects he sees, with the feelings and volitions of which he is conscious himself" (Richard Congreve, in Bray 1863: 174–75).

141   "Fiction" should not be confused with "make believe," "pretend," or the whims of the subjective imagination, etc., but in the literal sense of fashioned or formed. The middle english word for "fiction" was "fixion" and the connection to the Latin *fixus* seems fairly clear to me as is the connection to the word "fix" which, in relation to the operations of the mind, refers to stabilization of meanings, constancy, and definitions, etc. In Marx, for example, we have a concept of fictional capital that is both unreal and real (in its effects) simultaneously. Capitalism and all religions run to a great extent on fictions di- vorced from the real. Our special quality as a species is the capacity to live "outside the real" (EFRL: 425) which puts us in the world of "fictions." We do not so much play "make believe" but are made through our beliefs that rise up as powers through our collective, organized praxis, which we seldom grasp intellectually, except without specialized effort. Our capacity for creating and understanding representations is bound up with processes of misrecognition and misunderstanding what we ourselves have done (EFRL: 363). Vai- hinger fails to comprehend that concepts like "force" are social products projected onto nature, not fictions borrowed from nature to imperfectly explain the moral aspects of life (EFR: 369–70). As for misunderstandings, it might seem that when common understand- ings are lacking we are suffering a logonomic breakdown but it may also be that misun- derstandings are actually built into systems as constitutive elements in order to keep the

religious baggage smuggled into science and philosophy. Wittgenstein, for example,

> shared an inspiration that he had come across as a teen-ager in 'The Principles of Mechanics,' by Heinrich Hertz .... [who] ... suggested a novel way to deal with the puzzling concept of force in Newtonian physics: the best approach was not to try to define it but to restate Newton's theory in a way that eliminates any reference to force. Once this was done, according to Hertz, 'the question as to the nature of force will not have been answered; but our minds, no longer vexed, will cease to ask illegitimate questions.' [Wittgenstein's] big idea was to apply this method to philosophical problems.
>
> GOTTLIEB 2009: 74

The concept of "force" was the centerpiece of Newtonian physics and, before the end of the 18th century, "it had become one of those words – like the key words in science ever since – that had captured the popular and the philosophical imagination. 'Force' had become a metaphor for any below-the-surface activity which could be used to explain movements and transformations.... [and was] the dominant explanatory principle of science" (Solomon 1983: 367–68). Later philosophers, principally Hegel, criticized the traditional, metaphysical and *infinite* notions of "force" as an empty abstraction that instituted a world-behind-the-world. For Hegel, there is only this world and no recourse to a counter-world was permissible. Hegel's *finite* conceptualization of "force" places the notion upon a social or moral foundation (rather than on an all-encompassing metaphysics) that is decisive, both directly and indirectly, for later attempts to theorize the emergence and logic of the modern world.

Durkheim founds his sociology and method on the concept of force being known through its expressions and effects; representations are expressions and condensations of forces. Whether analyzing suicide rates or exploring the defects of the social division of labor, the underlying forces are known through their representational expressions: "... social solidarity is a wholly moral phenomenon which by itself is not amenable to exact observation and especially not to measurement.... [W]e must therefore substitute for this internal datum, which escapes us, an external one which symbolizes it, and then study the former through the latter" (DOL: 24). It might appear that "forces" and external

---

sign system humming along. Society might fall apart if people "understood" everything. Constitutive ignorance means, at the bottom, that things are ignored. Some things are better left alone.

"symbols" are two separate objects, but like Hegel and Marx, Durkheim grasps that the underlying "force" is bound to representations: the world is a system of forces and the world is a system of representations (RSM: 253).[142] To have actual force, moral currents must be represented in the mind. Durkheim's sociology of forces has been written off as nothing more than a misleading use of metaphor and that "force" can be dropped without suffering sociological damage but without "forces" there would not only be no Durkheim but no sociology at all.

It is not Durkheim's contention that the laws of nature dominate society and history, that society is reducible to a physics, or that the study of amoral nature can lead to a better comprehension of society, rather, his point is that conceptions of nature and even concepts deployed by physics are unconsciously drawn from the logic of social organization and social processes, especially religious thought and practice (EFRL: 17). Religious conceptions pertaining to "supernatural" power are the prototypical forms of thought for ensuing revolutions in natural scientific thought. The "idea of natural forces is very likely derived from that of religious forces" (EFRL: 24). The study of, say, thermodynamics can tell us nothing about moral life since the former is the rationalized and transfigured reflection of the latter. According to Smith, "the word *physis* itself was originally conceived less as a proto-scientific notion than as a kind of spiritual force. The Greeks '... were not concerned with an abstract conception of nature, but conceived it as a kind of essence ... or force, *dynamis*, with vague spiritual properties, which nonetheless have a corporeal basis'" (1988: 18). The true sociological operation would be to explain how the development of physics and the natural sciences as a whole, the structure of its thought, runs in an imperfect parallel with the evolution of social organization. If we want to know the Durkheimian basis of energy we have to place the concept in the context of self-alienation.

As we saw previously, the *externality* of social facts does not mean that "facts" exist outside of the mind, rather, the point is that the human mind is not one-sided; we have a personal or private mind and a public mindedness and the latter precedes and weighs on the former – like a nightmare at times. Apart from consciousness, energy is also dual: we eat, rest, and toil but the *splitting of the mind* results in a metaphorical "fission" in the sense that we are driven to go beyond bare existence in order to devote time to culture, play,

---

142   Takla and Pope indicate that "the force imagery" in Durkheim's work is key, a "basic, integral, and synthesizing element ... something that permeates and integrates the conceptual, explanatory, methodological, and metatheoretical frameworks of Durkheim's sociological *summa*" (1985: 76–7).

and science, etc. If we had remained at the level of animal instincts we would use tools, for example, but we would not develop technology. Likewise, if we were single-minded[143] we would live in shelters but would not plunge into the absurdities of mansions, shopping malls, and amusement parks; likewise, we would eat but we would not have developed the culinary arts or cuisine – indeed, we would not have even worked ourselves up to "good eats" to go with our live bait; and while we would move from one point to another we would not tour, endure vacations, or journey to the moon. It is the splitting and dividing of the mind and the *fusion* of ideas and representations that results in the liberation of free physical and mental energies that can be mobilized for social ends.[144] Rituals generate collective effervescence and the experience of external forces that cause a bifurcation of the mind but when participants return to the banal routines of daily life they take that duality and capacity for surplus creation with them. It endures in memory. Mindfulness is memory.[145] Memory arises from the memorial, the rite, but lives on in routines. "Routine" comes form the classical Latin *rupta* for "broken" and is close to the root for "rupture" – *rites unite the group but divide the mind.* Everyday routines are not always the profane tasks we normally take them to be but pattern traces originating under extraordinary circumstances. Having a social mind is like possessing a "dynamo" that pushes the individual beyond mere self-interest. The person in his or her "right mind" is literally "rite-minded," going beyond self-interests and seeking collective goals. Having personal *discipline* to function independently means being a *disciple* (the root of "discipline") and simply means following a collective representation, e.g., a disciple of Christ – a god is just an alienated representation that a society has of itself, society, that is, in its hypostatized and projected form (S: 312). The communication between our two minds and our projective and objectifying capacities are grounded in language.

3   Projection and Externalization

"Projection" comes from the Latin *projectio* from *proicere* for "throw forth." The common, everyday psychological meaning of projection is illustrated in the

---

143   The person who is single-minded is often characterized as having "dogged determination."

144   When discussing the "combinatory power of the signifier" (Forrester 1981: 54) we have to remember that the fusion of representations and ideas is immaterial but produces material or physical effects, or as Hume puts it, the "extraordinary effects" of the union of ideas (1896: 12–13).

145   "Memory" comes from the Latin *memoria,* from *memor,* which means mindful or remembering.

following anecdote provided by Smith: when the famous chef Julia Childs was asked "'Why do you massage the chicken with butter?' she replied, 'Well, I think it likes it'" (1988: 335).[146] What Becker calls the "miracle" of projection (1973: 212) involves the transfer of feelings from one representation to another (S: 335) that we can think of as a process of auto-valuation and auto-devaluation where representations such as emblems and signs gain and lose prestige and authority (DOL: 42) or are objects of "investment" and "disinvestment" with regards to meaning. From one angle, projection involves the ejection of mate- rial from "internal perception into the external world, and thus detached from them and pushed on to someone else." The energetic relief is "exchanged" for a feeling of "oppression from without" (Freud [1913] 1950: 79).

> The projection outwards, of internal perceptions is a primitive mecha- nism, to which, for instance, our sense perceptions are subject, and which therefore normally plays a very large part in determining the form taken by our external world. Under conditions whose nature has not yet been sufficiently established, internal perceptions of emotional and in- tellectual processes can be projected outwards in the same way as sense perceptions; they are thus employed for building up the external world, though they should by rights remain part of the internal world.
>
>   FREUD [1913] 1950: 81

From what we know of Durkheim's theory of social consciousness and the *externality* of social facts (the absolute psychology of the collective domain) not only should materials "by rights remain part of the internal world" they do remain in the "internal" world but appear in consciousness *as if* they exist independently and exterior to it. The lynchpin connecting the domains of the material and ideal, the fluid and the fixed, and the personal and impersonal is signification.

    Signification processes create a condensed, external and tangible (EFRL: 208) focal point and a name to the currents generated through practice; be- tween energy creation and the reality produced is the discharge of words (Cas- sirer 1946: 36, 37, 81). A sign is a word, gesture, process, or picture, etc., that has been interpreted and therefore has meaning for us and others. All our thinking

---

146   "The Roman doctrine of lawful domination is the source of other crucial ideas ... includ- ing the concept of projection, which has roots in the idea of 'transferred' or 'translated' authority. Analyzing [the] idea of transfer makes it possible to differentiate several kinds of projection – a fact of some relevance, given the significance ... attach[ed] to *projectio*" (Smith 1988: 335).

is done on the basis of signs (Chandler 2007: 14). "Anything can be a sign as long as someone interprets it as "signifying" something – referring to or *standing for* something other than itself. We interpret things as signs largely unconsciously by relating them to familiar systems of conventions" (Ibid.).

A sign consists of a *signifier* (some kind of "carrier," "bearer," "prop," "en-velope," "vehicle," or "raft" like bodily motions, blood, ink, sounds, or wood, stones, etc.)[147] and a *signified* concept. The *linguistic* sign is where we focus on the signification of words and language proper (Chandler 2007: 14). The division of the signifier and the signified follows the line between the form (signifier) and the content (signified) of signification – i.e., the real and the ideal or material and the immaterial aspects.[148] For example, Saussure made a distinction between the physical *sound* and the non-physical sound *pattern* ([1916] 1983: 66; see also Chandler 2007: 14). Fetish thinking misplaces meaning by finding it in the material aspects of communication itself.[149] The anthro-pologist Leslie White referred to the carrier as a "physical structure" but the relationship between the carrier and the signified is not reducible to a dualistic or mechanistic bolting together of things or of signifiers "merely attached" to a "physical structure" (see Boon 1982: 122–23) as some kind of laminate of matter and meaning that can simply fall apart or be unbolted at will. No, the sign is a

147 The term "envelope" is striking and essentially identical with Marx's use of the term "bearer" in describing the use-value of the commodity or Weber's notion of a "carrier" of charismatic gifts – again, the ideas are virtually identical: the material element is the non-essential "body" of the objective but immaterial "spiritual" substance that has "taken possession" of, alienated, the material thing. Incidentally, the Melanesians imagined the human body as a "support" for the "living one" or *kamo* (Leenhardt 1979: 24).

148 The split between the real and the ideal or the physical and immaterial departs from Saussure who says that both the signifier and the signified are non-physical or merely *psychological*. This departure fits not only our sociological project but also follows later trends: "Nowadays, while the basic 'Saussurean' model is commonly adopted, it tends to be a more materialist model than that of Saussure himself. The *signifier* is now commonly interpreted as the *material (or physical) form* of the sign – it is something which can be seen, heard, touched, smelled or tasted – as with Roman Jakobson's *signans*, which he described as the ... perceptible part of the sign" (Chandler 2007: 14–15).

149 In phonosemantics, the theory of sound symbolism (literally, the sound is the symbol) misplaces meaning in the physical carrier itself, in other words, transforms matter into something moral on the basis of its own physical properties. This fetishism has plagued human thought from time immemorial, continues today (e.g., Blasi et al. 2016; Ornstein 2003: 72). Likewise, when we find a worker projecting meaning into a labor product through the expenditure of muscle we have a replication of this very fetishism (e.g., Ea-gleton 2016: 97): "To carve stone is to invest a chunk of matter with meaning, converting it into a signifier of spirit." It is not in the carving itself nor in the finished product that meaning is found.

stranger thing yet that appears to ordinary consciousness as, to borrow from Hegel, a thing "ensouled."

> When we speak, in gestures or signs, we fashion a real object in the world; the gesture is seen, the words and the song are heard. The arts are simply a kind of writing, which, in one way or another, fixes words or gestures, and gives body to the invisible. These new objects, poems or temples, are made of the same material as the world.... A Greek temple has no within; it announces that its marble is only marble; and poetry itself, and music above all, show by other means the same grain and the same homogeneous crystal.
>
>   ALAIN [1934] 1974: 14

Though we cannot achieve it here, comprehensiveness would require that we disentangle or defetishize the "ensoulment" by distinguishing between sound, voice, word, meaning, reference, interpretation, logonomy, and communication. We will have to be content with merely indicating that even though "our dealings are in the air" (Gracián [1647] 2015: 49) when signification enters the physical stage of delivery, meaning ends, there is a "cutting free" and we enter a purely profane or *infraliminal* dimension (the real of communication) where air molecules, in the case of speech, are merely "sensory residues" (Freud [1913] 1950: 81). Sound itself is "sunken" or "without value or content" (Hegel 1975a: 89).[150] Air molecules bump into one another activating the aural system of another person who synthesizes or constructs an image.[151] This process operates retroactively to confer upon the speaker a voice and subjectivity. It is important to remember that there is no meaning itself in the material aspects of communication. I have something I want to say, I think I say what I think I mean, but as soon as the words are transmitted as carriers they no longer have meaning "out there" in the domain of the real. I can only hope that the sounds and the enacted delivery and the references are interpretable in such a way that the receiver can "see what I am saying." The hope is that there is a sufficiently robust logonomy – e.g., ritual stereotyping, etc. (Mannheim 1982: 221) – to lift the voice up from a puff of air into an object of fascination that inspires "peace, friendship, [and] the end of useless struggle" (Greene 1929: 37). Of course, not all words inspire actions and passionate reactions – only those we might call the energy words (Mandeville [1732] 1924, 2: 293) or technical

---

150   Linguistic materialism and onomatopoeias are dead ends for sociology. See Bracken (2007: 138–48) for an interesting discussion of this problem.
151   We make "living music" out of "dead air" (Carlyle [1836] 1987: 92).

and specialist terminologies, especially the terms associated with money, loans, and contracts (Bourdieu 2005: 159) as well as winged words filled with a rising nobility (Hausman 1975: 105). Some words are too hot and steamy to use without upsetting the social equilibrium.[152]

Shared meaning implicates a complex process of mediation between reference, logonomic systems,[153] and interpretation that keeps signifiers and their signifieds entangled somewhere between the zero eccentricity of the total and reified meaning and the infinite eccentricity of planar chaos (postmodern, hyper-Fordist deregulation). Once the "fact of names" dissolves we are lost and drift along without confidence (Rosenzweig [1944] 1999: 57–58). Symbolic[154] objectivity is found in a zone between the elliptical and the hyperbolic and, as such, we can find acceptable degrees of eccentricity:

Brutality	$e = 0$	circular	Thing
	$e < 1$	elliptical	~ Obj
Logonomy	$e = 1$	parabolic	Object
	$e > 1$	hyperbolic	~ Obj
Anarchy	$e = \infty$	linear	Monster

Objectivity is not a problem of logic per se but a matter of "practical-critical activity" (MECW, 5: 6) and the preservation and vitality of duality (*Homo duplex* again). Under the heel of the dictator, language is reduced to the function of invocation and the differentiation between the written word and the oral commands of the ruler are obliterated; the totalitarian linguistic model is based on

---

152 "We even reject the word *fame* – a hot word. A steaming word. We abhor 'personality.' We eschew difference" (Barker 2017: 8).

153 "Logonomic systems" is a phrase coined by Kress and Hodge (1988). The idea of "logonomic system is something I haven't taken up much. Largely because I have not continued with description or analysis of text a lot. Because my interests moved more to an understanding of mode rather than a continued interest in text or the social aspects of text" (Kress 2008). See Koselleck (1985: 75 ff.) for an analysis of Hardenberg's "September Memorandum" of 1807 and the role it played in attempting to gut and redefine the meaning of *Stand* such that the old vertical meaning of social rank was flattened, equalized, and rationalized.

154 The icon does not represent as much of a problem for objectivity and the index even less so. Indices are "non-arbitrary" as are icons, to some extent, but the icon, since it is "intentional" in contrast to the non-intentionality of the index, is more plastic by virtue of its entanglement with a cultural grammar. It is the symbol, since it is characterized by an arbitrary connection between form and meaning, that presents the decisive problem area for objectivity (see Everett 2017: 84–88).

the shouting and haranguing of the "rabble-rouser" (Klemperer [1957] 2000: 22–23). The obverse, the anarchy of criticism and expression found in the Weimar Republic that preceded and conditioned the rise of the Nazis, was itself self-destructive:

> The Republic, almost suicidally, lifted all controls on freedom of expression; the National Socialists used to claim scornfully that they were only taking advantage of the rights granted them by the constitution when in their books and newspapers they mercilessly attacked the state and all its institutions and guiding principles used every available weapon of satire and belligerent sermonizing. There were no restraints whatsoever in the realm of the arts and sciences, aesthetics and philosophy. Noody was bound to a particular moral dogma or ideal of beauty, everyone was free to choose. This motley intellectual freedom was celebrated as a tremendous and decisive leap forward compared with the imperial age.
>
> KLEMPERER [1957] 2000: 20

Objectivity can endure a degree of deviation (hyperbole and ellipsis) but excessive tilting results in terror, fatalism, fetishism, pragmatic liquidity, and absurdity. Where we find a disintegration of logic and linguistic hyper-fluidity, where signifiers and the things they signify no longer exhibit an elective affinity the way they used to we can be sure that the underlying social organization that served as its model has come undone (EFRL: 16). Social media, granular participation, propaganda, and so on, have contested traditional meanings from the top, bottom, and sides (see Rose 2012: 141–43) leading to a crumbling of the integrity of expressions and a loosening of referentiality. This is the ground from which demagogues and horror arise.

The spatial and temporal latency in the process leaves open the possibility for the unraveling of communication:

> The problem is the problem that has troubled western thought since the pre-Socratics recognized the separation between what was said and the act of saying. This separation must be thought both as time and space – as the space, which in the distance from page to eye or mouth to ear allows the possibility of misunderstanding – as the time taken to traverse the page or listen to an utterance which ensures the deferred interpretation of words which are always only defined by what follows.
>
> MACCABE 1985: 35

The communication process where we find rapid alternations between the infraliminal and supraliminal dimensions is roughly analogous with the contrasting slow-motion movement and transformation of money into coin and back into money (CPE: 127). With understanding we have communication, a communing of people. The image is no mere "picture" (although we sometimes do engage in "picture thinking")[155] but, at the apex of praxis, the image is an active social force, a collective representation.[156] To the average person the *carrier* has what appears to be magical powers (AJ: 221) which corresponds with the naive realism of mythology (Cassirer 1946: 3–6).

> Words were originally magic and to this day words have retained much of their ancient magical power. By words one person can make another blissfully happy or drive him to despair, by words the teacher conveys his knowledge to his pupils, by words the orator carries his audience with him and determines their judgements and decisions. Words provoke affects and are in general the means of mutual influence among men.
>
> FREUD [1917] 1966: 20

As Hume says, it is never "will alone" that causes mutual obligations but those expressed in signs that tie us together (1896: 523).[157] Words are transformative, they do not change physical matter but have real and physical effects and alter human relations. In other words, human communication almost always involves the production of a surplus. "Nothing said in words ever [comes] out quite even" in a mathematical sense (Le Guin 1974: 31). With words we can never make the books balance, it seems.

For normal (normalized) people, "words to a great extent make things, and that changing words, and, more generally representations … is already a way of changing things" (Bourdieu 1990: 54). If one is in a position to do so, if one possesses the requisite authority, the "imposition of a name" imposes on the named, their "social essence" (Bourdieu 1991: 120).[158]

---

155   "Thinking in pictures is … only a very incomplete form of becoming conscious. It some way, too, it stands nearer to unconscious processes than does thinking in words, and it is unquestionably older than the latter both ontogenetically and phylogenetically" (Freud [1923] 1960: 11).

156   "Temples have their sacred images, and we see what influence they have always had over a great part of mankind. But in truth the ideas and images in men's minds are the invisible powers that constantly govern them, and to these they all universally pay a ready submission" (Locke [1706] 1966: 31–32).

157   "[W]ords carry suggestions the way the wind carries pollen and leaves and dust particles. And music" (Barker 2017: 16).

158   "There is no social agent who does not aspire, as far as his circumstances permit, to have the power to name and to create the world through naming…" (Bourdieu 1991: 105). "The way men usually are, it takes a name to make something visible for them. – Those with originality have for the most part also assigned names" (Nietzsche [1887] 1974: 218).

It is hard, I found, to be called traitor. Strange how hard it is, for it's an easy name to call another man; a name that sticks, that fits, that convinces. I was half convinced myself.

LE GUIN 1969: 78

Names seem to devour things in a process of transformation where the living is destroyed ("The Letter Killeth"), the lifeless is animated, and things that did not previously "exist" suddenly spring forward in symbolic interaction (Mead [1934] 1962: 78). The word is a bridge between the dimensions of the real and the ideal. "[T]he articulated Word sets all hands in Action" (Carlyle [1836] 1987: 43). The word transforms the imperceptible into the perceived – and *vice versa* – and makes the subjective appear as objective – and *vice versa*.

> The part played by word-presentation ... [is] perfectly clear. By their interposition internal thought-processes are made into perceptions. It is like a demonstration of the theorem that all knowledge has its origin n external perception. When a hypercathexis of the process of thinking takes place, thoughts are *actually* perceived as if they came from without and are consequently held to be true.
>
> FREUD [1923] 1960: 13

Far from a mere dumb "tool" language is "'the god gone astray in the flesh'" (Valery, in Fanon 1967: 18). However, the extent of the reification and fetishization of the word is variable. For people unlucky enough to have their social system melt, i.e., forced to endure what amounts to a "psychotic structuration" of society reduced to interpersonal conflict, words have equal weight as material things; for example, peasants thrown out of stable feudal order into a world of destabilized and particularized symbolic authority experience words as material things with magical powers (Krier and Feldmann 2016: 212). Where conservative critics of "politically correct" neoliberal culture have a point is in the tendency for "progressives" to equate the material and the spiritual. For hard-boiled detectives or altruistic zealots solidly connected to their god, enemy words cannot hurt them. For the common neurotic, words are more than air but less than demons; our normal social reality is a kind of "virtual reality" (Žižek passim) where our normality, our status and class coordinates, are dependent upon sustaining fantasies that glitter like stars and prevent us from slipping into the abyss of the Real. Generally speaking, though we have to eat, sleep, and so on, we find our real pleasures in words and representations – with words we are very often "easily satisfied" (Safouan 1981: 86).

The field of empirical reality as a constellation of *names* is a mirror for psyche and only a psychotic sees right down to bare, lifeless bones.[159] Once a person has a name for something the object begins to shine,[160] reflect, and seems to spontaneously form connections with other objects. It seems, once one has the name or all the names, a problem has been solved.

> So the universe has always appeared to the natural mind as a kind of enigma, of which the key must be sought in the shape of some illuminating or power-bringing word or name. That word names the universe's *principle*, and to possess it is, after a fashion, to possess the universe itself. 'God,' 'Matter,' 'Reason,' 'the Absolute,' 'Energy,' are so many solving names. You can rest when you have them. You are at the end of your metaphysical quest.
>
> JAMES [1907] 1995: 21

James overestimates the quest-ending power of the word or name. Names are themselves questers.

Since the word can never express the totality of an object (some things must go unsaid) a mystical leftover is inevitable (Wittgenstein 1922). "The organization of things, even when in the context of technical enterprise it has every appearance of being objective, always remains a powerful springboard for projection and cathexis" (Baudrillard 2005: 28). To think about and understand the named thing sets into motion a 'speculative' journey around the field of interconnected objects linked by the dynamic, projective mind. The social space appears to sparkle with radiant objects. And these objects, named, and therefore more opaque than if they were theorized, mark a line of transition from object to thing. "Through all the superfluities of verbalism, through the magical illusion of the word (the world renewed, the new life, aesthetic transformation via the word), language takes on substance. It becomes reified, an extreme example of alienation" (Lefebvre 1995: 176). We can all think of more extreme forms of alienation but the point is well taken.

---

159 "I was out of my mind with sobriety, teetotalled – I felt lightheaded, I felt downright drunk, eating dinner up here with this sicko who saw nothing in me but myself. Jesus, what kind of pervert am I dealing with now?" (Amis 1984: 200).

160 Hegel's use of *"Schein"* is multifaceted and revealing (no pun intended). Not only does it mean "appearance" but also "shine" or "glow" and is correlated with essence and reflections such that the essence of a thing shines forth but is shrouded by a veil of appearances and illusions that, through a speculative or reflective method, can be known. See Inwood (1992: 38–39) for the various meanings and connotations.

The name *per se* provides us with no vital information but the projection of a name does animate an object and, metaphorically, makes it shine or sparkle.[161] Like crows and chimps, we do like shiny things.[162] Though the image is the active element, it appears to animate the passive carrier such that the whole ensemble itself appears within inverting consciousness as a power: gold is valuable, that's why we dig it up! It seems to be the profession of the word to become an outward, tangible, and visible representation (EFRL: 208) that encourages the mind to confuse reflections for reflectors. The word "gold" has a power over the imagination: fetishists put their faith in the "*gold* standard" when, sociologically, it is not the gold that is the important aspect but the existence of some kind of external *standard*.[163] Even people who should know better fall prey to fetishism. For example, in the case of gold once again:

> As a universal equivalent, gold is both a universally valid and always coveted form of value and wealth accumulation. It would be senseless to accumulate legal tender paper money, since it appears as value only in the domestic circulation of a country. Gold, on the other hand, is ... international money and constitutes a reserve for all expenditures. Hence its accumulation is always a rational act. Gold is an independent bearer of value even when it is not in circulation.... money with an intrinsic value— such as gold – is always needed as a means of storing wealth in a form in which it is always available for use
>
> HILFERDING [1910] 1981: 55, 58

---

161   If we meet a man named "Eric" we cannot know *a priori* that this man is intelligent but merely lacking motivation or whether or not he is destined to marry a woman named "Penelope." Wittgenstein makes some interesting points about names as "primitive signs" (1922: 22–23) that are worth considering.

162   Virtually everything here runs in opposition to the evolution of Baudrillard's thought on objects, signs, things, and mirrors. Where, in the late 60s, there were objects filling out the social space (2005) by the 80s there were only blank screens and networks (1983c). From objects to incomprehensible things. "Baudrillard's work often appears simply to recycle Adorno's vision of the totally administered society, but without any of the latter's sensitivity to its fissures and contradictions" (Dews 1987: 285–86).

163   Naming (nomination) and language would seem to put the world in order and make it comprehensible, yet, the symbolic order is to a great extent "senseless" and promotes "deregulation" (Žižek 2014a: 163) or anomie and words are especially important forces in ideological struggles. "Now the cat is out of the bag. You are attacking the profit motive and that leads to Communism.... It doesn't get anywhere and it doesn't mean anything. However, it makes both sides feel that God is with them. It is a form of prayer.... The words 'budget balancing' and 'social cost' contain all sorts of hidden polar terms. They are completely meaningless except as moving forces" (Arnold 1937: 170).

Beware those who use the terms "always" and "intrinsic." Because he fe-tishized gold, Hilferding also did not believe a pure paper currency was pos-sible and that the *gold* standard was basically necessary and eternal. Exactly 30 years after his death at the hands of the Gestapo in occupied France, the United States abandoned the gold standard, ushering in the era of limitless-ness and an empire driven by anomie. However, again, it was not the jettison-ing of the *gold* standard that opened the way to the devil of limitlessness but the negation of the gold *standard*.

One could approach fetishism from the side of primitivism or infantilism but, either way, we have a case of the name not merely confused with the object it points to,[164] but the name actually creating the thing, welding together name, material, and image (Hegel [1840] 1995b: 283). There is, therefore, tremendous power in knowing the names of things (Moret 1927: 366) and the enjoyment of life and power by virtue of having a name.[165] Our social honor is bound to our names and the desire for a good name forces us to maintain our contacts with others.[166] The name is essential (AJ: 142). "Names go to the bone" (Hemingway 1986: 141).[167] Names are our destinies (Schnitzler [1926] 1999: 84).[168] "They are everything.... From a label there is no escape!" (Wilde [1890] 1995: 221, 222). In modernity, tribalism is supposed to have receded into the past. However, we seem to be plagued, if not by literal tribalism in the social-organizational sense, at least by the residual tyranny of labels, titles, and names. Once you

---

164   People are hoodwinked by the signifier: "The signifier is treated as if it were identical with a pre-existing signified and ... the reader's role is purely that of a consumer... Signifier and signified appear not only to unite, but the signifier seems to become transparent so that the concept seems to present itself, and the arbitrary sign is naturalized by a spuri-ous identity between reference and referents, between the text and the world" (Tagg, in Chandler 2007: 68).

165   Arendt says that "a dog with a name has a better chance to survive than a stray dog who is just a dog in general" (1968: 287).

166   Egoists take note: "The passion to withdraw, to leave no trace, is inaccessible to anyone attached to his name and to his work ..." (Cioran 1974: 80).

167   "The structure of truth ... demands a mode of being which in its lack of intentionality resembles the simple existence of things, but which is superior in its permanence. Truth is not an intent which realizes itself in empirical reality; it is the power which determines the essence of this empirical reality. The state of being, beyond all phenomenality, to which alone this power belongs, is that of the name" (Benjamin [1963] 1998: 36).

168   "Strongly do the Russian folk express themselves! and if they bestow a little word on someone, it will go with him and his posterity for generations, and he will drag it with him into the service, and into retirement, and to Petersburg, and to the ends of the earth. And no matter how clever you are in ennobling your nickname later, even getting little scriven-ers to derive it for hire from ancient princely stock, nothing will help: the nickname will caw itself away at the top of its crow's voice and tell clearly where the bird has flown from. Aptly uttered is as good as written, an axe cannot destroy it (Gogol [1842] 1996: 123).

know the name of something, you know all you need to know, apparently. Lee Ross experimented with the power of names in the context of the Israeli and Palestinian conflict:

> Even when each side recognizes that the other side perceives the issues differently, each thinks that the other side is biased while they themselves are objective and that their own perceptions of reality should provide the basis for settlement. In one experiment, Ross took peace proposals created by Israeli negotiators labeled them as Palestinian proposals, and asked Israeli citizens to judge them. 'The Israelis liked the Palestinian proposal attributed to Israel more than they liked the Israeli proposal attributed to the Palestinians .... Closer to home ... Geoffrey Cohen found that Democrats will endorse an extremely restrictive welfare proposal, one usually associated with Republicans, if they think it has been proposed by the Democratic Party, and Republicans will support a generous welfare policy if they think it comes from the Republican Party'
>
> TAVRIS AND ARONSON 2015: 55

Label a suicide machine a "Tremendous, tremendous tax cut for the middle class" and tens of millions of forlorn Americans will think "bunko" is the brand.

Under certain circumstances, a minority of people are able to monopolize definitions and terminology, restrict the use of, and determine the lexicon of an entire branch of human affairs. In short, there are times when no more than a half dozen individuals are capable of not only defining a situation but creating an entire social fantasy.[169] In other situations, a whole new paradigm may erupt "all at once, sometimes in the middle of the night, in the mind of a man deeply immersed in crisis" (Kuhn 1970: 90). And sometimes, the combined power of an industry can twist minds so far off balance that people can be persuaded to forsake the living for the dead.

Illustrating the essential power of symbols, a childhood obesity study found that when children were asked to choose between a banana and a rock bearing a cartoon character for breakfast, it was reported that the overwhelming majority of them chose the rock.

---

169   "At one point, philosophers like [C.S.] Peirce could determine the very language we use. They had the power to define reality. But no longer, and this was, at least for me, no small tragedy. Over the last century, mainstream philosophy had retreated into the upper reaches of the ivory tower, and as it specialized and professionalized, it largely lost touch with the existential questions that drove [William] James and Peirce" (Kaag 2016: 25).

> We discovered the enormous swaying powers of spokescharacters when.... we asked three and four year olds to choose between a cupcake with the American flag and one with a familiar cartoon character. Almost all the kids picked a character over the red white and blue. So we upped the ante and went for the battle parents lose all the time – a fattening dessert versus fruit. We asked these pre-schoolers to choose between a cupcake and a banana. This time, we recruited Scooby and Shrek to pitch the fruit. Most went with what Shrek and company seemed to endorse. So finally, to see just how far these characters could sway kids, we asked: what would they rather have for breakfast? A banana or...a rock? We decorated the rock [with] character stickers this time. It seemed pretty clear companies can count on Scooby-Do when they've got some work to do. An overwhelming majority went straight for the rock.[170]

Likewise, researchers noted that children preferred the taste of food if they believed it originated from a fast food restaurant (Robinson, Borzekowski, Matheson, and Kraemer 2007).[171] Are children simply irrational and easily manipulated or do their choices illustrate a fundamental truth about social life, namely, that symbolic identification and symbolic nourishment are just as much essential elements for life as the physical energy provided by food? Sure, even little kids know that when push comes to shove they really cannot eat rocks for breakfast but corporate logos have an irresistible leverage over immature minds (of all ages). In other words, cartoon characters, logos, words, and images are active *forces* that energize, drive, and structure conduct. After the rise of the advertising industry and mass media, consumption of useful objects is always simultaneously the consumption of culture and signs (Ewen 1976: 42).[172] To the extent that a representation or an image has the "capacity to overcome resistance" it has "power" (Smith 1988: 339) or, really, *is* power.[173] A mere

---

170 "Who's to Blame for the U.S. Obesity Epidemic?" 19 August, 2006, *Dateline* NBC.

171 "By the early age of 3 to 5 years, low-income preschool children preferred the tastes of foods and drinks if they thought they were from McDonald's, demonstrating that brand identity can influence young children's taste perceptions. This was true even for carrots, a food that was not marketed by or available from McDonald's. These taste preferences emerged despite the fact that 3 of the foods were from McDonald's and only the branding was changed, indicating that the effects were not due to familiarity with the taste or smell of McDonald's food. Even the children with the lowest frequency of eating food from McDonald's had average positive total preference scores, indicating they preferred more of the branded foods (Robinson *et al.* 2007: 6).

172 On the origins of advertising aimed at children, see Ewen (1976: 143 ff.).

173 If we extend the benefit of doubt to these children and view them as not simply as mindless imitators we can be fairly certain that the power of corporate logos and collective

word, then, can become a "cult" (Cassirer 1946: 61)[174] and ideology consumes and reorganizes the real into social reality – they are doing it, but they don't know it, and even if they did know it, they would continue, cynically, to do it anyways (Žižek passim). From one angle, with regards to rock-eaters, it would be more accurate to say that from the intersubjective standpoint, they were attracted not to rocks at all but power or, from another angle, objectivated psyche (Freyer [1928] 1998). Minds and McNuggets. And, here, at the moment of externalization and projection, at this scale of social life, it is still possible to talk about the vital importance of an intersubjective perspective but, even here, things become opaque for these little rock-eaters because today's rock-eaters did not receive direct instructions from yesterday's rock-eaters on how to act, think, and feel about substituting rocks for sugar beets. If so, we could legitimately talk about "inter-individual traditions" and the transmission of an act from one person to another, one generation to another, and so forth. But this is not the case (S: 308–9). Our signs do not merely circulate on a flat horizontal plane from mouth to ear or eye to hand. There exists an irreducible depth to human language and signs compared to signals used by other animals. This depth is represented in the triadic structure of human communication; face to face conversations between individuals involves a third dimension lacking in animal dyadic communication – our symbols are used "to get someone else to attend to something outside the immediate relationship between speaker and hearer" (Evans 2014: 61).[175]

---

effervescence overwhelmed the countervailing power of their families to create an aura around bananas, carrots, and broccoli. When these studies were conducted, television was still the primary way children were exposed to corporate propaganda. The behaviorist fear is that children (with their "black box" minds) are capable of being brainwashed and transformed into drooling morons that want nothing more out of life than to prop up free-market capitalism. However, the dynamic view, while admitting that media content is an obvious problem, insists that the solution resides on the receiving side. It is more important what children bring to the image rather than what the image brings to them: "If children are relatively normal and adjusted, if they experience ... [e.g.] violence of TV in homes where love and support abound, neurotic antisocial behavior does not result" (Fore 1970: 99).

174   The insatiable desire to *be* a "name" can also drive a person toward the abyss of infinity: "And Ben! when he walks into a business office his name will sound out like a bell and all the doors will open to him! I've seen it, Ben, I've seen it a thousand times! You can't feel it with your hand like timber, but it's there" (Miller 1950: 86).

175   "It was as if I was a character in a movie and the real action was about to start at any minute. But I think some people wait forever, and only at the end of their lives do they realize that their life has happened while they were waiting for it to start. Do you know what I mean, Pasquale?' He did know what she meant! It was just how he felt – like someone sitting in the cinema waiting for the film to start. 'Yes!' he said.... He felt drained from trying

The sign or representation expands to account for the signifier, a word, and its signified, the concept (Saussure [1916] 1983). For example, the utterance of the word or profane carrier (signifier) "apple" points not to any particular apple in experience but to the idea or concept of apple in itself. Effectively synthesized, the sign manifests itself as a meaningful image in the minds of socialized individuals. Following Peirce ([1908] 1998: 481) we can reduce the most socially important types of signs down to three: index, icon, and symbol. An index indicates the presence of something; for example, a price tag is normally indicative of the presences of a certain magnitude of value or worth.[176] An icon (from the Greek *eikon* for "likeness" or "image") *stands for* something – an image of an envelope for "mail" or the likeness of a clock for "time." Finally, a symbol functions to link signifiers together in a chain: "baseball" might conjure the ideas of a spring afternoon, pine tar, peanuts, America, apple pie, mom, and so on. A sign is a part of the presentation and re-presentation process of intersubjective meaning-making. Here, the coherency of the terms seems to destabilize – a problem that worried many thinkers. What is the difference and relationship between, say, an idea, a concept, a representation, and so on? Kant exhorted "those who have the interests of philosophy at heart" to keep their terminological ducks in a row rather than letting it all fall apart "in a happy-go-lucky confusion, to the consequent detriment of science."

> Their serial arrangement is as follows. The genus is *representation* in general.... Subordinate to it stands representation with consciousness.... A *perception* which relates solely to the subject as the modification of its state in *sensation* ... an objective perception is *knowledge*.... This is either *intuition* or *concept*.... The pure concept, in so far as it has its origin in the understanding alone ... is called a *notion*. A concept formed from notions and transcending the possibility of experience is an *idea* or concept of reason.
>
> KANT 1929: 314; SEE WARTENBERG 1993: 116[177]

---

to speak English, but pleased to have communicated something abstract and personal ..." (Walter 2012: 54, 104).

176   "The guardian of the commodities must ... lend them his tongue, or hang a ticket on them, in order to communicate their prices to the outside world" (C: 189).

177   Karl Leonhard Reinhold was, for a time, the most famous Kantian professor in Germany. Reinhold's whole approach to presenting Kant was to focus on the processes of *representation*. Representations became the first principle, elemental, the foundation for all philosophy (see Pinkard 2002). Reinhold was important for putting "representations" on the lips of European philosophers.

"Representation" is here the master signifier, the signifier that commands, under which all other terms are species of representations.[178] The sign functions as a collective representation when it is a fact (authority) for some social collectivity. A good example of this kind of sign, the collective representation, is a national flag. Writing about the American culture wars of the Reagan era, Rodgers packs it all in to a couple of pages. The American flag was the "symbolic centerpiece" to this conflict:

> The flag was a partisan rallying point, a weapon in the culture wars.... [T]he flag was also a symbol of common ties and obligations.... It made visible the claims and ambitions that the nation as a whole embodied... [T]he flag was a vessel for ideals that went beyond identity, self, and markets. It carried aspirations for a common culture and a common set of public values.... But if the flag stood for aspirations for a common national culture, it also symbolized the nation's claims on the individuals who composed it. It condensed into an image the obligations that citizenship in the nation required: its demands for loyalty and affection, its webs of mutual obligation and support ... its requirements of sacrifice for the common good.... [T]he flag stood for the collective imperatives of the whole, the claims of each for all.
>
> 2011: 180–81

Here we see how the flag is a composite of signs that link concepts and ideas, standing for this and that, and even pointing in vague ways towards how much inequality "America" can tolerate and still be "America." But most importantly, the flag sign qua collective representation commands certain ways of acting, thinking, and feeling.

Signs are, as Saussure claims, arbitrary but the work of society puts a halt to arbitrariness (Levi-Strauss 1963: 91; see also G: 145; Quine 1960: 6).[179] "A dogmatic assertion that signs are all and equally 'arbitrary' is unjustifiable and unhelpful for general semiotics" (Hodge and Kress 1988: 22). In other words, the signifier is arbitrary in the material sense (Whitehead [1927] 1955: 2; see also

---

178   Importantly, representational thought at the institutional level is, in Hegel's word, *Entzweiung* ([1807] 2008: 712). While society is constituted by its representations the task of critical sociology is to raise collective consciousness to the "level" of collective self-consciousness, getting behind the representation and arriving at a world of rational praxis and conceptual thought (cf. Hegel [1807] 2008: 712).

179   "[S]ome things are arbitrary in the symbols we use and ... some things are not" (Wittgenstein 1922). "[I]f a symbol is not to be arbitrary, certain conditions are demanded of the material in which it is represented. The symbol for words, for example the alphabet etc. have an analogous history" (G: 145; Goux 1990 also addresses this passage).

Deutscher 2013: 10) but is not arbitrary in the immaterial, from the standpoint of shared and authoritative meanings (Chandler 2007: 76).[180] Successful paternal repression that negates the incestuous imaginary relation between the child and maternal caretaker (socialization) results in a link between signifier and the signified "that will never break" (Fink 1997: 93).

But not everything rises to the level of crystallized collective representation as Mauss indicates: "There is something other than collective representations in society, however important or dominant they may be ..." (1979: 7). Even though "representation" was already on the tongues of Europeans it was Hegel who transferred the concept of "representation" to the ground of moral authority and legitimation processes: for something to be a representation it "must have that status bestowed" on it "by being taken up into the practice of giving and asking for reasons" (Pinkard 2002: 260).[181]

4   Objectification and Internalization

Beyond productivity for the satisfaction of organic needs, objectification is an essential aspect of human life in that it humanizes the world and, in their creative activities, people duplicate their existence (Sayers 2011: 16–25; see also Becker 1973: 185). "In creating a *world of objects* by his practical activity, in *his work upon* inorganic nature, man proves himself a conscious species being ...." (PM: 113). The world is, in so far as it has been *altered* by humans, the external transfigured form of humanity itself, or, at least, the vision and ideas of the ruling class made concrete by their servants (MECW, 5: 59).[182] Here, though, we are still squarely in the domain of relatively transparent praxis:

> The production of ideas, of conceptions, of consciousness, is at first directly interwoven with the material activity and the material intercourse

---

180   It is a feature of children and some "primitives" to disallow the arbitrary nature of the signifier (Chandler 2007: 74–5). It is a feature of psychosis to confuse the signifier with the object signified (Chandler 2007: 73–4).

181   "As Michel Foucault has shown, only in the early modern period did scholars come to see words and other signifiers as representations which were subject to conventions rather than as copies.... By the seventeenth century, clear distinctions were being made between representations (signifiers), ideas (signifieds) and things (referents). Scholars now regarded signifiers as referring to ideas rather than directly to things. Representations were conventionalized constructions which were relatively independent both of what they represented and of their authors" (Chandler 2007: 75).

182   "'Alienation is not objectification. Objectification is natural. It is not a way for consciousness to become alien to itself, but a way to express itself naturally'" (Hyppolite, in Aron 1965: 230).

of men – the language of real life. Conceiving, thinking, the mental
intercourse of men at this stage still appear as the direct efflux of their
material behaviour. The same applies to mental production as expressed
in the language of the politics, laws, morality, religion, metaphysics, etc.,
of a people. Men are the producers of their conceptions, ideas, etc., that
is, real, active men, as they are conditioned by a definite development of
their productive forces and of the intercourse corresponding to these, up
to its furthest forms.

MECW, 5: 36

When we make objects, when we as subjects objectify, we are still in a realm
of freedom in the sense that "in what confronts the subject there is nothing
alien.... [O]n the contrary, the subject finds himself in it.... [T]he subject is rec-
onciled with the world, satisfied in it, and every opposition and contradiction
is resolved" (Hegel 1975a: 97). In other words, objectification is not the null fi-
cation of the individual but the actual confirmation of individual activity (PM:
140). This world of transparent activities, objectifications, and non-mysterious
relations may have the aire of fiction (C: 169; EFRL: 292) and they may also be
felt to "stand against" us (Freyer [1928] 1998: 24) but we are nonetheless not
doomed to alienation qua massive reification at this point. At this precise moment "The horizon is not too vast; the consciousness ... can easily embrace it"
(Durkheim 1961: 231). Objective life is open to transparent constructions and
meanings and, while much if not most of our representations and objectifications are obscure, many are crystal clear to us. We must reject a statement like
that from DeLuca (1977: 13) where objectification and idolization are inseparable, at least at this scale of life, although, with Durkheim we might find out
later that a bit of reification is inevitable and even *necessary*, but this does not
mean we are doomed to fetishism[183] even as we admit that the moment of objectification lies along a continuum with the possibility of eventual "loss of the
object" (PM: 108). Objectification is only metaphorically the crystallization of
mind[184] and energy (EFRL: 422) but objectification is also inextricably bound
up with introjections (Durkheim [1912] 1915: 252) and identifications, the
presence of an object in the mind as a representation due to its reflection back
into consciousness (EFRL: 47)[185] not to mention the fact of accretion whereby

---

183   See Spero (1992: 88–89) for a critique of DeLuca's identification of objectification and
fetishism.
184   Refer again to Marx's comparison of the bee and the architect. "Because the course of the
world has handed down to us the precipitate of [its] ... activity, even if in ruins, a mind
now stands face to face, over time and space, with another mind" (Freyer [1928] 1998: ■.
185   "Spirit itself and the moments distinguished within it generally belong to representational thought and the form of objectivity. The *content* of representational thought is absolute

that which is "stored up in earlier works asserts itself in any new creations and moves the execution of the individual work in the direction of the collective process" (Mannheim 1982: 232). Even when we sense that we are working only for ourselves with our own comprehensible products we are nonetheless fated, so long as our private actions impinge upon the public sphere in any way, to never freely choose what is internalized. Just as an infant does not choose its mother, it has no object-choice of its own because it lacks an ego (Parsons 1964: 92), the even slightly-integrated member of the group does not have much choice in rejecting or choosing its internalized object-representation if that person wishes to remain in the group.[186]

"To represent something ... is to give a thing an internal idea.... Representation ... is the process by which human practices breaks down the rigid dichotomy between subject and object upon which sociological materialism is based.... The material world is subjectified and, at the same time, the subjective world is objectified" (Alexander 1982: 249). A representation[187] is an idea that is formed from the socially mediated process of communication. Our signs are dynamic, charged with effervescence, and, to jump ahead, once they become authoritative, determine conduct.[188] We engage in energetic association such as rituals, effervescence is projected onto something external via signification, the ritually-produced force is imagined to inhabit an object at the center of the cult and, consequently, that object is set aside, becomes taboo and therefore

---

spirit, and the sole remaining issue is that of sublating this mere form, or, rather, because the form belongs to *consciousness as such*, its truth must have already resulted from the shapes consciousness has assumed" (Hegel [1807] 2008: 715).

186   Of course, people often dissemble and dissimulate. In a theoretical condensation (formal results chapter) I will try to map out a model of dyspraxia following some ideas by Austin (1975).

187   "Representation is the production of the meaning of the concepts in our minds through language" (Hall 1997: 17). Representations are systematized twice over, once when objects and things are "correlated with a set of concepts or *mental representations* which we carry around in our heads," i.e., organized systems of classification, conceptual maps, and so on, and, secondly, the translation of these maps and classifications "into a common language, so that we can correlate our concepts and ideas with certain written words, spoken sounds or visual images" (Hall 1997: 17–18).

188   "How is one to explain, for example, that a Negro who has passed his baccalaureate and has gone to the Sorbonne to study to become a teacher of philosophy is already on guard before any conflictual elements have coalesced round him? Rene Menil accounted for this reaction in Hegelian terms. In his view it was 'the consequence of the replacement of the repressed [African] spirit in the consciousness of the slave by an authority symbol representing the Master, a symbol implanted in the subsoil of the collective group and charged with maintaining order in it as a garrison controls a conquered city'" (Fanon 1967: 145).

negatively sacred, and is "elevated" from an *object* to an ambiguous *thing* bearing special emblems that evoke an array of contradictory feelings and sentiments. The process of painful expenditure (loss) is rewarded by a recovery in
the form of introjected object identification (Freud [1923] 1960: 18–20). This
new object, not only set up in the ego of the individual but all the egos of the
participants, marks the arrival of a collective image. "Feelings evoked by a person or a thing spread contagiously, from the idea or that thing or person to the
representations associated with it, and from there to the objects with which
those representations become associated" (EFRL: 326).[189] The sceptic "knows
that the emotions result form mere plays of images" but the believer feels awe
and fear and "From the fear, the conclusion: A majestic and awesome force
does indeed live in it, so he keeps his distance from that thing and treats it as if
it was sacred, even though it is in no way entitled to be" (EFRL: 326).

Representations are mental realities yet nonetheless objectively real across
particular and universal linguistic and sign worlds. The relationship between
material and immaterial objectivities is unique. Even though we "bump into
stuff" when we move around our material environment it is important to remember that the material world is experienced by ordinary consciousness as
being consumed by signs (Hegel [1840] 1974: 109–10) and can be "read" like a
"text." As shared ways of acting, thinking, and feeling, social facts are identical
with what Durkheim called objective manifestations of collective consciousness and the system of "collective representations" that constitute the objective manifestations of our reality. "Everything occurs in the sphere of public
opinion, but this latter is precisely what we call the system of collective representations. Social facts are therefore causes ... [due to the fact that] they are
representations or act on representations. At the inner foundation of social
life stands a whole group of representations" (Mauss 2005: 17). These representations offer not simply an "image of reality, a motionless shadow projected
into us by things." Instead, a representation is "a force that stirs up around us a
whole whirlwind of organic and psychological phenomena" (DOL: 53). The emphasis on the *force* of representations represents the definite limits of symbolic
interactionism, pragmatism, and hard constructionism with respect to representations as more than a problem of ordinary communication and informa-
tion-sharing. Moscovici, for example, argued for ditching the term "collective
representations" for "social representations" because the word "collective"

---

189   Mannheim also shows us that the internalization process involves *contagion* whereby
      what gets taken back up by the ego is infected with an alien supplement (1982: 188–80).
      We seem to always get not enough or too much of what we need and want.

implies "constraining force on the individuals swept up in it. It left the implication that the representations conveyed by language and nourished by tradition had a coercive power on the members of a given society. In fact, this power is the very symbol of their collective nature. Representations thus took on, if not a transcendental, at least a supraindividual character." Moscovici continues:

> It was thought that each person bore their imprint but without knowing how the representations were conceived and shaped. A great mystery hovered over the way in which they came into being and how they made us function in society.... And yet we should not be led to underestimate the autonomy of the present and the contribution each member of a given society makes in creating and maintaining the beliefs and behaviors shared by all. In other words, what counts is not the separateness of individual representations but the transformation of each individual imposes on group representation and the converse.[190]
> 1984: 949–50

Unlike the majority of my critical colleagues, I do reserve a place for constructionism and intersubjectivity within the sociogony, to deny it is to remain obstinately dogmatic and to render individuals nothing more than cog-like automatons in a vast, transcendental machinery – without attention to this scale of life we are left with little more than theoretical fatalism or ridiculous prophecies centered around automatic laws of history.[191] The fact of a hegemony of structure does not permit us to ignore an entire scale of social life. Postone, for example, claims that within capitalism the "essential social relations are social in a peculiar manner. They exist not as overt interpersonal relations but as a quasi-independent set of structures that are opposed to individuals, a sphere of impersonal, 'objective' necessity and 'objective dependence'" (1993: 125). In this world we are ruled not by others but by abstractions. Far be it for me to argue against the reality of structural domination but, frankly, this perspective

---

190 Moscovici's lack of attentiveness to power and domination leaves representations functioning as little more than *tools* for making sense of the world. I think we know who the tool is.

191 If intersubjectivity and constructionism were irrelevant I'm not sure what is supposed to happen once a social order disintegrates, but, at the same time, the pragmatic emphasis on fluidity (where any universal equivalent merely "comes and goes" with each passing dyadic moment as we see in the accidental value form) and the lack of a crystallized universal normative order (and a Big Other) qua universal third term rendered Marx's theory of communist association a complete failure both in thought and in practice (Worrell and Krier 2018).

is populated with ghosts.[192] However, we do not want to error on the opposite end of the spectrum, where, for example, Moscovici is clearly overstating the agency of individuals and it is a fiction he shares with those who believe in liquid constructions and pragmatist traditions (i.e., egoists and mystics). The powers of individuals depends upon many things including the scale of life, status, legitimacy, inequality, and a thousand other things that cannot be reduced to scientistic variables, not to mention all the unconscious dynamics swirling in the underground. The problem with Moscovici is one that most theorists share when they think of the difference between individual and collective consciousness and representations, as we saw in the chapter on social facts.

There exists in conscious minds, collective representations which are distinct from individual representations.[193] Of course, the active side of society is made up *only* of individuals[194] and, consequently, collective representations are only due to the manner in which individuals can act and react upon each other within a constituted group.These actions and reactions, however, generate *external* psychic phenomena of a new type (refer to the preceding chapter)[195] that are capable of evolving independently, of mutually modifying one another, and whose grouping forms a definite system.... [Representations] translate (or, to employ

---

192   Postone falls into the class of "robot Marxists" that pin their hopes on the rise of the dead as the precondition for the liberation of the living (1993: 357). What robot Marxists fail to realize is that the establishment of full automation and the enlargement of negative freedom (*from* work) does not guarantee the enlargement of the sphere of positive freedom.

193   Individual or psychological representations and collective representations are different species of thought that appear to be nothing more than slight alterations or extensions of one another but the two classes of things are unique and while one can map what appears to be a continuous line from one to the other they nonetheless occupy separate domains of reality (Mauss 2008: 18).

194   "The individual *is* the *social being* ...." (Marx, in Lichtman 1982: 64). "For society is no more intelligible without the individual than is the individual without society" (Lichtman 1982: 64). Nowhere is this dynamic and reciprocating relation better expressed than toward the end of *Elementary Forms* where Durkheim says: "Like ritual life, social life in fact moves in a circle. On the one hand, the individual gets the best part of himself from society – all that gives him a distinctive character and place among other beings, his intellectual and moral culture. On the other hand, however, society exists and lives only in and through individuals" (EFRL: 351).

195   Connecting the material on externality in the first chapter to the concept of repression: "For the mental process which has been turned into a symptom owing to repression now maintains its existence outside the organization of the ego and independently of it" (Freud [1926] 1959: 18).

philosophical language, they 'symbolize') its actual structure.... The psychic life of society is, therefore, constituted from quite different material from that of the individual.

Fauconnet explained collective representations well when he emphasized their energized quality and their capacities to mobilize people for particular actions: "societies have representations which are peculiar to them, collective representations charged with collective emotions; and that these representations (beliefs, myths, aesthetic images, moral notions, scientific concepts, technical ideas), form the greater part of thought and sensibility strictly human.... these collective representations express not only the exterior world and the individual consciousness, but society itself, a real being and a system of forces, which dominate individuals and act through them" (1927: 16).

If collective consciousness is to appear, a *sui generis* synthesis of individual consciousnesses must occur. The product of this synthesis is a whole world of feelings, ideas, and images that follow their own laws once they are born. They mutually attract one another, repel one another, fuse together, subdivide, and proliferate; and none of these combinations is directly commanded and necessitated by the state of the underlying reality. Indeed, the life thus unleashed enjoys such great independence that it sometimes plays about in forms that have no aim or utility of any kind, but only for the pleasure of affirming itself.[196]

EFRL: 426

This description of the free play of collective consciousness sounds strikingly similar to Žižek's depiction of the autonomous forms of the cinematic Real in Part Three of *The Pervert's Guide to Cinema*: forms are autonomous and express their own meanings. "Beneath the level of meaning ... we get a more elementary level of forms themselves communicating with each other, interacting, reverberating, echoing, morphing, transforming, one into the other. And it is this background ... of proto-reality, a Real which is more dense, more fundamental than the narrative reality." Žižek's error is to interpret this play of forms as a "cinematic materialism." A "transcendental materialism" would presuppose an "empirical idealism." And characterizing the play of forms as a "proto-reality" confuses rather than clarifies their nature as *social a priori*, i.e., the dance of

---

196 It is no doubt true that "Social existence determines consciousness" (Dunayevskaya 1965) but it is no less true that social consciousness determines existence.

collective consciousness à la Durkheim. Clearly, this is a nonstarter for any reasonable social ontology. In confusing material effects and appearances for the
forms per se, Žižek's materialism signals a regression from the achievements of
Hegel, Marx, and Durkheim.

In the foregoing, it might seem that collective representations are only ideas
running in our heads but Durkheim, not exactly an idealist, makes perfectly
clear that these representations find material *supports*, that they, in a sense,
mount the physical world ([1914] 1960: 335–36).[197] Through productive activity the human externalizes consciousness but in a contradictory way – these
contradictions "frustrate man's attempt to integrate himself into his world"
(Avineri 1972: 90).

Everything we have mapped out to this point, from assemblage to objectification, can be summarized from Durkheim's portrayal of the crowd:

> A number of men in assembly are similarly affected by the same occur-
> rence and perceive this at least partial unanimity by the identical signs
> through which each individual feeling is expressed. What happens
> then? Each one imperfectly imagines the state of those about him. Im-
> ages expressing the various manifestations emanating, with their different
> shades, from all parts of the crowd, are formed in the minds of all. Nothing
> to be called imitation has thus far occurred; there have been merely per-
> ceptible impressions ... sensations, wholly identical with those produced
> in us by external bodies. What happens then? Once aroused in my con-
> sciousness, these various representations combine with one another and
> with my own feeling. A new state is thus formed, less my own than its pre-
> decessor, less tainted with individuality and more and more freed, by a se-
> ries of repeated elaborations analogous to the foregoing, from all excessive
> particularity.... [T]his combination of forces results in something new.[198]
>
>   S: 125–6

The crowd, that temporary and fluid proto-society (Durkheim 1961: 62) can
whip itself up to the stature of a "fearful monster" due to a quantity-quality

---

197   Importantly, Durkheim's self-professed "qualified idealism" avoids the pitfalls of realism
      that materializes the sacred and, as such, confuses the sacred and the profane; Durkheim's
      dialectical analyses are identical in spirit and intent to Marx's where the sacred and the
      profane, the ideal and the material, are fastidiously separated at all stages of inquiry.
198   "It has often been observed that, caught in a crowd, hurried along in its current, the indi-
      vidual soon comes to feel as though taken out of himself. He is carried away by emotions
      to which, if left alone, he would never either have raised or lowered himself" (Bouglé
      [1926] 1970: 30).

dialectic (S: 126) where quantitative increases of "the original state" are transformed into qualitatively new feelings and expressions. This process is described as a "reaction" and a "fusion" whereby an assemblage of individuals
transforms into a group with its own, irreducible, objective consciousness and
definite feelings and prescribed courses of action. And this brings us to another important consideration regarding internalization, which is, the necessity
for continuous re-internalizations; it is not only insufficient but also impossible to "energize" representations once and for all. Foucault on punishment
gives us what we need:

> To find the suitable punishment for a crime is to find the disadvantage
> whose idea is such that it robs for ever the idea of a crime of any attrac-
> tion. It is an art of conflicting energies, an art of images linked by associa-
> tion, the foregoing of stable connections that defy time: it is a matter of
> establishing the representation of pairs of opposing values, of establish-
> ing quantitative differences between the opposing forces, of setting up a
> complex of obstacle-signs that may subject the movement of the forces
> to a power relation.... The role of the criminal in punishment was to rein-
> troduce, in the face of crime and the criminal code, the real presence of
> the signified – that is to say, of the penalty which, according to the terms
> of the code, must be infallibly associated with the offence. By produc-
> ing this signified abundantly and visibly, and therefore reactivating the
> signifying system of the code, the idea of crime functioning as a sign of
> punishment, it is with this coin that the offender pays his debt to society.
>   1977: 104, 128

The reflected arousal of representations[199] where individuality and immediacy recede into naturalization and second nature, is the point at which
internalization, re-internalization, introjections, and so forth, shade off into
identification (Freud [1921] 1959: 47–50) where estrangement and, later, violence break out between subjects (see volume two). To the extent that the relation between the objectification and the internalization of that product evades

---

199   The paradoxical nature of words is that they simultaneously provide us with the capacity
      for externalization and projection, gaining objective control over perceptions and grasp-
      ing ever-larger swaths of experience but under certain circumstances (ceremonials, etc.)
      words act like the breath of gods resulting in enhancement and estrangement. "So mar-
      vellous was his achievement that, down to our own day, man has persistently sought to
      apply the magic of words to realms where it is worthless. Since words often to bring about
      changes in human conduct, acting as a trigger if not as a bludgeon, primitive man sought
      to apply this power to non-human objects as well: were not clouds and trees alive? By
      word magic, he would invoke rain or fertility, health or energy" (Mumford 1973: 417).

conceptualization, such that it lacks an adequate concept of itself, consciousness will remain estranged from itself and externality will be more or less permanent (Hegel 2007: 27).

5   Estrangement, Fetishistic Reversals and Inversions, or, the Problem
         with Straw Hats

"The good *is* the bad. One cannot take Hegel literally enough here" (Gadamer 1976: 51).[200] As we will see in the second volume this dramatic statement requires qualification. What is meant is that, within the structure of the concept, with an eye toward the inner syllogism, the universal singular enjoys its moral good standing on the back of the impure particular equivalent that, in its reciprocal sacrifice (functional one-sidedness), raises it out of the bad and also into the good, unless, of course, after receiving its gift of recognition, the singular disposes of its alter ego and, in so doing, brings down the entire absolute order. Alienation dynamics, in other words, continue to provide the crucial insight into identification and moral statuses. Progress = misery (PM: 71).

Estrangement or dispossession, reversals, and inversions are essential aspects moving "laterally" or "forward" into the increased obfuscation of the social process. Inversions occur at both the intimate, face-to-face level as well as the aggregate. In the *Grundrisse* Marx indicates that the "process of objectification in fact appears as a process of dispossession from the standpoint of labour or as appropriation of alien labor from the standpoint of capital – to that extent, this twisting and inversion [*Verdrehung und Verkehrung*] as a *real*

---

200   "Thus every Part was full of Vice, Yet the whole Mass a Paradise" (Mandeville [1732] 1924, 1: 24). All action, says Durkheim, is altruistic (S: 279–80) and "*action* is itself nothing else but negativity" (PS: 238). "And pious action we do sugar o'er / The devil himself" (Shakespeare 2001: 64). "Present day psychology is increasingly turning back to Spinoza's idea that things are good because we like them, rather than that we like them because they are good.... An act is socially evil because it is rejected by society" (DOL: 40). As the old saying goes, "The good is the evil we choose to ignore" (Nelson [1917] 1957: 90). If we're all selling our talents it is no longer prostitution (G: 163). Evil, then, is simply the good we cannot get enough of. Good and evil are polarities of an "excess in two contrary directions" (Bataille [1962] 1991: 78). "The opposition between good and evil lacks the radical character ascribed to it by the popular conscience. Imperceptible gradations lead from one to the other and frontiers are often unclear" (S: 371). And, anyways, "In the final analysis, to understand everything means to forgive everything" (Weber 1988: 375). "When all tend to debauchery none appears to do so. He who stops draws attention to the excess of others, like a fixed point" (Pascal 1941: 124). "Irreligion is simply a word for other people's religion; immorality, a term for behavior different from our own" (Hook 1934: n.p.).

[phenomenon], not merely supposed one existing merely in the imagination of the workers and the capitalists" (G: 831). "Ascending from earth to heaven" we finally encounter the world in its distorted image, the threshold of "camera obscura" inversions and "phantoms" or "sublimates of ... life process" that plague consciousness (MECW, 5: 36). Inversion creates a "magical effect" (CPE: 152) in the minds of creators such that their creations come back to the ego, are introjected and set up in the ego (Freud [1923] 1960: 18–20), as autonomous and enigmatic forces. A couple of things are worth pointing out here.

As Marx says in his *Resultate*, "The objective conditions essential to the realization of labour are alienated from the worker and become manifest as fetishes endowed with a will and a soul of their own" (C: 1003). No argument here, however, what is meant in this passage by "alienation" is best conceived of as "estrangement" or "dispossession" such that the object of, in this case, labor, is seized by the owner of the means of production for the purpose of exchange rather than consumption and needs-satisfaction. It is basically loss of goods or a *separation* of product from producer that leads, according to Marx, to the rise of a miscomprehension of products and a *forgetting* of one's actual role in creation and of one's normative value. There is quite a complicated social psychology at work here that Marx attempts to sketch out, if only in a rudimentary fashion: the work that is "just effort and torment" for the laborer is, for the capitalist, "a substance that creates and increases wealth." Reduced to a "variable component" in the labor process, living workers experience life as the "rule of things over man, of dead labour over the living, of the product over the producer." This inversion of the means (things) over the end (human beings) such that "the dead" becomes an end in itself over "the living" results in the "personification" of objects and the dehumanization of subjects: things perceived as living beings and people confronted as dead objects. The entire process of production for exchange rather than needs-satisfaction is "a process of enslavement" (C: 990). But note well, Marx is always racing ahead from the point of objectification to enslavement – e.g., we find that as soon as we are at the moment of "inversion" we are already moving from the world of alienated impersonality to a world dominated by "monstrous objective power" belonging to the "personified conditions of production" (G: 831). Once our productions come back to us in inverted and mystical forms they call and command, prohibit, and demand more repressions and self-negations – now, even if our desire for companions and comrades wanes we can count on external injunctions to maintain and even increase our capacities for energetic discharge.[201]

---

201 A society that has not devolved to full egoism has built into it, as a necessity, a way to channel built up aggravations and hostilities (see Fanon 1967: 145).

Before racing on we should look at this desire for companions in a more intimate situation where an unexpected reversal or spin throw us for a loop.

Conscientious manners extended toward another may have the effect of
changing our feelings or throwing a situation into a new light – even a well-
played miscommunication can make all the difference. Powell sketches a
humorous portrait of misplaced affection whereby a young man, anxious to
let a young woman know of his feelings before departing, mistakes another
woman for the object of his affection, resulting in a curious transformation of
sentiment:

> As she turned, I immediately realized that the hand was, in fact, Madame
> Dubuisson's, who, as she left the house, must have taken up Suzette's
> straw hat to shield her eyes while she crossed the garden.
>
> It was now too late to retreat. I had prepared a few sentences to express
> my feelings, and I was already half-way through one of them. Having
> made the mistake, there was nothing for it but to behave as if it were
> indeed Madame Dubuisson who had made my visit to La Grenadière
> seem so romantic. Taking her other hand, I quickly used up the remain-
> ing phrases that I had rehearsed so often for Suzette.
>
> The only redeeming feature of the whole business was that Madame
> Dubuisson herself gave not the smallest sign of being in the least sur-
> prised. I cannot remember in what words she answered by halting as-
> surance that her presence at La Grenadière would remain for me by far
> its sweetest memory; but I know that her reply was entirely adequate...
>
> This scene, although taking up only a few minutes, exhausted a good
> deal of nervous energy. I recognized that there could now be no ques-
> tion of repeating anything of the same sort with Suzette herself, even if
> opportunity were to present itself in the short time left to me. That par-
> ticular card had been played, and the curious thing was that its effect had
> been to provide some genuine form of emotional release. It was almost
> as if Madame Dubuisson had, indeed, been the focus of my interest while
> I had been at La Grenadière. I began to feel quite warmly towards her,
> largely on the strength of the sentiments I had, as it were, automatically
> expressed.
>
> [1951] 1962: 164–5

What still needs answering is, at this moment in the sociogony, why loss and
inversion necessarily lead to fetishism. Fetishism is not merely the mystification of an object but also the notion that an object is not a merely everyday

object but somehow invested with a special moral quality or *force* and capable of extraordinary effects.

> The word 'fetishism' derives from the Latin for *making*. It was used by Portuguese voyagers to describe African religion. The idea is that a fetish, or *feitiço,* is an object *made by people* which they think contains super-natural powers. 'Fetishism,' then, is the system of beliefs that people hold about the fetishes they make. The critical point is that, even though they make these fetishes themselves, people in the grip of fetishism believe that these objects have power *intrinsically.*
>
> SMITH 2016: 29

Marx repeatedly draws the parallel between the labor process and religious and ideological inversions. It seems impossible that a worker could confuse a manufactured good with a god, however, as Durkheim shows, how we regard and treat objects determines their moral statuses (cf. G: 412). Forbid contact with an object[202] and it is transposed from the realm of the profane to the realm of the sacred. Indeed, we do not venerate an object because it is sacred, rather, an object confronts us as a sacred entity because we feel obligated to venerate it. When a thing that is profane encroaches upon something vener-ated the group and therefore the psyche launch into self-defense mode.

Take for example the intrusion of straw into the world of felt. Freytag's sketch of hostilities between neighboring hat-makers, Hummel and Hahn illustrates nicely the power of material objects as carriers of status, marks of distinction, and tokens of differentiation that generate, direct, and maintain hostilities. Hummel, the maker of felt hats, is vexed by the intrusion of Hahn, the manufacturer of straw hats, into his once-exclusive neighborhood:

> Mr. Hahn was respectable; there was nothing to be said against his fam-ily; but he was Mr. Hummel's natural opponent, for the business of the new settler was also in hats, although straw hats. The manufacture of this light trash was never considered as dignified, manly work; it was not a guild handicraft; it never had the right to make apprentices journeymen; it was formerly carried on only by Italian peasants; it had only lately, like other bad customs, spread through the world as a novelty; it is, in fact, not a business – the plait-straw is bought and sewed together by young girls

---

202　"The later Deuteronomic and priestly conception occasionally enjoins strict ritualistic prohibition of the enjoyment of blood on the grounds that one must eat the soul neither of man nor animal. It would result in evil charm and possibly possession" (AJ: 141).

who are engaged by the week. And there is an old enmity between the felt hat and straw hat. The felt hat is an historical power consecrated through thousands of years – it only tolerates the cap as an ordinary contrivance for work-days. Now the straw hat raises its pretensions against prescribed right, and insolently lays claim to half of the year. And since then approbation fluctuates between these two appurtenances of the human race. When the unstable minds of mortals wavered toward straw, the most beautiful felts, velveteen, silk, and pasteboard were left unnoticed and eaten by moths. On the other hand, when the inclinations of men turned to felt, every human being – women, children, and nurses – were men's small hats; then the condition of straw was lamentable – no heart beat for it, and the mouse nestled in its most beautiful plaits.[203]

[1887] 1890: 22–3

For it to retain its prestige, felt cannot simply allow straw to waltz right in unopposed.[204] Straw is trash.[205] Unlike any other article of clothing or accessory the hat is a representation and makes reference to a code. Hats embody and express ideas (Bernays 1928)[206] and function to mark important lines of demarcation such as gender and class distinctions.[207] Here, the hat is an instrument of social regulation, a sign that something has a hold on the person (Certeau 1984: 147). It is not simply a case of a new fashion alternative, rather, there is felt and, then, there is that which is not-felt that disturbs custom and offends

---

203   "My new clothes had put me instantly into a new world. Everyone's demeanor seemed to have changed abruptly. I helped a hawker pick up a barrow that he had upset. 'Thanks, mate,' he said with a grin. No one had called me mate before in my life – it was the clothes that had done it. For the first time I noticed, too, how the attitude of women varies with a man's clothes. When a badly dressed man passes them they shudder away from him with a quite frank movement of disgust, as though he were a dead cat. Clothes are powerful things" (Orwell [1933] 1961: 129; see especially Malraux 1961: 247 on the transformative power of attire in the eyes of others; also Mann [1924] 1952: 343).

204   The syntagmatic concern, here, is the either-or tension between felt and straw (the materials) whereas the paradigmatic concern is the hat itself as an object to be worn on the head; for those who value felt, straw is impossible; they cannot both be worn on the head at the same time and they can never be combined (Barthes 1964; Chandler 2007: 86).

205   On hostilities between felt hats and berets see Hertz ([1913] 1987: 58). On the monstrosity of composite headgear see Flaubert (1957: 4).

206   "How mean and comically a Man looks, that is otherwise well dress'd, in a narrow-brim'd Hat when every Body wears broad ones; and again, how monstrous is a very great Hat, when the other extreme has been in fashion for a considerable time?" (Mandeville [1732] 1924, 1: 328). On 'hat terror' see Dostoyevsky's *Crime and Punishment* (1994: 6).

207   On the orchestrated velvet hat invasion of America and the decline of felt see Bernays (1928). See also the chapter on hats in Gilman (2002).

sensibilities.[208] The things we wear, the food we eat, our bad habits, etc., are "the machinery by which a society represents itself in living beings and makes them its representation" (Certeau 1984: 147). The clothed and fed individual becomes the *Vorstellungsrepräsentanz* or the representative of the representation (see Fink 1997: 167). This is, unfortunately, an inevitable and ubiquitous aspect of any "general economy" – we will fight over straw and felt. "We make a comedy of our life, a web of lies and pretensions. We are nevertheless doomed to a contempt for others, expressed in violent prejudices against them. The inescapable cause of this is the desire to be *more human*" (Bataille [1976] 1991: 337–38). We all draw distinctions between ourselves and others, lines separating one group from another, and, as such, the setting one thing apart from others, introduces a mark of distinction, of a higher value of sacralization compared to others. "Something sublime is the principle of our being, which maintains the millennial contest in which men have always tried to be more worthy of admiration than their fellows" (Bataille [1976] 1991: 343). As we will see in volume three, valorization is always preceded by a radical devaluation.

As with the product that is *separated* from the worker, the fact of loss, of spatial-temporal distance, collective production, or multiplication, etc., injects a quantum of mysticism into the moment. Here, Lévy-Bruhl's *participation mystique* ([1910] 1926; [1923] 1966) is relevant: the subject-object identity of "this is what I have done" (this is my objectification) is transformed into "they are doing it but they don't know it" whereby the product, whatever it is, seems to take on a life of its own, and ego and object blend.[209] For its own sake "society often needs us to see things from a certain standpoint and feel them in a certain way. It therefore modifies the ideas we would be inclined to have about them, and the feelings to which we would be inclined if we obeyed only our animal nature – even to the extent of replacing them with quite opposite feelings" (EFRL: 62).

Many powerful social facts have remained within the pre-reified moment of the sociogonic arc for decades and even generations. The meaning of Jesus

---

208 Although, today's trash is often tomorrow's treasure (Wharton 1924: 9–80). It must be noted that this kind of "'generic'" animosity toward something as mundane as a hat or article of clothing (as signifier of class or status position) is the mark of the "'semi-feudal'" mentality (Gramsci 1971: 273) that one finds, still, among the downwardly mobile and déclassé elements of society.

209 "In Weininger the feeling of omnipotence was instigated by his primary narcissism, which was clearly related to his pronounced self-esteem. The result was that he developed a peculiar brand of speculative metaphysics. For him all objects gradually became concrete ego-qualities. His ego was penetrated by the world, and the world was penetrated by his ego" (Abrahamsen 1946: 165).

prior to the consolidation of the New Testament under Irenaeus was highly fluid as numerous Christian communities constructed their own representations
of Christ in stories, some of which were written down in the form of gospels
(the good news). Those that were perceived to undermine church authority
by promoting mysticism and direct, unmediated access to the sacred, were
branded as heretical, a process that left the church with only four books out of
dozens to choose from. This process of creating an orthodox Christianity out of
a multitude of Christianities took nearly 200 years to complete.

6   Reification and Sublation

There are things and then there are Things. Leiris reports of having his pronun-
ciation corrected by a parent – we clearly see the difference between a thing
and some other kind of thing:

> The word which until then I had used as a pure interjection, without any
> awareness of its real meaning ... was suddenly inserted into the whole se-
> quence of precise meanings. The sudden apprehending of the complete
> word, which until then I had always slurred, took on the quality of a dis-
> covery .... It was no longer a thing that belonged to me alone. It partook
> of the reality which was the language of my brothers and sister and also
> of my parents. What had been a thing peculiarly mine became a common
> and open thing. All at once, in a flash, it had become a shared, or rather
> a socialized thing.
>
>   IN SARTRE [1952] 1963: 43

What had been a personal thing without meaning is transformed "in a flash"
into a social object, not "socialized thing." After the correction, the word had
not only meaning for Leiris but for everybody, a precision where there had
been opacity and isolation – a new rationality and illumination was created.
This is what we strive for. However, social life is not restricted, in the final analysis, to the intersubjective relations and the face-to-face correctives and the
arriving at understandings.

    The result of inversion and fetishism is the appearance of human praxis,
spirit not merely in its objective guise, but in the form of things as carriers of supernatural *forces* and capacities. Look no further than the first few lines of *Capital* and we find that "The commodity is, first of all, an external object, a thing .."
(C: 126). More precisely, it was an *object* but now its objectivity has moved beyond the horizon of inversion and mystification and into the reified space of a

sublated thing (objectivity is preserved but has become additionally *weird*).[210] Reification means "thingification" – where an object becomes weirdly unrecognizable and perceived as unalterable, inevitable, and even eternal. Reification renders invisible the social relations that animate it (Lukács 1971: 83)[211] as well as its historical development. The thing does not come from somewhere it simply is.[212] According to Berger and Luckmann, "... as soon as an objective social world is established, the possibility of reification is never far away."[213]

> The objectivity of the social world means that it confronts man as something outside of himself. The decisive question is whether he still retains the awareness that, however objectivated, the social world was made by men – and, therefore, can be remade by them. In other words, reification can be described as an extreme step in the process of objectivation, whereby the objectivated world loses its comprehensibility as a human enterprise and becomes fixated as a non-human, non-humanizable, inert facticity.[214]
> 1966: 89

---

210 We are with Adorno on the connection between the reified thing and the enchanted fetish: "a peculiar pathology of the material in which the former solid things of a world of use values are transmogrified into abstract equivalencies which none the less now project the mirage of a new kind of libidinally invested materiality..." (Jameson 1990: 180).

211 "There is both an objective and a subjective side to this phenomenon. *Objectively* a world of objects and relations between things springs into being ... [and] ... confront him as invisible forces that generate their own power.... *Subjectively* ... a man's activity becomes estranged from himself..." (Lukács 1971: 87). Reification, really, is the transformation of the *objects* springing up into overbearing and incomprehensible *things*.

212 "For us ... accustomed to thinking in units of one or a few lifetimes, the permanence of the state and its administered space seems an inescapable constant of our condition" (Scott 2017: 13).

213 Note well that reification is a *possibility* and not an *inevitability*. "The school of Lukács has overestimated the theory of reification to the point of making it the foundation of a philosophy and sociology" (Lefebvre [1966] 1968: 48).

214 Berger and Luckmann, however, cannot keep the distinction between objects and things clear: "I am constantly surrounded by objects that 'proclaim' the subjective intentions of my fellowmen, although I may sometimes have difficulty being quite sure just what is that a particular object is 'proclaiming,' especially if it was produced by men whom I have not known well or at all in face-to-face situations" (1966: 35). The everyday world is filled not with objects proclaiming subjective intentions but things that keep their mouths shut. Their over-reliance on the primacy of face-to-face, symbolic interaction leads constantly back to the land of pragmatic intersubjectivity that, combined with other problems noted earlier, render *The Social Construction of Reality* a flawed classic. Heidegger, as well, did not understand the distinction between objects and things, or willfully distorted matters for the sake of maximizing authenticity-value (Adorno [1964] 1973: 7) when he proposed to transform Kant's Thing-in-itself into the Object-in-itself (1971: 177). Kant knew well what he was doing when he chose the word "thing" rather than "object." John Carpenter's *The Thing* would be absurd if it had it been titled *The Object*.

Here people do not have the experience of having created or given birth to anything, rather, they feel as if they are pushed around by unseen but palpably real entities with a will of their own and a resistance to being comprehended: "A thing is any object of knowledge which is not naturally penetrable by the understanding" (RSM: 36). Life takes on a religious tinge – we feel compelled to take the side of this or that idea in the field of "warring gods" (FMW: 152) and whereby we feel that we make "imperishable" contributions "to a super-personal realm" (FMW: 155). Thingification "tempts the subjects to ascribe their own social circumstances of production to the noumena" (Adorno 1973: 189)

The veiled essence of reification is contained in the Latin *differre* (defer) delay, to set beside oneself,[215] to put off until a later time, and which is the root of *deference*, yielding to superiority. On the one hand, the problem of reification, the transformation of the object into a thing, is the problem of time[216] and space:

> The distance between a systematized delusion and the first impressions that gave birth to it is often considerable. The same applies to religious thought. As it progresses historically, the causes that called it into existence, though still at work, are seen no more except through a vast system of distorting interpretations. The popular mythologies and the subtle theologies have done their work: They have overlaid the original feelings with very different ones that, although stemming from primitive feelings of which they are the elaborated form, nevertheless allow their true nature to show only in part. The psychological distance between the cause and the effect, and between the apparent cause and the effective cause, has become wider and more difficult for the mind to overcome.[217]
>   EFRL: 7

On the other hand, reification is a problem of deference to superiority, the superiority of, say, public opinion or an authoritative representation or prestigious person that stands apart even as they stand within. Whereas an object is ordinary a thing can be simultaneously less than and more than ordinary – a

---

215   Recall that any time we set certain objects aside or set them apart from others, the remainders, we set into motion the valuation of objects.

216   "Firstly ... most social institutions have been handed down to us already fashioned by previous generations; we have had no part in their shaping" (RSM: 37).

217   On the spatial-temporal aspects of "differ" and "defer" see Goux (1990: 27).

thing taken for granted that, when one stops to consider it, reveals an abyss of meaning and origins.[218]

For an example of the spatial-temporal dimension whereby an object of comprehension from one angle is, from another, an incomprehensible thing, take the case of a guru expounding upon the meaning of a graph to credential-seeking neophytes. Present from the beginning, the graph, built up piece by piece and explained point by point, is an *object* to all in attendance, so long as they are paying attention. "Consider the object for a moment: the object as humble and receptive supporting actor, as a sort of psychological slave or confidant – the object as directly experienced in traditional daily life ..." (Baudrillard 2005: 26). The assembled know who presented the graph-object, how it was conceived and built, what it means according to the guru's explanation and, importantly, they have been held responsible for knowing it and reproducing (representing) it during future examinations.[219] In short, the graph as an object has arisen out of interaction, discourse, defining, interpretations, and it means something and is comprehended by reason. It is a social object (Blumer 1969: 10–11, 68–69). The object possesses a reason and we can not speak "of *things* at all, i.e., of something which would be for consciousness merely the negative of itself" (PS: 143). After the figure has been completed and the presentation has moved on to other matters, a straggler arrives and is barred entrance, left to wonder the meaning of the day's teachings. The origin and meaning of the graph is uncertain for this latecomer; here the graph is not a concrete object but an enigmatic and esoteric thing to this individual separated from their cohort.[220] Held responsible for knowing the meaning of the

---

218   "To the most, indeed, he had become not so much a Man as a Thing; which Thing doubtless they were accustomed to see, and with satisfaction; but no more thought of accounting for than for the fabrication of their daily *Allgemeine Zeitung*, or the domestic habits of the Sun. Both were there and welcome; the world enjoyed what good was in them, and thought no more of the matter. The man Teufelsdröwwckh passed and repassed, in his little circle, as one of those originals and nondescripts, more frequent in German Universities than elsewhere; of whom, though you see them alive, and feel certain enough that they must have a History, no History seems to be discoverable; or only such as men give of mountain rocks and antediluvian ruins: that they have been created by unknown agencies, are in a state of gradual decay, and for the present reflect light and resist pressure; that is, are visible and tangible objects in this phantasm world, where so much other mystery is" (Carlyle [1836] 1987: 14).

219   Our "objects" are far from the mystical confusions of Latour (see 1993: 112). "Today, at last, these objects emerge absolutely clear about the purposes they serve" (Baudrillard 2005: 16).

220   There are object and there are things. Sometimes, though, the object contains some enigmatic aspect from the standpoint of the subject, or, what is thing-like in one sphere is, in contrast, an altogether well-known object in another: "There are persons who exist in the

figure, without further assistance, the estranged latecomer must construct the meaning of the thing from past experiences, guesswork, and rationalizations. The outcome will, inevitably, be far from the shared conceptual meaning possessed by the the community of insiders. In other words, the straggler is recast as a primitive among moderns (Simmel 1955: 127).

The extreme nature of reification means that people become *estranged* from their own products and relations, or what should be their own products and relations. Estrangement is, literally, becoming a stranger in one's own land, confronting ourselves in transfigured, unrecognizable and impersonal forms, and, ultimately, finding oneself on the outside looking in with bewilderment. Things seem to come from, or present themselves to us, from some "transcendental" (external) dimension separate from our world or from a different time. When it comes to graphs and other things "our minds seem to be incapable of imagining the birth of the [thing] at all, for we are latecomers and the heirs of time" (Burckhardt [1943] 1955: 108–109). The temporal dimension is important. Perhaps the guru is indulgent with those arriving a minute late and is willing to get them "caught up" but is inflexible toward those that attempt entry later – with each passing minute we move away from object and closer to thing, from insider to outsider, from person to pariah.[221] With respect to our latecomer, the graph, like the self, is a fraction and they will have to rely on the goodness of others, through deference, on completing the picture, literally, and also the completion of their fractured self picture, estranged as they are from the community (Goffman 1967: 84). But space and time work against the completion of the picture. With the passage of time we forget much that would be helpful in preserving the object status of what has devolved into a thing. With regard to the categories of totemic classification, for example, Durkheim and Mauss tell us "The reasons which have led to the establishment of the categories have been forgotten, but the category persists and is applied, well or ill, to new ideas ..." ([1903] 1963: 21). Circling back around to the beginning of the chapter, we can see that since flexible and symbolic communication between humans enables us to interact, cooperate, and produce not only in face-to-face contexts with intimates but also with strangers and other generations, we are in a sense "doomed" to live in a world of things and not just

---

world not as objects, but as alien specks or spots on objects. They sit in the same place, hold their head in the identical manner, one is ready to take them for furniture and thanks that in all their born days no word has ever passed those lips; but somewhere in the servants' quarters or the pantry it turns out simply – oh-ho-ho!" (Gogol [1842] 1996: 110).

221   There is an inevitability here as well. The guru knows in advance, statistically, that two out of twenty candidates will fail to maintain an "objective" orientation to the teaching and will fall into a reified confusion, will fall into alienation. From the very beginning, two are already rogues – only time will tell who is fated.

objects. I look around my domestic environment I have no idea where most of this stuff originated, who made it, how it was made, and so on.

The object *per se* is present to us in its lack of mystery (subjective intention and all that jazz) whereas a thing is strange and lacks humanity. Our ignorance and our attitude of responsibility toward that ignorance sets up the transition from subject to subjugated. We are on the threshold between freedom and unfreedom. "The ignorant man is not free, because what confronts him is an alien world, something outside him and in the offing, on which he depends, without his having made this foreign world as in something his own" (Hegel 1975a: 98). Industrial capitalism and the commodification and mass-marketing of everything means that we are mostly doomed to living in a world of mysterious things. But this is not a solid crystal. There are a range of objects and things and we can get to know them to a fair degree.

One of my possessions, a former commodity, is a musical instrument that even though I had no hand in its creation it is also not exactly a mysterious thing to me. I do know where it was made, I know when it was made, I know exactly how it was made and the entire labor process from beginning to end – I even know how many days it took to shape the neck of this instrument. I also know what all the materials are and where they originated. I know how the instrument functions. I know its "name" (in this case, a serial number and a model designation). If I had the inclination I could even find out the names of the people who cooperated in its manufacture. In some cases, it is possible to determine the names of every employee who had a hand in making an instrument in a factory back in the 1960s because each worker wrote their initials in a body cavity or a neck pocket as the instrument moved from one job station to the next. There is a whole cult devoted to revealing the meanings of these marks and establishing the provenance of these instruments. The cult is so developed that ordinary factory employees are tracked down and interviewed regarding their experiences working in old, mythologized factories and those that can be connected to some operation such as winding wire around magnets or the shaping of a neck of an instrument that found its way to Woodstock, etc., become minor celebrities in their own right and suddenly find their wages increasing or even using their new celebrity leverage to launch their own small business winding and sanding. It is certainly weird that mass-manufactured goods can sometimes hide codes in out of the way places and under paint. With more automation being used every day in the musical instrument industry the chances of finding these intriguing signs are becoming more remote, however, at the same time, we live in what amounts to a golden age of boutique craftsmanship and pseudo-boutique assemblage work ("fauxtique") that promises to collapse the distance between producer and consumer.

There is a measurable distinction between an object that I make, on the one hand, and one that is made for me according to my specifications and another distance yet down the scale of obscurity to the object selected on the basis of qualities. Each step along the continuum leads to greater obfuscation, from pure object to thing. And even an object that emerges from my efforts may undergo a transvaluation such that it is transposed from the domain of objects to some old thing that winds up in the recycling bin or garbage. When we cease to care, objects and things both collapse into another dimension of non-objects and non-things. We cannot produce a complete catalog of objects and things but the world is filled with many different types: objects, partial objects, anti-objects, non-objects, lost objects, dark or invisible objects, positive and negative, material and immaterial, and so on, and then the whole sequence begins anew with things – dark, partial, negative, etc., concluding with *the* Thing.

Sociologically, though, we can see that both object and thing fall on "this side" of the process of representation and regardless of whether or not a thing is known or a mystery it is still represented in ordinary consciousness. When estrangement goes beyond external transfiguration to feeling uncanny, weird, or hostile (truly alien) we have moved beyond reification and into alienation proper and the oppression of people by their own thoughts, emotions and creations. Representations become more than a problem, riddles, and hieroglyphics, they return as commanding powers demanding obedience.

7   Alienation and Domination

The social character of activity, as well as the social form of the product, and the share of individuals in production here appear now as something not only external and objective but, beyond that, as alien, confronting the individuals, not as their relation to one another, but as their active subordination to relations which subsist independently of them and which arise out of collisions between mutually indifferent or antagonistic individuals. The general exchange of activities and products, which has become a vital condition for each individual, their mutual interconnections, here appears as something autonomous, as an enigmatic thing. Immersed in the sphere of exchange value, the social connection between persons is transformed into a social relation between things (G: 157).

Marx's "Estranged Labor" from the 1844 manuscripts hones in on four aspects of alienation:
1.   estrangement from the product of labor;
2.   estrangement from the process of labor;

3.   estrangement from species being, and;
4.   estrangement from one another.

Drawing the problem of alienation out along these four lines reveals a well-worn path rooted in preexisting philosophical debates between critical and absolute idealists as well as debates between idealists and materialists during the 19th century. Of paramount importance was, and remains, the interdigitated and paradoxical nature of *autonomy* and *heteronomy*. It is upon this axis that Marx's essay rotates. The first two forms appear to hang together logically and bear most directly on the problem of *heteronomy*.

Form one (from *product*) exposes the reduction of the working class to the status of slaves and we see an entire social class in bondage (PM: 109). Form two (from *process*) emphasizes the "cretinism" of workers: subjecting workers to barbaric mechanization and the reduction of human life to the level of human creatures (caught between the twin poles of humanity and beasts) and the sacrifice and loss of self (PM: 110–111).

Forms three and four revolve, in a somewhat jumbled manner, around the problem of *autonomy*, and, importantly, the nature of universality and individuality.

Form three (from *species being*) explores the destruction of productive freedom and universality (PM: 112). Capital breaks down the life of the species "into a means of individual life" (PM: 112) and reduces "individual life into its abstract form" (PM: 112–13). Here we find reversals, duplications, and inversions of life such that the only element of universality left for workers is in production (objectification) and consumption of individual commodities via the particular medium of cash exchanges,[222] while the self is cast off into what Sartre might call "molecular exile at the boundary of life and death" – of singular isolation and powerlessness and incomprehensible duplications of subjective spirit in its alien, objective forms ([1960] 2004: 733). Of special note is the falling of the individual into the "wrong" where abstractions, money, i.e., crystals of value, mediate the individual's relationship to the means of existence (use-values). Marx draws this out in his *Critique* where C–M–C, the sale of labor power, in exchange for wages, and the purchasing of use-values for survival, conform to this "wrong" syllogistic form of P–U–S or P–U–I (CPE: 94; see Hegel [1821] 1991: 115–32). Form four, however, represents another weird formation (alienation *between individuals*) and the sundering of both universality and

---

222   "Production, distribution, exchange and consumption ... form a proper syllogism; production represents the general [universal], distribution and exchange the particular, and consumption the individual [or singular] case which sums up the whole" (CPE: 194).

individuality with relations particularized and instrumentalized. Relations are
incapable of immediate gratifications or spontaneous associations.

Forms three and four are blended as Marx demonstrates when he says "...
the proposition that man's species nature is estranged from him means that
one man is estranged from the other, as each of them is from man's essential
nature" (PM: 114). The logical differentiation between forms three and four is
that between *universality* (species being) and *singularity* (individual or singularity contra particular): "man and man" (the other as the social mirror for the
individual). Here we see the influence of classical "mirror philosophy" made
popular by Goethe (philosophically by Fichte) and the mystification involved
in the breakdown of freedom between "man and man" into the coercive relationship between worker and owner (PM: 115) or between workers thrown
into competition against one another. Durkheim passes over the same theoretical territory in *Suicide* where we find four modes of alienation emerging in
the "social octahedron" (the problem of volume two), corresponding with the
four primary types of self-destruction: egoism and estrangement; anomie and
splitting;[223] altruism and possession; and fatalism and bondage. We will map
these dimensions in the volume on self-destruction.

For now we can see that building a social psychology bridge out of Durkheimian materials, as a mediating conceptual matrix connecting Marx to the
domain of subjective spirit, yields interesting dividends. From the standpoint
of *Suicide* we correlate the four forms of suicide (egoism, altruism, anomie,
and fatalism) with the four types of alienation worked out by Marx (see Worrell 2015a, 2015b; 2014a; 2014b). A self-destructive society is arrived at when
some force disrupts the social equilibrium and solidarity and regulation are
lost; where there had been a society now an abyss opens and begins to drag
institutions and individuals to their total or partial demise – perhaps in the
wake of a charismatic savior (Neumann 1944: 96). The purely negative currents
that had previously been fused into a positive "alloy" (the "four horsemen of
the apocalypse" canceled upward or sublated into the "positive hell" of a normal society, cf. Hegel [1807] 1977: 278) now, acting independently or in weird
conjunctions, lure individuals to self-destruction. The spirit of *anomie* induces
people to strive for the impossible and promises a world of limitlessness advancement but delivers aggravation and the sorrow of the ego *split or divided*
within itself – we become strange to ourselves, our selves and alter egos in

---

223   "Rooms divide, rooms multiply. Houses split – houses are tripleparked [sic]. People are
        doubling also, dividing, splitting. In double trouble we split our losses. No wonder we're
        bouncing off the walls" (Amis 1984: 64; see also Wilde [1890] 1995: 165).

unmediated conflict;[224] *egoism* preaches *detachment* and isolation leading to depression, materialism, or sorrowful introspection due to the lack of anything but a molecular flow of egos and their fleeting and accidental contacts; *altruism* might seem good on the surface but, beneath its platitudes, it leads to the *possession* of people and renders them either *tools* to some terrifying (negative) Other (instrumentalization) or leads them to seek *absorption* within the infinity of some ethereal and holy substance and its crystallization in the (positive) Other; and, finally, the spirit of *fatalism* corresponds to *bondage* to some other that holds all the power. In each case we find some broken down form or another of the dialectic of mediation: a flow of singularities; the unmediated terror of a chiding absolute over a one-sided subject bent on achieving the impossible; the individual who misplaces his or herself within the coordinates of the imagined absolute; the lone ego devoid of others.

Heteronomy
estrangement from the product of labor = slavery and bondage = fatalism;
estrangement from the process of labor = possession = altruism;

Autonomy
estrangement from species being = splitting, multiplying, and doubling = anomie;
estrangement from one another = estrangement and atomization = egoism.

Within the Durkheimian register we find that Marx's four modes of alienation correspond well with the conceptual matrix worked out in *Suicide* and impinge on the above distinction between autonomy and heteronomy.

Heteronomy, in simple terms, is the negative identity of fatalism and altruism in their pure forms. The identity of egoism and anomie is what Durkheim calls "the disease of the infinite" but also corresponds to the polar opposite of heteronomy, namely, *autonomy*. As we have seen, Marx argues for what amounts to autonomy of individuals from any restraining Other and an autonomy to do whatever strikes their fancy whenever they want ("just as I have a mind"). But this notion of autonomy is built from either an assumption regarding instinctual self-regulation or Enlightenment-era notions regarding the

---

224   This multiplication is built into the foundations of capitalist society: "The reproduction of labor-power which must incessantly be re-incorporated into capital as its means of valorization, which cannot get free of capital, and whose enslavement to capital is only concealed by the variety of individual capitalists to whom it sells itself, forms ... a factor in the reproduction of capital itself. Accumulation of capital is therefore multiplication of the proletariat" (Marx 1976: 763–64).

rationality of the individual. Reason is not a psychological fact but a social fact. The *ethic* of this autonomy, however, is Faustian:

> ... Faust attempts to establish that he is indeed independent, that he, as Faust the individual, is capable of doing as he pleases in that world ... For Faust, independence is thus simply unimpeded freedom to do 'as he pleases' unconstrained by past convention or mores. Faust desires to see himself affirmed as free in the sense of being unimpeded in his doing what he wants. In this way, Faust stands for the darkly self-realizational romantic side of modern self-understanding, the desire to cast away the past and push all limits simply in order to have it affirmed for himself that he *can* do so, that there is nothing in the past or in current mores that *could* count as a reason against his doing anything.
>
> PINKARD 1996: 93–94

From the critical sociological perspective, autonomy (abstract self-rule) is not only undergirded by a hidden heteronomy where you are free to choose so long as you make the right choice (Žižek passim) but is just as pathological as the ideal-type of automatonism or the idea of being ruled by an alien other that utilizes others as mere instruments or beasts of burden. Marx, in his utopic de-mystification and banishment of the Big Other and the reduction of syllogistic particularity to the function of a procession of singularities, actually falls into a re-positing of what amounts to egoism and deregulation (anomic striving), the negative identity of which we know of as "the disease of the infinite" or *autonomy*.

The various moments of the sociogony up to this point can be summarized as such: the product of repression within the interaction setting is the generation of a current of what Durkheim calls "collective effervescence" or "ebullience"[225] that, if it is not to go to waste by way of, e.g., the pragmatic method,[226] must be projected or transferred, as we will see, via some process of *signification* involving, among other things, correct utterances, syntactical-ly-correct formulas, and the performance of (possibly mimetic) gestures. The whole point of signification is to, essentially, provide a *name* for the collective

---

225 Simmel says that groups "exhibit something one might call collective nervousness – a sensitivity, a passion, an eccentricity that will hardly ever be found in anyone of their members in isolation" (SGS: 35).

226 The essence of the pragmatic method as described by James is the assuagement of ebullience, i.e., being a party-pooper ([1907] 1995: 18). Though, this method might come in handy when it comes to the return of the repressed. Pragmatism is good for people who need a rest or to have their uncertainties and doubts tamed.

effervescence generated by ritualists and get people moving in the right (rite) way.[227] Fauconnet explained representations perhaps best when he emphasized their "charged" natures and their capacities to energize masses of people and move them in particular directions: "societies have *representations* which are peculiar to them, collective representations charged with collective emotions; and that these representations (beliefs, myths, aesthetic images, moral notions, scientific concepts, technical ideas), form the greater part of thought and sensibility strictly *human.* ... these collective representations express not only the exterior world and the individual consciousness, but society itself, a real being and a system of forces, which dominate individuals and act through them" (1927: 16).

8   Derealization and Desublimation, or, Treitschke in Narnia

Derealization (*Entwirklichung*) is our final sociogenic moment, the fall into agony or the collapse of social reality into (a) the world full of monstrosities[228] or, (b) at the final limit, a lapse into the "desert of the Real" (Žižek).[229] Berger calls this last phase of the process of disintegration "de-objectivation" and it can descend to a point where a meaningful social existence melts down into anomic terror, horror, and insanity (1967: 170) before finally blinking out.

> It is the moment ... when everything will fall into lawlessness, sons will raise their hands against fathers, wives will plot against husbands, husbands will bring wives to law, masters will be inhuman to servants and servants will disobey their masters, there will be no more respect for the old, the young will demand to rule, work will seem a useless chore to all, everywhere songs will rise praising license, vice, dissolute liberty of behavior. And after that, rape adultery, perjury, sins against nature will follow in a great wave, and disease, and soothsaying, and spells, and flying bodies will appear in the heavens, in the midst of the good Christians

---

227 Though it is too long to quote, Hermann Hesse's description of the ecstasy and effervescence of a festive dance scene in Steppenwolf is perfect (1963: 190–94).

228 "Where men cant [sic] live gods fare no better" (McCarthy [2006] 2012: 145).

229 "The world shrinking down about a raw core of parsible entities. The names of things slowly following those things into oblivion. Colors. The names of birds. Things to eat. Finally the names of things once believed to be true. More fragile than he would have thought. How much was gone already? The sacred idiom shorn of its referents and so of its reality" (McCarthy [2006] 2012: 75). The place where language fails is called Hell (Mann 1948: 245).

false prophets will rise, false apostles, corrupters, impostors, wizards, rap-
ists, usurers, perjurers and falsifiers; the shepherds will turn into wolves,
priests will lie, monks will desire things of this world, the poor will not
hasten to the aid of their lords, the powerful will be without mercy, the
just will bear witness to injustice. All cities will be shaken by earthquakes,
there will be pestilence in every land, storm winds will uproot the earth,
the fields will be contaminated, the sea will secrete black humors, new
and strange wonders will take place upon the moon, the stars will abandon their courses, other stars – unknown – will furrow the sky, it will
snow in summer, and in winter the heat will be intense. And the times of
the end will have come, and the end of time.

ECO 1983: 453–4

Are we there yet? Where previously in the sociogony we encountered potentialities, mutable energies, forces for potential good and evil, alien powers and
domination, we now find destiny and demons.[230] Each moment in the continuum, from energy to monstrosity represents greater reification, disorder,
coercion, and the debasement of validity. Far from Spirit coming to know itself
or gaining self-certainty, the terminus (while it does contain all of its earlier
moments) leads not higher but lower and, circling back, into explosive dissolution and inchoate energies. There is a great difference, morally, between effervescence objectified and *force*.[231] Before total collapse into nothingness we
are plagued by "sorcerers" and monsters of various kinds. But make no mistake,
before the collapse into the Real, the kind of negative heaven we find in the
next volume on suicide is one that is fully sacred; anti-gods are, as Durkheim

---

230   In *Socialism: Utopian and Scientific*, Engels says: "As long as we obstinately refuse to un-
      derstand the nature and the character of these social means of action – and this under-
      standing goes against the grain of the capitalist mode of production and its defenders –so
      long these forces are at work in spite of us, in opposition to us, so long they master us, as
      we have shown above in detail. But when once their nature is understood, they can, in the
      hands of the producers working together, be transformed from master demons into will-
      ing servants. The difference is as that between the destructive force of electricity in the
      lightning of the storm, and electricity under command in the telegraph and the voltaic
      arc; the difference between a conflagration, and fire working in the service of man. With
      this recognition at last of the real nature of the productive forces of to-day, the social an-
      archy of production gives place to a social regulation of production upon a definite plan,
      according to the needs of the community and of each individual" (MECW, 24: 320).
231   "Force is a physical power; I do not see how its effects could produce morality. To yield to
      force is an act of necessity, not of will; it is at best an act of prudence" (Rousseau [1762]
      1968: 52).

says, still fully gods (EFRL: 423).[232] "Ghosts, vampires, monsters, the undead dead, etc., flourish in an era when you might expect them to be dead and buried, without a place. They are something brought about by modernity itself" (Dolar 1991: 7).[233]

> The fear of bourgeois civilization is summed up in two names: Franken-stein and Dracula. The monster and the vampire are born together, one night in 1816, in the drawing room of the Villa Chapuis near Geneva, out of a society game among friends to while away a rainy summer. Born in the full spate of the industrial revolution, they rise again together in the critical years at the end of the nineteenth century, under the names of Hyde and Dracula.... Frankenstein and Dracula lead parallel lives. They are two indivisible, because complementary, figures; they are two horrible faces of a single society, its *extremes*: the disfigured wretch and the ruthless proprietor. The worker and capital.
>
> MORETTI 1988: 83

But any and all societies contain monsters, that is, monstrosity is a "permanent" social feature (RSM: 105)[234] and even essential.[235] Evil, pathology, crime, moral degeneration, disease, and monstrously bad public art,[236] exist for a

---

232 "The whole of religious life [recall that everything is religious] gravitates around two opposite poles ... their opposition being the same as that between the pure and the impure, the saint and the sacrilegious person, the divine and the diabolical" (EFRL: 413). "Monsters exist because they are part of the divine plan, and in the horrible features of those same monsters the power of the Creator is revealed" (Eco 1983: 48). "Monstrous forms of life do exist, are not at all rare, and perhaps represent a form of decline and death" (Lefebvre [1966] 1968: 29).

233 We should also keep monsters and the monsterization of the humanities foregrounded (never has so much been written about monsters). When one form of life dies and a new one has yet to fully emerge to replace it, social discourse becomes fixated on monsters and the supernatural in general. The function of these monster discourses (ghost stories, etc.) is to negate egoism and draw people back together. It is through horror stories and the undead that "we learn the value of the hearth and of our fellow men" (Alain [1934] 1974: 76). There's no place like home.

234 Just as Durkheim claims that, ultimately, "everything is religious" the young Benjamin says that "In everything there is something monstrous that we have to keep quiet about" (1996: 16).

235 "Moreover, to employ the somewhat theological language of our adversaries, whatever is necessary must have some perfection in it" (S: 362).

236 "It is not accidental that our greatest art is intimate and not monumental, nor is it accidental that today only within the smallest and intimate circles, in personal human situations, in *pianissimo*, that something is pulsating that corresponds to the prophetic *pneuma*, which in former times swept through the great communities like a firebrand,

reason (RSM: 32) and we can comprehend their functions.[237] The real is rational (Hegel). In *Macbeth*, a good tale of anomie,[238] we find the witches functioning on the fringes of society as the living embodiments of social contradictions
(Orgel 2000). It is another thing altogether when monstrosities come rushing
in from the fringes to play a dominating role in normal life. The capitalist era
of value divination and neoliberal fusion of markets and conflict is the epoch
par excellence for monsters and sorcerers.[239]

   Hegel equates the rise of machine production with the demise of artisan
labor as a developmental force in the life of the human spirit (Avineri 1972: 87–
98). The mechanization of labor means, "this deceit that he practices against
nature ... takes its revenge upon him; what he gains from nature, the more he
subdues it, the lower he sinks himself." Work as a whole becomes more mechanistic, deadening to consciousness, and substantively worthless, increasing
the quantity of mindless labor for the individual trapped in the world of mass
production while making productivity superfluous for other segments of society (Hegel [1802–04] 1979: 247; cf. Marcuse 1941: 77–79). Hegel's prognosis is

---

welding them together. If we attempt to force and to 'invent' a monumental style in art,
such miserable monstrosities are produced as the many monuments of the last twenty
years" (FMW: 155).

237 On "functions" see RSM: 123. For an example of function, crime serves the needs for punishment. We do not punish a person or group because they have committed a crime,
rather, something is a crime because it is punished (DOL: 40). In the aftermath of the 1968
Tet Offensive it became obvious (with the Korean debacle in the rearview mirror) that
the US did not have what it takes to defeat adversaries on the ground the way it did still in
the 1940s. What also became obvious was that the new forms of guerrilla warfare encountered in Vietnam did not dispose of surplus young men the way the previous wars did; the
US was involved in Vietnam from the moment of the French defeat in 1952 until the final,
ignominious liftoff in 1975 and the sum total of dead was approximately 55,000 for the
US. With so many young males piling up in the domestic core, and so many servicemen
returning from Vietnam as heroin addicts, a new "war" had to be waged in order to soak
up potential trouble and the "war on drugs" was cooked up by the Nixon administration
in 1971. Whatever the unwanted are doing, criminalize that, then throw them in jail. Well-
off whites abuse drugs and get treatment; blacks abuse drugs and are thrown in prisons
to function as slave laborers. Durkheim makes an analogous argument in EFRL regarding
the social psychology of demonization and enemy-creation. So, crime and enemies are
"constructs" after all. Yes, but try telling that to victims and prisoners. I don't think addiction knows it is a construct.

238 "I have no spur / To prick the sides of my intent, but only / Vaulting ambition, which
o'erleaps itself / And falls on th' other" (Shakespeare 2000: 21).

239 "Capital doesn't give a damn about the idea of the contract which is imputed to it – it is
a monstrous unprincipled undertaking, nothing more.... Capital in fact has never been
linked by a contract to the society it dominates. It is a sorcery of the social relation, it is a
challenge to society and should be responded to as such" (Baudrillard 1983a: 29–30).

grim: "Need and labor, elevated into this universality, then form on their own account a monstrous system of community and mutual interdependence in a great people; a life of the dead body, that moves itself within itself, one which ebbs and flows in its motion blindly, like the elements, and which requires continual strict dominance and taming like a wild beast." Enslaved labor is reduced to the "movement of the living dead" and life is turned away from ethical relations with other humans toward the fretting over of property and possessions ([1802–04] 1979: 249; cf. DOL: 1–5; also Kojève [1947] 1969: 15–16). Below the administrative and managerial office monster (Kracauer 1998: 49) dwell the industrial living dead, the dregs, the total waste of humanity, the "tramp-monsters" (Orwell [1933] 1961: 201), and "carnivorous swamp monsters" (Isenberg 2016: 55).[240] Marx is a keen theoretician of this "movement of the living dead" and his magnum opus is woven in a rich tapestry of blood and horror.

The desire for money is voracious appetite; it is the "great huge monster" of usury that "like a were-wolf ... lays waste to all ..." (C: 740) and the appetite of the vampire for labor power, excess and unpaid labor, and surplus value, is insatiable, or, to use Durkheim's term, anomic. In reference to the shift system, for example, Marx says "The prolongation of the working day beyond the limits of the natural day, into the night, only.... slightly quenches the vampire thirst for the living blood of labour" (C: 367). His use of the term shifts from metaphor ("vampire-like") to analogy (money is the congealed residue of abstract human life). The vampire representation in particular can be found in various locations including *The German Ideology, Class Struggle in France, The Eighteenth Brumaire, The Grundrisse,* and *The Holy Family.* Marx's economic writings are also filled with the dynamic tension between the living and the dead (e.g., variable capital as living labor and constant capital as dead labor). The fetishization of technology meant that dead things (the instruments of production, tools, machinery, "dead labor") were tended to as if it they were founding fathers of the Kingdom of Ends while, conversely, those that were truly alive (human beings) were consumed as mere objects – another form of capital (human resources in our contemporary jargon).[241] Dead labor absorbs living labor and animates the realm of lifeless objects circulating through society as if somehow by magic. We can save the details for the volume on capitalism

---

240 Orwell gives us a sense of social function of useless, suffering dregs – their function, created and maintained by business and law, is to simply exist and suffer for no purpose whatsoever but to provide an inert base of subhuman life upon which to build bourgeois society. The planter elite of Virginia held a dim view of the lazy, swamp-dwelling subhumans of North Carolina (Isenberg 2016: 43–63).

241 For more on the relationship between the vampire metaphor and the organic composition of capital in Marx's *Capital* see Neocleous (2003).

but, for now, this process of "monsterization" is located within the portions of *Capital* dealing with valorization. There are two shifts and three moments to be located at this point from two radically opposed points of view: on the one hand, the concrete and qualitative and, on the other, the abstract and quantitative: When we examine the concrete labor process we find people producing things capable of being used, needs-satisfiers if you will, but when we shift from the register of the concrete to the abstract (seeing with the alien profit-eye) we see not labor products made by flesh and blood human beings but "value creation" and crystals of value. Valorization, as seen from the concrete gaze reveals nothing more than a prolongation of the workday beyond what is necessary for the reproduction of labor power (here, valorization appears to be nothing more than more of the same: labor and more labor, surplus labor). However, if one pays attention to the texture of Marx's argument it becomes clear that valorization is not merely *more of the same,* in a purely quantitative sense, but that valorization involves a dialectical shift into a new condition a different register of life, as if alienation and abstraction were pushed along a continuum into surplus alienation, literally "delta alienation" or alienation on top of alienation whereby the merely abstract and impersonal is transformed into the horror of sub-human deformation. We can see now why sublime objects like Jesus or Big Macs are monsters. The commodity is, today, the ultimate monstrosity (Worrell 2014) and while Marx is the master theorist of the horror of the commodity world, radicals were not alone in characterizing the modern economy as a giant blood-sucking monster.

The vampire was a popular trope in 19th and 20th century antisemitic propaganda where Jews were portrayed as evil parasites feeding off the souls of good Christians.[242] The Nazis reduced Jews to ashes or the *musselmann* – living corpses awaiting their final biological death. For both German and American antisemites, Jews were the embodiment of unproductive capital, i.e., financialists, as well as fringe parasites soiling the economic sphere. The radical critique of capital treats it as a totality to be undone by the working class itself (those zombie-like proletariat) whereas the fascist backlash against capital dismembers the object and calls forth the "vampire slayer" (the demagogic hero) to save the "little man" from the predator.

The zombie and the vampire seem to represent extreme juxtapositions or ideal-typical endpoints along a macabre continuum of modern, capitalist

---

242 The belief that Jews could make fortunes out of pennies was supposedly a testament to a kind of "Jewish magic" and, likewise, the ability to "split" capital, and even capitalism (into two separate species of good and bad, Christian and Jewish, productive and financial) was imagined as a kind of "magic" as well (Worrell 2008).

exploitation: the *dehumanized* victim and the *inhuman* devourer. Indeed, the stereotypical zombie is the embodiment of pure drive (without desire) and, as such is reduced to being a virtual puppet controlled by an alien force (Žižek 1991: 22) whereas the vampire (e.g., Dracula) appears to be a self-consciously desiring master over mindless victims. But the dichotomy is not as clear-cut as it may appear: like the zombie, the vampire also lives an alienated existence (as Marx and Weber note with regard to the capitalist) ensnared by abstract forces beyond their control; the sociological difference between these two species of monsters lies in their coordinates within the system of subordination to impersonal forces beyond their control; in short, both represent un-free subjects of misery and desire:

> ... if there is a phenomenon that fully deserves to be called the 'fundamental fantasy of contemporary mass culture,' it is this fantasy of the return of the living dead: the fantasy of a person who does not want to stay dead but returns again and again to pose a threat to the living. The unattained archetype of a long series ... is still George Romero's *The Night of the Living Dead*, where the 'undead' are not portrayed as embodiments of pure evil, of a simple drive to kill or revenge, but as sufferers, pursuing their victims with an awkward persistence, colored by a kind of infinite sadness (as in Werner Herzog's *Nosferatu*, in which the vampire is not a simple machinery of evil with a cynical smile on his lips, but a melancholic sufferer longing for salvation).
> ŽIŽEK 1991: 22–23

Capitalism, then, "the Thing *par excellence*" today, reduces people to the status of the suffering undead longing for redemption or escape.[243] Even the so-called master class is a category of the 'living dead' – though, the "possessing class.... experiences the alienation as a sign *of its own power*, and possesses in it the *appearance* of a human existence" (Marx and Engels 1972: 104). By taking seriously the comparison with the zombie and the vampire we might come away with an analysis of capitalist relations that exposes something interesting that is not easily perceivable.

"Monster" comes from the Latin *monstrum* ("portent" or "monster") – itself derived from *monere* ("warn"). There appears to be no form of social organization or particular society that has not concerned itself with monstrosities

---

243 Capital is "a chimeric apparition which, although it can nowhere be spotted as a positive, clearly delimited entity, nonetheless functions as the ultimate Thing regulating our lives" (Žižek 2001: 123).

because all societies are continuously preoccupied with instability, egoism, decay, evil, and the dissolution of law and order; where one encounters *fin de siècle* anomie one is sure to find a deep fascination for monstrosity (Laqueur 1996). Wilson tells us that the imagined Jew of antisemitic propaganda is an objectification of contradictory social processes that not only provides an explanation for they way things are but a feeling of power over impersonal forces (1982: 637). In the anthropological sense, monsters reside in the realm of morality (they are sacred) but their sacredness is, like any devil or demon, of an *impure* form (EFRL passim; see also Caillois 1959).[244] The function of the morally impure element is to pursue and punish good residents of the domain of light while increasing the population of the domain of darkness. Since all people suffer ambivalence, and few are saints, the fear of monsters like the walking dead is virtually universal.[245]

"Zombie" apparently comes from the word *zumbi* (fetish) in Kikongo (a Bantu language spoken in the Congo).[246] The zombie is imagined[247] to be a corpse that has been animated in either one of two ways: ritual production or demonic possession.[248] The ritually produced zombie is created by a necromancer for purely personal reasons. Basing his observations on the Tibetan context, Wiley referred to this ritual production of zombies as the "tantric" form. Opposite this ritual production of zombies we have the "demonic" zombie that "is activated by an evil demon without benefit of conjuration. Greatly feared, this type of zombie seeks to turn other people into [zombies] ... and drastic measures are taken to prevent the spread of its contamination" (Wylie 1964: 72). Further, we find that zombies are corpses that have had either their bodies (material zombies) or their souls (immaterial zombies) possessed.

---

244   The sacred "means at the same time the worst and the best" (Alain [1934] 1974: 109).

245   "There is no religion in the world but has its demons or evil monsters who represent pain, misery, and destruction" (Carus [1900] 1996: 440).

246   Alternatively, Davis says that zombie (or zombi) "probably comes from the Kongo word *nzambi*, which more or less means 'spirit of a dead person.' This is yet another example of the African roots of the vodoun religion and society" (1985: 12).

247   Sometimes zombies are just lethargic idiots misidentified by the locals as the corpse of a person who died years ago. "The common people do not trouble themselves with ... subtleties. For them the *zombi* are the living dead – corpses which a sorcerer has extracted from their tombs and raised by a process which no one really knows" (Metraux 1959: 281).

248   As Davis points out, some zombies are chemically produced with toxic powders while others, the "astral" zombies, are the product of magical spells only – the true, powerful *houngan* (vodoun priest) has "disdain for such powders." Though, most decisively, both types of zombies are, ultimately, the product of socialization and social expectations (1985: 166–69). As Levi-Strauss says, the effectiveness of magic depends upon the *belief* in magic (1963: 168).

In some cultures, the boundaries between the living and the dead are flu-id.[249] As Simpson says with regard to northern Haiti,

> In the vodun cult ... the dead rank second only to the loas [spirits]. We have already stated that some of the dead become loas, but not all of them do, and those who do not achieve this distinction must also be treated respectfully. The dead are here, there, and everywhere. They are simply the invisible living. They retain an interest in this world, and, like the loas, they favor or destroy its inhabitants.
>
> 1945: 52

As Simpson reports, "zombie" is a classification of dead people in general but it is also used in a specific sense; it is worth quoting at length:

> The term *zombie* is often employed to designate persons who have been killed by sorcerers, or those who have met death in other ways, and have been resurrected by 'bad' *houngans*. Such *zombies* have no souls, are completely dominated by their masters, and are utilized by them for evil purposes. *Zombie errants* are the spirits of human beings who died in accidents. They inhabit the woods by day and walk on the roads at night, as they live out the periods of earthly existence assigned to them by God. *Diablesses* are evil spirits who must live in the woods for several years before they can be admitted to Heaven. These devil-women are being punished for the crime of being virgins at the time of their deaths. *Lutins* are the ghosts of children who died before baptism. *Bakas* are *zombies* who have been converted into animals, usually dogs, by sorcerers. These creatures are sent out to steal for their masters. *Spectres* and *fantomes* are inhabitants of the other world who appear before the living stripped of their bodies.
>
> SIMPSON 1945: 53

The essence of the zombie is total alienation or absolute possession of the subject to the point of pure otherness: the reduction of the subject to the level of a beast, or abomination – the "obscene" other or, in other words, the total presence of the inhuman. What separates the zombie's pure otherness from Durkheimian *altruisme* is the essential gap between ego and collective consciousness. The notion of purely altruistic horde members lacking any and all signs of individual identity was what Mauss calls "an error of genius" (on the part of Morgan) and "only a hypothesis ... but, in our view, a necessary

---

249   "A zombi sits on the cusp of death ..." (Davis 1985: 180).

hypothesis [for Durkheim], to postulate amorphous societies at the origin of all our societies" (2005: 66). Crucially, though, for Durkheim "there is a sphere of psychological life which, no matter how developed the collective type may be, varies from one person to another and belongs by right to each individual.... This primal basis of all individuality is inalienable and does not depend upon the social condition" (DOL: 145). Given this "primal basis" of individuality, the human being (as far as we care to go back in history, presumably) possesses a form of consciousness that is potentially at odds or in opposition with the demands of the collective consciousness.

Membership in the collectivity entails a variable amount of repression and alienation. The zombie, by contrast, represents the prototype of pure alienation – as Durkheim might say, in the case of the zombie, collective consciousness has eclipsed the member wholly to a theoretical zero point and necessity is pure and absolute; here we find the ideal type of the heteronomous automaton. This total or absolute possession provides the collective fascination with the zombie: might some force wholly possess me? Might I "lose" my mind or self?[250] Is there already some zombie-like "thing" that runs my mind automatically? Are we being stalked by something that might deprive us of our very selves? In the popular imagination, where one finds zombies, one is sure to find the vampire counterpart.

The word "vampire" comes from the Hungarian *vampir* (which may itself derive from the Turkish word *uber* or "witch"; see Wilson 1985). Like the zombie, vampires are categorized as members of the living dead – the vampire is a corpse capable of leaving its grave to prey on the living. In cinematic representations, the vampire is generally not a mindless instrument inhabiting an underworld but a prime mover of sorts.[251] There are at least two distinct types of vampires: the *dead* of the living dead and the *living* of the living dead. The dead vampire is a corpse that has been reanimated:

> In Russia, Roumania, and the Balkan States there is an idea – sometimes vague, sometimes fairly definite – that the soul does not finally leave the body and enter into Paradise until forty days after death. It is supposed that it may even linger for years, and when this is the case decomposition is delayed. In Roumania, bodies are disinterred at an interval of three

---

250   Recent work on models of consciousness suggest there may be a "zombie within" already (Place 2000; Revonsuo, Johanson, Wedlund, and Chaplin 2000).
251   The lure of the vampire, the promises of pleasure, lure the individual from living others, from life itself: "Look at me naked, and I will replace / sun and moon and every star in the sky" (Baudelaire 1993: 189). From the poem "Metamorphoses of the Vampire."

years after death in the case of a child, of four or five years in the case of young folk, and of seven years in the case of elderly people. If decomposition is not then complete, it is supposed that the corpse is a vampire; if it is complete, and the bones are white and clean, it is a sign that the soul has entered into eternal rest. The bones are washed in water and wine and put in clean linen, a religious service is held, and they are re-interred. In Bukovina and the surrounding districts there was an orgy of burials and re-burials in the years I919 and 1920, for not only were people dying of epidemics and hardships, but the people who had died in the early years of the War had to be disinterred.

MURGOCI 1926: 320

Living vampires, on the other hand, are those who, "destined to become vampires after death may be able in life to send out their souls, and even their bodies, to wander at crossroads with reanimated corpses. This type may be called the live-vampire type. It merges into the ordinary witch or wizard, who can meet other witches or wizards either in the body or as a spirit" (Murgoci 1926: 321).[252]

Interestingly, vampires are imagined to form hierarchies and even puppet regimes. For example, in parts of Africa, it is believed that behind the local vampire resides a master: the European vampire (White 2000). This European vampire is not hidden away in Europe but appears in the form of the local missionaries and priests:

In what is today the Northern Province of Zambia, accusations that Africans working for Europeans captured other Africans in order to remove their blood were commonplace between the mid-1920s and the mid-1950s.... [I]n almost every outbreak of these accusations that reached the attention of the *boma* (local administrative headquarters), one order of Catholic priests – the Society of Missionaries for Africa, known in Africa and among themselves as White Fathers, because of their robes – was named as the Europeans behind the *banyama* [local vampires]

WHITE 1993: 750

---

252 "... Cameroonian President Paul Biya urged citizens to use witchcraft against Boko Haram, the Islamic State-affiliated militants who have terrorized West Africa for years. 'We expect every village to have brilliant actions in this direction,' said Midjiyawa Bakari, governor of the Far North region of the country, echoing the president. 'We want to hear that this or that village has wiped out or limited the sect's damage through witchcraft. Fight for your country'" (Locka 2017).

The vampire, then, appears at first glance to be something qualitatively different from the zombie just as the exploited worker appears to be something wholly different from the capitalist. As different as the zombie and vampire are, one seems to be a pure victim while the other seems to be a demonic master, they are nonetheless both fully possessed by impersonal forces and estranged. Monsters are capable of being only slaves or an enslaved master of slaves[253] – even though one segment of the monster world enjoys subjugation appreciably more.[254] Apart from monsters the derealized society is plagued by sorcerers and magicians promising salvation.

The idea of the "magician" comes from the Persian *magi* – a priest or, better, a sorcerer.[255] But surely, the era of magic is behind us and to reflect upon it would be a waste of time. However,

> Magic works. In the life of childhood words really make things appear; first the servant, then his services, the keys to the doors, the garden, the toy, the bottle. In adult life many miracles take place because of words. Authority, favor, reputation, disapproval, contempt, excommunication either encourage or disrupt activity, and therefore health.
>
> ALAIN [1934] 1974: 49

---

253   "The Southern planter suffered, not simply for his economic mistakes – the psychological effect of slavery upon him was fatal. The mere fact that a man could be, under the law, the actual master of the mind and body of human beings had to have disastrous effects. It tended to inflate the ego of most planters beyond all reason; they became arrogant, strutting, quarrelsome kinglets; they issued commands; they made laws; they shouted their orders; they expected deference and self-abasement; they were choleric and easily insulted. Their 'honor' became a vast and awful thing, requiring wide and insistent deference" (Du Bois 1935: 52).

254   As Hegel says: "The one who serves lacks a self and has another self in place of his own; so that in the Master he has alienated and annulled himself as an individual Ego and now views another as his essential self. The Master, on the contrary, sees in the Servant the other Ego as annulled and his own individual will as preserved" (1986: 62). Yet, according to his master-slave model in the *Phenomenology*, Hegel argues that relations of domination are always dynamic and prone to upward cancellation: today the master, tomorrow superfluous and plowed into the ground. Cf. Weil (1965: 11, 22–23) on the "pitiless" possession of force over the subjected as well as those who wield force – both fated to thingification in the uniformity of horror.

255   The term "magic" is derived "from the religious world of the Persians, in which the *magos* is a priest or, in any case, a specialist in religion. It is Herodotus who first speaks to us of them: the *magoi*, who for a secret Persian tribe or society, are responsible for the royal sacrifices, funeral rites, and for the divination and interpretation of dreams; Xenophon describes them as 'experts' 'in everything concerning the gods'" (Graf 1997: 20).

Social life is not fully comprehended without a consideration of magic and magicians. Unlike monsters, the magician is not a victim but a master of spiritual forces, so masterful, in fact, that according to Weber "Whoever possesses the requisite charisma for employing the proper means is stronger even than the god, whom he can compel to do his will" (ES, 1: 422). Unlike the monster, the magician brings in his or her wake, not only doom, impurity, and profanation (Halbwachs 1962: 22–23) but also the potential for happiness (Voeks 1993: 72). However, the magician, by virtue of participating in non-localized forces, incurs the status of an anti-social outsider "wielding a mysterious and dreaded power. He is no longer regarded by others as a "brother." In fact, he has become another being.... He becomes a virtual outcast from the community ... he incarnates ... the very forces of dissolution" (Caillois 1959: 55).[256] The magician is an "audacious" and self-centered manipulator of "existing powerful symbols" (O'Keefe 1982: 73). The happiness the magician can bring is in the form of the satisfied client or customer – unlike religion, there is no church of magic (EFRL: 39–42, 199–200; Halbwachs 1962: 23).[257] "A magical rite is *any rite which does not play a part in organized cults* – it is private, secret, mysterious and approaches the limit of a prohibited rite" (Mauss 1972: 24).[258]

Whereas religious forces are connected to periodic rites (collective, orgiastic gatherings) magic is "continuous" and connected with the being of the

---

256   Magic is dangerous and represents a real threat to common morality: "power may be stretched for a moment beyond its due and normal limits, so that Gods, and even men, may achieve the impossible. But there is a strong sense that such feats are undesirable and dangerous. For Gods and men alike there are certain destined bounds which normally and rightly circumscribe their power. It is just possible to exceed them; but only at the cost of provoking an instant *nemesis*" (Cornford [1912] 2004: 14).

257   Where religion is essentially social in its end, magic is individual and while religions may utilize magical *means* the end is always social (Harrison 1962: xxii). Davis does a fine job in demonstrating the fluidity that permeates the distinction between priests (*houngan*) and magicians (*bokor*) as well as the relative difference between good and evil (1985). However, in highly anomic contexts, for example frontier life accompanied with a flourishing of mobile prophets, maniacs, and fanatics, religion and magic can melt into one another (e.g., the early days of Mormonism).

258   But it is crucial to stress that the magical ritual or formula must still be collectively recognized, i.e., magic is still *social*: "magic and magical rites, as a whole, are traditional facts. Actions which are never repeated cannot be called magical. If the whole community does not believe in the efficacy of a group of actions, they cannot be magical. The form of the ritual is eminently transmissible and this is sanctioned by public opinion. It follows from this that strictly individual actions, such as the private superstitions of gamblers, cannot be called magical" (Mauss 1972: 19).

magician (Weber [1922] 1991: 3).[259] Essentially, the cult ceremony is a communal affair whereas the individual turned to the magician for help:

> The individual, in order to avoid or remove evils that concerned himself – above all, sickness – has not turned to the cult of the community, but as an individual he has approached the sorcerer as the oldest personal and 'spiritual advisor.' The prestige of particular magicians, and of those spirits or divinities in whose names they have performed their miracles, has brought them patronage, irrespective of local or of tribal affiliation.[260]
>
> FMW: 272

Interestingly, though the magician loses the status of insider he or she is not simultaneously estranged or separated from society; the magician may be "despised" by upright society but also "accepted" and considered institutionally "essential" for the maintenance of social equilibrium (Davis 1985: 96). Indeed, following a logic that is reminiscent of Durkheim's mapping of the evolution of the division of labor from the mechanical to the organic system of interdependence, the magician becomes an indispensable member of society. As we will see in the volume on suicide, any society maps onto itself imagined replicas of itself. Magicians and their forces belong naturally with the "underground" but communicate and interact with the physical model upon which they are based. Religious and magical forces are essentially identical (magic could even conceivably be termed "magic religion")[261] but the two can be distinguished on the bases of organizational function, individual versus collective goals, and prohibition. Metaphorically, if religion is moral and within society, immoral

---

259   The well-known formula of the magician profaning the sacred is underlined by the essentially egoistic and individuated nature of magical practices and magic's inclinations toward the concrete. Magic "'leans toward the concrete as religion leans toward the abstract'" (Mauss and Hubert, in Bouglé [1926] 1970: 159).

260   "Thus the magician has transformed himself into the mystagogue; that is, hereditary dynasties of mystagogues or organizations or trained personnel under a head determined in accordance with some sort of rules have developed. This head has either been recognized as the incarnation of a superhuman being or merely as a prophet, that is, as the mouthpiece and agent of his god. Collective religious arrangements for individual 'suffering' per se, and for 'salvation' from it, have originated in this fashion" (FMW: 272).

261   Magic is reducible to the concept of mana "once it has shed its outer form" (Mauss 1972: 118). Malinowski loses sight of the origins of magical forces from the religious (1948: 7) but is correct that, in a sense, magic has a counter-polarity to religious power if we maintain the focus on the split between the collective (we) and the personal (me) as well as the division between ends and means. Magical practices are always singular or particular in contrast to the relative universality of religion.

magic, by contrast, is perceived as existing somehow "below" society (Beidelman 1974: 41) or in some kind of subterranean counterworld.

Magic may be attributed to any number of individuals based on purely contingent criteria or they may be attributed to whole classes of people – some occupational groups such as blacksmiths, barbers, and so forth – as well as other outsiders and "strangers" of various kinds. Magic may acquire a hereditary quality as well with particular clans monopolizing magical functions for themselves. Some significant degree of development within the division of labor must occur within the tribal system for a class of religious officiates to coalesce within the social system and, likewise, we find that a distinct class of "full-time" magicians can only sustain itself once specialization has developed to a great extent. Magicians, like priests, may revolve around a specialized clan or, as we find later with the Persians, a wandering population of ritual specialists. The social functions of the magician are many.

Magicians provide services including preventative, curative, and good magic. Preventative magic (basically a "negative" form) is used as a kind of antidote to bad magical practices that may have been wielded against a person by vengeful neighbors, etc. Curative magic is, as implied, used to cure illnesses or promote health in general. Good magic (magic's "positive" form) may be used to empower a client – e.g., obtaining a sexual partner (Simpson 1940). Magicians may work for purely private ends or may render social services such as helping to empower political or opposition leaders; magicians may operate as agents of good or as terrorists (Simpson 1945: 36–37). At the end of the day, however, the magician is, at bottom, always an egoist and anti-social.[262] "Magicians are excluded from friendship, and they know it. It is their particular job to play only upon the basest part of man; and it is their consolation to despise him" (Alain [1934] 1974: 97).[263] The magician combines the will-mania of Treitschke's political philosophy (Durkheim 1915) with the absolutism of a Queen Jadis.

Possession is central to the practices of the professional magician but the differences between the magician and a monster are decisive. The magician

---

262   A society may be able to sharply differentiate between social and anti-social practices and rites (Evans-Pritchard 1976: 176) but the magician per se does not escape the class of egoists even though the magician serves self through serving the other (see FMW: 290). There may be "good magic" (Ibid.) but there is no such thing as a good magician in ideal-typical purity. A magician can never be ignored.

263   "No doubt they would never have chosen this sad occupation for themselves; more likely they were exiled and condemned to it, by an involuntary power. But we must also consider the effect of that childhood injustice which looks for magicians everywhere, and which divides the world into good and evil, thus confirming the one and the other" (Alain [1934] 1974: 97).

is possessed, or "mounted" as Davis (1985) puts it, by an impersonal power not dissimilar to mana (Simpson 1945: 46) and, in this sense, the same forces are at work on magicians and monsters but, in the case of the former, possession is intentionally brought on by the magician and remains under his or her control. Possession entails the *doubling* of either the magician's body or spirit.[264] One side of the double may die a temporary death while the spirit leaves the body to operate as a single entity[265] but this is less interesting than when the magician is doubled and the union becomes one of cooperation or, better, where the magician gains an obedient deputy. "In general, any individual who has the power to send forth his soul is a magician."

> A soul is a person's double, that is, it is not an anonymous part of his person, but the person himself. It is transported at will to any place and its activities there are physical ones. In some cases even, the magician is said to split himself in two.... The two parts of the double are identical to the point that they are strictly interchangeable, one for the other.... [T]he double may be quite separate from the magician, a person to some degree independent of his control, who from time to time appears to carry out his will. The magician may be escorted by a retinue of assistants, animals or spirits, who are none other than his doubles or external souls.... When the sorcerer is possessed he not only feels the presence of a new person within him, but his own personality succumbs to the power of the demon.... [W]e find that we are dealing with the splitting of a person's personality. It is a remarkable fact that a magician, to a certain extent, can control his possession; he brings it on by appropriate practices.... A magician is seen in terms of his relationship with animals as well as his relationship with spirits, and in the last analysis he is seen in

---

264   One of the most impressive powers of the magician is "the power to send forth his soul.." (Mauss 1972: 34). "A soul is a person's double, that is, it is not an anonymous part of his person, but the person himself. It is transported at will to any place and its activities there are physical ones. In some cases even, the magician is said to split himself in two (Mauss 1972: 34–35).

265   Intimate associations can a problem for the sorcerer. Hegel recounts the case of the Greek philosopher and magician Hermotimus who "possessed the peculiar gift of being able to make his soul quit his body. But this did him bad service in the end, since his wife, with whom he had a dispute, and who besides knew very well how matters stood, showed to their acquaintances this soul-deserted body as dead, and it was burnt before the soul reinstated itself – which soul must have been astonished" ([1892] 1995: 321). Despite his reputation as pedantic and dour, Hegel possessed a wicked sense of humor.

terms of his own soul. The liaison between a magician and his spirit often develops into a complete identity one with the other.

MAUSS 1972: 34–39; SEE ALSO MAUSS [1909] 2003: 80

Essentially, though the magician is a master of power he or she is nonetheless subject to alienation just as the monster. In the popular imagination (at least in Haiti) all these abysmal things, monsters and sorcerers frequently blend together, the lines separating one from another are blurred (Metraux 1959: 303–4). For us, what separates the magician from the monster, however, is that possession does not absolutely or even relatively estrange the magician from his or her "soul" or multiform "souls." In some cases the magician is in total command of his or her alienated aspects – *alienation without estrangement or dispossession*, at least from the viewpoint of the duped customer. The magician can appear to others to have achieved the Nietzschean trick for hovering over an abyss, defying the spirit of gravity, and, as such, enjoying a special dreaded glory.

Simultaneously entertaining and a plague on the psyche, "humans are forever vulnerable to the machinations of magicians and sorcerers" (Voeks 1993: 72). Rational adults can appreciate monsters and magicians as scintillating fiction but, unfortunately, as Vyse reports, thinking unencumbered by superstitions and mysticism, even in our modern world, is not the norm but the exception: Gallup polls conducted for nearly twenty years from the late 70s and into the mid-90s reveal deep and widespread beliefs in devils, miracles, ghosts, and so forth (1997: 16–19).[266] And for much of the underdeveloped world, steeped in superstition and tradition, monsters and magicians are imagined as serious problems (McNally 2011: 175 ff).[267] Universally, what lies behind monsters and magicians is the belief in impersonal, supernatural, and domineering forces of gargantuan proportions. Sociologically, we know that emanations of evil are projections, conferred powers, and social constructs. However, as Erikson says, people "who fear witches soon find themselves surrounded by them" (1966:

---

266 We would do well to remember Fromm's insight that much of what people consider to be normal social behavior is predicated upon the existence of a "magic helper" – the objectification of external moral powers that sustain and promote life ([1941] 1969: 172–73).

267 Tylor notes that societies frequently impute upon, and fear, the imagined magical and occult superiority of others perceived to be "lower" on the scale of socio-cultural or spiritual development. In Europe, e.g., Gypsies were believed to possess "powers of sorcery" not accessible to "civilized" peoples. And in Scotland and Germany it was believed that relief from devils and mental illness required a Catholic priest: "Protestants get the aid of Catholic priests and monks to help them against witchcraft, to lay ghosts, consecrate herbs, and discover thieves" (Tylor [1873] 1958: 115).

22).[268] Far from irrelevance to developed modernity, the enjoyment-value of monsters and magicians attests to the fact that these forms of belief are rooted, as Durkheim might say, in some kernel of social reality.[269] Even witchcraft, alchemy, and astrology have, at bottom, an idea that is plausible (Ruskin 2015: 33).

When he claimed that we moderns have the mindset of primitives (EFRL: 25) Durkheim was prefacing the work of critical sociologists that found the widespread persistence of necrophilia (Fromm 1973) and magical thinking – forms of thinking that get people into all kinds of trouble.[270]

Classical sociology, using a variety of terms, converged on the problem of alienation as "inevitable" or as a precondition for the construction of the self and the relation of the self to others. Indeed, "self-consciousness is only possible as double" or in a process of self-duplication (Gadamer 1976: 62, 63, 67). Monstrosity is a reflection of the play of being as it is turned back upon itself, relating with itself in an inverted and perverted form. The sorcerer is, to use a phrase Simmel coined to refer to the modern person, both divided and multiplied – in other words, like us, the magician is double. Human duality is *not* best understood as the traditional Cartesian split between body (organism) and mind, but the split between our private and social existence – we are simultaneously private and public, individual and social, I and we ruled by an Other.[271] On the one hand, the expansiveness of the self makes possible the

---

268   Had space permitted, an account of monster-makers (e.g., Mary Shelley's *Frankenstein*) and those who elect to show fidelity toward monsters (e.g., Stephen Crane's short story "The Monster") as well as numerous variations on the monster within (e.g., *Dr. Jekyll and Mr. Hyde* by Stevenson) and monster-hunting (say, *Moby Dick* or the film *Jaws* as two examples) could be pursued; for a quick take on *Jaws* see Worrell and Krier (2012).

269   Not that this "kernel" persists as an unchanged "survival." "In a dialectical process no original part remains unchanged" (Lichtman 1982: 65). But as a sublated "kernel" the changed thing lives on as a dynamic element that has to be taken into consideration. Totemism is dead, for example, but the logic of totemism and fetishism must be grasped if we are to comprehend the social world of today. "The intellectual life of mankind develops by gradual growth. The old views are, as a rule, preserved but transformed. There is nowhere an absolutely new start" (Carus [1900] 1996: 444).

270   See Mann (1931: 52) for the connection between magic and authoritarianism.

271   Matheson draws out the alien nature of our subjective duality via the reduction of the population, save one, to night-prowling monsters. The protagonist, Robert Neville, lashes out at himself, "beginning to suspect his mind of harboring an alien. Once he might have termed it conscience. Now it was only an annoyance. Morality, after all, had fallen with society. He was his own ethic" ([1954] 1995: 61–62). Neville's duality becomes nearly a source of madness: "Two in the morning. Two days since he'd buried her. Two eyes looking at the clock, two ears picking up the hum of its electric chronology, two lips pressed together, two hands lying on the bed. He tried to rid himself of the concept, but everything in the world seemed of twos" ([1954] 1995: 75–76). On society reduced to a dyad see McCarthy's *The Road*.

creation of an expansive citadel of selfhood that that can withstand the shocks and tribulations of existence. As William James says,

> ... a man's Self is the sum total of all that he CAN call his, not only his body and his psychic powers, but his clothes and his house, his wife and children, his ancestors and friends, his reputation and works, his lands and horses, and yacht and bank-account. All these things give him the same emotions. If they wax and prosper, he feels triumphant; if they dwindle and die away, he feels cast down ...
>
> 1918: 291; CF. MAUPASSANT [1883] 1999: 209

On the other hand, this expansive self has left itself open on all fronts to subversion and attack; our greatest strength seems to also be our greatest weakness: "Properly speaking, a man has as many social selves as there are individuals who recognize him and carry an image of him in their mind. To wound any one of these his images is to wound him" (James 1918: 294). Fame and flagellation would seem to be coterminous. So long as duality-in-unity is more or less preserved we avoid being reduced to brutes, or, beyond brutalization, the ultimate fall into monstrosity, the penultimate station before the Real of biological (the second) death. There appears to be no duality of monsters – is not the zombie just a mindless pursuer lacking a soul? This observation points in two directions. First, the monster is a thing that has misplaced or lost a part of itself. Second, the monster (even the zombie) can assume a completely abstract, ghostly form. Ackermann and Gauthier indicate that the zombie is itself a double concept "that has gone largely unnoticed by the general public outside of Haiti."

> Most investigators have focused on the flesh-and-blood zombi, a body without a soul, the same type of zombi that has become famous through portrayal on film. The other variety of the zombi, a soul without a body, remains little known if at all, both to scholars and to the general public.
>
> 1991: 467

In other words, the living may be pursued, on the one hand, by material remains or, on the other, a disembodied "spirit" or spectral energy. Alienation as possession by an alien power, negation, splitting apart, doubling, misplacement, and forgetting, etc., plays a decisive role in the development of the self and the formation of social identity (the construction of positive and negative social forms).

Solidarity with a group, either ideal or concrete, means that we must each set aside or forget (repress) some aspects of our individuality. The ego becomes a site of antagonism between individual desire and the expectations of others. The negative moment in this dialectic is the loss of self due to its possession by the other. In this sense we are rendered "less than" what we think of as a full self. However, just as the labor product is transformed into a moral object (a commodity) by virtue of its alienation, we are "reborn" as a moral entity, recognized, by virtue of our eclipse. In this sense, we are "more than" what we think of as our mere selves. In short, the social processes of personal negation transforms us into something that is simultaneously more than and less than an individual, a subject – a subjugated self. A diseased society, one undergoing derealization is imagined as a plague of monstrosities where the former or imagined positive hell of divine life has fallen into a state of impurity: we are pursued by ghosts, ghouls, demons, and so on, and fear that we will be devoured by them, and finally dragged down into the terrifying void of nothingness that pulsates at the center of the derealized social system. But perhaps Hegel would say that, finally, things are getting interesting. Just when things cannot get any more polarized and weird, perhaps, there is great potential to transform "the alien into the kindred" and affirm "the self in and through the other" (Bosanquet 1912: 60). Monsterization does not, in other words, *necessarily* lead to the gateway of the abyss, though that seems to be our ultimate destination. But monsters may also signify a new era of de-reification and objectivity.

• • •

Building upon the present work, volume two will hopefully demonstrate that social life is not, at bottom and despite appearances, just a system of contingent rules, routines, habits, imitations, and so on, but an energetic system of currents generated by a system of primary and secondary negations or alienations, and undergoing processes of crystallization, desublimation, inversion, reversal, debasement, and diabolicalization built upon the bases of voluntary and involuntary submission and respect for things sacred, repulsion with regard to things impure, and indifference toward the domain of the infraliminal. Society is built on a coordinated system of human sacrifice and, as such, a mapping out of the world of self-destruction will take us some way into this decisive fact of life.[272] Before we make it to the second installment, however, I will briefly encapsulate a few ideas that we have encountered so far and condense them down into a few formal models in a brief intermezzo.

---

272   Classical sociology, rooted in the problem of the sacred, "is also constituted as a discourse about *sacrifice*" (Milbank 2006: 68) and, in the final analysis, this book is really about voluntary human sacrifice and self-destructiveness as acts of obedience and disobedience.

CHAPTER 3

A Formal Intermezzo

James Henry Breasted wraps up his disquisition on the historical emergence of conscience thusly:

> I am discussing the history of man and something which, especially in its earlier stages, is quite unmistakably disclosed as a force visibly present and operative for several hundred thousand years, and which I believe is still at work. No one can define it, or tell what it is, but like the force of gravitation, we can observe what it does.
>
> 1933: 408

But, of course, there have been no shortages of names and definitions when it comes to this something-force. Most theologies assure us that this "something" is god. Philosophy has attempted to wrestle it to the ground but philosophical answers have not quite gotten ahold of the whole thing.

> That there is "something" is not open to doubt. And that this "something" is a force of some kind (what the Greeks called *energeia*, what Spinoza called *conatus*, what modern physics calls energy) is self-evident to anyone capable of observing nature. The question is not *whether* but *why* there is something. Why nature? Why energy? Why being? Why becoming?.... The question of being is primordial and recurs constantly. Yet no one can answer it.
>
> COMTE-SPONVILLE 2007: 85

Psychology, too, runs into dead ends. Jaynes opened *The Origins of Consciousness in the Breakdown of the Bicameral Mind* with an amazing passage that eloquently encapsulates the overall problem of the Western intellectual tradition as seen from the vantage point of psychology.

> O' what a world of unseen visions and heard silences, this insubstantial country of the mind! What ineffable essences, these touchless rememberings and unshowable reveries! And the privacy of it all! A secret theater of speechless monologue and prevenient counsel, an invisible mansion of all moods, musings, and mysteries, an infinite resort of disappointments and discoveries. A whole kingdom where each of us reigns and reclusively alone, questioning what we will, commanding what we can. A hidden

hermitage where we may study out the troubled book of what we have done and yet may do. An introcosm [sic] that is more myself than anything I can find in a mirror. This consciousness that is myself of selves, that is everything, and yet nothing at all – what is it?

1990: 1

The "bicameral mind" thesis is ultimately incorrect but the book belongs to that class of works we might call the "intellectual hellride" that should be read for their sheer audaciousness (another in this genre, to name only one, is Brown's *Life Against and Death*). Earlier, M.C. Otto came at the same basic problem of this "something" from a different angle toward the end of one of his works:

For there is a rock fact of human nature against which the waves of rhetoric and logic dash in vain; a rock fact which, after all the proofs and disproofs have fallen back into the sea of words from which they came, stands forth the clearer for the spray dashed over it. What is this stubborn fact? It is the fact that human beings refuse to be psychically alone in the universe; the fact that they demand that somehow there shall be a Power at the heart of things which will not let them suffer ultimate defeat, let appearances be what they may.

1924: 283–84

Between the passages from Breasted, Comte-Sponville, Otto, and Jaynes we encounter a bundle of fundamental riddles that resisted even partial solutions until the end of the 19th Century: the ontic status of surplus moral energy; the crystallization and organization of what Alain calls this "human fire" into a constellation of inhuman mirrors;[1] consciousness of this reflected energy; the emergent self-conscious awareness that the subject and object are dynamically linked and even identical in some way (subject-object identity); and, if all goes well, self-consciousness raised to consciousness of self-consciousness and the emergence of Spirit into the noontime of reason. But it can be darkest at noon. "Man" "looks in vain for himself, he turns the universe upside-down, trying to find himself, he finds masks, and behind the masks death" (Maritain 1939: 3). In the final analysis we live in a demon-haunted world (Sagan 1995).[2] And, as Žižek says somewhere, this excess is with us *forever*.

Just as we think we have a grasp of the ultimate Thing we tend to continue circling around it rather than penetrating its depths. "I would like to add, in

---

1 "Such then is this human fire, as inhuman as any other, which burns within the hearth of hearts" (Alain [1934] 1974: 115).

2 "Skepticism doesn't sell newspapers" (Sagan 1995: 57).

anticipation, that the spirit searches for itself as legitimately in the external world as within; however, the exact critique of this notion of notions would be out of place here" (Alain [1934] 1974: 117). Whether it is the Party, the movement, the state, or whole civilizations, the end is the same:

> For the movement was without scruples; she rolled towards her goal unconcernedly and deposed the corpses of the drowned in the windings of her course. Her course had many twists and windings; such was the law of her being. And whosoever could not follow her crooked course was washed on to the bank, for such was her law.
> KOESTLER [1941] 1968: 76

At the end of *The Critique of Pure Reason* Kant famously asserted that the rhapsodic spread of human knowledge would crystallize into a unified system "under one idea" (1929: 653). And what was this one idea? It was more or less the same idea that occupied Hegel in the *Phenomenology*. "This idea is the concept provided by reason – of the form of a whole – in so far as the concept determines *a priori* not only the scope of its manifold content, but also the positions which the parts occupy relatively to one another" (Ibid.). When we arrive at the end of Hegel's *Phenomenology* we are greeted not merely with a passing from religion to philosophy (the usual reading) or an act of sacrifice pure and simple – Calvary, where Jesus dies on the cross – but, if we take the *Gospel of Judas* seriously, a suicide. Judas is informed that he will "exceed" all the other disciples:

> For you will sacrifice
> the man who bears me.
> Already your horn has been raised,
> and your wrath has been kindled,
> and your star has passed by, and
> your heart has [become strong].
> KASSER and WURST 2007: 231

Death by Pilate via Judas (indirect, positive, optional altruistic suicide) was a good career move, of that there can be no doubt. However, it must be stated bluntly at this point that if we aspire to a "cult of man in the concrete" (in contrast to Christianity and its "cult of man in the abstract") then the proper object of devotion vis-a-vis the Jesus cult is not the resurrected (objectified) Christ but the helpless, broken, and forsaken bag of bones hanging on the cross. "Up there" Jesus was reduced to a one-sided sacrificial victim; sublated, the representation of Jesus Christ does not represent a double sided figure (profane body and sacred spirit) but an eight-sided enigma – notice what happens at the moment of the disjunctive syllogism in Hegel's big logic: the sacrifice gives birth to a doubled, four-sided representation, or, a new universal envelope that contains itself in addition to the other moments of the syllogism, but is also stalked by a shadowy double and, as such, is constantly plagued by the return of the repressed that exceeds the capacities of institutional mediation to deal with this return. Not to lose sight of it, however, the main point is that apex moments in the life of the absolute hinge on annihilation and calamity out of which another generation rises.

Hegel is normally presented as one who deceived himself in believing that philosophy reached the historical pinnacle of reasoning and that *"the world had become transparent, when, in fact, it was simply a matter of a world becoming visible to itself"* (Mannheim 1982: 179). I think, however, that we should take Hegel at his word: the Idea does not realize itself in triumphal perfection. There are no utopias in the Hegelian odyssey, only a spiraling sequence of violence and conflagrations. The "highpoints" of spiritual perfection are ideal-typical purities. When absolute knowing is actually realized, and Spirit knows itself as Spirit, it annihilates itself.[3] Absolute knowing *was* achieved by Hegel; the young Marx found the Hegelian mode of presentation to be lacking and attempted to whittle the dynamics of Spirit down to the ground of labor;[4] Durkheim "completed" the work of Hegel by grounding Spirit in the much broader ground of social organization, myriad effervescent practices, and the procession of social forms.[5] I think it is fair to say that in the span between the so-called Jena Circle and the publication of *Elementary Forms* in 1912, Spirit found and comprehended itself, at least philosophically and sociologically, but it had no power to prevent mass suicide, twice, at a total price of over 120 million dead between 1914 and 1945. It was not simply that only *a world*, as Mannheim puts it, grasped itself directly, *it was the only world that could possibly do so.*[6] Let us examine the simplified process whereby humans create this "transcendental"

---

3   The Absolute Idea is not "something in heaven or the stratosphere, but in fact in the objective world whose very ground is the Notion [concept] ..." (Dunayevskaya 1980: n.p.).

4   Hegel is normally treated as if Spirit was a disembodied entity or autonomous mind at work behind the world somewhere but Hegel's philosophy was saturated in political economy and the new industrial armies of the living dead and urban rabble. The Hegelian Spirit is covered in blood and filth and terminates always in an act of self-destruction, sometimes total but usually partial.

5   By all means see the neglected but important *From Tribe to Empire* (Moret and Davy [1926] 1970).

6   "It is impossible for all men to be scientists" says Carus, but it is also "not necessary that their minds and hearts should be enslaved by blind faith" ([1900] 1996: 450).

something that haunts every epoch in a kaleidoscope of forms at various scales of life.

1   Hyper-Praxis

When it comes to us, as Otto Hintze says, "All human activity, political and religious, stems from an undivided root" (in Bendix 1978: 17). The common root metaphor is germane but we will have to go our own way. Burckhardt says that "In the course of any material activity carried on with independent power, and not merely slavishly, a spiritual surplus is generated, be it ever so little" ([1943] 1955: 126). In the sociogony we saw that human objectivation amounts to an open-ended procession of particular metamorphoses of an underlying substance (*hypokeimenon*) mounting itself onto the material world and, along the way, simultaneously altering physical existence and providing the education of Spirit – at least, that's the optimistic version: the eruption of and the ascendency of reason out of the dung heap of superstition, ignorance, and common sense through a spiraling helix of negations and sublations. Simplistically, we can say that human assemblage[7] (A) is productive of special effects (Collective Effervescence) that, to avoid having this current going to waste,[8]

---

7   Our first social necessity is association (C: 447). Here we have "joint action" and the "fitting together" of individuals not out of any shared values but out of necessity (Blumer 1969: 76). This effervescence, once it starts to take form rather than wasting away is our sociological *arche* or underlying principle. Assemblage is the precondition for cooperation (C: 439–54) and organization. Assemblage is the milieu in which the individual, the undividable, will be divided, will become double and possessed by external and alien forces. But mere assemblage and cooperation can be achieved through a spatial and temporal "restriction" that extends "effectiveness" (C: 446) of the collective endeavour (work, ritual, etc.) to the widest possible extent. In other words, the assembled individuals must be compressed into a defined and bounded space-time and they must must all expend their energy or be employed "simultaneously" (C: 447). The result is a "concentration" of bodies and energies (S: 208). The moment of energetic creation is also the moment where energy has the potential to slip away from us and become "irresponsible power" (Dicks 1972: 256). Our creations (objects) are often transmogrified into objectivities, things, and finally monsters, despite our best intentions.

8   The pleasure of discharge of energies must be avoided such that it does not go to waste. In other words, we need a shift from the pleasure principle to a pleasure beyond the pleasure principle, such that "When discharge comes, it already includes the Other ..." (Fink 1997: 226). To hitch Lacan to Durkheim we can see that the organization of effervescence, its production, exchange, and accumulation marks the transition from mere excitement and collective frenzy to a crystallized and symbolically "bridled" or regulated *jouissance* where we mark the transition from profane satisfactions (the individual pleasure principle) to the sacred (and substitute) satisfactions of association and participation in symbolic life and culture. The yield is a quantum of "useful effect" (C: 445) that has been liberated from the

must be transferred via Projection (signification and mimetic gestures, etc.)[9] and mounted upon some material prop or carrier that is set apart (alienated and objectified)[10] and thereby acquiring the status of a sacred entity, e.g., a Totem that embodies a simultaneously awesome and terrifying force. This thing (fluid, jelly, or crystal) is regarded not as a simple product but an enigmatic power that demands respect, worship, and sacrifice – and that also embodies all the hopes, dreams, fears, and contradictions of the collectivity that unwittingly gave birth to it: A - CE - P - T.

Another way of looking at this process of objectivation is to conceive of human interaction giving rise to a current that we could represent in the form of a simple band that can be metaphorically pinned together with a signifier. If no signifier can join the two ends the band simply dissolves into nothing – it would be as if the interaction never took place. But suppose a signifer does join the ends of the band: at one extreme the signifier can mean anything to anybody and the whole affair inevitably devolves into linguistic anarchy, and, on the other, the shared meaning collapses down to a single referent and the

---

diffusion and waste of a gathering that fails to organize itself. The quantum of "useful effect" is dependent upon the quantitative volume (C: 445) or "density" (S: 198) of participants; the greater the volume and density, the larger the "useful effect." The factors that most dramatically increase the quantum of effectiveness is *specialization* of tasks, functions, or roles and, secondly, the restriction of goals or aims to the least number possible (S: 208) for the telos of the single-minded and determined group is a definite point in time and space and more assured of success. The "allocation of personnel" is concerned with getting "the 'right' people ... into the right roles, and that people stay 'where they belong' in terms of status" (Parsons 1951: 133–34). Quoting Talleyrand's "very fine passage" Durkheim says that "'One should ... consider society as a vast studio. It is not enough that everyone should be at work in it, it is essential that everyone be in their rightful place; otherwise forces will work against one another instead of working in that harmony which they become multiplied ....'" (1977: 290).

9   Here we have the ritual energizing of representations (EFRL: 349–50).
10   In signification, less crucial is the status of the profane carrier or prop compared to the image that is produced. The image has the tricky job of shocking consciousness by connecting contextualized concepts that "summon each other on one level, and repel each other on another" (Caillois 2003: 316–17). As soon as a sign is affixed to an object it becomes emblematic of a social relation and is shifted to an autonomous dimension apart from creative intentionality (Buber 1965: 66). The problem with signification is that the "operation of signifying representation never comes off without producing some disturbing surplus, some leftover ..." (Žižek 1993: 130). Drawing a line across the profane world and placing some things and people in the position of the prohibited marks the emergence of the sacred and the demand for inhibition. There can be no social world without the delineations and difference-making. That's just what humans do. To live as a human means to live in an organized fashion and to be organized means to have lines drawn all over the place. Well all need someone to tell us "Well, you's arthurized, ain't ya?"

whole thing devolves into signaling; in either case, human duality is lost in chaos or under the iron heel of the dictator.[11] But let us suppose that the signifier and the signified are bound together but with a varying degree of eccentricity such that the band is linked but not just simply, joined with a twist in it, the "twist" representing some degree of eccentricity (imagine a Mobius band). The product of successful association is, in very simple terms, the formation of a "parabolic allegory" that, with correct mass, bends the intersubjective plane into a gentle hyperbola or parabola (basically, we are referencing an object with an eccentricity between circular zero and linear infinity) generating rotation

---

11   In the one case, there is no authority, just communal liquidity and the "happy go lucky" world of pragmatic play as Durkheim puts it. On the other, authority has passed over into authoritarian domination. Sociology can have neither anarchy nor despotism. The requirement for simultaneity in praxis (labor or ritual) means that the assembled must be under the direction of a supervisor, leader, guide, psychopompos, or what have you. Somebody has to keep an eye on things. "All directly social or communal labour on a large scale requires, to a greater or lesser degree, a directing authority, in order to secure the harmonious co-operation of the activities of individuals, and to perform the general functions that have their origin in the motion of the total productive organism, as distinguished from the motion of its separate organs" (C: 448). We can refer to this aspect as rational *coordination* in contrast to irrational *subordination* (Fichte 1847: 33). Coordination is not an auxiliary function but for humans is as necessary as food and shelter for survival (Whitehead [1933] 1955: 76). "As a matter of fact, the division of labor which involves cooperation is possible only when all the members are guided by a common idea, so that each member responds to, and to some degree influences, the directing purpose of the whole. In order that there shall be genuine cooperation in any spiritual enterprise – and all enterprises involving human individuals are at bottom spiritual – the parts must be members, and to be a member implies a constant interplay and interchange taking place between the different points of the system" (Creighton 1925: 53). The same discipline, training, and coordination can manifest itself in wildly different and sociologically antagonistic forms. For example, the Athenian hoplite and the naval rower were almost equally trained, disciplined, and coordinated but the rower, facing backwards, "had to act blindly as part of a machine" (McNeill 1963: 256–57) whereas the hoplite, face-to-face with his adversary had to improvise a bit in hand-to-hand combat – especially if the phalanx broke apart. Once Athenian military power became dualistic (land and sea, farmers and *thetes*, phalanx and fleet) a split widened also between the communal and altruistic solidarity of rowers and the individualized service of the hoplite (Ibid.). Even though rowers consisted of different classes of people hoplite ideology reduced them to a homogenous "mob" compared to to the landed hoplites (Strauss 1996). The authoritative function, e.g., the ritual psychopompos, consists of signifying and objectivating currents of effervescence generated by the assemblage – signification is essentially the *aesthetic* moment in transforming nothing more than a felt excitement into a named object with value (authority) capable of normative direction once it has become reified. Basically, what we have here is an *axiomatization* process where energy is cancelled upward or sublated into definite value forms (political, religious, and economic).

of individuals, dyads, and larger units around a churning vortex – the telos of
the infraliminal domain. If the volume and mass or "bulk" (Augustine) of this
absolute is insufficient the intersubjective plane will flatten out and structures
will disintegrate, leaving nothing but atomic drift following the chaotic permis-
sibility of planar infinity; too great a "bulk" and the intersubjective space will
warp into an elliptical nightmare of rapid and violent descent into the moral
vortex or the closed totality of a circular, zero eccentricity life of mass incar-
ceration or society reduced to a gulag. "Alcmaeon declares that men perish because they cannot link together the beginning to the end" (Aristotle 1984: 1420).
However, social death occurs when the "beginning" and the "end" are connected in a totalitarian infinity just as moral suicide awaits those who drift along the
flat plane of aimless infinity. Through periodic repetition,[12] expansion, division
of statuses, ranks, and responsibilities, the proliferation of taboos and positive
norms, the band is more fully organized, *more tightly wound around itself* that is,
and acquires a more complicated structure. This Thing can be a totem, a charismatic hero, king, god, devil, scapegoat, commodity, or what have you.

Once something like a totem is brought into existence the entire social
ground is reconstituted "vertically" as well as "horizontally" around the group
name such that life acquires an ontic depth as well as mythological origins.[13]
The totemic powers have the capacity to spread contagiously but are controlled and regulated following the contours of social organization, taboo, customs, and unequal statuses.[14] Even though the sacred is in a sense beyond time
and space it is nonetheless organized because it is modelled on the underlying
shape of the society that has produced and renewed it.[15] Lacking organization
an angry mob, for example, fails to generate a moral surplus of any value (RSM:
129, 131) or crystallize into the permanent crowd, i.e., society (Durkheim 1961:
62). In society, all put in what they can and receive a quantum of moral power
in return. The thing depends upon them and they, in return, depend upon their
collective representation. As society becomes more organized and sharply
delineated groups proliferate, and where individuals are free to participate in
a multiplicity of groups divided by function, the vitality of individual life s

---

12   Repetition of metaphors leads to a contraction and labeling of a thing, the creation of a
      new object (Jaynes 1990: 49). To move from the domain of the temporary and fluid to that
      of permanence requires periodicity and duration (S: 202). Duration is linked to volume:
      if the volume of the group is insufficient, nothing durable will be achieved and without
      duration, society dies.

13   Cf. Levinas on metaphysical "height" and the "Most High" (1979: 34 ff.).

14   It would be more accurate to say that contagion actually depends upon communication
      and social organization.

15   "Association is not established and does not produce its effects all at once; it requires time
      and there are consequently moments at which the reality is indeterminate" (S: 313).

heightened (Simmel 1955: 133). Sounding much like Marx, Durkheim says that "in the end, man finds himself a captive in this imaginary world, even though he is its creator and model. He becomes the vassal of those spiritual forces that he has made with his own hands and in his own image" (EFRL: 49). Moreover, we suffer for this "misguided" devotion. "How all times mischoose the objects of their adulation and reward. And how the same inexorable price must still be paid for the same great purchase" (Whitman 2002: 10). Still, this purchase, as misguided as it is, means that life is no longer lived exclusively upon the horizontal plane of profane labor, consumption, and excretion but becomes deeper and more articulated whereby the Individual person (P) is linked to the Universal tribal status (T) via the mediating function of clan Particularity (C).

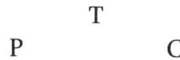

$$T$$
$$P \qquad\qquad C$$

One of the unique features of modern society is the veneration of a hyper-praxis, the overdoing it, that was exceptional in the premodern world of tradition and, where it existed, was considered morally suspect. Hegelian and neo-Hegelian social philosophy (and here we can include Marx) went most of the way in solving the problem but it was not completely grasped until sociology proper, in the form of Durkheim and his disciples, completed the project begun in Jena generations earlier.[16] Following Labriola,

> we are only searching for the explicit conditions of human association in so far as it is no longer simply animal. It is not for us to support our inductions or our deductions upon the data of biology, but, on the contrary, to recognize before all else the peculiarities of human association, which form and develop through the succession and the growing perfection of the activity of man himself in given and variable conditions, and to find the relations of co-ordination and subordination of the needs which are the substratum of will and action.
>
> 1896: n.p.

From the Durkheimian point of view, "society begins in an ecstatic moment of creativity, it comes into existence in relation to its already given relations which the sacred transfigures. It is the drive of the energy which is essential

---

16   Part of me is inclined to say that Marx did have it all figured out but getting "bogged down" in the critique of political economy prohibited him from rounding out the bulk of his intellectual project that embraced the totality of capitalist civilization and its historical origins.

and this forces itself to be represented: the basic structure of this energy is contagious and infinitely divisible, but essentially it can only come into existence in the medium of the symbolic order itself ..." (Gane 1992: 80–81). The result is not natural but "supernatural" – "humans are not simply alive, they are possessed by the strange drive to enjoy life in excess, passionately attached to a surplus which sticks out and derails the ordinary run of things" (Žižek 2006b: 62). This surplus is what we add to our world through hyper-praxis and this surplus is, make no mistake, an autonomous subject-substance that exhibits qualities of autonomous existence. This surplus, its power to make us stronger and to put us in bondage, as well as our consciousness of (and our miscomprehension of it) are the fundamental problems of sociology for this is the seat of the phenomenon of authority.[17]

2   The Dynamistic Circle

For Marx, labor was the decisive engine of human creativity whereas for Durkheim the labor ontology takes its place within a larger matrix of a general economy of energetic association as the base for the spread of a vast and enigmatic web of consubstantial modalities. Laboring for vast millenia was simply profane activity whereas religion and magic were the domains of sacred productions. As such, periodic rites and rituals are the "engines" from which people generate and then project moral energy.

However we must be careful not to confuse the physical with the social just as we must always avoid confusing reflections for the mirrors. For example, labor may "create value" (and we must remember that this "creation" is retroactively constituted through appropriation, reckoning, calculations, measuring, pricing, i.e., compound alienation) "but is not itself value" (C: 142). Likewise, ritual conduct may create the mana that will be projected onto the totemic shell (carrier, prop, envelope, bearer, etc.) but it is not itself mana. Mana, like value, belongs to the domain of substantial or absolute subjectivity. We are not referring to logical universals or mere categories of the understanding but to social absolutes or constraining ideals (Bouglé [1926] 1970: 35, 75).

As Weber put it in "Rise of Religions" the "distinctive subjective condition" known as ecstasy was produced through "communal" forms of "religious association" ([1922] 1991: 3). And this productive nature of the rite is central: "rites are eminently effective; they are creative; they *do* things" (Mauss 1972: 19). In

---

17   Contra Mannheim, this surplus does not "derive from" representations (1982: 207) but is expressed and reproduced as representations.

some cases even, ritual derives its name from a reference to these effective characteristics: in India the word which best corresponds to our word ritual is *karman*, action .... The German word *Zauber* has the same etymological meaning; in other languages the words for magic contain the root *to do*" (Mauss 1972: 19). Since the 16th Century, however, labor has shifted from being merely profane activity to being a conduit to the sacred, at least in North America and Europe. If we combine the models of Marx and Durkheim regarding the origins of moral surpluses – let us for now just refer to them all generically as *axia* (values)[18] of one sort or another that have separated out – we find down in the arena of organized human assemblage and interaction a strikingly similar and compatible set of ideas.

A recurring image in Durkheim's *Elementary Forms* is the social circle: the periodic ascendency of the group from profane everyday activity into the "higher" sacred life. The cult is the engine for the periodic renewal of moral life. This cult association is productive of what he calls "special effects" (S: 310). This effect is the collective effervescence or a core of moral fire (Buber 1965: 107) produced under special circumstances. This "fire" can and often does go to waste – never crystallizing into anything with moral importance. However, if the ebullience or "fire" that erupts from the ritual circle is "captured" and mounted on a prop something new enters the world. Based on what we will see in the next volumes on suicide and the moral geometry and topology of capitalist society, I think a suitable metaphor to describe this unique product is, to pick back up where we left off, the Mobius loop.

For a simple demonstration, take an ordinary belt and wrap it around itself three times and fasten the buckle to the running end. Why three times? Stories have a beginning, a middle, and an end; jokes possess a tripartite structure – a priest, a rabbi, and a minister walk into a bar ...; "Weave a circle round him

---

18   It would be appropriate, I think, to conceive of our overall project as a kind of "axiology" if we were to follow Lepley's suggestion that axiology should raise itself up to the analysis and theory of values (not just exchange-value) across the domains of the economy, politics, and so on (1949: 391). There are multiple fields of value (Morris 1949) each with their own "axial principle" (Bell 1976: 10) and techniques of value "production" (ritual, manufacturing, deal-making, stump speeches, etc.) but, in the final analysis, values are essentially manifestations of objectified surplus energy that have undergone a moralization process. I disagree with Daniel Bell in that a society can have a disjunctive structure while also enjoying a holistic totality. In the *Logic*, Hegel provides us with insight into the structure of disjunctive development and the unfolding of the absolute. What Bell does not have is a theory of the Value of values or the universal-equivalent of the universal-equivalent, the Law of the law, the Other of the Big Other.

thrice, And close your eyes with holy dread ..." (Coleridge: 1816: 58). After the belt is secured separate the bands evenly and attempt to form a perfect sphere out of the belt. Let us refer to this resulting sphere as a "parabolic allegory." The problem with the sphere is that there is always an excess that "sticks out" – a kind of disturbing and unwanted supplement that prevents the sphere from completing itself to our satisfaction. Let us refer to this unwanted protuberance that disrupts the integrity of the sphere as the "return of the repressed." Since we can never smooth things over and complete the perfect sphere we will just give up and, aggravated, pull the sphere apart – resulting in a Mobius loop in the shape of the symbol for mathematical infinity. Most of us will be familiar with Mobius bands from the artwork of M.C. Escher (Bool et al. 1982) but what you may not know is that if you cut a Mobius strip lengthwise in half the result is another Mobius strip. If we take this metaphor of the Mobius structure seriously, we can imagine that, like the twisted loop, we can be split or divided (doubled) and still retain our individual integrity. In fact, our doubled unity acquires new qualities that the original materials and structures lack. Where an uncut Mobius loop possesses the quality of a single half "twist" the divided loop will possess four half twists and all four of these half twists will reside on a single side of the loop leaving one side flat (linear). Two Mobius loops of opposing chirality (one is right-handed and the other left-handed, i.e., they are mirror images of one another – "chirality" from the Greek *kheir* for "hand") joined at right angles to one another and split down the middle result in the surprising figure of paradromic rings (intertwined hearts). As such, when the two strips are cut they remain entangled – and apparently in love or chained together at least. One can replicate this with paper, tape, and a pair of scissors or consult the demonstrations performed by the Cambridge mathematician Tadashi Tokieda. We could plunge into the Euler characteristic and mathematical aspects of the topology of the Mobius strip but a more germane example is provided by Bach's *Goldberg Variations*.

Canon 5 from the *Variations* is basically a musical Mobius. Leaving aside the individual notes and symbols themselves, the pitches, what is interesting for us is the unique property of the composition once it is bent into shape: two distinct voices plus their inversions (four total voices) singing four different lines forming *mirror* identities with one another once they are "alienated" from their two-dimensional compositional space, i.e., looped, and finally twisted. In other words, when the voices are structured in a particular manner (a Mobius band) something new emerges that lives *in* and only *within* the loop – not *on* the surface of the band, topologically, but in it (Phillips 2015).

3   The Inhuman Equivalent

Let us return to the image of the protuberance of repression we found in the
Mobius structure. If love were universal we would have no problems:

> *Love* one another, unite in spirit, and your hearts will be filled with that
> blessedness which you have so vainly sought for *outside* of yourselves, in
> God. *Organise,* unite in the real world, and by your deeds and works you
> will possess all the wealth, which you have so vainly sought, in *money.*
> So long as you do not strive to develop your own nature, so long as you
> strive to be not *human* but *superhuman* and *inhuman* creatures, you will
> become inhuman, you will look down contemptuously upon human na-
> ture, whose real nature you do not recognize and treat "the masses" as
> if they were a wild beast. The beast which you see in the people is in
> yourself.
>
> MOSES HESS, in *HOOK* 1934: n.p.

However, love is, in the best of times, a positive hate. It is the return of the repressed that causes problems for individuals and their relation to the universal
because the flow of the return passes through the particularity of the alter ego.
The more organization a social system has the more "negative entropy" and
"improbability" it enjoys (Boulding 1964: 139). Regulated social systems strive
for the improbable and resist dissolution into entropy whereas in social systems that are falling apart, fear and hatred battle in the name of entropy and
diminution of social potentials. The spectacle of Trumpism and the dream of
high walls surrounding the United States (keeping the -X out of America) offers a perfect example of the embrace of entropy and collective suicide. Where
there is love, *agape*, entropy has met its countervailing substance (Boulding
1964: 146).

   A minimal degree of repression and self-repression are necessary to lift a society above the subsistence level of hunting and gathering but for both Freud
and Durkheim the problem of modern civilization is not repression per se but
excessive or surplus repression. For Marx, an opponent of all repression, surplus value is traced back through dialectical analysis to the discovery that any
surplus is rooted, in the final analysis, in surplus labor, aided by the detailed
division of labor and a dehumanizing instrumental rationality. Marx did not
have a lot to say about the structure and quality of communist association in
the post-capitalist future but it is difficult to imagine how a modern civilization could be rewired to prevent the production and accumulation of surplus.

Like mana, surplus value is also society in its alienated formlessness, however, far from the object of cooperative mediation, the commodity and capital
forms are terrifying monsters that reign with absolute hegemony over nearly
the entire planet. It is important to note that religions most closely associated
with the capitalist spirit were those that were also plagued by a god that was
distant and indifferent, so remote that, had the devil (the negative god) not
persisted, it would have led to a practical atheism. Thank god for the devil.

Bibliography

Abrahamsen, David. 1946. *The Mind and Death of a Genius*. New York: Columbia University Press.

Abrams, Philip. 1982. *Historical Sociology*. Ithaca: Cornell University Press.

Ackermann, Hans W. and Jeanine Gauthier. 1991. "The Ways and Nature of the Zombie." *The Journal of American Folklore* 104 (414): 466–94.

Ackermann, Robert John. 1990. *Nietzsche*. Amherst. The University of Massachusetts Press.

Acton, H.B. 1967. "Idealism." pp. 110–118 in *The Encyclopedia of Philosophy*, Vol. 8. New York: Macmillan and The Free Press.

Adams, Marilyn McCord. 1983. "Introduction." pp. 1–33 in *Predestination, God's Foreknowledge, and Future Contingents*, 2nd ed., by William Ockham, tr. M. Adams and N. Kretzmann. Indianapolis: Hackett.

Adams, Phillip, interviewed by Paul Holdengräber. 2014. "The Art of Nonfiction, No. 7." *The Paris Review*, Spring. Online: (www.theparisreview.org/interviews/6286/the-art-of-nonfiction-no-7-adam-phillips).

Adams, Richard George. [1972] 2000. *Watership Down*. New York: Scribner.

Adams, Richard Newbold. 1978. "Man, Energy, and Anthropology: I Can Feel the Heat, but Where's the Light?" *American Anthropologist* 80 (2): 297–309.

Adler, Alfred. 1954. *Understanding Human Nature*. Greenwich: Fawcett.

Adorno, Theodor W. 1950. "Democratic Leadership and Mass Manipulation." pp. 418–435 in *Studies in Leadership*, ed. Alvin W. Gouldner. New York: Harper.

Adorno, Theodor W. [1964] 1973a. *The Jargon of Authenticity*, tr. Knut Tarnowski and Frederic Will. Evanston: Northwestern University Press.

Adorno, Theodor W. 1967. *Prisms*, tr. Samuel and Shierry Weber. Cambridge: MIT Press.

Adorno, Theodor W. 1973b. *Negative Dialectics*, tr. E.B. Ashton. New York: Continuum.

Adorno, Theodor W. 1974. *Minima Moralia*, tr. E.F.N. Jephcott. London: Verso.

Adorno, Theodor W. [1975] 2000. *The Psychological Technique of Martin Luther Thomas*. Stanford: Stanford University Press.

Adorno, Theodor W. 1976. "Sociology and Empirical Research." pp. 68–86 in *The Positivist Dispute in German Sociology* by Theodor W. Adorno, Hans Albert, Ralf Dahrendorf, Jürgen Habermas, Harald Pilot, and Karl R. Popper. London: Heinemann.

Adorno, Theodor W. 1989. *Kierkegaard*, tr. Robert Hullot-Kentor. Minneapolis: University of Minnesota Press.

Adorno, Theodor W. 1997. *Aesthetic Theory*, tr. Robert Hullot-Kentor. Minneapolis: University of Minnesota Press.

Adorno, Theodor W. 1993. *Hegel: Three Studies*, tr. Shierry Nicholsen. Cambridge: The MIT Press.

Adorno, Theodor W. 1998. *Critical Models*, tr. Henry W. Pickford. New York: Columbia University Press.

Adorno, Theodor W. and Hellmut Becker. 1983. "Education for Autonomy." *Telos* 55: 103–110.

Adorno, T.W., Else Frenkel-Brunswik, Daniel J. Levinson, and R. Nevitt Sanford. 1950. *The Authoritarian Personality*. New York: W.W. Norton.

Agamben, Giorgio. 2004. *The Open: Man and Animal*. Stanford: Stanford University Press.

Agger, Ben. 1989. *Socio(onto)logy*. Urbana: University of Illinois Press.

Alain. [1934] 1974. *The Gods*, tr. Richard Pevear. New York: New Directions.

Alexander, Jeffery C. 1982. *Theoretical Logic in Sociology, Volume Two, The Antinomies of Classical Thought: Marx and Durkheim*. Berkeley: University of California Press.

Alexander, Jeffery C. 1986. "Rethinking Durkheim's Intellectual Development I: On 'Marxism' and the Anxiety of Being Misunderstood." *International Sociology* 1(1): 91–107.

Ali, Farhana and Jerrold Post. 2008. "The History and Evolution of Martyrdom in the Service of Defensive Jihad." *Social Research* 75 (2): 615–654.

Alighieri, Dante. 1995. *The Divine Comedy*, tr. Allen Mandelbaum. New York: Knopf.

Alperovitz, Gar and Lew Daly. 2008. *Unjust Deserts*. New York: The New Press.

Alpert, Harry. 1939. *Emile Durkheim and his Sociology*. New York: Columbia University Press.

Alpert, Harry. 1958. "The Growth of Social Research in the United States." pp. in *The Human Meaning of the Social Sciences*. New York: Meridian Books.

Altemeyer, Bob. 2006. *The Authoritarians*. Online: (http://home.cc.umanitoba.ca/~altemey).

Althusser, Louis. 1969. *For Marx*. New York: Vintage.

Althusser, Louis. 1970. "Ideology and Ideological State Apparatuses." Online: (www.marxists.org/reference/archive/althusser/1970/ideology.htm).

Alvarez, A. 1972. *The Savage God*. New York: Random House.

Amin, Samir. 1994. *Re-Reading the Postwar Period*. New York: Monthly Review Press.

Amis, Martin. 1984. *Money: A Suicide Note*. New York: Penguin.

Anderson, Kevin. 1993. "On Hegel and the Rise of Social Theory: A Critical Appreciation of Herbert Marcuse's *Reason and Revolution*, Fifty Years Later." *Sociological Theory* 11 (3): 243–267.

Antonio, Robert J. 1995. "Nietzsche's Antisociology: Subjectified Culture and the End of History." *American Journal of Sociology* 101(1): 1–43.

Antonio, Robert J. 2003. "Introduction: Marx and Modernity." pp. 1–50 in *Marx and Modernity*, ed. Robert J. Antonio. Malden: Blackwell.

Antonio, Robert J. 2017. "Immanent Critique and the Exhaustion Thesis: Neoliberalism and History's Vicissitudes." pp. 655–676 in The Palgrave Handbook of Critical Theory, ed. Michael J. Thompson. New York: Palgrave.

Appadurai, Arjun. 1986. "Introduction: Commodities and the Politics of Value." pp. 2–63 in *The Social Life of Things*, ed. Arjun Appadurai. Cambridge: University of Cambridge Press.

Appleby, Julie. 2017. "Obesity-LInked Diagnoses on the Rise Among Kids and Teens." *National Public Radio*, 12 January. Online: (www.npr.org/sections/health-shots/2017/01/12/509374443/obesity-linked-diagnoses-on-the-rise-among-kids-and-teens).

Apuleius. 1994. *The Golden Ass*, tr. P.G. Walsh. Oxford: Oxford University Press.

Aquinas, Thomas. 1947. *Summa Theologica*. Grand Rapids: Christian Classics.

Arendt, Hannah. 1968. *The Origins of Totalitarianism*. New York: Harcourt.

Aristotle. 1984. *Complete Works of Aristotle, Volume 2*. Princeton: Princeton University Press.

Arnold, Matthew. [1869] 1990. *Culture and Anarchy*. Cambridge: Cambridge University Press.

Arnold, Thurman W. 1937. *The Folklore of Capitalism*. New Haven: Yale University Press.

Aron, Raymond. 1964. *German Sociology*. New York: The Free Press.

Aron, Raymond. 1965. *Main Currents in Sociological Thought, Vol. 1*. New York: Doubleday.

Aron, Raymond. 1967. *Main Currents in Sociological Thought, Vol. 2*. New York: Doubleday.

Aron, Raymond. 1968. *Progress and Disillusion*. New York: The New American Library.

Aronowitz, Stanley. 1994. *Dead Artists, Live Theories, and Other Cultural Problems*. London: Routledge.

Artaud, Antonin. 1958. *The Theater and its Double*, tr. Mary Richards. New York: Grove.

Ashley-Cooper, Anthony (Earl of Shaftesbury). 1904. *An Inquiry Concerning Virtue or Merit*. Heidelberg: Carl Winter's Universitätsbuchhandlung.

Auerbach, Erich. 1953. *Mimesis*, tr. Willard Trask. Princeton: Princeton University Press.

Augustine. 1876. *Works*, Vol. 15 (3). Edinburgh: T. and T. Clark.

Austin, J.L. 1975. *How to do Things with Words*. Cambridge: Harvard University Press.

Avineri, Shlomo. 1972. *Hegel's Theory of the Modern State*. Cambridge: Cambridge University Press.

Bacevich, Andrew J. 2009. *The Limits of Power*. New York: Holt.

Bacon, Francis. 1872. *The Works of Francis Bacon, I: Philosophical Writings*. New York: Hurd and Houghton.

Badiou, Alain. 2003. *Saint Paul*. Stanford: Stanford University Press.

Badiou, Alain. 2009. *Theory of the Subject*, tr. Bruno Bosteels. New York: Continuum.

Bageant, Joe. 2007. *Deer Hunting with Jesus*. New York: Three Rivers Press.

Bageant, Joe. 2010. *Rainbow Pie*. Melbourne: Scribe.

Bakhtin, M.M. 1993. *Toward a Philosophy of the Act*, tr. Vadim Liapunov. Austin: University of Texas Press.

Bakker, J.I. 2009. "Peirce, Pragmaticism and Public Sociology: Translating an Interpretation into Praxis." *Current Perspectives in Social Theory* 26: 229–57.

Baldwin, James M (ed.). 1902. *Dictionary of Philosophy and Psychology*. New York: Macmillan.

Baldwin, James M. 1915. *Genetic Theory of Reality*. New York: Putnam's Sons.

Baldwin, Neil. 2001. *Henry Ford and the Jews*. New York: Public Affairs.

Bales, Kevin. 2012. *Disposable People*. Berkeley: University of California Press.

Balzac, Honoré de. [1846] 1991. *Cousin Bette*, tr. James Waring. New York: Knopf.

Barker, Nicola. 2017. *H(a)ppy*. London: William Heinemann.

Barnes, Jonathan. 2001. *Early Greek Philosophy*. New York: Penguin.

Barth, Karl. 1933. *The Epistle to the Romans*. London: Oxford University Press.

Barthes, Roland. 1964. *Elements of Semiology*. Online: (www.marxists.org/reference/ subject/philosophy/works/fr/barthes.htm).

Barthes, Roland. 1976. *Sade, Fourier, and Loyola*, tr. Richard Miller. Berkeley: University of California Press.

Barthes, Roland. 1982. *Empire of Signs*, tr. Richard Howard. New York: Hill and Wang.

Barzun, Jacques. 1964. *Science: The Glorious Entertainment*. New York: Harper.

Bataille, Georges. [1962] 1991a. *The Impossible*, tr. Robert Hurley. San Francisco: City Lights.

Bataille, Georges. [1967] 1989a. *The Accursed Share, Vol. 1*, tr. Robert Hurley. New York: Zone Books.

Bataille, Georges. [1976] 1991b. *The Accursed Share, Vol. 2*, tr. Robert Hurley. New York: Zone Books.

Bataille, Georges. 1989b. *Theory of Religion*, tr. Robert Hurley. New York: Zone Books.

Bataille, Georges. 2004. *Divine Filth*, tr. Mark Spitzer. Creation.

Bateson, Gregory. 1972. *Steps to an Ecology of Mind*. New York: Ballantine Books.

Baudelaire, Charles. 1993. *Poems*, tr. Richard Howard. New York: Knopf.

Baudelaire, Charles. 2002. *On Wine and Hashish*, tr. Andrew Brown. London: Hesperus Press.

Baudrillard, Jean. 1983a. *Simulations*, tr. Paul Foss, Paul Patton, and Philip Beitchman. New York: Semiotext(e).

Baudrillard, Jean. 1983b. *In the Shadow of the Silent Majorities*, tr. Paul Foss, John Johnston, and Paul Patton. New York: Semiotext(e).

Baudrillard, Jean. 1983c. "The Ecstasy of Communication." pp. 126–34 in *Anti-Aesthetic*, ed. Hal Foster. Port Townsend: Bay Press.

Baudrillard, Jean. 1988. *America*, tr. Chris Turner. London: Verso.

Baudrillard, Jean. 2005. *The System of Objects*. London: Verso.

Baumeister, Roy. 2010. "Understanding Free Will and Consciousness on the Basis of Current Research Findings in Psychology." pp. 24–42 in *Free Will and Consciousness*, eds. Mele Baumeister, and Vohs. New York: Oxford University Press.

Bearman, Peter S. 1991. "The Social Structure of Suicide." *Sociological Forum* 6 (3): 501–24.

Bechdel, Alison. 2006. *Fun Home*. New York: Houghton Mifflin Harcourt.

Becker, Ernest. 1973. *The Denial of Death*. New York: The Free Press.

Beidelman, T.O. 1974. *W. Robertson Smith and the Sociological Study of Religion*. Chicago: The University of Chicago Press.

Beiser, Frederick. 2002. *German Idealism*. Cambridge: Harvard University Press.

Beiser, Frederick. 2005. *Hegel*. New York: Routledge.

Bell, Daniel. 1976. *The Cultural Contradictions of Capitalism*. New York: Basic Books.

Bellah, Robert N., Richard Madsen, William M. Sullivan, Ann Swidler, and Steven M. Tipton. 1985. *Habits of the Heart*. New York: Harper.

Bendix, Reinhard. [1956] 1974. *Work and Authority in Industry*. Berkeley: University of California Press.

Bendix, Reinhard. 1960. *Max Weber*. Garden City: Doubleday.

Bendix, Reinhard. 1978. *Kings or People*. Berkeley: University of California Press.

Benjamin, Jessica. 1988. *The Bonds of Love*. New York: Pantheon.

Benjamin, Walter. [1963] 1998. *The Origin of German Tragic Drama*. London: Verso.

Benjamin, Walter. 1996. *Selected Writings, Volume 1*. Cambridge: Harvard University Press.

Benjamin, Walter. 1999a. *Selected Writings, Volume 2, Part 2*. Cambridge: Harvard University Press.

Benjamin, Walter. 1999b. *The Arcades Project*, tr. Howard Eiland and Kevin McLaughlin. Cambridge: Harvard University Press.

Berger, Bennett M. 1995. *An Essay on Culture*. Berkeley: University of California Press.

Berger, Jonah. 2016. *Invisible Influence*. New York: Simon and Schuster.

Berger, Peter. 1967. *The Sacred Canopy*. New York: Anchor.

Berger, Peter. 1969. *A Rumor of Angels*. New York: Anchor.

Berger, Peter and Stanley Pullberg. 1965. "Reification and the Sociological Critique of Consciousness." *History and Theory* 4 (2): 196–211.

Berger, Peter and Thomas Luckmann. 1966. *The Social Construction of Reality*. New York: Anchor.

Berger, Peter, Brigitte Berger, and Hansfried Kellner. 1973. *The Homeless Mind*. New York: Vintage.

Bergson, Henri. 1920. *Mind-Energy*, tr. H. Wildon Carr. New York: Henry Holt.

Bering, Jesse. 2013. *Perv: The Sexual Deviant in All of Us*. New York: Scientific American/Farrar, Straus, and Giroux.

Berman, Marshall. 1988. *All that is Solid Melts into Air*. New York: Penguin.

Bernays, Edward L. 1928. "Manipulating Public Opinion: The Why and the How." *American Journal of Sociology* 33(6): 958–71.

Bernhard, Thomas. 1979. *Correction*, tr. Sophie Wilkins. New York: Vintage.

Bernhard, Thomas. 1987. *Woodcutters*, tr. David McLintock. New York: Vintage.

Bernstein, Richard J. [1971] 1999. *Praxis and Action,* new edition. Philadelphia: University of Pennsylvania Press.

Berthold-Bond, Daniel. 1995. *Hegel's Theory of Madness*. Albany: SUNY Press.

Besnard, Philippe. 2000. "The Fortunes of Durkheim's *Suicide*. pp. 97–125 in *Durkheim's Suicide*, eds. W.S.F. Pickering and Geoffrey Walford. London: Routledge.

Besnard, Philippe. 2005. "Durkheim's Squares: Types of Social Pathology and Types of Suicide." pp. 70–79 in *The Cambridge Companion to Durkheim*, eds. Jeffrey C. Alexander et al. Cambridge: Cambridge University Press.

Bettelheim, Bruno. 1960. *The Informed Heart: Autonomy in a Mass Age*. New York: Avon.

Bettelheim, Bruno. 1982. *Freud and Man's Soul*. New York: Vintage.

Bhaskar, Roy. 2008. *Dialectic: The Pulse of Freedom*. New York: Routledge.

Bienenstock, Myriam. 2011. "Between Hegel and Marx: Eduard Gans on the 'Social Question.'" pp. 164–78 in *Politics, Religion, and Art: Hegelian Debates*, ed. Douglas Moggach. Evanston: Northwestern University Press.

Binion, Rudolph. 2005. *Past Impersonal*. Dekalb: Northern Illinois University Press.

Blackburn, Simon. 2001. *Being Good*. Oxford: Oxford University Press.

Blackmar, Frank W. 1905. *The Elements of Sociology*. New York: Macmillan.

Blanc, Paul Le. 2016. *Lenin and the Revolutionary Party*. Chicago: Haymarket.

Blasi, Damian, Soren Wichmann, Harald Hammarstrom, Peter F. Stadler, and Morten H. Christiansen. 2016. "Sound-Meaning Association Biases Evidenced Across Thousands of Languages." *Proceedings of the National Academy of Sciences*. Online: (www.pnas.org/content/early/2016/09/06/1605782113).

Bloch, Ernst. 1988. *The Utopian Function of Art and Literature*. Cambridge: The MIT Press.

Bloch, Marc. 1953. *The Historian's Craft*. New York: Vintage.

Bloch, Marc. 1961. *The Royal Touch*, tr. F.E. Anderson. New York: Dorset.

Blumenthal, Albert. 1936. "The Nature of Culture." *American Sociological Review* 1(6): 875–93.

Blumer, Herbert. 1969. *Symbolic Interactionism*. Berkeley: University of California Press.

Boas, Franz. 1916. *The Mind of Primitive Man*. New York: Macmillan.

Boas, Franz. 1938. "Language." pp. 124–145 in *General Anthropology*, ed. Franz Boas. Boston: D.C. Heath and Co.

Boethius, Anicius Manlius Severinus. [524] 1962. *The Consolation of Philosophy*, tr. Richard Green. New York: Macmillan.

Boétie, Etienne de la. [1552–53] 1975. *The Politics of Disobedience: The Discourse of Voluntary Servitude*. Montreal: Black Rose Books.

Bogardus, Emory. 1922. *A History of Social Thought*. Los Angeles: University of Southern California Press.

Bonhoeffer, Dietrich. 2005. *Ethics*. Minneapolis: Fortress Press.

Bonhoeffer, Dietrich. 2009. *Letters and Papers from Prison*. Minneapolis: Fortress Press.

Bonilla-Silva, Eduardo. 1999. "The Essential Social Fact of Race." *American Sociological Review* 64(6): 899–906.

Bool, Flip, et al. 1982. *M.C. Escher: His Life and Complete Graphic Work*. New York: Abrams.

Boon, James A. 1982. *Other Tribes, Other Scribes*. Cambridge: Cambridge University Press.

Boothby, Richard. 2001. *Freud as Philosopher*. New York: Routledge.

Borkenau, Franz. 1981. *End and Beginning*. New York: Columbia University Press.

Borneman, Ernest (ed.). 1976. *The Psychoanalysis of Money*. New York: Urizen Books.

Bortkiewicz, Ladislaus. [1907] 1952. *Value and Price in the Marxian System*. London: Macmillan. Online: (http://classiques.uqac.ca/classiques/Bortkiewicz_ladislaus_von/value_and_price_marxian_system/value_price_marxian_system.pdf).

Bosanquet, Bernard. 1912. *The Principle of Individuality and Value*. London: Macmillan.

Bosanquet, Bernard. 1913. *Mind and its Object*. Manchester: Manchester University Press.

Bosanquet, Bernard. 1920. *What Religion Is*. London: Macmillan.

Bosanquet, Bernard. [1923] 1965. *The Philosophical Theory of the State*. New York: St Martin's.

Bosserman, Phillip. 1968. *Dialectical Sociology*. Boston: Porter Sargent.

Bouglé, Celestin. [1926] 1970. *The Evolution of Values*. New York: Augustus M. Kelley.

Boulding, Kenneth E. 1964. *The Meaning of the Twentieth Century*. New York: Harper.

Bourdieu, Pierre. 1977. *Outline of a Theory of Practice*. Cambridge: Cambridge University Press.

Bourdieu, Pierre. [1980] 1990a. *The Logic of Practice*. Stanford: Stanford University Press.

Bourdieu, Pierre. 1990b. *In Other Words*. Stanford: Stanford University Press.

Bourdieu, Pierre. 1991. *Language and Symbolic Power*. Cambridge: Harvard University Press.

Bourdieu, Pierre. 2005. *The Social Structures of the Economy*. Malden, MA: Polity Press.

Bourdieu, Pierre et al. 1999. *The Weight of the World*. Stanford: Stanford University Press.

Boutroux, Emile. 1914. *Natural Law in Science and Philosophy*, tr. Fred Rothwell. New York: Macmillan.

Bowersock, G.W. 1994. *Fiction as History*. Berkeley: University of California Press.

Bracken, Christopher. 2007. *Magical Criticism: The Recourse of Savage Philosophy*. Chicago: University of Chicago Press.

Bradley, F.H. 1916. *Appearance and Reality*. London: George Allen and Unwin.

Brandom, Robert. 2013. "A Spirit of Trust." Online: (www.pitt.edu/~brandom/spirit_of_trust.html).

Braudel, Fernand. 1980. *On History*, tr. S. Matthews. Chicago: The University of Chicago Press.

Braverman, Harry. 1974. *Labor and Monopoly Capital*. New York: Monthly Review Press.

Bray, Charles. 1863. *The Philosophy of Necessity*, 2nd ed. London: Longman.

Breasted, James H. 1933. *The Dawn of Conscience*. New York: Scribner's Sons.

Breckman, Warren. 2013. *Adventures of the Symbolic*. New York: Columbia University Press.

Breunig, Charles. 1970. *The Age of Revolution and Reaction, 1789–1850*. New York: Norton.

Brinton, Crane. 1950. *Ideas and Men*. New York: Prentice-Hall.

Brinton, Crane. 1963. *The Shaping of Modern Thought*. Englewood Cliffs: Prentice-Hall.

Brown, Norman O. 1959. *Life Against Death*. London: Routledge and Kegan Paul.

Brown, Phil. 1974. *Toward a Marxist Psychology*. New York: Harper.

Brown, Richard Harvey. 1977. *A Poetic for Sociology*. Chicago: The University of Chicago Press.

Brown, Steven D. and Rose Capdevila. 1999. "*Perpetuum Mobile*: Substance, Force, and the Sociology of Translation." pp. 26–49 in *Actor Network Theory and After*, eds. John Law and John Hassard. Oxford: Blackwell.

Buber, Martin. 1965. *The Knowledge of Man*. New York: Harper.

Burckhardt, Jacob. [1943] 1955. *Force and Freedom*. New York: Meridian Books.

Burckhardt, Jacob. [1943] 1979. *Reflections on History*. Indianapolis: Liberty.

Burke, Christopher. 2010. "Introduction." pp. vii–xviii in *From Hieroglyphics to Isotype* by Otto Neurath. London: Hyphen Press.

Burke, Peter. 1992. *History and Social Theory*. Ithaca: Cornell University Press.

Burroughs, William S. [1959] 2001. *Naked Lunch*. New York: Grove.

Burton, Robert. [1621–1638] 2001. *The Anatomy of Melancholy*. New York: New York Review of Books.

Byron, G.G. 1880. *The Poetical Works of Lord Byron*. New York: A.L. Burt.

Caillois, Roger. 1959. *Man and the Sacred*. Urbana: University of Illinois Press.

Caillois, Roger. 2003. *The Edge of Surrealism*, ed. Claudine Frank. Durham: Duke University Press.

Cain, James M. [1934] 1997. *The Postman Always Rings Twice*. pp. 1–95 in *Crime Novels: American Noir of the 1930s and 40s*. New York: The Library of America.

Caird, John. 1880. *An Introduction to the Philosophy of Religion*. Glasgow: James Maclehose.

Caird, John. 1885. *The Social Philosophy and Religion of Comte*. Glasgow: James Maclehose.

Caird, John. 1886. *Hegel*. Philadelphia: J.B. Lippincott.

Caird, John. 1893. *Hegel*. Edinburgh and London: William Blackwood and Sons.

Calvin, John. [1559] 1981. *Institutes of the Christian Religion*, tr. Henry Beveridge. Grand Rapids, MI: Wm. B. Eerdmans.

Calvino, Italo. 1974. *Invisible Cities*, tr. William Weaver. San Diego: Harcourt.

Camus, Albert. 1955. *The Myth of Sisyphus and Other Essays*, tr. Justin O'Brien. New York.

Capek, Karel. [1923] 1961. *R.U.R.* Oxford: Oxford University Press.

Capra, Fritjof. 1982. *The Turning Point*. New York: Bantam.

Carey, Henry C. [1872] 1967. *The Unity of Law*. New York: Augustus M. Kelley.

Carlyle, Thomas. [1836] 1987. *Sartor Resartus*. Oxford: Oxford University Press.

Carnot, Sadi. 1824. *Reflections on the Motive Power of Fire and on Machines Fitted to Develop that Power*, tr. R.H. Thurston. Paris: Chez Bachelier, Libraire.

Carr, Edward Hallett. 1961. *What is History?* New York: Vintage.

Carus, Paul. [1900] 1996. *The History of the Devil and the Idea of Evil*. New York: Gramercy.

Cassano, Graham. 2008. "Radical Critique and Progressive Traditionalism in John Ford's *The Grapes of Wrath*." *Critical Sociology* 34 (1): 99–116.

Cassano, Graham. 2016. "Critical Pragmatism's Status Wage and the Standpoint of the Stranger." pp. 217–39 in *Capitalism's Future*, ed. Dan Krier and Mark P. Worrell. Leiden and Boston: Brill.

Cassirer, Ernst. 1946. *Language and Myth*. New York: Harper.

Cassirer, Ernst. 1955a. *The Philosophy of Symbolic Forms, Vol. 1*. New Haven: Yale University Press.

Cassirer, Ernst. 1955b. *The Philosophy of Symbolic Forms, Vol. 2*. New Haven: Yale University Press.

Cassirer, Ernst. 1996. *The Philosophy of Symbolic Forms, Vol. 4*, The Metaphysics of Symbolic Forms. New Haven: Yale University Press.

Cassirer, Ernst. 2013. *The Warburg Years*, tr. S.G. Lofts with A. Calcagno. New Haven: Yale University Press.

Castoriadis, Cornelius. 1987. *The Imaginary Institution of Society*, tr. Kathleen Blamey. Cambridge: The MIT Press.

Cavan, Ruth Shonle. [1928] 1965. *Suicide*. New York: Russell.

Certeau, Michel de. 1984. *The Practice of Everyday Life*, tr. Steven Rendall. Berkeley: University of California Press.

Champagne, Claudia M. 1991. "Adam and His 'Other Self' in *Paradise Lost*: A Lacanian Study in Psychic Development. *Milton Quarterly* 25 (2): 48–59.

Chandler, Daniel. 2007. *Semiotics*, 2nd ed. New York: Routledge.

Chandler, Raymond. 1995. *Later Novels and Other Writings*. New York: Library of America.

Chasseguet-Smirgel, Janine. 1985. *Creativity and Perversion*. London: W.W. Norton.

Chateaubriand de, René-François. 1962. "Progress." pp. 99–107 in *Catholic Political Thought*, ed. Bela Menczer. Notre Dame: University of Notre Dame Press.

Chen, Chung-Hwan. 1956. "Different Meanings of the Term Energia in the Philosophy of Aristotle." *Philosophy and Phenomenological Research* 17 (1): 56–65.

Cheney, Dorothy L. and Robert M. Seyfarth. 2008. *Baboon Metaphysics*. Chicago: The University of Chicago Press.

Chesterton, G.K. 1986. *Collected Works, Volume 1*. San Francisco: Ignatius Press.

Choron, Jacques. 1972. *Suicide*. New York: Charles Scribner's Sons.

Cioran, E.M. 1974. *The New Gods*, tr. Richard Howard. Chicago: The University of Chicago Press.

Cladis, Mark S. 2012. "Suffering to Become Human: A Durkheimian Perspective." pp. 81–100 in *Suffering and Evil*, eds. W.S.F. Pickering and Massimo Rosati. New York: Durkheim Press/Berghahn.

Clark, Terry. 1973. *Prophets and Patrons*. Cambridge: Harvard University Press.

Clegg, Stewart R. and Tyrone S. Pitsis. 2012. "Phronesis, Projects and Power Research." pp. 66–93 in *Real Social Science*, eds. Bent Flyvbjerg, Todd Landman, and Sanford F. Schram. Cambridge: Cambridge University Press.

Cohen, Maurice. [1950] 1970. *Language: Its Structure and Evolution*. Miami, FL: University of Miami Press.

Cohn, Norman. 1970. *The Pursuit of the Millennium*. New York: Oxford University Press.

Cohn, Norman. 1993. *Cosmos, Chaos and the World to Come*. New Haven: Yale University Press.

Coleridge, Samuel Taylor. 1798. *The Rime of the Ancient Mariner*. Online: (www.gutenberg .org/files/151/151-h/151-h.htm).

Coleridge, Samuel Taylor. 1816. *Christabel, Kubla Khan, The Pains of Sleep,* and *Zapolya*. London: Murray.

Collingwood, R.G. 1946. *The Idea of History*. Oxford: Oxford University Press.

Collins, Hugh. 1982. *Marxism and Law*. Oxford: Oxford University Press.

Collins, Randall. 1998. *The Sociology of Philosophies*. Cambridge: Harvard University Press.

Collins, Randall. 2004. *Interaction Ritual Chains*. Princeton: Princeton University Press.

Comte, Auguste. 1853. *The Positive Philosophy, Volume 2*. London: John Chapman.

Comte, Auguste. 1969. *Auguste Comte: Sire of Sociology*. New York: Thomas Y. Crowell Company.

Comte-Sponville, Andre. 2004. *The Little Book of Philosophy*. London: Heinemann.

Comte-Sponville, Andre. 2007. *The Little Book of Atheist Spirituality*. New York: Viking.

Congreve, Richard. 1874. *Essays: Political, Social, and Religious*. London: Longmans.

Conrad, Joseph. [1904] 1961. *Nostromo*. New York: Heritage Press.

Cooley, Charles Horton. [1909] 1962. *Social Organization*. New York: Schocken.

Copleston, Frederick. 1946. *Greece and Rome from the Pre-Socratics to Plotinus*. New York: Doubleday.

Copleston, Frederick. 1950. *Medieval Philosophy*. New York: Doubleday.

Cornford, F.M. [1912] 2004. *From Religion to Philosophy*. Mineola: Dover.

Cox, Gary. 2012. *The Existentialist's Guide to Death, the Universe, and Nothingness*. London: Continuum.

Creighton, James Edwin. 1925. *Studies in Speculative Philosophy*. New York: Macmillan.

CrimethInc. 2001. *Days of War, Nights of Love*. Salem: CrimethInc.

CrimethInc. 2011. *Work*. Salem: CrimethInc.

Croce, Benedetto. 1915. *What is Living and What is Dead of the Philosophy of Hegel*. London: Macmillan.

Crombez, Joel. 2016. "The Other Side of Critical Theory." Paper presented at the annual meeting of the International Social Theory Consortium, 10 June, Iowa State University, Ames, IA.

Cunha, Euclides da. 1944. *Rebellion in the Backlands*, tr. Samuel Putnam. Chicago: The University of Chicago Press.

Cutler, Jonathan. 2011. *Literary Theory*. New York: Oxford University Press.

Dahms, Harry F. 2011. *The Vitality of Critical Theory: Current Perspectives in Social Theory* 28. Bingley: Emerald.

Dahrendorf, Ralf. 1959. *Class and Class Conflict in Industrial Society*. Stanford: Stanford University Press.

Damasio, Antonio. 1999. *The Feeling of What Happens*. San Diego: Harcourt.

Darwin, Charles. 1897. *The Descent of Man*. New York: Appleton.

Davies, Christie and Mark Neal. 2000. "Durkheim's Altruistic and Fatalistic Suicide." pp. 36–52 in *Durkheim's Suicide*, eds. W.S.F. Pickering and Geoffrey Walford. London: Routledge.

Davis, Michael M. 1906. "Gabriel Tarde: An Essay in Sociological Theory." (Doctoral dissertation). New York: Columbia University.

Davis, Mike. 1990. *City of Quartz*. London: Verso.

Davis, Mike. 2006. *Planet of Slums*. London: Verso.

Davis, Wade. 1985. *The Serpent and the Rainbow*. New York: Simon and Schuster.

Davy, Georges. 1957. "Introduction." pp. xliii–lxxiv in *Professional Ethics and Civic Morals* by Emile Durkheim. London and New York: Routledge.

Debord, Guy, Attila Kotanyi, and Vaneigem Raoul. [1962] 1981. "Theses on the Paris Commune." pp. 314–17 in *Situationist International Anthology*, edited by Ken Knabb. Berkeley: Bureau of Public Secrets.

Debord, Guy. 1983. *Society of the Spectacle*. Detroit: Black & Red.

Degré, Gerard. 1985. *The Social Compulsions of Ideas*. New Brunswick: Transaction.

DeLanda, Manuel. 2006. *A New Philosophy of Society*. London and New York: Bloomsbury.

Deleuze, Gilles and Felix Guattari. 1983. *Anti-Oedipus: Capitalism and Schizophrenia*. Minneapolis: University of Minnesota Press.

Derrida, Jacques. 1976. *Of Grammatology*. Baltimore: The Johns Hopkins University Press.

Descartes, Rene. 1954. *Philosophical Writings*, eds. Elizabeth Anscombe and Peter Thomas Geach. Wokingham, UK: Van Nostrand Reinhold.

Desmonde, William H. 1976. "The Origin of Money in the Animal Sacrifice." pp. 113–33 in *The Psychoanalysis of Money*, ed. Ernest Borneman. New York: Urizen.

Deutscher, Guy. 2010. *Through the Language Glass*. New York: Henry Holt.

Dewey, John. 1903. *Ethical Principles Underlying Education*. Chicago: The University of Chicago Press.

Dewey, John. 1929. *The Quest for Certainty*. New York: Capricorn.

Dewey, John. 1946. *Problems of Men*. New York: Philosophical Library.

Dews, Peter. 1987. *Logics of Disintegration*. London: Verso.

Dicker, Georges. 1993. *Descartes: An Analytical and Historical Introduction*. New York: Oxford University Press.

Dicks, Henry V. 1972. *Licensed Mass Murder*. New York: Basic Books.

Diderot, Denis. 1966. *Rameau's Nephew* and *D'Alembert's Dream*, tr. Leonard Tancock. New York: Penguin.

Diderot, Denis. 1999. *Jacques the Fatalist*, tr. David Coward. Oxford: Oxford University Press.

Dilthey, Wilhelm. 1961. *Pattern and Meaning in History*. New York: Harper.

Dolar, Mladen. 1991. "'I Shall Be with You on Your Wedding-Night': Lacan and the Uncanny." *October* 58: 5–23.

Donoghue, Frank. 2008. *The Last Professors*. New York: Fordham University Press.

Dostoyevsky, Fyodor. 1994. *Crime and Punishment, The Gambler,* and *Notes from the Underground*. London: Chancellor Press.

Douglas, Jack D. 1967. *The Social Meanings of Suicide*. Princeton: Princeton University Press.

Drapeau, C.W. and J.L. McIntosh. 2015. *U.S.A. Suicide 2014*. Washington, DC: American Association of Suicidology. Online: (www.suicidology.org).

Draper, Hal. 1978. *Karl Marx's Theory of Revolution, Vol. 2*. New York: Monthly Review Press.

Droge, Arthur and James D. Tabor. 1992. *A Noble Death*. New York: Harper.

Du Bois, W.E. Burghardt. [1903] 1969. *The Souls of Black Folk*. New York: New American Library.

Du Bois, W.E. Burghardt. 1935. *Black Reconstruction in America*. New York: Harcourt, Brace and Co.

Du Bois, W.E. Burghardt. 1965. *The World and Africa*. New York: International Publishers.

Dunayevskaya, Raya. 1943. "A Restatement of Some Fundamentals of Marxism Against 'Pseudo-Marxism.'" Online: (https://web.archive.org/web/20130821153517/http://newsandletters.org/issues/1999/June/6.99_rd.htm).

Dunayevskaya, Raya. 1961. "Notes on the *Logic* from Hegel's *Encyclopedia of Philosophical Sciences*." Online: (www.marxists.org/archive/dunayevskaya/works/newslet/5_00_rd.htm).

Dunayevskaya, Raya. 1965. "The Theory of Alienation: Marx's Debt to Hegel." Online: (www.marxists.org/archive/dunayevskaya/works/articles/alienation.htm).

Dunayevskaya, Raya. 1980. *Hegel's Absolute as a New Beginning*. News and Letters Reprint.

Durkheim, Emile. [1893] 1984. *The Division of Labor in Society*, tr. W.D. Halls. New York: The Free Press.

Durkheim, Emile. [1897] 1951. *Suicide*, tr. J. Spaulding and G. Simpson. New York: The Free Press.

Durkheim, Emile. [1901] 2006. "Technology." pp. 31–32 in *Marcel Mauss: Techniques, Technology and Civilization*, ed. Nathan Schlanger. New York: Durkheim Press/Berghahn.

Durkheim, Emile. [1912] 1915a. *The Elementary Forms of the Religious Life*, tr. Joseph Ward Swain. New York: The Free Press.

Durkheim, Emile. [1912] 1995. *The Elementary Forms of Religious Life*, tr. Karen E. Fields. New York: The Free Press.

Durkheim, Emile. [1914] 1960a. "The Dualism of Human Nature and its Social Conditions." pp. 325–40 in *Emile Durkheim, 1858–1917, A Collection of Essays*, ed. Kurt H. Wolff. Columbus: The Ohio State University Press.

Durkheim, Emile. 1915b. *Germany Above All*. Paris: Librairie Armand Colin.

Durkheim, Emile. 1957. *Professional Ethics and Civic Morals*, tr. Cornelia Brookfield. London and New York: Routledge.

Durkheim, Emile. 1958. *Socialism*. New York, NY: Collier.

Durkheim, Emile. 1960b. *Montesquieu and Rousseau*. Ann Arbor: The University of Michigan Press.

Durkheim, Emile. 1961. *Moral Education*, tr. Everett K. Wilson and Herman Schnurer. Mineola: Dover.

Durkheim, Emile. 1973. *On Morality and Society*. Chicago: The University of Chicago Press.

Durkheim, Emile. 1974. *Sociology and Philosophy*, tr. D.F. Pocock. New York: The Free Press.

Durkheim, Emile. 1977. *The Evolution of Educational Thought: Lectures on the Formation and development of Secondary Education in France*, tr. Peter Collins. London: Routledge and Kegan Paul.

Durkheim, Emile. 1978. *On Institutional Analysis* ed. and tr. Mark Traugott. Chicago: University of Chicago Press.

Durkheim, Emile. 1981. "The Realm of Sociology as a Science." *Social Forces* 59 (4): 1054–70.

Durkheim, Emile. 1982. *The Rules of Sociological Method*, ed. Steven Lukes and tr. W.D. Halls. New York: The Free Press.

Durkheim, Emile. 1983. *Pragmatism and Sociology*, tr. J.C. Whitehouse and ed. John B. Allcock. Cambridge: Cambridge University Press.

Durkheim, Emile. 1993. *Ethics and the Sociology of Morals*, tr. Robert T. Hall. Buffalo: Prometheus.

Durkheim, Emile. 2004. *Durkheim's Philosophy Lectures: Notes from the Lycée de Sens Course, 1883–1884*, eds. Neil Gross and Robert Alun Jones. Cambridge: Cambridge University Press.

Durkheim, Emile and Marcel Mauss. [1903] 1963. *Primitive Classification,* tr. and ed. Rodney Needham. Chicago: University of Chicago Press.

Durkheim, Emile and Marcel Mauss. [1913] 2006. "Note on the Concept of Civilization." pp. 35–39 in *Marcel Mauss: Techniques, Technology and Civilization*, ed. Nathan Schlanger. New York: Durkheim Press/Berghahn.

Duveen, Gerard. 2001. "Introduction: The Power of Ideas." pp. 1–17 in *Social Representations* by Serge Moscovici. New York: New York University Press.

Eagleton, Terry. 2016. *Materialism*. New Haven: Yale University Press.

Eastman, Max. 1955. *Reflections on the Failure of Socialism*. New York: Grosset.

Eco, Umberto. 1983. *The Name of the Rose*, tr. William Weaver. New York: Knopf.

Eco, Umberto. 1984. *Semiotics and the Philosophy of Language*. Bloomington: Indiana University Press.

Eco, Umberto. 2016. *Chronicles of a Liquid Society*, tr. R. Dixon. New York: Houghton Mifflin Harcourt.

Edmonds, David and John Eidinow. 2001. *Wittgenstein's Poker*. New York: HarperCollins.

Ehrbar, Hans G. 1998. "Marxism and Critical Realism." Meeting of the Heterodox Economics Students Association, 25 September. Online: (http://content.csbs.utah.edu/~ehrbar/marxre.pdf).

Einstein, Albert. 1982. *Ideas and Opinions*. New York: Crown.

Eldridge, J.E.T. (Ed.). 1971. *Max Weber: The Interpretation of Reality*. New York: Charles Scribner's Sons.

Elias, Norbert. [1939] 1994. *The Civilizing Process*, tr. Edmund Jephcott. Oxford: Blackwell.

Eliot, George. [1871–72] 2015. *Middlemarch*. New York: Penguin.

Eliot, T.S. 1922. *The Waste Land*. New York: Boni and Liveright.

Ellis, Havelock. 1911. *The World of Dreams*. New York and Boston: Houghton Mifflin

Ellul, Jacques. 1975. *The New Demons*, tr. C. Edward Hopkin. New York: Seabury.

Emerson, Ralph Waldo. [1837] 1981. "The American Scholar." pp. 51–71 in *The Portable Emerson*, ed. Carl Bode. New York: Penguin.

Emerson, Ralph Waldo. 1950. *The Selected Writings of Ralph Waldo Emerson*. New York: Modern Library.

Epictetus. 2004. *Enchiridion*. Mineola: Dover.

Erasmus. [1509] 1913. *The Praise of Folly*, tr. Wilson, John. London: Oxford University Press.

Erikson, Kai T. 1966. *Wayward Puritans*. New York: Wiley.

Evans, Vyvyan. 2014. *The Language Myth*. Cambridge: Cambridge University Press.

Evans-Pritchard, EE. 1976. *Witchcraft, Oracles, and Magic among the Azande*. Oxford: Oxford University Press.

Everett, Charles. C. 1882. *The Science of Thought*. Boston: Hall and Whiting.

Everett, Daniel L. 2008. *Don't Sleep, There are Snakes*. New York: Vintage.

Everett, Daniel L. 2016. *Dark Matter of the Mind*. Chicago: University of Chicago Press.

Everett, Daniel L. 2017. *How Language Began*. New York: Liveright.

Ewen, Stuart. 1976. *Captains of Consciousness*. New York: McGraw-Hill.

Eysenck, Hans. [1967] 2006. *The Biological Basis of Personality*. New Brunswick: Transaction.

Fadiman, Anne. 1998. *Ex Libris*. New York: Farrar, Straus and Giroux.

Fanfani, Amintore. 1935. *Catholicism, Protestantism and Capitalism*. London: Sheed and Ward.

Fanon, Frantz. 1963. *The Wretched of the Earth*. New York: Grove Press.

Fanon, Frantz. 1967. *Black Skin, White Masks*. New York: Grove Press.

Fauconnet, Paul. 1923. "The Pedagogical Work of Emile Durkheim." *The American Journal of Sociology* 28 (5): 529–53.

Fauconnet, Paul. 1927. "The Durkheim School in France." *Sociological Review* 19 (1): 15–20.

Fedden, Henry Romilly. 1938. *Suicide*. London: Peter Davies Ltd.

Fellman, Gordon. 1998. *Rambo and the Dalai Lama*. Albany: SUNY Press.

Fenichel, Otto. [1945] 1996. *The Psychoanalytic Theory of Neurosis*. New York: Norton.

Fermi, Enrico. 1936. *Thermodynamics*. New York: Dover.

Festinger, Leon, Henry W. Riecken, and Stanley Schachter. 1956. *When Prophecy Fails*. New York: Harper.

Feuerbach, Ludwig. 1986. *Principles of the Philosophy of the Future*. Indianapolis: Hackett.

Fichte, Johann Gottlieb. 1847. *The Vocation of the Scholar*, tr. W. Smith. London: Chapman.

Fichte, Johann Gottlieb. 1848. *The Vocation of Man*, tr. William Smith. London: Chapman.

Findlay, J.N. 1958. *Hegel: A Re-Examination*. New York: Collier.

Fink, Bruce. 1995. *The Lacanian Subject*. Princeton: Princeton University Press.

Fink, Bruce. 1997. *A Clinical Introduction to Lacanian Psychoanalysis: Theory and Technique*. Cambridge: Harvard University Press.

Fischer, David Hackett. 1989. *Albion's Seed*. New York and Oxford: Oxford University Press.

Flaubert, Gustave. 1957. *Madame Bovary*, tr. Francis Steegmuller. New York: Knopf.

Fodor, Jerry A. 1981. *Representations*. Cambridge: The MIT Press.

Fore, William F. 1970. *Image and Impact*. New York: Friendship Press.

Forrester, John. 1981. "Philology and the Phallus." pp. 45–74 in *The Talking Cure*, ed. Colin MacCabe. London: Macmillan.

Forster, Michael N. 1998. *Hegel's Ideal of a Phenomenology of Spirit*. Chicago: The University of Chicago Press.

Foster, John Bellamy and Fred Magdoff. 2009. *The Great Financial Crisis*. New York: Monthly Review Press.

Foucault, Michel. 1970. *The Order of Things*. New York: Vintage.

Foucault, Michel. 1977. *Discipline and Punish*. New York: Vintage.

Fournier, Marcel. 2006. *Marcel Mauss*, tr. J.M. Todd. Princeton: Princeton University Press.

Frankel, Charles. 1956. *The Case for Modern Man*. Boston: Beacon.

Frankfurt Institute for Social Research. 1972. *Aspects of Sociology*. Boston: Beacon.

Franklin, Benjamin. 2008. *The Way to Wealth*. Best Success Books.

Freire, Paulo. 1993. *Pedagogy of the Oppressed,* revised edition. New York: Continuum.

Freud, Sigmund. [1900] 1965. *The Interpretation of Dreams*. New York: Avon.

Freud, Sigmund. [1913] 1950. *Totem and Taboo*. New York: Norton.

Freud, Sigmund. [1914] 1959a. "On Narcissism: An Introduction." pp. 30–59 in *Collected Papers, Vol. 4*. New York: Basic Books.

Freud, Sigmund. [1915] 1959b. "Thoughts for the Times on War and Death." pp. 288–317 in *Collected Papers, Vol. 4*. New York: Basic Books.

Freud, Sigmund. [1917] 1966. *Introductory Lectures on Psycho-Analysis*. New York: Norton.

Freud, Sigmund. [1919] 1959c. "The Uncanny." pp. 368–07 in *Collected Papers, Vol. 4*. New York: Basic Books.

Freud, Sigmund. [1921] 1959d. *Group Psychology and the Analysis of the Ego*. New York: Norton.

Freud, Sigmund. [1925] 1959e. "Negation." pp. 181–85 in *Collected Papers, Vol. 5*. New York: Basic Books.

Freud, Sigmund. [1923] 1960. *The Ego and the Id*. New York: Norton.

Freud, Sigmund. [1926] 1959f*Inhibitions, Symptoms, and Anxiety*. New York: Norton.

Freud, Sigmund. [1927] 1959"Fetishism." pp. 198–204 in *Collected Papers, Vol. 5*. New York: Basic Books.

Freud, Sigmund. [1930] 1961. *Civilization and its Discontents*. New York: Norton.

Freud, Sigmund. 1939. *Moses and Monotheism*. New York: Vintage.

Freud, Sigmund. [1940] 1969. *An Outline of Psycho-Analysis*. New York: Norton.

Freud, Sigmund. 1962. *Three Essays on the Theory of Sexuality*. New York: Avon.

Freud, Sigmund. 1963. *The History of the Psychoanalytic Movement*. New York: Collier.

Freud, Sigmund. 2002. *The Schreber Case*. New York: Penguin.

Freyer, Hans. [1928] 1998. *Theory of Objective Mind*, tr. Steven Grosby. Athens: Ohio University Press.

Freytag, Gustav. [1887] 1890. *The Lost Manuscript, Vol. 1*. Chicago: The Open Court.

Friedman, Milton. 1962. *Capitalism and Freedom*. Chicago: The University of Chicago Press.

Frisby, David. 1983. *The Alienated Mind*. Atlantic Highlands: Humanities Press.

Fromm, Erich. 1941. *Escape from Freedom*. New York: Henry Holt and Company.

Fromm, Erich. 1957. "The Authoritarian Personality." Online: (www.marxists.org/archive/fromm/works/1957/authoritarian.htm).

Fromm, Erich. 1968. *The Revolution of Hope*. New York: Harper.

Fromm, Erich. 1970. *The Crisis of Psychoanalysis*. Greenwich: Fawcett Publications.

Fromm, Erich. 1973. *The Anatomy of Human Destructiveness*. New York: Holt, Rinehart and Winston.

Fromm, Erich. 1976. *To Have or to Be?* New York: Continuum.

Fromm, Erich. 1981. *On Disobedience*. New York: The Seabury Press.

Fromm, Erich. 1984. *The Working Class in Weimar Germany*. Cambridge: Harvard University Press.

Fultner, Barbara. 2017. "Collective Agency and Intentionality: A Critical Theory Perspective." pp. 523–45 in *The Palgrave Handbook of Critical Theory*, ed. Michael J. Thompson. New York: Palgrave.

Fustel de Coulanges, Numa Denis. [1873] 1956. *The Ancient City*. New York: Doubleday.

Gabriel, Markus and Slavoj Žižek. 2009. *Mythology, Madness, and Laughter*. London: Continuum.

Gadamer, Hans–Georg. 1976. *Hegel's Dialectic*. New Haven: Yale University Press.

Gagnier, Regenia. 2000. *The Insatiability of Human Wants*. Chicago: The University of Chicago Press.

Galbraith, John Kenneth. 1969. *The Affluent Society*. New York: New American Library.

Galen, Clemens Graf von. 1941. "Sermon Delivered by Bishop Clemens August Count of Galen on July 13, 1941, at the Church of St. Lambert, Muenster." Online: (http://www.priestsforlife.org/preaching/vongalen07-13.htm).

Gane, Mike (ed.). 1992. *The Radical Sociology of Durkheim and Mauss*. London: Routledge.

Gane, Mike. 2006. *Auguste Comte*. New York: Routledge.

Gangas, Spyros. 2007. "Social Ethics and Logic: Rethinking Durkheim Through Hegel." *Journal of Classical Sociology* 7(3): 315–38.

Gangas, Spyros. 2017. "Recognition, Social Systems and Critical Theory." pp. 547–63 in *The Palgrave Handbook of Critical Theory*, ed. Michael J. Thompson. New York: Palgrave.

Garver, Eugene. 1994. *Aristotle's Rhetoric*. Chicago: University of Chicago Press.

Gary, Romain. 2017. *The Kites*, tr. M. Mouillot. New York: New Directions.

Gay, Peter. 1993. *The Cultivation of Hatred*. New York: Norton.

Gay, Peter. 2006. *Freud: A Life for Our Time*. New York: Norton.

George, Henry. [1879] 1956. *Progress and Poverty*. New York: R. Schalkenbach Foundation.

Gerth, Hans and C. Wright Mills. 1953. *Character and Social Structure*. New York: Harcourt.

Giddens, Anthony. 1965. "The Suicide Problem in French Sociology." *The British Journal of Sociology* 16(1): 3–18.

Giddens, Anthony. 1984. *The Constitution of Society*. Berkeley: University of California Press.

Giedion, Siegfried. 1975. *Mechanization Takes Command*. New York: Norton.

Gilbert, Margaret. 1989. *On Social Facts*. Princeton: Princeton University Press.

Gillespie, Michael Allen. 2008. *The Theological Origins of Modernity*. Chicago: University of Chicago Press.

Gilman, Charlotte Perkins. [1915] 1998. *Herland*. Mineola: Dover.

Gilman, Charlotte Perkins. 2002. *The Dress of Women*. Westport: Greenwood.

Gissing, George. 1897. *The Whirlpool*. London: Lawrence and Bullen.

Godlove, Terry F (ed.). 2005. *Teaching Durkheim*. New York: Oxford University Press.

Goethe, J.W. [1809] 1971. *Elective Affinities*, tr. R.J. Hollingdale. New York: Penguin.

Goethe, J.W. [1808] 1961. *Faust*, tr. Walter Kaufmann. New York: Anchor Books.

Goethe, J.W. 1976. *Faust*, tr. Walter Arndt and ed. Cyrus Hamlin. New York: Norton.

Goethe, J.W. 1984. *Faust*, tr. Stuart Atkins. Princeton: Princeton University Press.

Goethe, J.W. 1989. *The Sorrows of Young Werther*, tr. Michael Hulse. New York: Penguin.

Goffman, Erving. 1963. *Behavior in Public Places*. New York: The Free Press.

Goffman, Erving. 1967. *Interaction Ritual*. New York: Pantheon.

Goffman, Erving. 1974. *Frame Analysis*. Boston: Northeastern University Press.

Gogol, Nikolai. [1842] 1996. *Dead Souls*, tr. R. Pevear and L. Volokhonsky. New York: Knopf.

Goldmann, Lucien. 1969. *The Human Sciences and Philosophy*. London: Cape.

Goldmann, Lucien. 1976. *Cultural Creation*. Saint Louis: Telos Press.

Goodchild, Philip. 2009. *Theology of Money*. Durham: Duke University Press.

Goodman, Russell B. 2002. *Wittgenstein and William James*. Cambridge: Cambridge University Press.

Gopnik, Adam. 2018. "The Made-Up Man." *The New Yorker*, 1 January. Online: (https://www.newyorker.com/magazine/2018/01/01/the-made-up-man).

Gottlieb, Anthony. 2009. "A Nervous Splendor." *The New Yorker*, 6 April: 70–74.

Gouldner, Alvin W. 1970. *The Coming Crisis of Western Sociology*. New York: Basic.

Goux, Jean-Joseph. 1990. *Symbolic Economies*. Ithaca: Cornell University Press.

Gracia, Jorge J.E. 2011. "Introduction." pp. 1–27 in *Suarez on Individuation*. Milwaukee: Marquette University Press.

Gracián, Baltasar. [1647] 2015. *How to Use Your Enemies*, tr. J. Robbins. New York: Penguin.

Graf, Fritz. 1997. *Magic in the Ancient World*. Cambridge: Harvard University Press.

Gramsci, Antonio. 1971. *Selections from the Prison Notebooks*. New York: International Publishers.

Granet, Marcel. 1951. *Chinese Civilization*. New York: Barnes and Noble.

Green, T.H. 1895. *Lectures on the Principles of Political Obligation*. London: Longmans, Green, and Co.

Greenblatt, Stephen. 1988. *Shakespearean Negotiations*. Berkeley: University of California Press.

Greene, Graham. 1929. *The Man Within*. New York: Penguin.

Greene, Graham. [1948] 2004a. *The Heart of the Matter*. New York: Penguin.

Greene, Graham. [1951] 2004b. *The End of the Affair*. New York: Penguin.

Grene, David and Richmond Lattimore (eds.). 1960. *Greek Tragedies, Vol. 1*. Chicago: The University of Chicago Press.

Groddeck, Georg. [1949] 1961. *The Book of the It*. New York: Vintage.

Gurvitch, Georges. 1964. *The Spectrum of Social Time*, tr. M. Korenbaum. Dordrecht: Reidel.

Gurvitch, Georges. 1971. *The Social Frameworks of Knowledge*, tr. Margaret A. Thompson and Kenneth A. Thompson. New York: Harper.

Habermas, Jurgen. 1970. *Toward a Rational Society*. Boston: Beacon.

Habermas, Jurgen. 1973. *Legitimation Crisis*. Boston: Beacon.

Hacker, Jacob S. and Paul Pierson. 2016. *American Amnesia*. New York: Simon and Schuster.

Hadden, Richard W. 1994. *On the Shoulders of Merchants*. Albany: SUNY Press.

Haidt, Jonathan. 2012. *The Righteous Mind*. New York: Vintage.

Haimson, Leopold H. 1955. *The Russian Marxists and the Origins of Bolshevism*. Boston: Beacon Press.

Halbwachs, Maurice. [1930] 1978. *The Causes of Suicide*, tr. Harold Goldblatt. London: Routledge and Kegan Paul.

Halbwachs, Maurice. 1958. *The Psychology of Social Class*, tr. Claire Delavenay. Glencoe: The Free Press.

Halbwachs, Maurice. 1962. *Sources of Religious Sentiment*, tr. John A. Spaulding. New York: The Free Press.

Halevy, Elie. 1965. *The Era of Tyrannies*, tr. R.K. Webb. New York: NYU Press.

Hall, Stuart. 1997. "Representation, Meaning and Language." pp. 15–64 in *Representation*, ed. Stuart Hall. London: Sage.

Hamid, Mohsin. 2017. *Exit West*. New York: Riverhead/Penguin.

Hanzel, Igor. 2014. "'The Circular Course of Our Representation': 'Schein', 'Grund', and 'Erscheinung' in Marx's Economic Works. pp. 214–39 in *Marx's Capital and Hegel's Logic*, eds. Fred Moseley and Tony Smith. Chicago: Haymarket.

Harari, Yuval Noah. 2017. *Homo Deus*. New York: Harper Collins.

Hardimon, Michael O. 1994. *Hegel's Social Philosophy: The Project of Reconciliation*. Cambridge: Cambridge University Press.

Harding, Esther M. 1947. *Psychic Energy*. Princeton: Princeton University Press.

Hardinge, Frances. 2012. *A Face Like Glass*. New York: Amulet.

Hardy, Thomas. [1894–95] 2006. *Jude the Obscure*. Mineola: Dover.

Harman, Graham. 2010. *Towards Speculative Realism*. Winchester, UK: Zero Books.

Harman, Graham. 2011. *The Quadruple Object*. Winchester, UK: Zero Books.

Harmetz, Aljean. 1977. *The Making of* The Wizard of Oz. New York: Limelight Editions.

Harms, John B. 1981. "Reason and Social Change in Durkheim's Thought." *Pacific Sociological Review* 24(4): 393–410.

Harrington, Michael. 1965. *The Accidental Century*. Baltimore: Penguin.

Harris, H.S. 1993. "Hegel's Intellectual Development to 1807." pp. 25–51 in *The Cambridge Companion to Hegel*, ed. Frederick C. Beiser. Cambridge: Cambridge University Press.

Harrison, Jane Ellen. 1962. *Epilegomena to the Study of Greek Religion* and *Themis*. New Hyde Park: University Books.

Harvey, David. 1989. *The Urban Experience*. Baltimore: Johns Hopkins University Press.

Harvey, David. 1990. *The Condition of Postmodernity*. Cambridge: Blackwell.

Harvey, David. 2006. *Paris, Capital of Modernity*. New York: Routledge.

Hausman, Carl. 1975. *A Discourse on Novelty and Creation*. The Hague: Martinus Nijhoff.

Hawkins, Mike. 1999. "Durkheim's Sociology and Theories of Degeneration." *Economy and Society* 28 (1): 118–37.

Hearn, Frank. 1985. *Reason and Freedom in Sociological Thought*. London: Allen and Unwin.

Hegel, G.W.F. [1802–1804] 1979. *System of Ethical Life* and *First Philosophy of Spirit*, ed. and tr. H.S. Harris and T.M. Knox. Albany: SUNY Press.

Hegel, G.W.F. [1807] 1967. *The Phenomenology of Mind*, tr. J.B. Baillie. New York: Harper.

Hegel, G.W.F. [1807] 1977. *Phenomenology of Spirit*, tr. A.V. Miller. Oxford: Oxford University Press.

Hegel, G.W.F. [1807] 2008. *Phenomenology of Spirit*, tr. Terry Pinkard. Unpublished

Hegel, G.W.F. [1812] 1969. *Science of Logic*, tr. A.V. Miller. Atlantic Highlands, NJ: Humanities Press International.

Hegel, G.W.F. [1821] 1991a. *Elements of the Philosophy of Right*, tr. H.B. Nisbet. Cambridge: Cambridge University Press.

Hegel, G.W.F. [1830] 1991b. *The Encyclopedia Logic, Part I of the Encyclopedia of Philosophical Sciences with the Zusätze*, tr. T.F. Geraets, W.A. Suchting, and H.S. Harris. Indianapolis/Cambridge: Hackett Publishing.

Hegel, G.W.F. [1840] 1974. *Lectures on the Philosophy of Religion, Volume 1*, tr. E.B. Speirs and J. Burdon Sanderson (Reprint). New York: The Humanities Press.

Hegel, G.W.F. [1840] 1995a. *Lectures on the History of Philosophy, Vol. 2*, tr. E.S. Haldane and Frances H. Simson. Lincoln: University of Nebraska Press.

Hegel, G.W.F. [1840] 1995b. *Lectures on the History of Philosophy, Vol. 3*, tr. E.S. Haldane and Frances H. Simson. Lincoln: University of Nebraska Press.

Hegel, G.W.F. [1892] 1995. *Lectures on the History of Philosophy, Volume 1*, tr. E.S. Haldane. Lincoln: University of Nebraska Press.

Hegel, G.W.F. 1948. *Early Theological Writings*. Philadelphia: University of Pennsylvania Press.

Hegel, G.W.F. 1956. *The Philosophy of History*, tr. J. Sibree. Mineola: Dover.

Hegel, G.W.F. 1975a. *Aesthetics, Vol. 1*, tr. T.M. Knox. Oxford: Oxford University Press.

Hegel, G.W.F. 1975b. *Aesthetics, Vol. 2*, tr. T.M. Knox. Oxford: Oxford University Press.

Hegel, G.W.F. 1975c. *Lectures on the Philosophy of World History: Introduction*, tr. H.B. Nisbet. Cambridge: Cambridge University Press.

Hegel, G.W.F. 1983. *Hegel and the Human Spirit*, tr. Leo Rauch. Detroit: Wayne State University Press. Online: (www.marxists.org/reference/archive/hegel/jlindex.htm).

Hegel, G.W.F. 1986. *The Philosophical Propaedeutic*, tr. A.V. Miller. Oxford and New York: Basil Blackwell.

Hegel, G.W.F. 2002. *Miscellaneous Writings of G.W.F. Hegel*, ed. Jon Stewart. Evanston: Northwestern University Press.

Hegel, G.W.F. 2007. *Philosophy of Mind*, tr. W. Wallace and A.V. Miller. Oxford: Oxford University Press.

Heidegger, Martin. 1971. *Poetry, Language, Thought*. New York: Harper.

Heilbroner, Robert. 1972. *The Worldly Philosophers,* fourth edition. New York: Simon and Schuster.

Hemingway, Ernest. 1986. *The Garden of Eden*. New York: Scribner.

Henderson, James P. and John B. Davis. 1991. "Adam Smith's Influence on Hegel's Philosophical Writings." *Journal of the History of Economic Thought* 13(2): 184–204.

Heraclitus. 2001. *Fragments*, tr. Brooks Haxton. New York: Penguin.

Herder, Johann Gottfried. 1993. *Against Pure Reason*, ed. and tr. Marcia Bunge. Fortress Press: Minneapolis.

Herf, Jeffrey. 1984. *Reactionary Modernism*. Cambridge: Cambridge University Press.

Herrera, Yuri. 2015. *Signs Preceding the End of the World*, tr. Lisa Dillman. London: And Other Stories.

Hertz, Robert. [1913] 1987. "St Besse: A Study of an Alpine Cult." pp. 55–100 in *Saints and their Cults*, ed. Stephen Wilson. Cambridge: Cambridge University Press.

Hertz, Robert. 1994. *Sin and Expiation in Primitive Societies*, tr. Robert Parkin. Oxford: British Centre for Durkheimian Studies.

Hess, Moses. 1845. "The Essence of Money." Online: (www.marxistsfr.org/archive/hess/1845/essence-money.htm).

Hesse, Hermann. [1925] 1965. *Demian*. New York: Harper.

Hesse, Hermann. 1963. *Steppenwolf.* New York: Modern Library.

Hessler, Peter. 2016. "Making Peace with Trump's Revolutionaries." *The New Yorker*, 20 October. Online: (www.newyorker.com/news/news-desk/making-peace-with -trumps-revolutionaries).

Hetherington, Marc J. and Jonathan D. Weiler. 2009. *Authoritarianism and Polarization in American Politics.* Cambridge: Cambridge University Press.

Higgins, Kathleen. 1990. "Nietzsche and Postmodern Subjectivity." pp. 189–215 in *Nietzsche as Postmodernist*, ed. Clayton Koelb. Albany: SUNY Press.

Hilbert, Richard A. 1986. "Anomie and the Moral Regulation of Reality: The Durkheimian Tradition in Modern Relief." *Sociological Theory* 4(1): 1–19.

Hilferding, Rudolf. [1910] 1981. *Finance Capital.* London: Routledge & Kegan Paul.

Hinshaw, John and Peter N. Stearns. 2014. *Industrialization in the Modern World.* Santa Barbara: ABC-CLIO.

Hirst, R.J. 1967. "Realism." pp. 77–83 in *The Encyclopedia of Philosophy, Vol. 7.* New York: Macmillan and The Free Press.

Hobbes, Thomas. 1651. *Leviathan.* London: Andrew Crooke. Online: (socserv2.socsci. mcmaster.ca/econ/ugcm/3ll3/hobbes/Leviathan.pdf).

Hobbes, Thomas. 1889. *Behemoth*, ed. F. Tönnies. London: Simpkin, Marshall, and Co

Hocart, A.M. [1936] 1970. *Kings and Councillors.* Chicago: The University of Chicago Press.

Hocking, William Ernest. 1918. *Morale and its Enemies.* New Haven: Yale University Press.

Hocking, William Ernest. 1926. *Man and the State.* New Haven: Yale University Press.

Hocking, William Ernest. 1956. *The Coming World Civilization.* New York: Harper.

Hodge, Robert and Gunther Kress. 1988. *Social Semiotics.* Ithaca: Cornell University Press.

Hofstadter, Douglas. 1995. *Fluid Concepts and Creative Analogies.* New York: Basic Books.

Hölderlin, Friedrich. 2008. *Hyperion*, tr. Ross Benjamin. New York: Archipelago Books.

Hollingworth, H.L. 1923. "Review of *Outline of Psychology* by William McDougall." *The Journal of Philosophy* 20(25): 679–86.

Holzner, Burkart. 1968. *Reality Construction in Society.* Cambridge: Schenkman.

Homer. 1944. *The Odyssey*, tr. Samuel Butler. Roslyn: Walter J. Black.

Hook, Sidney. 1934. "Karl Marx and Moses Hess." Online: (www.marxistsfr.org/history/ etol/writers/hook/1934/12/hess-marx.htm).

Hopkins, Gerard Manley. 2015. *As Kingfishers Catch Fire.* New York: Penguin.

Horkheimer, Max. 1972. *Critical Theory.* New York: Continuum.

Horkheimer, Max. 1978. *Dawn and Decline.* New York: Seabury.

Horkheimer, Max and Theodor W. Adorno. [1944] 1972. *Dialectic of Enlightenment*, tr. John Cumming. New York: Continuum.

Horney, Karen. 1939. *New Ways in Psychoanalysis*. New York: Norton.

Horney, Karen. 1945. *Our Inner Conflicts*. New York: Norton.

Houellebecq, Michel. 2011. *The Map and the Territory*. New York: Vintage.

Houellebecq, Michel. 2015. *Submission*. New York: Farrar, Straus and Giroux.

House, Patrick. 2016. "Werner Herzog Talks Virtual Reality." *The New Yorker*, 12 January. Online: (www.newyorker.com/tech/elements/werner-herzog-talks-virtual-reality).

Howard, Dick. 1972. *The Development of the Marxian Dialectic*. Carbondale: Southern Illinois University Press.

Hubert, Henri and Marcel Mauss. 1964. *Sacrifice*. Chicago: The University of Chicago Press.

Hughes, H. Stuart. 1977. *Consciousness and Society: The Reorientation of European Social Thought: 1890–1930*, revised edition. New York: Vintage Books.

Hugo, Victor. 1887. *The Works of Victor Hugo: Les Misérables, Volume Two*, tr. I.F. Hapgood, et. al. New York: The Kelmscott Society.

Huizinga, Johan. 1924. *The Waning of the Middle Ages*. New York: St. Martin's Press.

Hume, David. 1896. *A Treatise of Human Nature*. Oxford: Clarendon Press.

Huxley, Aldous. [1932] 1946. *Brave New World*. Cutchogue, NY: Buccaneer Books.

Huysmans, Joris-Karl. [1884] 1998. *Against Nature*, tr. Margaret Mauldon. Oxford: Oxford University Press.

Hyatt-Williams, Arthur. 1998. *Cruelty, Violence, and Murder*. Northvale: Aronson.

Ibbotson, Paul and Michael Tomasello. 2016. "Evidence Refutes Chomsky's Theory of Language Learning." *Scientific American*, 7 September. Online: (www.scientificamerican.com/article/evidence-rebuts-chomsky-s-theory-of-language-learning).

Ilyenkov, Evald. 1960. *Dialectics of the Abstract and the Concrete in Marx's* Capital. Online: (www.marxists.org/archive/ilyenkov/works/abstract).

Institute of Social Research. 1945. *Antisemitism Among American Labor*. Unpublished, four-volume report. Columbia University.

Inwood, Michael. 1992. *A Hegel Dictionary*. London: Blackwell.

Isenberg, Nancy. 2016. *White Trash*. New York: Viking.

Ivimey, Muriel. 1946. "What is a Neurosis?" pp. 61–92 in *Are You Considering Psychoanalysis?*, ed. Karen Horney. New York: Norton.

Jacoby, Russell. 1981. *Dialectic of Defeat*. Cambridge: Cambridge University Press.

James, William. [1907] 1995. *Pragmatism*. New York: Dover.

James, William. 1918. *The Principles of Psychology, Volume 1*. Mineola: Dover.

Jameson, Fredric. 1990. *Late Marxism*. London: Verso.

Jameson, Fredric. 1991. *Postmodernism*. Durham: Duke University Press.

Jameson, Fredric. 2009. *Valences of the Dialectic*. London: Verso.

Jankélévitch, Sophie. 2012. *"Le Suicide* and Psychological Suffering." pp. 31–48 in *Suffering and Evil*, eds. W.S.F. Pickering and Massimo Rosati. New York: Durkheim Press/ Berghahn.

Jaspers, Karl. 1986. *Basic Philosophical Writings*, ed. and tr. Edith Ehrlich, Leonard H. Ehrlich, and B. George Pepper Amherst: Prometheus Books.

Jay, Martin. [1973] 1996. *The Dialectical Imagination*. Berkeley: University of California Press.

Jay, Martin. 1984. *Marxism and Totality*. Berkeley: University of California Press.

Jaynes, Julian. 1990. *The Origin of Consciousness in the Breakdown of the Bicameral Mind*. Boston: Houghton Mifflin.

Jenkyns, Richard. 2007. "Introduction." pp. vii–xxiii in *The Nature of Things* by Lucretius. New York: Penguin.

Jennings, Richard. [1855] 1969. *Natural Elements of Political Economy*. New York: Augustus M. Kelley.

Johnson, Ian. 2018. "Who Killed More: Hitler, Stalin, or Mao?" *The New York Review of Books*, 5 February. Online: (www.nybooks.com/daily/2018/02/05/who-killed-more -hitler-stalin-or-mao).

Johnston, David. 2003. *Perfectly Legal*. New York: Penguin/Portfolio.

Jones, Susan Stedman. [2000] 2006. "Representations in Durkheim's Masters: Kant and Renouvier." pp. 37–58 in *Durkheim and Representations*, ed by W.S.F. Pickering. London: Routledge.

Jones, Susan Stedman. 2001. *Durkheim Reconsidered*. Cambridge: Polity.

Jones, W.T. 1969. *The Medieval Mind: A History of Western Philosophy, Vol. 2*, 2nd ed. San Diego: Harcourt.

Jones, W.T. 1970. *A History of Western Philosophy, Volume I: The Classical Mind*, 2nd ed. San Diego: Harcourt.

Jost, John T., Jack Glaser, Arie W. Kruglanski, and Frank J. Sulloway. 2003. "Political Conservatism as Motivated Social Cognition." *Psychological Bulletin* 129(3): 339–75.

Jung, Carl. 1969. *The Archetypes and the Collective Unconscious*, 2nd ed. Princeton: Princeton University Press.

Kaag, John. 2016. *American Philosophy: A Love Story*. New York: Farrar, Straus and Giroux.

Kaag, John. 2017. "Me for the Woods." *The Paris Review*, 30 June. Online: (www.the parisreview.org/blog/2017/06/30/me-for-the-woods).

Kalberg, Stephen. 1985. "The Role of Ideal Interests in Max Weber's Comparative Historical Sociology." pp. 46–67 in *A Weber-Marx Dialogue*, eds. Robert J. Antonio and Ronald M. Glassman. Lawrence: University of Kansas Press.

Kalberg, Stephen. 1994. *Max Weber's Comparative-Historical Sociology*. Chicago: The University of Chicago Press.

Kamen, Henry. 1971. *The Iron Century*. New York: Praeger.

Kammari, M.D. and G.L. Kabaev. 1965. "Problems of Historical Materialism and Concrete Sociological Research." pp. 101–08 in *Social Sciences in the* USSR, Unesco. Paris: Mouton.

Kant, Immanuel. 1929. *Critique of Pure Reason*, tr. Norman Kemp Smith. New York: St. Martin's Press.

Kant, Immanuel. 1951. *Critique of Judgement*, tr. J.H. Bernard. New York: Hafner.

Kant, Immanuel. 1964. *Groundwork of the Metaphysics of Morals*, tr. H.J. Paton. New York: Harper & Row.

Kant, Immanuel. 1983. *Perpetual Peace and Other Essays*, tr. Ted Humphrey. Indianapolis: Hackett.

Kapur, Akash. 2016. "The Return of the Utopians." *The New Yorker*, 3 October. Online: (www.newyorker.com/magazine/2016/10/03/the-return-of-the-utopians).

Karatani, Kojin. 2001. "Introduction: What is Transcritique." Online: (https://web.princeton.edu/sites/sics/What_is_transcritique.pdf).

Karatani, Kojin. 2014. *The Structure of World History*. Durham: Duke University Press.

Karr-Morse, Robin, and Meredith S. Wiley. 1997. *Ghosts from the Nursery: Tracing the Roots of Violence*. New York: The Atlantic Monthly Press.

Kasser, Rudolphe and Gregor Wurst (eds.). 2007. *The Gospel of Judas*, tr. R. Kasser, M. Meyer, G. Wurst, and F. Gaudard. Washington, DC: National Geographic.

Katz, Michael B. 1986. *In the Shadow of the Poorhouse*. New York: Basic.

Kaufmann, Walter. 1958. *Critique of Religion and Philosophy*. Princeton: Princeton University Press.

Kaufmann, Walter. 1965a. *Hegel: A Reinterpretation*. Notre Dame: University of Notre Dame Press.

Kaufmann, Walter. 1965b. *Hegel: Text and Commentary*. Notre Dame: University of Notre Dame Press.

Kaufmann, Walter. 1980. *Discovering the Mind: Freud, Adler, and Jung*. New Brunswick: Transaction.

Kautsky, Karl. 1888. *Thomas More and his Utopia*. Online: (www.marxists.org/archive/kautsky/1888/more/ch13.htm).

Kaye, F.B. 1924. "Introduction: Mandeville's Thought." pp. xvii–xxxii in *The Fable of the Bees* by Bernard Mandeville, Vol. One. Oxford: Clarendon Press.

Kenkō, Yoshida. 2015. *A Cup of Sake Beneath the Cherry Trees*, tr. Meredith McKinney. New York: Penguin.

Kerrigan, William. 1983. *The Sacred Complex*. Cambridge: Harvard University Press.

Keynes, John. Maynard. 1953. *The General Theory of Employment, Interest, and Money*. San Diego: Harcourt.

Khazan, Olga. 2015. "Middle-Aged White Americans are Dying of Despair." *The Atlantic*, 4 November. Online: (www.theatlantic.com/health/archive/2015/11/boomers-deaths-pnas/413971).

Khazan, Olga. 2016. "Why are so Many Middle-Aged White Americans Dying?" *The Atlantic*, 29 January. Online: (www.theatlantic.com/health/archive/2016/01/middle-aged-white-americans-left-behind-and-dying-early/433863).

Kierkegaard, Søren. 1940. *For Self-Examination*. Minneapolis: Augsburg Publishing House.

Kierkegaard, Søren. 1954. *Fear and Trembling and Sickness Unto Death*, tr. Walter Lowrie. Princeton: Princeton University Press.

Kierkegaard, Søren. 1987. *Either/Or*. Princeton: Princeton University Press.

Kimmel, Michael. 2013. *Angry White Men*. New York: Nation Books.

King, D. Brett and Michael Wertheimer. 2005. *Max Wertheimer and Gestalt Theory*. New Brunswick: Transaction Publishers.

King, Jerry. P. 1992. *The Art of Mathematics*. Mineola: Dover.

Kintz, Linda. 1997. *Between Jesus and the Market*. Durham: Duke University Press.

Kitto, H.D.F. 1950. *Greek Tragedy*. Garden City: Doubleday.

Klein, Richard G. with Blake Edgar. 2002. *The Dawn of Human Culture*. New York: Wiley.

Klemperer, Victor. [1957] 2000. *The Language of the Third Reich*, tr. Martin Brady. New York: Bloomsbury.

Kliman, Andrew. 2000. "Marx's Concept of Intrinsic Value." *Historical Materialism* 6 (1). Online: (https://libcom.org/files/kliman.pdf).

Kliman, Andrew. 2007. *Reclaiming Marx's 'Capital.'* Lanham: Lexington Books.

Knapp, Peter. 1986. "Hegel's Universal in Marx, Durkheim, and Weber: The Role of Hegelian Ideas in the Origin of Sociology." *Sociological Forum* 1 (4): 586–609.

Knausgaard, Karl Ove. 2018. "A Literary Road Trip Into the Heart of Russia." *The New York Times Magazine*, 14 February. Online: (www.nytimes.com/2018/02/14/magazine/a-literary-road-trip-into-the-heart-of-russia).

Koepping, Klaus-Peter. 1983. *Adolf Bastian and the Psychic Unity of Mankind*. St. Lucia: University of Queensland Press.

Koestler, Arthur. [1941] 1968. *Darkness at Noon*. New York: Scribner.

Kojève, Alexandre. [1947] 1969. *Introduction to the Reading of Hegel*. Ithaca: Cornell University Press.

Kolbert, Elizabeth. 2017. "Why Facts Don't Change Our Minds." *The New Yorker*, 27 February. Online: (www.newyorker.com/magazine/2017/02/27/why-facts-dont-change-our-minds).

Kolhatkar, Sheelah. 2017. "National Disaster." *The New Yorker*, 18 September: 21.

Kolnai, Aurel. 1922. *Psychoanalysis and Sociology*, tr. Eden and Cedar Paul. New York: Harcourt.

Körner, Stephan. 1955. *Kant*. New York: Penguin.

Korsch, Karl. 1970. *Marxism and Philosophy*. New York: Monthly Review Press.

Koselleck, Reinhart. 1985. *Futures Past*, tr. Keith Tribe: Cambridge: The MIT Press.

Kotulak, Ronald. 1996. *Inside the Brain: Revolutionary Discoveries of How the Mind Works*. Kansas City, Mo: Andrews and McMeel.

Kracauer, Siegfried. 1995. *The Mass Ornament*. Cambridge: Harvard University Press.

Kracauer, Siegfried. 1998. *The Salaried Masses*. London: Verso.

Kracht, Christian. 2015. *Imperium*, tr. Daniel Bowles. New York: Farrar, Straus and Giroux.

Krakauer, Jon. [1990] 2009. *Eiger Dreams*. Guilford: The Lyons Press.

Kramer, Lawrence (ed.). 2011. *Hart Crane's 'The Bridge'*. New York: Fordham University Press.

Kress, Gunther, interviewed by Fredrik Lindstrand. 2008. "Interview with Gunther Kress." *Designs for Learning* 1(2): 59–71.

Krier, Dan. 2005. *Speculative Management*. Albany: State University of New York Press.

Krier, Dan. 2008. "Critical Institutionalism and Finance Globalization: A Comparative Analysis of American and Continental Finance." *The New York Journal of Sociology* 1: 130–86.

Krier, Dan. 2017. "Debt, Value, and Economic Theology." *Continental Thought and Theory* 1 (2). Online: (https://ir.canterbury.ac.nz/bitstream/handle/10092/13076/Krier-CTT-v1-2-2017.pdf).

Krier, Dan and Tony Feldmann. 2016. "Social Character in Western Pre-Modernity: Lacanian Psychosis in Wladyslaw Reymont's *The Peasants*." pp. 175–216 in *Capitalism's Future*, edited by Dan Krier and Mark P. Worrell. Leiden and Boston: Brill.

Krier, Dan and Mark P. Worrell. 2017. "The Social Ontology of Capitalism." pp. 1–11 in *The Social Ontology of Capitalism*, eds. Dan Krier and Mark P. Worrell. New York: Palgrave.

Krier, Dan and Mark P. Worrell. 2017b. "The Organic Composition of the Big Mother." *Continental Thought and Theory* 4. Online: (http://ctt.canterbury.ac.nz).

Kripke, Saul A. 1980. *Naming and Necessity*. Cambridge: Harvard University Press.

Kroner, Richard. 1961. *Speculation and Revelation in Modern Philosophy*. Philadelphia: Westminster Press.

Kuhn, Thomas S. 1970. *The Structure of Scientific Revolutions*, 2nd ed. Chicago: University of Chicago Press.

Kuo, Zing Yang. 1921. "Giving up Instincts in Psychology." *The Journal of Philosophy* 18 (24): 645–64.

Kureishi, Hanif. 2017. *The Nothing*. London: Faber and Faber.

Kushner, Howard I. 1989. *Self-Destruction in the Promised Land*. New Brunswick: Rutgers University Press.

Labriola, Antonio. 1896. *Essays on the Materialist Conception of History, Part 2, Historical Materialism*. Online: (www.marxists.org/archive/labriola/works/alo1.htm).

Lacan, Jacques. 1988. *The Seminar of Jacques Lacan, Book II: The Ego in Freud's Theory and in the Technique of Psychoanalysis, 1954–1955*, tr. S. Tomaselli. New York: Norton.

Lacan, Jacques. 1993. *The Seminar of Jacques Lacan, Book III: The Psychoses, 1955–1956*, tr. Russell Grigg. New York: Norton.

Lacan, Jacques. 2002. *Écrits*, tr. Bruce Fink. New York: Norton.

Lacan, Jacques. 2008. *My Teaching*, tr. David Macey. London and New York: Verso.

Lacan, Jacques. 2014. *The Seminar of Jacques Lacan, Book X: Anxiety*, tr. A.R. Price. Cambridge: Polity.

Lacan, Jacques interviewed by Emilio Granzotto. 1974. "There can be no Crisis of Psychoanalysis." *Panorama*. Online: (www.versobooks.com/blogs/1668-there-can-be-no-crisis-of-psychoanalysis-jacques-lacan-interviewed-in-1974).

Laing, R.D. 1969. *Self and Others*. New York: Penguin.

Lakoff, George and Mark Johnson. [1980] 2003. *Metaphors We Live By*. Chicago: The University of Chicago Press.

Laqueur, Walter. 1996. "Fin-de-siecle: Once More with Feeling." *Journal of Contemporary History* 31(1): 5–47.

Lasch, Christopher. 1977. *Haven in a Heartless World*. New York: Norton.

Lasswell, Harold D. 1933. "The Psychology of Hitlerism." *The Political Quarterly* 4(1–2): 373–84.

Latour, Bruno. 1993. *We Have Never Been Modern*. Cambridge: Harvard University Press.

Latour, Bruno. 1998. "On Recalling ANT." pp. 15–25 in *Actor Network and After*, ed. John Law and John Hassard. London: Blackwell. Online: (www.bruno-latour.fr/sites/default/files/P-77-RECALLING-ANT-GBpdf.pdf).

Latour, Bruno. 2005. *Reassembling the Social*. New York: Oxford University Press.

Leach, William. 1993. *Land of Desire*. New York: Pantheon.

Lears, T.J. Jackson. 2003. *Something for Nothing*. New York: Viking.

Leatherbarrow, W.J. and D.C. Offord. 1987. *A Documentary History of Russian Thought: From Enlightenment to Marxism*. Ann Arbor: Ardis.

Le Bon, Gustave. 1913. *The Psychology of Revolution*. London: Unwin.

Leenhardt, Maurice. 1979. *Do Kamo: Person and Myth in the Melanesian World*, tr. Basia Miller Gulati. Chicago: The University of Chicago Press.

Lefebvre, Henri. [1966] 1968. *The Sociology of Marx*. New York: Penguin.

Lefebvre, Henri. [1968] 2009. *Dialectical Materialism*, tr. John Sturrock. Minneapolis: University of Minnesota Press.

Lefebvre, Henri. 1995. *Introduction to Modernity*, tr. John Moore. London: Verso.

Le Guin, Ursula K. 1969. *The Left Hand of Darkness*. New York: Ace.

Le Guin, Ursula K. 1974. *The Dispossessed*. New York: Harper Collins.

Leites, Edmund. 1985. "The Duty to Desire: Love, Friendship, and Sexuality in Some Puritan Theories of Marriage." *Comparative Civilizations Review* 10–11: 117–49.

Lenin, V.I. 1909. "Freedom and Necessity." *Collected Works, Volume 14*. Online: (www.marxists.org/archive/lenin/works/1908/mec/three6.htm).

Lepenies, Wolf. 1988. *Between Literature and Science: The Rise of Sociology*. Cambridge: Cambridge University Press.

Lepley, Ray (ed.). 1949. *Value: A Cooperative Inquiry*. New York: Columbia University Press.

Lessing, Gotthold Ephraim. [1772] 1979. *Emilia Galotti*, tr. Edward Dvoretzky. New York: Mary S. Rosenberg, Inc.

Levi-Strauss, Claude. 1963. *Structural Anthropology*. New York: Basic.

Levi-Strauss, Claude. 1966. *The Savage Mind*. Chicago: The University of Chicago Press.

Levinas, Emmanuel. 1979. *Totality and Infinity*, tr. A. Lingis. The Hague: Martinus Nijhoff.

Levy–Bruhl, Lucien. 1899. *History of Modern Philosophy in France*. Chicago: Open Court.

Levy–Bruhl, Lucien. [1910] 1926. *How Natives Think*. London: Allen and Unwin.

Levy–Bruhl, Lucien. [1923] 1966. *Primitive Mentality*. Boston: Beacon Press.

Lewin, Bertram D. 1961. *The Psychoanalysis of Elation*. New York: Psychoanalytic Quarterly.

Lewitzky, Anatole. [1939] 1988. "Shamanism." pp. 248–61 in *The College of Sociology*, ed. Denis Hollier. Minneapolis: University of Minnesota Press.

Libertson, Joseph. 1982. *Proximity, Levinas, Blanchot, Bataille, and Communication*. The Hague: Martinus Nijhoff.

Lichtheim, George. 1967. *The Concept of Ideology*. New York: Vintage.

Lichtman, Richard. 1982. *The Production of Desire*. New York: The Free Press.

Lieberman, Lisa. 2003. *Leaving You*. Chicago: Ivan R. Dee.

Liebersohn, Harry. 1988. *Fate and Utopia in German Sociology, 1870–1923*. Cambridge: MIT.

Lilla, Mark. 2016. *The Shipwrecked Mind*. New York: The New York Review of Books.

Lilla, Mark. 2017. *The Once and Future Liberal*. New York: Harper Collins.

Linton, Ralph. 1936. *The Study of Man*. New York: D. Appleton-Century.

Lippit, Victor D. 2004. "Class Struggles and the Reinvention of American Capitalism in the Second Half of the Twentieth Century." *Review of Radical Political Economics* 36 (3): 336–43.

Lloyd, J. William. 1931. *The Karezza Method*. Roscoe, CA.

Lloyd, Seth. 2006. *Programming the Universe*. New York: Vintage.

Locka, Christian. 2017. "Cameroon has Been Using Witchcraft to Fight Boko Haram." *Public Radio International*, 11 January. Online: (www.pri.org/stories/2017-01-11/cameroon-has-been-using-witchcraft-fight-boko-hara).

Locke, John. [1706] 1966. *Of the Conduct of the Understanding*. New York: Teachers College Press.

London, Jack. [1908] 2006. *Iron Heel*. New York: Penguin.

Lowenthal, David. 1985. *The Past is a Foreign Country*. Cambridge: Cambridge University Press.

Lowenthal, David. 1998. *The Heritage Crusade and the Spoils of History*. Cambridge: Cambridge University Press.

Lowenthal, Leo. 1961. *Literature, Popular Culture, and Society*. Palo Alto: Pacific Books.

Lowenthal, Leo and Norbert Guterman. 1949. *Prophets of Deceit*. New York: Harper and Brothers.

Löwith, Karl. 1964. *From Hegel to Nietzsche*. New York: Columbia University Press.

Löwith, Karl. 1995. *Martin Heidegger and European Nihilism*. New York: Columbia University Press.

Luckmann, Thomas. 1967. *The Invisible Religion*. New York: Macmillan.

Lukács, Georg. 1926. "Moses Hess and the Problems of Idealist Dialectics." Online: (www.marxistsfr.org/archive/lukacs/works/1926/moses-hess.htm).

Lukács, Georg. 1971. *History and Class Consciousness*. Cambridge: The MIT Press.

Lukács, Georg. 1978a. *The Ontology of Social Being, 1, Hegel*. London: Merlin.

Lukács, Georg. 1978b. *The Ontology of Social Being, 2, Marx*. London: Merlin.

Lukács, Georg. 1978c. *The Ontology of Social Being, 3, Labour*. London: Merlin.

Lukes, Steven. 1968. "Methodological Individualism Reconsidered." *British Journal of Sociology* 19 (2): 119–29.

Lukes, Steven. 1973. *Emile Durkheim*. Stanford: Stanford University Press.

Lundskow, George. 2008. "Toyota's Willing Stooges." *New York Journal of Sociology* 1: 92–117. Online: (http://facultyweb.cortland.edu/tnyjs/TNYJS.html).

Luxemburg, Rosa. [1900] 1970. *Reform or Revolution*. New York: Pathfinder Press.

Lynd, Robert S. 1939. *Knowledge for What?* Princeton: Princeton University Press.

Lynd, Robert S. and Helen Merrell Lynd. 1937. *Middletown in Transition*. New York: Harcourt.

MacCabe, Colin. 1985. *Tracking the Signifier*. Minneapolis: University of Minnesota Press.

MacCabe, Colin. 2002. "Introduction." pp. vi–xxii in *The Schreber Case* by Sigmund Freud. New York: Penguin.

MacGregor, David. [1984] 2015. *The Communist Ideal in Hegel and Marx*. London: Routledge.

Machiavelli, Niccolò. [1532] 2005. *The Prince*, tr. Peter Bondanella. New York: Oxford University Press.

MacIntyre, Alasdair. 1984. *After Virtue*, 2nd ed. Notre Dame: University of Notre Dame Press.

MacPherson, C.B. 1962. *The Political Theory of Possessive Individualism*. Oxford: Oxford University Press.

Malabou, Catherine. [1996] 2005. *The Future of Hegel*. New York: Routledge.

Malinowski, Bronisław. 1948. *Magic, Science and Religion*. New York: Doubleday.

Malisoff, William Marias. 1940. "Physics: The Decline of Mechanism." *Philosophy of Science* 7(4): 400–14.

Malraux, Andre. 1961. *Man's Fate*, tr. Haakon M. Chevalier. New York: Random House.

Man, Hendrick de. 1985. *The Psychology of Marxian Socialism*. New Brunswick: Transaction.

Manders, Dean. 2006. *The Hegemony of Common Sense*. New York: Peter Lang.

Mandeville, Bernard. [1732] 1924. *The Fable of the Bees*. Oxford: Clarendon Press.

Mann, Erika. 1938. *School for Barbarians*. Mineola: Dover.

Mann, Thomas. [1924] 1952. *Buddenbrooks*, tr. H.T. Lowe-Porter. New York: Vintage.

Mann, Thomas. [1927] 1955. *Magic Mountain*, tr. H.T. Lowe-Porter. New York: Heritage Press.

Mann, Thomas. 1931. *Mario and the Magician*, tr. H.T. Lowe-Porter. New York: Knopf.

Mann, Thomas. 1948. *Doctor Faustus*, tr. H.T. Lowe-Porter. New York: Knopf.

Mann, Thomas. 1951. *The Holy Sinner*, tr. H.T. Lowe-Porter. New York: Knopf.

Mannheim, Karl. 1936. *Ideology and Utopia*. New York: Harcourt.

Mannheim, Karl. 1982. *Structures of Thinking*. London: Routledge and Kegan Paul.

Manzotti, Riccardo and Tim Parks. 2016. "The Color of Consciousness." *New York Review of Books*, 8 December. Online: (www.nybooks.com/daily/2016/12/08/color-of-consciousness).

Mao, Zedong. 1927. "Report on an Investigation of the Peasant Movement in Hunan." Online: (www.marxists.org/reference/archive/mao/works/red-book/ch02.htm).

Marcus Aurelius. 1945. *Marcus Aurelius and His Times*. New York: Walter J. Black.

Marcus Aurelius. 1983. *The Meditations*, tr. G.M.A. Grube. Indianapolis: Hackett.

Marcuse, Herbert. 1941. *Reason and Revolution*. Atlantic Highlands: Humanities Press.

Marcuse, Herbert. 1955. *Eros and Civilization*. Boston: The Beacon Press.

Marcuse, Herbert. 1972. *From Luther to Popper*. London: Verso.

Marett, R.R. 1914. *The Threshold of Religion*. New York: Macmillan.

Maritain, Jacques. 1939. "Integral Humanism and the Crisis of Modern Times." *The Review of Politics* 1(1): 1–17.

Marsh, James L. 1999. *Process, Praxis, and Transcendence*. Albany: SUNY Press.

Martyris, Nina. 2015. "Death by Coconut." National Public Radio. Online: (www.npr.org/sections/thesalt/2015/12/03/457124796).

Marx, Gary T. 1990. "Reflections on Academic Success and Failure." Online: (http://web.mit.edu/gtmarx/www/success.html).

Marx, Karl. [1844] 1964. *The Economic and Philosophic Manuscripts of 1844*, ed. Dirk J. Struik and tr. Martin Milligan. New York: International Publishers.

Marx, Karl. [1857] 1973a. *Grundrisse*, tr. Martin Nicolaus. New York: Penguin.

Marx, Karl. 1859. *Zur Kritik der Politischen Ökonomie*. Berlin: Duncker. Online: (www.mlwerke.de/me/me13/me13_003.htm).

Marx, Karl. [1859] 1970. *A Contribution to the Critique of Political Economy*, tr. S.W. Ryazanskaya. New York: International Publishers.

Marx, Karl. 1867. *Das Kapital: Kritik der politischen Ökonomie*. Online: (http://www.arbeiterpolitik.de/Texte/Kapital/KAPITAL1.pdf)

Marx, Karl. [1867] 1976. *Capital: A Critique of Political Economy, Vol. 1*, tr. Ben Fowkes. New York: Penguin.

Marx, Karl. [1869] 1963a. *The Eighteenth Brumaire of Louis Bonaparte*. New York: International Publishers.

Marx, Karl. [1884] 1978a. *Capital: A Critique of Political Economy, Vol. 2*, tr. David Fernbach. New York: Penguin.

Marx, Karl. [1894] 1981. *Capital: A Critique of Political Economy, Vol. 3*, tr. David Fernbach. New York: Penguin.

Marx, Karl. 1904. *A Contribution to the Critique of Political Economy*, tr. N.I. Stone. Chicago: Charles H. Kerr.

Marx, Karl. 1935. *Value, Price, and Profit*. New York: International Publishers.

Marx, Karl. 1963b. *Theories of Surplus Value, Part I*. Moscow: Progress Publishers.

Marx, Karl. 1969. "Feuerbach." Online: (www.mlwerke.de/me/me03/me03_017.htm#I_I).

Marx, Karl. 1973b. *The Revolutions of 1848*. New York: Penguin.

Marx, Karl. 1978b. "The Value-Form." *Capital and Class* 4, Spring: 130–50. Online: (www.marxists.org/archive/marx/works/1867-c1/appendix.htm).

Marx, Karl and Friedrich Engels. [1848] 1972. "The Communist Manifesto." in Robert C. Tucker, ed., *The Marx-Engels Reader*, pp. 331–62. New York: W.W. Norton.

Marx, Karl and Friedrich Engels. [1848] 1977. *Manifesto of the Communist Party*. Moscow: Progress Publishers.

Marx, Karl and Friedrich Engels. 1968. *Selected Works*. New York: International Publishers.

Marx, Karl and Friedrich Engels. 1970. *The German Ideology*. New York: International Publishers.

Marx, Karl and Friedrich Engels. 1972. *The Marx–Engels Reader*, ed. Robert C. Tucker. New York: Norton.

Marx, Karl and Friedrich Engels. 1975–2004. *Collected Works, Volumes 1–50*. New York: International Publishers.

Marx, Karl and Friedrich Engels. 1978. *The Socialist Revolution*. Moscow: Progress Publishers.

Marx, Karl and Friedrich Engels. 2008. *On Religion*. Mineola: Dover.

Massing, Paul W. 1949. *Rehearsal for Destruction*. New York: Harper.

Matheson, Richard. [1954] 1995. *I Am Legend*. New York: Tor.

Matterson, Stephen. 1990. "Introduction." in Herman Melville, ed., *The Confidence-Man*, pp. vii-xxxvi. New York: Penguin.

Matthews, Richard K. 1995. *If Men Were Angels*. Lawrence: University Press of Kansas.

Mattick, Paul. 1993. "Marx's Dialectic." in Fred Moseley, ed., *Marx's Method in Capital*, pp. 115–33. Atlantic Highlands: Humanities Press.

Maugham, William Somerset. 1915. *Of Human Bondage*. New York: The Modern Library.

Maupassant, Guy de. [1883] 1999. *A Life*, tr. R. Pearson. New York: Oxford University Press.

Maupassant, Guy de. [2004] 2015. *Femme Fatale*, tr. S. Miles. New York: Penguin.

Mauss, Marcel. [1909] 2003. *On Prayer*, tr. Susan Leslie. New York: Durkheim Press/ Berghahn Books.

Mauss, Marcel. [1920/1950] 2006. "The Nation." in Nathan Schlanger, ed., *Marcel Mauss: Techniques, Technology and Civilization*, pp. 41–48. New York: Durkheim Press/ Berghahn.

Mauss, Marcel. 1972. *A General Theory of Magic*. New York: Norton.

Mauss, Marcel. 1979. *Sociology and Psychology*, tr. B. Brewster. London: Routledge & Kegan Paul.

Mauss, Marcel. 1990. *The Gift*, tr. W.D. Halls. New York: Norton.

Mauss, Marcel. 2005. *The Nature of Sociology*, tr. William Jeffrey. New York: Durkheim Press/Berghahn Books.

May, Rollo. 1977. *The Meaning of Anxiety,* revised edition. New York: Norton.

Mayo, Elton. 1945. *The Social Problems of an Industrial Civilization*. Boston: Division of Research, Graduate School of Business Administration, Harvard University.

McCall, Brian M. 2017. "The New Protestant Bargain." in John C. Rao, Ed., *Luther and his Progeny*, pp. 175–95. Kettering: Angelico Press.

McCarthy, Cormac. [2006] 2012. *The Road*. New York: Knopf.

McCarthy, Cormac. 2010. *The Sunset Limited*. New York: Vintage.

McCarthy, Thomas. 1991. *Ideals and Illusions*. Cambridge: The MIT Press.

McCauley, Clark and Sophia Moskalenko. 2011. *Friction*. New York: Oxford University Press.

McClelland, David. 1961. *The Achieving Society*. New York: The Free Press.

McCloskey, David. 1976. "On Durkheim, Anomie, and the Modern Crisis." *The American Journal of Sociology* 81(6): 1481–88.

McDougall, William. 1924. "Can Sociology and Social Psychology Dispense with In-stincts?" *American Journal of Sociology* 29(6): 657–73.

McDowell, John. 1998. *Mind, Value, and Reality*. Cambridge: Harvard University Press.

McGreal, Chris. 2016. "Financial Despair, Addiction, and the Rise of Suicide in White America." *The Guardian*, 7 February. Online: (www.theguardian.com/us-news/2016/ feb/07/suicide-rates-rise-butte-montana-princeton-study).

McNally, David. 2011. *Monsters of the Market*. Leiden: Brill.

McNeill, William H. 1963. *The Rise of the West*. Chicago: The University of Chicago Press.

McWilliams, Susan. 2016. "This Political Theorist Predicted the Rise of Trumpism. His Name was Hunter S. Thompson." *The Nation*, 15 December. Online: (www.thenation. com/article/this-political-theorist-predicted-the-rise-of-trumpism-his-name-was-hunter-s-thompson).

Mead, George Herbert. [1932] 1977. "The Objective Reality of Perspectives." in *George Herbert Mead on Social Psychology*, pp. 342–54. Chicago: University of Chicago Press.

Mead, George Herbert. [1934] 1962. *Mind, Self, and Society*. Chicago: The University of Chicago Press.

Meillassoux, Quentin. 2008. *After Finitude*, tr. Ray Brassier. London and New York: Bloomsbury.

Meissner, W.W. 1992. *Ignatius of Loyola*. New Haven: Yale University Press.

Melville, Herman. [1851] 1988. *Moby-Dick*. New York: Knopf.

Melville, Herman. [1856] 2009. "Bartleby the Scrivener." in *Billy Budd, Sailor and Selected Tales*. New York: Oxford University Press.

Melville, Herman. [1857] 1990. *The Confidence-Man*. New York: Penguin.

Melville, Herman. 1892. *Moby-Dick*. Boston: St. Botolph Society.

Menand, Louis. 2002. "What Comes Naturally." *The New Yorker*, 25 November. Online: (www.newyorker.com/magazine/2002/11/25/what-comes-naturally-2).

Menninger, Karl. 1938. *Man Against Himself*. New York: Harcourt.

Merleau-Ponty, Maurice. 1968. *The Visible and the Invisible*, tr. Alphonso Lingis. Evanston: Northwestern University Press.

Merleau-Ponty, Maurice. 1973. *Adventures of the Dialectic*, tr. Joseph Bien. Evanston: Northwestern University Press.

Meštrović, S.G. 1985. "Durkheim's Renovated Rationalism and the Idea that 'Collective Life is Only Made of Representations'." *Current Perspectives in Social Theory* 6: 199–218.

Meštrović, S.G.. 1988. *Emile Durkheim and the Renovation of Sociology*. Totowa: Rowman & Littlefield.

Mészáros, István. 2010. *Social Structure and Forms of Consciousness, Vol. 1, The Social Determination of Method*. New York: Monthly Review Press.

Mészáros, István. 2011. *Social Structure and Forms of Consciousness, Vol. 2, The Dialectic of Structure and History*. New York: Monthly Review Press.

Metraux, Alfred. 1959. *Voodoo in Haiti*, tr. Hugo Charteris. New York: Schocken Books.

Mettrie, Julien Offray la de. [1748/1912] 1993. *Man A Machine*. Chicago: Open Court.

Milbank, John. 2006. *Theology and Social Theory*, 2nd ed. Malden: Blackwell.

Milgram, Stanley. 1974. *Obedience to Authority*. New York: Harper.

Miliband, Ralph. 1969. *The State in Capitalist Society*. New York: Basic Books.

Mill, John Stuart. 1881. *The Principles of Political Economy*. London: Longmans, Green and Co.

Miller, Arthur. 1950. *Death of a Salesman*. New York: Viking.

Miller, Henry. 1945. *The Air-Conditioned Nightmare*. New York: New Directions.

Miller, Henry. 1961. *Tropic of Cancer*. New York: Grove Press.

Miller, John W. 1982. *The Midworld of Symbols and Functioning Objects*. New York: Norton.

Miller, W. Watts. 1996. *Durkheim, Morals, and Modernity*. Montreal: McGill-Queen's University Press.

Mills, C. Wright. 1956. *The Power Elite*. Oxford: Oxford University Press.

Mills, C. Wright. 1959. *The Sociological Imagination*. New York: Oxford University Press.

Mills, C. Wright. 1962. *The Marxists*. New York: Dell.

Milton, John. [1667] 2000. *Paradise Lost*. New York: Penguin.

Mintz, Susannah B. 2003. *Threshold Poetics*. Newark: University of Delaware Press.

Mitscherlich, Alexander. 1969. *Society Without the Father*. New York: Harcourt.

Mohanty, Satya P. 1997. *Literary Theory and the Claims of History*. Ithaca: Cornell University Press.

Moliere. 2001. *The Misanthrope, Tartuffe, and Other Plays*, tr. Maya, Slater. Oxford: Oxford University Press.

Mommsen, Wolfgang J. 1984. *Max Weber and German Politics, 1890–1920*. Chicago: The University of Chicago Press.

Mommsen, Wolfgang J. 1989. *The Political and Social Theory of Max Weber*. Chicago: The University of Chicago Press.

Mommsen, Wolfgang J. 2006. "From Agrarian Capitalism to the 'Spirit' of Modern Capitalism: Max Weber's Approach to the Protestant Ethic." *Max Weber Studies* 5(2): 185–203.

Monnat, Shannon. 2016. "Deaths of Despair and Support for Trump in the 2016 Presidential Election." The Pennsylvania State University, Department of Agricultural Economics, Sociology, and Education Research Brief. Online: (http://aese.psu.edu/directory/smm67/Election16.pdf).

Montaigne. 1842. *The Complete Works of Michel de Montaigne* tr. W. Hazlitt. London: Templeman.

Montesquieu. 2002. *The Spirit of Laws*. Amherst: Prometheus.

Moore, John A. 1958. "The Idealism of Sancho Panza." *Hispania* 41(1): 73–76.

More, Thomas. [1516] 1999. *Utopia*, in *Three Early Modern Utopias*, ed. Susan Bruce. Oxford: Oxford University Press.

Moret, Alexandre. 1927. *The Nile and Egyptian Civilization*. Mineola: Dover.

Moret, Alexandre and Georges Davy. [1926] 1970. *From Tribe to Empire*, tr. V.G. Childe. New York: Cooper Square Publishers.

Moretti, Franco. 1988. *Signs Taken for Wonders, revised edition*. London: Verso.

Morris, Charles. 1949. "Axiology as the Science of Preferential Behavior." in Ray Lepley, ed., *Value*, pp. 211–22. New York: Columbia University Press.

Morris-Reich, Amos. 2005. "From Autonomous Subject to Free Individual in Simmel and Lacan." *History of European Ideas*, 31(1): 103–27.

Morton, Timothy. 2013. *Realist Magic: Objects, Ontology, Causality*. Ann Arbor: Open Humanities Press.

Moscovici, Serge. 1984. "The Myth of the Lonely Paradigm: A Rejoinder." *Social Research* 51(4): 939–67.

Moscovici, Serge. 2001. *Social Representations*. New York: New York University Press.

Moseley, Fred. 1993. "Marx's Logical Method and the 'Transformation Problem'." in Fred Moseley, ed., *Marx's Method in Capital*, pp. 157–83. Atlantic Heights: Humanities Press.

Mounier, Emmanuel. 1952. *Personalism*. Notre Dame: University of Notre Dame Press.

Muirhead, J.H. 1923. "Bernard Bosanquet as I Knew Him." *The Journal of Philosophy* 20(25): 673–79.

Mulgan, Geoff. 2018. *Big Mind*. Princeton: Princeton University Press.

Muller, Herbert J. 1966. *Freedom in the Modern World*. New York: Harper.

Mumford, Lewis. 1973. *Interpretations and Forecasts: 1922–1972*. New York: Harcourt.

Munkelt, Richard A. 2017. "Religious Evolution and Revolution in the Triumph of *Homo Economicus*." in John C. Rao, ed., *Luther and his Progeny*, pp. 143–74. Kettering: Angelico Press.

Murakami, Haruki. 1991. *Hard-Boiled Wonderland and the End of the World*, tr. Alfred Birnbaum. New York: Vintage.

Murakami, Haruki. 2014. *The Strange Library*, tr. Ted Goossen. New York: Knopf.

Murgoci, Agnes. 1926. "The Vampire in Romania." *Folklore* 37(4): 320–49.

Murphy, Caryle. 2015. "Most Americans Believe in Heaven … and Hell." Pew Research Center, 10 November. Online:(pewresearch.org/fact-tank/2015/11/10/most-americans-believe-in-heaven-and-hell).

Murphy, Robert F. 1971. *The Dialectics of Social Life*. New York: Basic Books.

Murray, Gilbert. 1915. *The Stoic Philosophy*. London: Watts.

Myers, Gerald. 2001. *William James*. New Haven: Yale University Press.

Nehamas, Alexander. 1985. *Nietzsche*. Cambridge: Harvard University Press.

Neill, A.S. 1960. *Summerhill: A Radical Approach to Child Rearing*. New York: Hart.

Nelson, Leonard. [1917] 1957. *Critique of Practical Reason*. Frankfurt: Verlag.

Nemedi, Denes. [2000] 2006. "A Change in Ideas." in W.S.F. Pickering, ed., *Durkheim and Representations*, pp. 83–97. London: Routledge.

Neocleous, Mark. 2003. "The Political Economy of the Dead: Marx's Vampires." *History of Political Thought* 24(4): 668–84.

Neumann, Franz. 1944. *Behemoth*. New York: Harper.

Nichols, Roy F. 1935. "The Dynamic Interpretation of History." *The New England Quarterly* 8(2): 163–78.

Niehoff, Debra. 1999. *The Biology of Violence: How Understanding the Brain, Behavior, and Environment can Break the Vicious Circle of Aggression*. New York, NY: The Free Press.

Nielsen, Donald A. 2005. *Horrible Workers*. Lanham, MD: Lexington Books.

Nietzsche, Friedrich. [1887] 1974. *The Gay Science*, tr. Walter Kaufmann. New York: Vintage.

Nietzsche, Friedrich. 1967. *Ecce Homo*, tr. Walter Kaufmann. New York: Vintage.

Nietzsche, Friedrich. 1968. *Will to Power*, tr. Walter Kaufmann. New York: Vintage.

Nietzsche, Friedrich. 1982. *The Portable Nietzsche*, ed. and tr. Walter Kaufmann. New York: Penguin.

Nietzsche, Friedrich. 1986. *Human, All too Human*, tr. R.J. Hollingdale. Cambridge: Cambridge University Press.

Nietzsche, Friedrich. 2015. *Aphorisms on Love and Hate*, tr. Faber and Lehmann. New York: Penguin.

Novalis. 1997. *Philosophical Writings*, ed. and tr. Stoljar, Margaret. Albany: State University of New York Press.

Nye, D.A. and C.E. Ashworth. 1971. "Emile Durkheim: Was He a Nominalist or a Realist?" *The British Journal of Sociology* 22(2): 133–48.

Nye, Robert A. 1984. *Crime, Madness, and Politics in Modern France*. Princeton: Princeton University Press.

Obeyesekere, Gananath. 1990. "Culturally Constituted Defenses and the Theory of Collective Motivation." in David K. Jordan and Marc J. Swartz, eds., *Personality and the Cultural Construction of Society*, pp. 80–97. Tuscaloosa: University of Alabama Press.

O'Brien, Miles. 2013. "Sins of the Sons." *PBS Newshour*, February 20. Online: www.pbs .org/newshour/updates/science/jan-june13/miles_blog_02-19.html

O'Connor, James. 1980. "The Division of Labor in Society." *Insurgent Sociologist* 10(1): 60–68.

O'Connor, James. 1984. *Accumulation Crisis*. New York: Basil Blackwell.

O'Keefe, Daniel Lawrence. 1982. *Stolen Lightning*. New York: Continuum.

O'Neill, Eugene. 1932. "Mourning Becomes Electra." pp. 683–867 in *Nine Plays*. New York: Modern Library.

Orgel, Stephen. 2000. "Introduction." in *Shakespeare's Macbeth*, pp. xxix-xliii. New York: Penguin.

Ornstein, Robert. 2003. *Multimind*. Cambridge: Malor Books.

Orr, David. 2015a. *The Road not Taken*. New York: Penguin.

Orr, David. 2015b. "The Most Misread Poem in America." *The Paris Review*, September 11. Online: (www.theparisreview.org/blog/2015/09/11/the-most-misread-poem-in-america).

Ortega y Gasset, José. 1932. *The Revolt of the Masses*, tr. anon. New York: Norton.

Ortega y Gasset, José. [1941] 1961. *History as a System*, tr. Weyl, Helen. New York: Norton.

Ortega y Gasset, José. 1957. *Man and People*, tr. Trask, Willard. New York: Norton.

Orwell, George. [1933] 1961. *Down and Out in Paris and London*. San Diego: Harcourt.

Otto, M.C. 1924. *Things and Ideals*. New York: Henry Holt.

Owen, Wilfred. [1963] 1965. *The Collected Poems of Wilfred Owen*. New York: New Directions.

Owens, Leslie Howard. 1976. *This Species of Property*. Oxford: Oxford University Press.

Packard, Vance. 1959. *The Status Seekers*. New York: David McKay Co.

Pannekoek, Anton. 1909. "The New Middle Class." Online: (www.marxists.org/archive/ pannekoe/1909/new-middle-class.htm).

Pannekoek, Anton. 1937. "Society and Mind in Marxian Philosophy." Online: (www. marxists.org/archive/pannekoe/society-mind/index.htm).

Pannekoek, Anton. 1947. "Religion." Online: (www.marxists.org/archive/pannekoe/ 1947/religion).

Paoletti, Giovanni. 2012. "Some Concepts of 'Evil' in Durkheim's Thought." in W.S.F. Pickering and Massimo Rosati eds., *Suffering and Evil*, pp. 63–80. New York: Durkheim Press/Berghahn.

Park, Robert Ezra. 1950. *Race and Culture*. Glencoe: The Free Press.

Parkin, Robert. 2012. "Robert Herz on Suffering and Evil: The Negative Processes of Social Life and Their Resolution." in W.S.F. Pickering and Massimo Rosati eds., *Suffering and Evil*, pp. 103–17. New York: Durkheim Press/Berghahn.

Parsons, Talcott. 1951. *The Social System*. New York: The Free Press.

Parsons, Talcott. 1964. *Social Structure and Personality*. New York: The Free Press.

Parsons, Talcott. 1977. *The Evolution of Societies*. Englewood Cliffs: Prentice-Hall.

Parsons, Talcott. 1978. *Action Theory and the Human Condition*. New York: The Free Press.

Partridge, G.E. 1919. *The Psychology of Nations*. New York: Macmillan.

Pascal, Blaise. 1941. *Pensées*, tr. W.F. Trotter. New York: Modern Library.

Pearce, Frank. 1989. *The Radical Durkheim*. London: Unwin Hyman.

Peirce, C.S. [1878] 1992a. "How to Make Our Ideas Clear." in Nathan Houser and Christian Kloesel, eds., *The Essential Peirce, Vol. 1*, pp. 124–41. Bloomington: Indiana University Press.

Peirce, C.S. [1892] 1992b. "Man's Glassy Essence." in Nathan Houser and Christian Kloesel, eds., *The Essential Peirce, Vol. 1*, pp. 334–51. Bloomington: Indiana University Press.

Peirce, C.S. [1908] 1998. "Excerpts from Letters to Lady Welby." in the Peirce Edition Project, ed., *The Essential Peirce, Vol. 2*, pp. 477–91. Bloomington: Indiana University Press.

Perry, Ralph Barton. [1926] 1950. *General Theory of Value*. Cambridge: University of Harvard Press.

Pessoa, Fernando. 2001. *The Book of Disquiet*, tr. Richard Zenith. New York: Penguin

Pessoa, Fernando. 2012. *Philosophical Essays*. New York: Contra Mundum Press.

Peters, F.E. 1967. *Greek Philosophical Terms*. New York: New York University Press.

Phillips, Tony. 2015. "Surface Topology in Bach Canons, I: The Mobius Strip." American Mathematical Society. Online: (www.ams.org/samplings/feature-column/ fc-2016-10).

Piaget, Jean. 1970. *Structuralism*, tr. Chaninah Maschler. New York: Harper.

Pickering, W.S.F. 2000. "Reading the Conclusion." in W.S.F. Pickering and Geoffrey Walford, eds., *Durkheim's* Suicide, pp. 66–80. London: Routledge.

Pickering, W.S.F. [2000] 2006a. "Representations as Understood by Durkheim." in W.S.F. Pickering, ed., *Durkheim and Representations*, pp. 11–23. London: Routledge.

Pickering, W.S.F. [2000] 2006b. "What do Representations Represent?" in W.S.F. Pickering, ed., *Durkheim and Representations*, pp. 98–117. London: Routledge.

Pickering, W.S.F. 2012. "Reflections on the Death of Emile Durkheim." in W.S.F. Pickering and Massimo Rosati, eds., *Suffering and Evil*, pp. 11–27. New York: Durkheim Press/Berghahn.

Piketty, Thomas. 2014. *Capital in the Twenty-First Century*. Cambridge: Belknap/Harvard.

Pinkard, Terry. 1996. *Hegel's Phenomenology*. Cambridge: Cambridge University Press.

Pinkard, Terry. 2000. *Hegel*. Cambridge: Cambridge University Press.

Pinkard, Terry. 2002. *German Philosophy*. Cambridge: Cambridge University Press.

Pinker, Susan. 2014. *The Village Effect*. New York: Spiegel and Grau.

Pippin, Robert B. 1989. *Hegel's Idealism*. Cambridge: Cambridge University Press.

Place, Ullin T. 2000. "Consciousness and the Zombie Within." in Yves Rossetti and Antti Revonsuo, eds., *Beyond Dissociation*, pp. 295–329. Amsterdam: John Benjamins Publishing Co.

Plato. 1945. *The Works of Plato*, tr. Jowett, Benjamin. New York: Tudor.

Poe, Edgar Allan. [1839] 1903. "William Wilson." in Sherwin Cody, ed., *The Best Tales of Edgar Allan Poe*, pp. 300–24. Chicago: McClurg.

Poe, Edgar Allan. [1841] 1920. *A Descent into the Maelstrom*. Paris: Devambez.

Polanyi, Karl. 1944. *The Great Transformation*. Boston: Beacon.

Polanyi, Michael. 1962. *Personal Knowledge*. Chicago: University of Chicago Press.

Poliakov, Leon. 1975. *The History of Anti-Semitism, Vol. 1, From the Time of Christ to the Court Jews*, tr. Richard Howard. Philadelphia: University of Pennsylvania Press.

Polkinghorne, John. 2007. *Quantum Physics and Theology*. New Haven: Yale University Press.

Pollin, Robert. 2003. *Contours of Descent*. London: Verso.

Pope, Whitney. 1976. *Durkheim's* Suicide: *A Classic Analyzed*. Chicago: The University of Chicago Press.

Popper, Karl. 1966. *The Open Society and its Enemies: The Spell of Plato*. Princeton: Princeton University Press.

Postone, Moishe. 1993. *Time, Labor, and Social Domination*. Cambridge: Cambridge University Press.

Powell, Anthony. [1951] 1962. *A Question of Upbringing*. Chicago: University of Chicago Press.

Proal, Louis. 1905. *Passion and Criminality*, tr. A.R. Allinson. London: Imperial Press.

Proust, Marcel. [1913] 2002. *Swann's Way*, tr. Lydia Davis. New York: Penguin.

Puett, Michael and Christine Gross-Loh. 2016. *The Path*. New York: Simon and Schuster.

Quincey, Thomas De. [1827] 2015. *On Murder Considered as One of the Fine Arts*. New York: Penguin

Quine, Willard van Orman. 1960. *Word and Object*. Cambridge: The MIT Press.

Rabelais, Francois. [1532–1564] 1944. *The Complete Works of Rabelais: The Five Books of Gargantua and Pantagruel*. New York: Modern Library.

Rabinbach, Anson. 1990. *The Human Motor*. Berkeley: University of California Press.

Radcliffe-Brown, A. 1952. *Structure and Function in Primitive Society*. New York: The Free Press.

Ramp, William. 2000. "The Moral Discourse of Durkheim's *Suicide*." in W.S.F. Pickering and Geoffrey Walford, eds., *Durkheim's* Suicide, pp. 81–96. London: Routledge.

Ramp, William. 2012. "*Le Malin Génie*: Durkheim, Bataille and the Prospect of a Sociology of Evil." in W.S.F. Pickering and Massimo Rosati, eds., *Suffering and Evil*, pp. 118–35. New York: Durkheim Press/Berghahn.

Rank, Otto. 1941. *Beyond Psychology*. New York: Dover.

Rappaport, Roy. 1971. "The Sacred in Human Evolution." *Annual Review of Ecology and Systematics* 2: 23–44.

Reich, Wilhelm. [1933] 1972. *Character Analysis*. New York: Farrar, Straus and Giroux.

Reich, Wilhelm. 1970. *The Mass Psychology of Fascism*. New York: Noonday.

Reich, Wilhelm. 1974. *Listen Little Man*. New York: Noonday.

Reinhold, K.L. [1791] 2000. "The Foundation of Philosophical Knowledge." in *Between Kant and Hegel*, pp. 51–103. Indianapolis: Hackett.

Reiser, Oliver L. 1932. "Energy the Soul of Matter." *The Journal of Religion* 12(1): 61–73.

Reitman, Janet. 2017. "How the Death of a Muslim Recruit Revealed a Culture of Brutality in the Marines." *The New York Times*, 6 July. Online: (www.nytimes.com/2017/07/06/magazine/how-the-death-of-a-muslim-recruit-revealed-a-culture-of-brutality-in-the-marines.html).

Remarque, Erich Maria. [1929] 2010. *All Quiet on the Western Front*, tr. Jonathan Cape. London: Folio Society.

Remmling, Gunter W. 1967. *Road to Suspicion*. New York: Appleton-Century-Crofts.

Revonsuo, Antti, Mirja Johanson, Jan-Eric Wedlund, and John Chaplin. 2000. "The Zombies Among Us." in Yves Rossetti and Antti Revonsuo, eds., *Beyond Dissociation*, pp. 331–51. Amsterdam: John Benjamins Publishing.

Reuten, Geert. 1993. "The Difficult Labor of a Theory of Social Value: Metaphors and Systematic Dialectics at the Beginning of Marx's *Capital*." in Fred Moseley, ed., *Marx's Method in* Capital, pp. 89–113. Atlantic Highlands: Humanities Press.

Rhodes, R. Colbert. 1978. "Emile Durkheim and the Historical Thought of Marc Bloch." *Theory & Society* 5(1): 45–73.

Richman, Michèle H. 2002. *Sacred Revolutions*. Minneapolis: University of Minnesota Press.

Riesman, David, Nathan Glazer, and Reuel Denney. [1950] 1953. *The Lonely Crowd*. New York: Doubleday.

Rikowski, Glenn. 2003. "Alien Life: Marx and the Future of the Human." *Historical Materialism*. Online: (www.researchgate.net/publication/249599115_Alien_Life_Marx_and_the_Future_of_the_Human).

Riley, Alexander T. 1999. "Whence Durkheim's Nietzschean Grandchildren? A Closer Look at Robert Hertz's Place in the Durkheimian Genealogy." *European Journal of Sociology* 40(2): 304–30.

Riley, Alexander T. 2002. "The Sacred Calling of Intellectual Labor in Mystic and Ascetic Durkheimianism." *European Journal of Sociology* 43(3): 354–85.

Rinofner-Kreidl, Sonja. 2004. "What is Wrong with Naturalizing Epistemology?" in Richard Feist, ed., *Husserl and the Sciences*, pp. 41–68. King Edward, Ottawa, Ontario: University of Ottawa Press.

Rintelen, Fritz-Joachim von. 1977. "Philosophical Idealism in Germany." *Philosophy and Phenomenological Research* 38(1): 1–32.

Ritzer, George and Jeffrey Stepnisky. 2018. *Sociological Theory, 10th Edition*. Los Angeles: Sage.

Robinson, Thomas N., Dina L.G. Borzekowski, Donna M. Matheson, and Helena C. Kraemer. 2007. "Effects of Fast Food Branding on Young Children's Taste Preference." *Archives of Pediatrics and Adolescent Medicine* 16(8): 792–97.

Roché, Henri-Pierre. [1953] 2006. *Jules et Jim*, tr. Patrick Evans. London: Marion Boyars.

Rodgers, Daniel T. 2011. *Age of Fracture*. Cambridge: Harvard University Press.

Roehr, Sabine. 1995. *A Primer on German Enlightenment, with a Translation of Karl Leonhard Reinhold's "The Fundamental Concepts and Principles of Ethics"*. Columbia: University of Missouri Press.

Romano, Carlin. 2012. *America the Philosophical*. New York: Knopf.

Rosati, Massimo. 2012a. "Suffering and Evil in *The Elementary Forms*." in W.S.F. Pickering and Massimo Rosati, eds., *Suffering and Evil*, pp. 49–62. New York: Durkheim Press/Berghahn.

Rosati, Massimo. 2012b. "Evil and Collective Responsibility." in W.S.F. Pickering and Massimo Rosati, eds., *Suffering and Evil*, pp. 136–47. New York: Durkheim Press/Berghahn.

Rose, Gillian. 2009. *Hegel Contra Sociology*. London: Verso.

Rose, Gillian. 2012. *Visual Methodologies*, third edition. London: Sage.

Rose, Todd. 2016. "How the Idea of a 'Normal' Person got Invented." *The Atlantic*, 18 February. Online: (www.theatlantic.com/business/archive/2016/02/the-invention-of-the-normal-person).

Rosen, Michael. 1996. *On Voluntary Servitude*. Cambridge: Harvard University Press.

Rosenzweig, Franz. [1945] 1999. *Understanding the Sick and the Healthy*, tr. Nahum Glatzer. Cambridge: Harvard University Press.

Rousseau, Jean-Jacques. [1762] 1968. *The Social Contract*, tr. Maurice Cranston. New York: Penguin.

Rousseau, Jean-Jacques. [1762] 1978. *On the Social Contract*, tr. Judith R. Masters. New York: St. Martin's Press.

Rousseau, Jean-Jacques. 1898. *Emile*, tr. Eleanor Worthington. Boston: D.C. Heath.

Royce, Josiah. 1892. *The Spirit of Modern Philosophy*. Boston and New York: Houghton Mifflin.

Royce, Josiah. 1914. *War and Insurance*. New York: Macmillan.

Royce, Josiah. 1948. *California*. New York: Knopf.

Royce, Josiah. 1969. *The Basic Writings of Josiah Royce, Vol. 1*, ed. John J. McDermott. Chicago: The University of Chicago Press.

Royce, Josiah. 1982. *The Philosophy of Josiah Royce*, ed. John Roth. Indianapolis: Hackett.

Royce, Josiah. 2005. *The Basic Writings of Josiah Royce, Vol. 2: Logic, Loyalty, and Community*, ed. John J. McDermott. New York: Fordham University Press.

Ruskin, John. 2015. *Traffic*. New York: Penguin.

Russell, James C. 1994. *The Germanization of Early Medieval Christianity*. Oxford: Oxford University Press.

Ryrie, Alec. 2017. *Protestants: The Faith That Made the Modern World*. New York: Viking.

Sabatier, Paul. 1909. *Modernism: The Jowett Lectures, 1908*. New York: Scribner.

Sade, Marquis de. 1966. *The 120 Days of Sodom and Other Writings*, tr. Austryn Weinhouse and Richard Seaver. New York: Grove.

Sade, Marquis de. 2006. *Philosophy in the Boudoir*, tr. Joachim Neugroschel. New York: Penguin.

Safouan, Moustapha. 1981. "Representation and Pleasure." in Colin MacCabe, ed., *The Talking Cure*, pp. 75–89. London: Macmillan.

Sagan, Carl. 1995. *The Demon-Haunted World*. New York: Random House.

Sahlins, Marshall. 1972. *Stone Age Economics*. New York: Aldine de Gruyter.

Sainsbury, Peter. 1955. *Suicide in London*. New York: Chapman and Hall.

Salkever, Stephen G. 2014. *Finding the Mean*. Princeton: Princeton University Press.

Samelson, Franz. 1993. "The Authoritarian Character from Berlin to Berkeley and Beyond: The Odyssey of a Problem." in Lederer Stone and Christie, eds., *Strength and Weakness*, pp. 22–43. New York: Springer-Verlag.

Santayana, George. [1905] 1932. *Reason in Society*. Charles Scribner's Sons.

Santayana, George. 1913. *Winds of Doctrine*. London: J.M. Dent and Sons.

Sappho. 1986. *Sappho*, tr. Barnard, Mary. Berkeley: University of California Press.

Sartre, Jean–Paul. [1946] 1976a. *No Exit*. New York: Vintage.

Sartre, Jean–Paul. 1948. *The Wall*, tr. Lloyd Alexander. New York: New Directions.

Sartre, Jean–Paul. 1950. *Baudelaire*, tr. Martin Turnell. New York: New Directions.

Sartre, Jean–Paul. [1952] 1963. *Saint Genet*, tr. Bernard Frechtman. New York: Pantheon.

Sartre, Jean–Paul. 1976b. *Critique of Dialectical Reason, Vol. 1: Theory of Practical Ensembles*, new edition, tr. Alan Sheridan-Smith. London: Verso.

Saunders, George. 2016. "Who are all These Trump Supporters?" *The New Yorker*, 11 and 18 July. Online: (www.newyorker.com/magazine/2016/07/11/george-saunders-goes-to-trump-rallies).

Saussure, Ferdinand de. [1916] 1983. *Course in General Linguistics*. Chicago: Open Court.

Sawyer, R. Keith. 2001. "Emergence in Sociology: Contemporary Philosophy of Mind and Some Implications for Sociological Theory." *The American Journal of Sociology* 107(3): 551–85.

Sawyer, R. Keith. 2002. "Durkheim's Dilemma: Toward a Sociology of Emergence." *Sociological Theory* 20(2): 227–47.

Sayers, Sean. 2011. *Marx and Alienation: Essays on Hegelian Themes*. New York: Palgrave.

Schachtel, Ernest G. 1959. *Metamorphosis*. New York: Basic Books.

Schaff, Philip. 1919. *The Creeds of Christendom, vol. 1*. New York: Harper.

Scheler, Max. 1973. *Selected Philosophical Essays*. Evanston: Northwestern University Press.

Schelling, Friedrich. [1813] 1997. *Ages of the World*, tr. Judith Norman. Ann Arbor: The University of Michigan Press.

Schiller, Friedrich. 1966. *On the Sublime*. New York: Frederick Ungar.

Schiller, Friedrich. 1967. *On the Aesthetic Education of Man*. Oxford: Clarendon Press.

Schmitt, Carl. 2003. *The Nomos of the Earth*, tr. G. Ulmen. New York: Telos Press.

Schneck, Stephen F. 1987. *Person and Polis*. Albany: SUNY Press.

Schneider, Michael. 1975. *Neurosis and Civilization*. New York: Seabury.

Schnitzler, Arthur. [1926] 1999. *Dream Story*, tr. J.M.Q. Davies. New York: Penguin.

Schueller, George K. 1951. *The Politburo*. Stanford: Stanford University Press.

Schulz, Kathryn. 2017. "Fantastic Beasts and how to Rank Them." *The New Yorker*, 6 November: 24–28.

Scott, James C. 2017. *Against the Grain*. New Haven: Yale University Press.

Screpanti, Ernesto. 2007. *Libertarian Communism*. New York: Palgrave Macmillan.

Seaford, Richard. 2004. *Money and the Early Greek Mind*. Cambridge: Cambridge University Press.

Seligman, Adam B. 2000. *Modernity's Wager*. Princeton: Princeton University Press.

Sellars, John. 2006. *Stoicism*. Berkeley: University of California Press.

Sennett, Richard. 1980. *Authority*. New York: Knopf.

Shakespeare, William. 1973. *Coriolanus*. New York: Penguin.

Shakespeare, William. 1999. *Much Ado About Nothing*. New York: Penguin.

Shakespeare, William. 2000. *Macbeth*. New York: Penguin.

Shakespeare, William. 2001. *Hamlet*. New York: Penguin.

Shand, Alexander F. 1914. *The Foundations of Character*. London: Macmillan.

Shelley, Mary. [1818] 1992. *Frankenstein*. New York: Knopf.

Simmel, Georg. [1907] 1990. *The Philosophy of Money*. London and New York: Routledge.

Simmel, Georg. [1921–1922] 1984. "On Love (A Fragment)." in Guy Oakes, tr. and ed., *Georg Simmel: On Women, Sexuality, and Love*, pp. 153–92. New Haven: Yale University Press.

Simmel, Georg. 1950. *The Sociology of Georg Simmel*, tr. and ed. Kurt H. Wolff. New York: The Free Press.

Simmel, Georg. 1955. *Conflict* and *The Web of Group Affiliation*. New York: The Free Press.

Simmel, Georg. 1959. *The Sociology of Religion*. New York: Philosophical Library.

Simmel, Georg. 1971. *On Individuality and Social Forms*, ed. Donald N. Levine. Chicago: University of Chicago Press.

Simon, M. 1914. "To Melt or Not to Melt." *The Maccabaean Magazine* 24(1): 180–81.

Simons Science News. 2014. "Have We Been Interpreting Quantum Mechanics Wrong This Whole Time?" *Wired*. Online: ⟨www.wired.com/2014/06/the-new-quantum-reality⟩.

Simpson, George Eaton. 1933. "Emile Durkheim's Social Realism." *Sociology and Social Research* 28: 2–11.

Simpson, George Eaton. 1940. "Haitian Magic." *Social Forces* 19(1): 95–100.

Simpson, George Eaton. 1945. "The Belief System of Haitian Vodun." *American Anthropologist* 47(1): 35–59.

Singer, Peter. 1983. *Hegel*. Oxford: Oxford University Press.

Skinner, E. Benjamin. 2008. *A Crime so Monstrous*. New York: The Free Press.

Slotkin, Richard. 1992. *Gunfighter Nation*. Norman: University of Oklahoma Press.

Smith, Adam. [1776] 1937. *The Wealth of Nations*. New York: Modern Library.

Smith, Cyril. 1994a. "Karl Marx and the Origins of 'Marxism'." Online: ⟨www.marxists.org/reference/archive/smith-cyril/works/millenni/smith4.htm⟩.

Smith, David Norman. 1988. "Authorities, Deities, and Commodities: Classical Sociology and the Problem of Domination." Ph.D. dissertation, University of Wisconsin–Madison.

Smith, David Norman. 1994b. *The Realm of the Social*. New York: McGraw–Hill.

Smith, David Norman. 1998. "Faith, Reason, and Charisma: Rudolf Sohm, Max Weber, and the Theology of Grace." *Sociological Inquiry*, 68: 32–60.

Smith, David Norman. 2001. "Anomie, Solidarity, and Conflict: French Sociology and the Limits of Dialogue." *The Sociological Quarterly* 42(1): 69–78.

Smith, David Norman. 2006. "Time is Money: Commodity Fetishism and Common Sense." in *The Hegemony of Common Sense* by Dean Wolfe Manders, pp. xix–lxiii. New York: Peter Lang.

Smith, David Norman. 2013. "Charisma Disenchanted: Max Weber and His Critics." *Current Perspectives in Social Theory* 31: 3–74.

Smith, David Norman. 2016. "Capitalism's Future: Self-Alienation, Self-Emancipation and the Remaking of Critical Theory." in Daniel Krier and Mark P. Worrell, eds., *Capitalism's Future*, pp. 11–62. Leiden: Brill.

Smith, David Norman. 2017. "Theory and Class Consciousness." in Michael J. Thompson, ed., *The Handbook of Critical Theory*, pp. 369–423. New York: Palgrave.

Smith, Norman Kemp. 1992. *Commentary to Kant's 'Critique of Pure Reason'*, 2nd ed. Atlantic Highlands, NJ: Humanities Press.

Smith, Tony. 1993a. *Dialectical Social Theory and its Critics*. Albany: SUNY Press.

Smith, Tony. 1993b. "Marx's *Capital* and Hegelian Dialectical Logic." in Fred Moseley, ed., *Marx's Method in* Capital, pp. 15–36. Atlantic Highlands: Humanities Press.

Sohn-Rethel, Alfred. 1978. *Intellectual and Manual Labor*. Atlantic Highlands: Humanities Press.

Solms, Mark and Oliver Turnbull. 2002. *The Brain and the Inner World*. New York: Other Press.

Solomon, Robert C. 1983. *In the Spirit of Hegel*. Oxford: Oxford University Press.

Solovyov, Vladimir. 1918. *The Justification of the Good*, tr. N. Duddington. London: Constable.

Sorel, Georges. 1950. *Reflections on Violence*, tr. T.E. Hulme. Mineola: Dover.

Spaulding, Edward Gleason. 1918. *The New Rationalism*. New York: Henry Holt.

Spengler, Oswald. 1950. *The Decline of the West, Vol. 2*, tr. C.F. Atkinson. New York: Knopf.

Spero, Moshe Halevi. 1992. *Religious Objects as Psychological Structures*. Chicago: University of Chicago Press.

Spinoza, Baruch. 2002. *Complete Works*, tr. Samuel Shirley. Indianapolis: Hackett.

Steinbeck, John. 2002. *America and Americans* and *Selected Nonfiction*. New York: Penguin.

Steinberger, Peter J. 1977. "Hegel as a Social Scientist." *The American Political Science Review* 71(1): 95–110.

Steiner, Franz. 1956. *Taboo*. London: Cohen and West.

Stevenson, Robert Louis. [1886] 1992. *Dr. Jekyll and Mr. Hyde and Other Stories*. New York: Knopf.

Stewart, Jon (ed.). 1996. *The Hegel Myths and Legends*. Evanston: Northwestern University Press.

Storr, Anthony. 1989. *Freud*. Oxford: Oxford University Press.

Strauss, Barry. 1996. "The Athenian Trireme, School of Democracy." in Josiah Ober and Charles Hedrick, eds., *Demokratia*, pp. 313–26. Princeton: Princeton University Press.

Strauss, David Friedrich. 1892. *The Life of Jesus*, tr. George Eliot. London: Swan Sonnenschein.

Streeck, Wolfgang. 2016. *How Will Capitalism End?* London: Verso.

Strenski, Ivan. 2006. *The New Durkheim*. New Brunswick: Rutgers University Press.

Strong, Tracy B. 1988. *Friedrich Nietzsche and the Politics of Transfiguration*, expanded edition. Berkeley: University of California Press.

Sullivan, Paul. 2017. "Who are the Richest of the Rich?" *The New York Times*, 19 February. Online: (www.nytimes.com/2017/02/19/your-money/who-are-the-richest-of-the-rich.html).

Sumner, William Graham. [1906] 1940. *Folkways*. New York: Mentor.

Sussman, Robert. W. "Why the Legend of the Killer Ape Never Dies." in Douglas P. Fry, ed., *War, Peace, and Human Nature*, pp. 97–111. Oxford: Oxford University Press.

Suzman, James. 2017. *Affluence without Abundance*. New York: Bloomsbury.

Svevo, Italo. [1923] 2001. *Zeno's Conscience*, tr. William Weaver. New York: Knopf.

Swart, William J. and Dan Krier. 2016. "Dark Spectacle." in Dan Krier and Mark P. Worrell, eds., *The Social Ontology of Capitalism*, pp. 240–76. New York: Palgrave.

Sweezy, Paul M. and Charles Bettelheim. 1971. *On the Transition to Socialism*. New York: Monthly Review Press.

Swift, Jonathan. 2015. *A Modest Proposal*. New York: Penguin.

Takla, Tendzin N. and Whitney Pope. 1985. "The Force Imagery in Durkheim: The Integration of Theory, Metatheory, and Method." *Sociological Theory* 3(1): 74–88.

Talmon, J.L. 1967. *Romanticism and Revolt*. San Diego: Harcourt.

Taussig, Michael. 1993. *Mimesis and Alterity*. New York: Routledge.

Taussig, Michael. 2009. *What Color is the Sacred?* Chicago: The University of Chicago Press.

Tavris, Carol and Elliot Aronson. 2015. *Mistakes Were Made (but Not by Me)*. New York: Houghton Mifflin Harcourt.

Taylor, Steve. 1990. "Suicide, Durkheim, and Sociology." in *Current Concepts of Suicide*, ed. David Lester, pp. 225–36. Philadelphia: Charles Press.

Teilhard de Chardin, Pierre. 1959. *The Phenomenon of Man*, tr. Bernard Wall. New York: Harper.

Tester, Keith. 1993. *The Life and Times of Post-Modernity*. London: Routledge.

Therborn, Göran. 1980. *Science, Class, and Society*. London: Verso.

Theweleit, Klaus. 1994. *Object-Choice*, tr. Malcolm R. Green. London: Verso.

Thompson, Derek. 2017. *Hit Makers*. New York: Penguin.

Thompson, E.P. 1963. *The Making of the English Working Class*. New York: Vintage.

Thoreau, Henry David. [1854] 1960. *Walden*. New York: New American Library.

Tillich, Paul. 1967. *My Search for Absolutes*. New York: Simon and Schuster.

Tilly, Charles. 1984. *Big Structures, Large Processes, Huge Comparisons*. New York: Russell Sage Foundation.

Tocqueville, Alexis de. [1835] 1956. *Democracy in America*. New York: Mentor.

Tocqueville, Alexis de. 1856. *The Old Regime and the Revolution*, tr. John Bonner. New York: Harper.

Tolinski, Brad and Alan DiPerna. 2016. *Play it Loud*. New York: Doubleday.

Tolstoy, Leo. [1869] 1992. *War and Peace, Volume 3*, tr. Louise and Aylmer Maude. New York: Knopf.

Tonnies, Ferdinand. 1988. *Community and Society*. New Brunswick: Transaction.

Tranströmer, Tomas. 2006. *The Great Enigma*, tr. Robin Fulton. New York: New Directions.

Troeltsch, Ernst. [1911] 1931. *The Social Teaching of the Christian Churches, Vol. 2*. Chicago: University of Chicago Press.

Troeltsch, Ernst. 1922. *Historism and its Problems*, tr. James Luther Adams, et al. Unpublished English translation of *Historismus*. Tübingen: Verlag von J.C.B. Mahr (Paul Siebeck).

Trotsky, Leon. 1939. "The ABC of Materialist Dialectic." Online: (www.marxists.org/archive/trotsky/1939/12/abc.htm).

Trow, George W.S. 1999. *My Pilgrim's Progress*. New York: Pantheon.

Turner, Mark. 1996. *The Literary Mind*. Oxford and New York: Oxford University Press.

Turner, Terence. 1989. "[Agnostic Exchange: Homeric Reciprocity and the Heritage of Simmel and Mauss]: A Commentary." *Cultural Anthropology* 4(3): 260–64.

Turner, Victor. [1969] 1995. *The Ritual Process*. New York: Aldine de Gruyter.

Twain, Mark. 1872. *The $30,000 Dollar Bequest and Other Stories*. New York: Greystone.

Twain, Mark. 1917. *A Connecticut Yankee in King Arthur's Court*. New York: Greystone.

Tylor, Edward B. [1873] 1958. *The Origins of Culture, Part I of 'Primitive Culture'*, 2nd ed. New York: Harper.

Urban, Wilber. 1909. *Valuation*. New York: Macmillan.

Vacherot, Étienne. 1870. *La Science et la Conscience*. Paris: Germer Bailliere.

Vaihinger, Hans. 1924. *The Philosophy of 'As if'*, tr. C.K. Ogden. London: Routledge and Kegan Paul.

Vandenberghe, F. 2013. "Reification: History of the Concept." *Logos* 14(2–3): Online: (logosjournal.com/2013/vandenberghe).

Veblen, Thorstein. 1914. *The Instinct of Workmanship*. New York: B.W. Huebsch.

Verheggen, Theo. 1996. "Durkheim's 'Représentations' Considered as 'Vorstellungen'." *Current Perspectives in Social Theory* 16: 189–219.

Vincent, George Edgar. 1897. *The Social Mind and Education*. Chicago: University of Chicago Press.

Voeks, Robert. 1993. "African Medicine and Magic in the Americas." *Geographical Review* 83(1): 66–78.

Voloshinov, V.N. [1927] 2012. *Freudianism*. London: Verso.

Voloshinov, V.N. 1973. *Marxism and the Philosophy of Language*. Cambridge: Harvard University Press.

Voltaire. 1962. *Philosophical Dictionary*, tr. Gay, Peter. New York: Harcourt.

Vygotsky, Lev. 1978. *Mind in Society*. Cambridge: Harvard University Press.

Vyse, Stuart A. 1997. *Believing in Magic*. New York: Oxford University Press.

Wach, Joachim. 1944. *Sociology of Religion*. Chicago: The University of Chicago Press.

Wagenvoort, Hendrik. [1947] 1976. *Roman Dynamism*. Westport: Greenwood Press.

Walter, Jess. 2009. *The Financial Lives of the Poets*. New York: Harper.

Walter, Jess. 2012a. *Beautiful Ruins*. New York: Harper.

Walter, Jess. 2012b. "In the Time of Galley Slaves." (Appendix) in *Beautiful Ruins*, pp. 6–12. New York: Harper.

Ware, Chris. 2000. *Jimmy Corrigan, the Smartest Kid on Earth*. New York: Pantheon.

Warminski, Andrzej. 1998. "Hegel/Marx: Consciousness and Life." in Stuart Barnett, ec., *Hegel after Derrida*, pp. 171–93. London: Routledge.

Wartenberg, Thomas E. 1993. "Hegel's Idealism: The Logic of Conceptuality." in Frederick C. Beiser, ed., *The Cambridge Companion to Hegel*, pp. 102–29. Cambridge: Cambridge University Press.

Wartofsky, Marx W. 1977. *Feuerbach*. London: Cambridge University Press.

Watters, Ethan. 2010. *Crazy Like Us: The Globalization of the American Psyche*. New York: The Free Press.

Webb, Jimmy. 1998. *Tunesmith*. New York: Hyperion.

Weber, Marianne. 1988. *Max Weber*, tr. Harry Zohn. New Brunswick: Transaction.

Weber, Max. [1905] 2002. *The Protestant Ethic and the Spirit of Capitalism*, tr. Peter Baehr and Gordon C. Wells. New York: Penguin.

Weber, Max. [1909] 1984. "Energetic Theories of Culture." tr. Jon Mark Mikkelsen and Charles Schwartz. *Mid–American Review of Sociology* 9(2): 33–58.

Weber, Max. [1922] 1991. *The Sociology of Religion*. Boston: Beacon.

Weber, Max. [1930] 2001. *The Protestant Ethic and the Spirit of Capitalism*, tr. Talcott Parsons. London: Routledge.

Weber, Max. 1946. *From Max Weber: Essays in Sociology*, eds. Hans H. Gerth and C. Wright Mills. New York: Oxford University Press.

Weber, Max. 1949. *The Methodology of the Social Sciences*. New York: The Free Press.

Weber, Max. 1952. *Ancient Judaism*. New York: The Free Press.

Weber, Max. 1958. *The Rational and Social Foundations of Music*. Carbondale: Southern Illinois University Press.

Weber, Max. 1978. *Economy and Society, Vol. 1*. Berkeley: University of California Press.

Weeks, Kathi. 2011. *The Problem with Work*. Durham: Duke University Press.

Weil, Simone. 1965. "The Iliad, or the Poem of Force." *Chicago Review* 18(2): 5–30.

Weinstein, Fred and Gerald M. Platt. 1969. *The Wish to be Free*. Berkeley: University of California Press.

Wesep, H.B. 1920. *The Control of Ideals*. New York: Knopf.

Westphal, Merold. 1990. *History and Truth in Hegel's Phenomenology*. New Jersey: Humanities Press International.

Wexler, Philip. 1996. *Critical Social Psychology*. New York: Peter Lang.

Wharton, Edith. 1924. *Old New York*. New York: Scribner.

White, Luise. 1993. "Vampire Priests of Central Africa: African Debates about Labor and Religion in Northern Zambia." *Comparative Studies in Society and History* 35(4): 746–72.

White, Luise. 2000. *Speaking With Vampires: Rumor and History in Colonial Africa.* Berkeley: University of California Press.

White, Morton. [1955] 1957. *The Age of Analysis.* New York: George Braziller.

Whitehead, Alfred North. [1927] 1955a. *Symbolism.* New York: Fordham University Press.

Whitehead, Alfred North. [1933] 1955b. *Adventures of Ideas.* New York: Mentor.

Whitehead, Alfred North. 1978. *Process and Reality.* New York: The Free Press.

Whitman, Walt. [1892] 1992. *Leaves of Grass.* New York: Book of the Month Club.

Wiese, Leopold and Howard Becker. 1932. *Systematic Sociology.* New York: Wiley & Sons.

Wiggershaus, Rolf. 1994. *The Frankfurt School.* Cambridge, MA: The MIT Press.

Wilde, Oscar. [1890] 1995. *The Picture of Dorian Gray.* Köln: Könemann.

Wilde, Oscar. [1891] 2003. "The Soul of Man Under Socialism." in *Complete Works of Oscar Wilde*, pp. 1174–97. New York: Harper-Collins.

Wilde, Oscar. [1892] 2011. *Lady Windermere's Fan.* Mineola: Dover.

Willett, John (ed). 1992. *Brecht on Theatre.* New York: Hill and Wang.

Williams, Raymond. 1958. *Culture and Society, 1780–1950.* New York: Harper.

Williams, Tennessee. 1947. *A Streetcar Named Desire.* New York: New Directions.

Williams, Tennessee. 1954. *Cat on a Hot Tin Roof.* New York: New Directions.

Wills, Garry. 2012. "Our Moloch." *The New York Review of Books*, December 15. Online: (www.nybooks.com/blogs/nyrblog/2012/dec/15/our-moloch).

Wilson, Edmund. [1940] 1967. *To the Finland Station.* New York: New York Review of Books.

Wilson, Katharina M. 1985. "The History of the Word 'Vampire'." *Journal of the History of Ideas* 46(4): 577–83.

Wilson, Stephen. 1982. *Ideology and Experience.* East Brunswick: Associated University Presses.

Winder, Joel. n.d. "The Tragedy of Concept Formation." MA thesis, University of Sussex.

Winfield, Richard Dien. 1988. *The Just Economy.* London: Routledge.

Winn, Patrick. 2016. "One of Japan's Most Popular Mascots is an Egg with Crippling Depression." Public Radio International, 31 July. Online: (www.pri.org/stories/2016-07-31/one-japan-s-most-popular-mascots-egg-crippling-depression).

Winnicott, D.W. 1965. *The Maturational Processes and the Facilitating Environment.* London: The Hogarth Press.

Wittgenstein, Ludwig. 1922. *Tractatus Logico-Philosophicus.* Online: (http://people.umass.edu/klement/tlp/tlp.pdf).

Wittgenstein, Ludwig. 1958. *The Blue and Brown Books.* New York: Harper.

Wittgenstein, Ludwig. 1969. *On Certainty*. New York: Harper.

Wolfe, Tom. 2016. *The Kingdom of Speech*. New York: Little, Brown and Co.

Wolff, Michael. 2018. *Fire and Fury*. New York: Henry Holt.

Wolin, Sheldon S. 2008. *Democracy Incorporated: Managed Democracy and the Spectre of Inverted Totalitarianism*. Princeton: Princeton University Press.

Wood, Allen W. 1993. "Hegel and Marxism." in Frederick C. Beiser, ed., *The Cambridge Companion to Hegel*, pp. 414–44. Cambridge: Cambridge University Press.

Woolf, Virginia. [1929] 2001. *A Room of One's Own*. Peterborough: Broadview Press.

Woozley, A.D. 1967. "Universals." in *The Encyclopedia of Philosophy, Vol. 8*, pp. 194–205. New York: Macmillan and The Free Press.

Worrell, Mark P. 1995. "Getting to Know You: Marx and Nietzsche in the Age of Post-modernism." *Humanity and Society* 20(4): 109–12.

Worrell, Mark P. 1998. "Authoritarianism, Critical Theory, and Political Psychology: Past, Present, and Future." *Social Thought and Research* 21(1–2): 3–33.

Worrell, Mark P. 1999. "The Veil of Piacular Subjectivity: Buchananism and the New World Order." *Electronic Journal of Sociology* 4(3). Online: (www.sociology.org/content/vol004.003/buchanan.html).

Worrell, Mark P. 2008. *Dialectic of Solidarity*. Chicago: Haymarket.

Worrell, Mark P. 2009a. "A Faint Rattling: A Research Note on Marx's Theory of Value." *Critical Sociology* 35(6): 887–92.

Worrell, Mark P. 2009b. "The Cult of Exchange Value." *Fast Capitalism* 5.2. Online: (www.uta.edu/huma/agger/fastcapitalism/5_2/Worrell5_2.html).

Worrell, Mark P. 2009c. "The Ghost World of Alienated Desire." *Critical Sociology* 35(5): 119–22.

Worrell, Mark P. 2011. *Why Nations go to War*. New York: Routledge.

Worrell, Mark P. 2013. *Terror: Social, Political, and Economic Perspectives*. New York: Routledge.

Worrell, Mark P. 2014. "The Commodity as the Ultimate Monstrosity." *Fast Capitalism* 11.1. Online: (www.uta.edu/huma/agger/fastcapitalism/11_1/worrell11_1.html).

Worrell, Mark P. 2015a. "Imperial Homunculi: The Speculative Singularities of American Hegemony." *Current Perspectives in Social Theory* 33: 217–41.

Worrell, Mark P. 2015b. "Discarding Simmel: Public Property, Neoliberalism, and Potlatch Capitalism." *Logos* 14(1). Online: (www.logosjournal.com).

Worrell, Mark P. 2017a. "The Social Psychology of Authority." in Michael J. Thompson, ed., *Handbook of Critical Theory*, pp. 463–80. New York: Palgrave.

Worrell, Mark P. 2017b. "The Sacred and the Profane in the General Formula for Capital: The Octagonal Structure of the Commodity and Saving Marx's Sociological Realism from Professional Marxology." in Dan Krier and Mark P. Worrell, eds., *The Social Ontology of Capitalism*, pp. 75–119. New York: Palgrave Macmillan.

Worrell, Mark P. and Dan Krier. 2012. "The Imperial Eye." *Fast Capitalism* 9.1. Online: (www.uta.edu/huma/agger/fastcapitalism/9_1/worrellkrier9_1.html).

Worrell, Mark P. and Dan Krier. 2018. "Atopia Awaits!" *Critical Sociology* 44(2): 213–39. Online: (https://doi.org/10.1177%2F0896920515620476).

Worrell, Mark P and Jamie Dangler. 2011. "Cafe Narcissism Redux." in Tim Luke and Ben Agger, eds., *Journal of no Illusions: The Legacy of Telos*, pp. 72–92. New York: Telos Press.

Wulf, Maurice de. [1911] 1915. "Nominalism, Realism, Conceptualism." *The Encyclopedia of Catholicism, Volume 11*. New York: Encyclopedia Press.

Wundt, Wilhelm. 1897. *Ethics: An Investigation of the Facts and Laws of the Moral Life.* London: Swan Sonnenschein.

Wylie, Turrell. 1964. "Ro–Langs: The Tibetan Zombie." *History of Religions* 4(1): 69–80.

Wyschogrod, Edith. 1990. *Saints and Postmodernism*. Chicago: The University of Chicago Press.

Yeaworth, Irvin, dir. 1958. *The Blob*. Distributed by The Criterion Collection.

Ypsilon. 1947. *Pattern for World Revolution*. Chicago: Ziff-Davis.

Zamyatin, Yevgeny. [1924] 1993. *We*, tr. Clarence Brown. New York: Penguin.

Zeeberg, Amos. 2016. "Alienation is Killing Americans and Japanese." *Nautilus*, 1 June. Online: (http://nautil.us/blog/alienation-is-killing-americans-and-japanese).

Ziemer, Gregor. 1941. *Education for Death*. London: Oxford University Press.

Zinnemann, Fred (Director). [1955] 1999. *Oklahoma!* (DVD). Los Angeles: 20th Century Fox.

Žižek, Slavoj. 1989. *The Sublime Object of Ideology*. London: Verso.

Žižek, Slavoj. 1991. *Looking Awry*. Cambridge: The MIT Press.

Žižek, Slavoj. 1993. *Tarrying with the Negative*. Durham: Duke University Press.

Žižek, Slavoj. 2000a. *The Fragile Absolute*. London: Verso.

Žižek, Slavoj. 2000b. *The Ticklish Subject*. London: Verso.

Žižek, Slavoj. 2000c. "From *History and Class Consciousness* to *The Dialectic of Enlightenment...and Back*." *New German Critique* 81: 107–23.

Žižek, Slavoj. 2001. *Enjoy Your Symptom,* 2nd ed. New York: Routledge.

Žižek, Slavoj. 2002. *For They Know not What They Do*, 2nd ed. London: Verso.

Žižek, Slavoj. 2006a. *How to Read Lacan*. New York: Norton.

Žižek, Slavoj. 2006b. *The Parallax View*. Cambridge: The MIT Press.

Žižek, Slavoj. 2008. *In Defense of Lost Causes*. London and New York: Verso.

Žižek, Slavoj. 2010a. *Living in the End Times*. London and New York: Verso.

Žižek, Slavoj. 2010b. "Thinking Backward: Predestination and Apocalypse." in *Paul's New Moment: Continental Philosophy and the Future of Christian Theology* by Milbank *et al.* Grand Rapids, pp. 185–210, MI: Brazos Press.

Žižek, Slavoj. 2012. *Less Than Nothing*. London: Verso.

Žižek, Slavoj. 2014a. *The Most Sublime Hysteric*, tr. Thomas Scott-Railton. Cambridge: Polity Press.

Žižek, Slavoj. 2014b. Absolute Recoil. London and New York: Verso.

Žižek, Slavoj, interviewed by Katie Forster. 2016. "Slavoj Žižek: We are all Basically Evil, Egotistical, Disgusting." *The Guardian*, 10 December. Online: (www.theguardian.com/lifeandstyle/2016/dec/10/slavoj-zizek-we-are-all-basically-evil-egotistical-disgusting).

Index